HC 79 E5 C897

D1499099

WITHDRAWN

Cut Carbon, Grow Profits – Business Strategies for Managing Climate Change and Sustainability

edited by Kenny Tang and Ruth Yeoh

Cut Carbon, Grow Profits – Business Strategies for Managing Climate Change and Sustainability

edited by Kenny Tang and Ruth Yeoh

First published in 2007 by Middlesex University Press

Copyright © Middlesex University Press

Authors retain copyright of individual chapters.

ISBN 978 1 904750 15 4

All rights reserved. No part of this publication may be reproduced, stored in any retrieval system or transmitted in any form or by any means, electronic, mechanical, photocopying, recording or otherwise, without the prior written permission of the copyright holder for which application should be addressed in the first instance to the publishers. No liability shall be attached to the author, the copyright holder or the publishers for loss or damage of any nature suffered as a result of reliance on the reproduction of any of the contents of this publication or any errors or omissions in its contents.

A CIP catalogue record for this book is available from

The British Library

Cover design by Helen Taylor

Typesetting by Carnegie Book Production, Lancaster

Printed in the UK by Cambridge Printing

Mixed Sources
Product group from well-managed
forests and other controlled sources
www.fsc.org Cert no. SA-COC-1527
© 1996 Forest Stewardship Council

Middlesex University Press
North London Business Park
Oakleigh Road South
London N11 1QS

Tel: +44 (0)20 8411 4162: +44 (0)20 8411 4161
Fax: +44 (0)20 8411 4167

www.mupress.co.uk

Contents

FOREWORD   v
Dato' Abdullah Badawi, Prime Minister of Malaysia

FOREWORD   x
Rt Hon Margaret Beckett, UK Foreign Secretary

FOREWORD   xii
Rt Hon David Cameron, Leader of the Opposition

INTRODUCTION   xv
Kenny Tang and Ruth Yeoh

SUSTAINABILITY PERSPECTIVES AND STRATEGIES

1   Sustainability and Capitalism as if the World Matters   3
**Jonathon Porritt, Forum for the Future and
Kenny Tang, Oxbridge Climate Capital**

2   Climate Change and the Global Common Good: Emerging
Corporate Responsibility Strategies In the Insurance Industry   19
**Henri-Claude de Bettignies, INSEAD and CEIBS and
François Lépineux, INSEAD**

3   Sustainability: a Risk Management Perspective   33
David Singleton, Arup

4   Sustainable Computing: Sun Microsystems' 3-Step Eco-Strategy of Innovate,
Act and Share   43
Kenny Tang, Oxbridge Climate Capital

CORPORATE GOVERNANCE AND INTERNATIONAL BUSINESS LEADERSHIP

5   Global Climate Governance: How the World's Largest Companies are
Responding to Global Warming   53
Douglas G Cogan, Institutional Shareholder Services

6   The Growing Risk of Climate Change: Implications and Strategies for
Asian Companies and Economies   75
Ruth Yeoh, YTL Corporation

7   The Coming Market Shift: Business Strategy and Climate Change   101
Andrew J Hoffman, University of Michigan

8   Carbon Constraints: Threat or Opportunity?   119
**Karl Schultz, Energy Edge and
Peter Williamson, Energy Edge and INSEAD**

INVESTMENT OPPORTUNITIES AND CORPORATE STRATEGIES

9   The New Business Model for Investing in the Green Space   137
     Peter C Fusaro, Global Change Associates

10   Upside of Climate Change – Opportunities in Cleantech   149
     A sector study of the auto sector
     Andrew White, Innovest

11   Business Leadership on Climate Change: Energy Efficiency and Beyond   165
     Mark Kenber and Sophy Bristow, The Climate Group

12   Coming Clean: Business Takes on the Climate Challenge   179
     Jennifer Layke and Samantha Putt del Pino, World Resources Institute

13   Integrating Climate Change into Mission-Based Business Strategy   193
     Tauni Brooker, URS Corporation

IMPLEMENTATION STRATEGIES

14   The Carbon-Positive Company   207
     Antony Turner, Peter Martin and Fraser Durham, CarbonSense

15   The Growing Voluntary Market for Carbon: Emerging Strategies   217
     Ricardo Bayon, Amanda Hawn and Katherine Hamilton,
     Ecosystem Marketplace

16   Co-operative Strategies for Ecological Sustainability – Environmental
     Results or Competitive Advantage   233
     Art Kleiner, strategy+business

17   From Energy Management to Carbon Management – a Strategic Approach   241
     Dana Hanby, Ecofys International

FINANCIAL STRATEGIES – VALUING CARBON AND CLIMATE CHANGE

18   Climate Change and Business Valuation Techniques   259
     Daniel Wells, Ernst & Young

19   Valuation Applications in a Carbon-Constrained World: Qualitative and
     Quantitative Tools for Investment Managers   275
     Daniel Wells, Ernst & Young

COMMUNICATIONS STRATEGIES – ENGAGING CONSUMERS AND EMPLOYEES

20   Companies, Customers and Climate Change: the Impact of Public Opinion   297
     Arlo Brady, Freud Communications and Judge Business School

21   Engaging Consumers through Corporate Marketing and PR Programs   313
     Cecilia (Sid) Embree, AtmosClear Climate Club

22   Engaging Employees in Climate Change   325
     Trewin Restorick, Global Action Plan

SECTOR PERSPECTIVES AND STRATEGIES: IN THEIR OWN WORDS

23   Climate Change and the Insurance Industry   339
      Trevor Maynard, Lloyd's of London

24   Valuing Carbon Requires a Fundamental Change in Thinking: How climate
      mitigation can become affordable and widely accepted   353
      Georg Rosenbauer, Siemens Power Generation

25   Sustainability and Sustainable Vehicle Strategy at Ford Motor Company   367
      Benjamin Diggins, Ford Motor Company

26   Tackling Climate Change is Vital for Business Success: BT as an Example   377
      Adrian Hosford, BT Group plc

STRATEGIES ON CLIMATE CHANGE – CITIES AND BUSINESSES

27   Local Governments for Climate Protection – a Sustainable Business Approach 385
      Margarita Maria Parra and Maryke van Staden, ICLEI

28   Moving London Towards a Sustainable Low-Carbon Energy Community   401
      Allan Jones and Tatiana Bosteels, London Climate Change Agency

29   Urbanisation in China: Designing the World's First Sustainable Eco-City in
      Dongtan   419
      Peter Head and Alejandro Gutiérrez, Arup

      APPENDIX   431
      Managing the Risks and Opportunities of Climate Change –
      A Practical Toolkit for Corporate Leaders **Ceres**

      POST-WORD   456
      Sir Martin Laing, Trustee Emeritus, WWF-UK

      POST-WORD   457
      Tan Sri Dr Francis Yeoh, YTL Corporation

      CONTRIBUTOR PROFILES   459

Dedicated to
Puan Sri Rosaline Yeoh
(1952–2006)

Foreword

Dato' Seri Abdullah Haji Ahmad Badawl
Prime Minister of Malaysia

I am delighted to write this foreword for *Cut Carbon, Grow Profits – Business Strategies for Managing Climate Change and Sustainability*, which celebrates the 2nd anniversary of the Kyoto Protocol becoming law. My congratulations to Dr Kenny Tang and Ruth Yeoh, the two Malaysians who conceived the book and put it together.

Climate change is an issue that is currently at the forefront of the international community's consciousness. The weather is something that affects everyone and the seemingly unusual and extreme weather patterns that are reported with increasing frequency indicate that a broader shift is taking place.

Malaysia has had firsthand experience of this – as I write this, unprecedented levels of rainfall have caused our worst floods in over a century, causing massive displacement and large-scale damage to property. The destruction underscores the fact that developing countries can least afford the consequences wrought by climate change – whether in the form of reconstruction, pollution clean-up, crop failure or water shortages.

But Malaysia is not the only nation affected. The weather is one of those things that are truly transnational. It does not recognize borders and is not constrained by boundaries. It therefore seems to me that such a global phenomenon requires a global response. I believe that it is possible for governments to work together to resolve issues of common concern and I take heart from the response that the world has shown in tackling recent events such as the Tsunami disaster. We must realise that environmental issues such as climate change must be tackled with the same urgency, and with the same positive and co-operative outlook.

The Kyoto Protocol is a useful place to start, given that it contains flexible mechanisms, including the Clean Development Mechanism (CDM).The CDM allows for developed nations to implement projects that reduce emissions in developing nations, in return for Certified Emission Reductions. This promotes a win–win situation where developed nations contribute towards emissions reduction while assisting developing nations to achieve sustainable development. Through innovative mechanisms such as the CDM, a whole new industry is developing in the areas of financing, investing, trading and insuring climate change related initiatives. Carbon, it can be said, is now a determinant of corporate and financial value.

Technologies also play an important role in going forward. More investment needs to be committed to developing new products and services that reduce the stresses that we place on our environment and increase energy efficiency and sufficiency. On Malaysia's part, we have been a strong proponent of biodiesel and in 2007, we expect to produce one million tonnes of palm-oil-based biodiesel. We are actively exploring the utilisation of renewable energy sources, such as harnessing wind power for rural electrification and also aim to equip 1,000 houses with solar photovoltaic roofs for electricity generation.

My government has made safeguarding the environment one of its key guiding principles. Malaysia's accession to the Rio de Janeiro declaration and the Kyoto Protocol marks our commitment in this regard. Our own Langkawi Declaration, which called for co-ordinated global effort in tackling transnational environmental problems and a balanced view of promoting environmental protection within the context of economic growth and sustainable development, was another key initiative.

Our efforts have already borne initial results. A study in 2006 ranked Malaysia ninth among 133 countries in terms of efforts taken to reduce environmental stress on human health and in protecting ecosystem vitality.

Nonetheless, the steps we take to preserve the sanctity of our environment must be commensurate with the demands of development and economic growth. The two must go hand in hand. Otherwise, we will be embarking on a dangerously short-sighted path, to the detriment of future generations.

Foreword

Rt Hon Margaret Beckett MP
Secretary of State for Foreign & Commonwealth Affairs

Today, the risk of massive and dangerous disruption to our global climate is a real and urgent one. Climate change poses a fundamental threat to the security and prosperity of developed and developing countries alike. So tackling climate change is now an imperative not a choice, a problem for today not tomorrow.

When I became Foreign Secretary, I made responding to this threat – I call it achieving climate security – a new strategic international priority for the United Kingdom. Foreign policy is not just about dealing with each crisis as it hits us. Our obligation to our citizens is to put in place the conditions for security and prosperity. An unstable climate will make it much harder for us to meet that obligation. Climate change is not just an environmental issue, it is a security issue. It is not a discrete problem we can attend to on the side while getting on with business as usual, it is a systemic problem that will undermine our ability to deliver on all the things we care about from growth to stability, from health to immigration. As Kofi Annan recently noted, it requires first-order political attention.

Security

Climate change will bring more frequent and more prolonged famines threatening nations' food security. Studies suggest that temperature rises of just 2–3 degrees will see crop yields in Africa, the Middle East and South Asia fall by as much as 30 to 40 per cent. It is a similar story in China.

Access to fresh water – water security – is already a problem across the globe. Climate change will make it worse. One billion people in the South Asian sub-continent are likely to suffer from a reduction in Himalayan melt-water and changes to the monsoon. The Middle East and Central Asia will both see significantly less rain.

And then there is energy security – vital not just for keeping the economies of the developed world running but also – crucially – for giving the developing world the means to lift itself out of poverty. Climate change threatens this too. An increase in the frequency and severity of extreme weather events will threaten port and drilling facilities across the world with its impact on oil and gas supplies.

And it's not just storms that we need to worry about. Melting permafrost will damage energy infrastructure – pipelines – in Russia. Melting glaciers in the Himalayas threaten India's plans to increase hydro-electric capacity. Plus there is the danger of increased instability in key oil producing regions such as the Middle East.

Immigration

If people find their homes permanently flooded they will have to up sticks and move. Simple as that. One study suggests that a sea-level rise of just 50 centimetres – half the most optimistic estimates – will displace two million people from the Nile Delta. A one metre rise will displace 25 million in Bangladesh. Environmental degradation is already driving economic migration out of sub-Saharan Africa and on to Europe's shores.

By tackling climate change we can lessen the push factors driving immigration. If we don't tackle it, we have to brace ourselves for population shifts on a scale we have never seen before.

International, regional and local conflicts

Wars fought over limited resources – land, fresh water, fuel – are as old as history itself. By drastically diminishing those resources in some of the most volatile parts of the world, climate change creates a new and potentially catastrophic dynamic.

The Middle East is a case in point. Five per cent of the world's population already has to share only one per cent of the world's water. Climate change will mean there is even less water to go round. Current climate models suggest that Saudi Arabia, Iran and Iraq will see the biggest reductions in rainfall anywhere on earth. Egypt – a pivotal country for regional stability – will suffer a double blow. Drastic loss of Nile flow from the South and rising sea-levels in the North will destroy its agricultural heartland across the delta.

The same pattern emerges elsewhere. In South Asia, migration into the Indian state of Assam from Bangladesh is already causing tension. Climate change will make this worse. In Central Asia, nations are increasingly at odds over water rights.

The added stresses of climate change increase the risk of fragile states dropping over the precipice into civil war and chaos. And it edges those countries that are not currently at risk into the danger zone. In short, a failing climate means more failed states, exacerbating conflicts over national borders.

Climate opportunity

In October 2006 we saw the most detailed and comprehensive study ever undertaken into the economics of climate change. In it, the UK's Chief Economist and former Chief Economist at the World Bank, Sir Nicholas Stern, showed that climate change will have a potentially devastating effect on the economies of developed and developing countries and that the benefits of strong, early action on climate change significantly outweigh the costs.

That same study also showed that moving to a low-carbon global economy does not mean sacrificing economic growth or condemning people to poverty. Indeed if we take this road, it is not only affordable: it offers huge opportunities for us all.

Some of these are economic – the Stern Review estimates renewable energy markets will be worth $500billion a year by mid-century. There are now more people employed in the US renewables sector than in the coal industry. New, cleaner technologies will reduce pollution, improving health and local environments. Increasing energy efficiency and reducing our reliance on fossil fuels will also help reduce competition for resources, easing tensions in producer regions and allowing us all to build a more secure and stable global community.

Climate change threatens the security and prosperity of every person on the planet; tackling it will require us all to play our part. That is why I warmly welcome this book, *Cut Carbon, Grow Profits*. It shows from the ground up what businesses and cities can do to address climate security. From large corporations to small start-ups, from CEOs to frontline employees, from mega cities to small communities across the world, this book outlines how each can play its part in meeting this global threat.

Foreword

Rt Hon David Cameron MP
Leader of HM Opposition

There is no longer a rational case for business to fail to recognise the threat of climate change. The compelling scientific advice is that this is the most serious physical challenge that faces the world. As a result and not before time, governments and international institutions are, with increasing urgency, fundamentally altering their taxation, regulatory, and incentive regimes. The global market place is changing fast as emission reduction, energy saving, and carbon trading take centre stage.

Businesses cannot act as if it is no concern to them, not least because it is their assets, customers, employees, and markets, not to mention their reputations which are at risk. This is a responsibility that the commercial world must accept but it is also an opportunity. As it was technology, trade, and industry that caused the problem, so it will be technology, trade, and industry that will solve it. We, who have grown prosperous on the back of pollution, must continue that growth by meeting the needs of our customers and of society in a new, sustainable way.

It is not just a duty but a market necessity. The national and international regulatory framework and the demands and expectations of customers will reward companies that meet the challenge and shun or even destroy those who don't. It is that business realisation that is changing attitudes, even in the USA.

Nor is it possible to hide from reality by putting the world into reverse, destroying the whole apparatus of prosperity, and confronting the future in hair-shirted, spartan simplicity. Poverty is no more an option for the world's nine billion people, than is unsustainable, pollution-laden growth.

Instead, every business, large or small, will need a strategy to cope with a new commercial climate in the low carbon world. We will be operating in societies that will demand sustainable growth. Each company will have to play its part in reducing its own footprint; getting more value out of less resource; cutting energy and water usage; reducing packaging and waste; and becoming more efficient and profitable as a result.

Business must be the engine of necessary change. The future of the planet depends, in large measure, on the speed and extent of the business response to the challenge of climate change.

Cut Carbon, Grow Profits details the strategies of companies and cities that are first movers and market leaders in the transition to a low carbon, socially responsible economy of the future.

Introduction

'... the debate is over. We know the science and we see the threat. Most of all, I say that we know the time for action is now.'

Governor Arnold Schwarzenegger in *New Perspective Quarterly* (2006)

Why produce this book?

We are on the cusp of a new era. In July 2005, we produced the first ever book on *'The Finance of Climate Change – A Guide for Governments, Corporations and Investors'* to coincide with the UK Presidency of the G8 Group of Nations Summit at Gleneagles, Scotland. In his foreword to our book, UK Prime Minister Tony Blair wrote: 'Climate change is now more than the subject of scientific analysis or environmental campaigning. It is on the board agendas of the world's financial institutions, multinational companies, and businesses'.[1]

Well, the Prime Minister is (half) right! The world has moved on at a tremendous pace in the 18 months since then. Climate change is now on the daily agendas of local authorities and policymakers, senior managers and employees of big and small companies, local politicians, Hollywood stars and even Hollywood film producers! Employees are now in the front line to do their bit for conservation and climate change, public opinion is shifting with demand for more carbon friendly products and services including the potential introduction of individual personal carbon allowances and personal carbon credit cards.

Tipping point moment

2006 is the year when we have reached a tipping point moment where the campaign against climate change is unstoppable. The debate is over. The rise and rise of oil prices and energy use together with the threats to the supply of gas in Europe has made energy security and energy use on the forefront of every politician and every business and residential consumer. 2006 also saw the publication of the Stern Review of the Economics of Climate Change – a comprehensive year-long study into the risks and economic impact of climate change which has taken the debate to a new level.

The groundswell of action is beginning. A UK mainstream political party changed its party logo to a green tree and the Official Leader of the Opposition nailed his (green) colours to the post by putting up a wind turbine on the rooftop of his home. Even a sceptical President of the United States is heard to challenge US citizens about their 'addiction to oil' in a key State of the Union address in 2006.

This year also saw a two-hour science lecture by a defeated US Presidential candidate turn into a documentary ('An Inconvenient Truth') which has attracted cinema-goers by the millions across the globe to become one of the biggest box office hit documentaries in recent years. Why? Scientists have known the probable effects of climate change for over two decades. What is new is the increasing sense of urgency among governments, politicians, businessmen, environmentalists and NGOs that the effects of climate change is becoming real, it is happening now and it is happening much faster than had been predicted.

The sense of urgency is particularly focused and striking in the business world. This book details the strategies of firms from Lloyd's to the London Climate Change Agency, from Siemens to Shell, from America to Australia, from the biggest to the smallest start-up firms, from insurance to investment, from the power sector to the pulp and paper sector, from the city of (Dongtan near) Shanghai to Stockholm. The list goes on.

The crucial roles of business and industry

Business and industry have a crucial role in reducing greenhouse gas (GHG) emissions. Private firms are involved, directly or indirectly, in significant proportions of resource depletion, energy use and carbon emissions. Business activity dominates every stage of the value creation and production chain, from sourcing of raw materials and resources, to production of manufactured goods, transport and logistics of intermediate components and finished goods to the collection and ultimate disposal of household and industrial waste. These business activities consume vast amounts of resources and utilise huge energy consumption with consequent impacts on greenhouse gas emissions and human-induced climate change.

In the same vein, businesses and industrial firms can also serve as powerful instruments and engines of change, which could deploy their leadership skills to potentially reshape their vast marketing, logistical and production machines and redirect their substantial financial, creative, technological and organisational resources toward addressing ecological and environmental concerns. The ecological and environmental impact of the firms' myriad business activities across the entire logistical and production chain makes them critical players in societal and business responses to ecological and environmental issues – both in terms of setting business leadership examples (in corporate governance, public communications and employee empowerment) as well as in generating early mover and competitive advantages for their firms – at a global, regional, local and community level.

The involvement of business is a critical factor in the fight against the effects of climate change – both in mitigation and in adaptation. It is business that will meet the ever increasing demands of the world's burgeoning population of consumers for more sophisticated energy-intensive goods and services. It is business that develops and deploys most of the world's technology that needs significant energy support and resource use. It is business that utilises the immense financial resources provided by the global financial community to fund the world's dash for economic growth (aided by its burgeoning population and voracious consumer appetites) [2]. It is business, therefore, that will be increasingly called upon to bear the burden of implementing and financing a substantial part of the world's efforts and initiatives to combat ecological and environmental concerns including resource use, pollution and emissions control and especially climate change adaptation and mitigation.

The role of cities

More than half of the current global population of 6 billion now lives in urban centres and cities; by 2050, cities will account for 75 per cent of the projected world population of 9 billion. Already, 75 per cent of all energy consumption is centred around the activities of the city. This means that cities, through their myriad activities, are major producers of GHG emissions and as such they hold tremendous power to influence both the causes of climate change as well as the potential solutions. Cities have an important role in the fight against climate change – in setting city leadership examples, in their own day-to-day activities and in working with local businesses and individuals.

The (emissions) harvest is plentiful but the labourers are few

To avoid the more extreme risks associated with higher GHG emissions in the atmosphere and the extreme effects of climate change, experts agree that reductions in GHG emissions are needed on a significant scale and in a relatively short period. The benefits of strong early action on climate change outweigh the costs[3]. What we do in the next 20 years will have a profound effect on the climate as we reach a critical juncture in the world's delicate climate situation with the risks of serious, irreversible impacts. If and when the real damages occur, it could be too late to reverse the process.

Despite the urgency of the situation that the world is facing right now, deep awareness of the significant problems and that significant action will be required by individuals, by businesses and industrial firms at all levels and by cities and governments throughout the world has been relatively low.

Furthermore even though climate change has been rising up the business and political agenda in recent years and particularly in the last 18 months, awareness is one thing; taking action is another. What the world needs now is action and fast. The world needs decisive leadership; the world needs examples on what needs to be done and how to do it. It needs action by governments, by local authorities, by cities, by businesses, by corporate leaders, by its employees and by the world's consumers (doing their own 'low-carbon' bit in the home and also by their own actions in purchasing the right low-carbon products and services). To paraphrase a common quotation: 'The emissions harvest is plentiful but the labourers are few.'[4]

None more so than in the developing countries where the dash for economic growth amidst the social needs and disruption of a burgeoning, migrating and voracious population require a very delicate balance. Climate change threatens the basic elements of life for people around the world – access to water, food production, health and use of the land and the environment. It is not just a climate issue or even an environmental issue – it is an issue of national security in water supply, food production and health. The Stern Review points out clearly that 'the impacts of climate change are not evenly distributed – the poorest countries and people suffer earliest and most. Climate change is likely to reduce further already low incomes and increase illness and death rates in developing countries.'[5]

The current climate is already posing problems for many developing countries with its impact on health, energy and food production. Mild climatic shocks such as modest climate change will create real setbacks to the delicate economic and social development in developing countries today – while severe climate change could upset the entire ecosystem upon which the slender economies of these countries entirely depend. Throw in the immense but unquantifiable cost of adaptation to the extreme effects of climate change that is urgently required and we have a ticking nuclear time bomb on our hands, especially if these impacts spill over national borders and create international security problems.

The impact of climate change on developing countries will be severe – yet they do not have the financial resources or the expertise needed to adapt to these impacts! As UK Chancellor of the Exchequer Gordon Brown said: 'Climate change is an issue of justice as much as economic development. It is a problem caused by the developed countries but whose effects will disproportionately fall on developing countries.' We hope this book is of particular help to advance the call for workers and call for action in the developing countries. This could entail raising billions of pounds via the issuance of triple rated *'Climate Bonds'* in the international capital markets, which are backed by 15-year irrevocable commitments, to frontload vital climate change adaptation projects in fresh water, food production, flood defences and other areas. (The term 'climate bonds' was first coined in a recent article by Kenny Tang and Ruth Yeoh in the *Financial Times*, 22 January 2007).

Structure

To date, the significant discussions about climate change have been largely dominated by policy issues and scientific debates, but much less attention has been paid to the role of business and to the role of cities, such as: what companies have shown leadership in setting climate change goals, how to translate climate change goals into targets for new product development, how to engage employees, etc. What are the business strategies to deal with climate change? What are the investment models? How to communicate with customers and suppliers? What is the nature of the response in individual sectors? What is the role of major cities in the fight against climate change?

This book aims to fill the gap with a wide ranging business perspective. It poses the question: *What are the characteristics of companies and cities that are successfully addressing the strategic challenges of climate change in terms of business leadership, corporate governance, investment analysis, business valuation, marketing, branding, risk management, new product development, corporate communications and employee engagement?*

This book is a business and strategy guide for forward-looking corporate leaders who want to seize the challenges and profit from the impending low- carbon economy. It illustrates what every corporation needs to know to manage the carbon and sustainability challenges facing societies, cities, individuals and businesses. With a global line up of leading international experts from around the world, *Cut Carbon, Grow Profits* shows how businesses create sustainable shareholder value, cut costs, increase revenues, build formidable corporate reputations, develop new low-carbon products and services, engage employees, and create powerful brands, through incorporating strategic aspects of carbon thinking into their business strategies and those of their customers and suppliers as they begin the low-carbon journey. With a clear focus on practical execution, this book offers insightful and inspiring road maps that companies can deploy to navigate through increased external ecological and environmental pressures and regulations while stimulating internal creativity and innovation that will drive long-term dynamic growth in the low-carbon economy.

This book is essential reading for business leaders wanting to learn about best practice in the sectors most likely to be seriously affected and tasked with acting in their company's strategic interests; functional directors and managers with responsibilities in marketing, branding, finance, sourcing, production, logistics, personnel and human resources, communications and public relations, investor relations, strategy development, business planning and new product development; businesses and their employees learning to apply best practice in their sectors for climate change reduction initiatives; policymakers searching for policy instruments that have proven business support in changing behaviour towards climate change both in the business world and in individual citizenship; city lawmakers searching for initiatives to control energy use and using their power to influence both the causes of climate change as well as the potential solutions; academics and researchers analysing the complexity of how cities, businesses and individuals are responding to the challenge of climate change; and enterprising entrepreneurs positioning themselves to exploit the myriad entrepreneurial opportunities in the transition to a low-carbon economy. We must acknowledge that many companies, cities, countries and individuals have taken a wait-and-see approach – this is a book for them.

In *Cut Carbon, Grow Profits*, we take you inside companies, across political jurisdictions and business pressures, across sectors and around three continents. Indeed no one can afford to ignore the issues of sustainability, and of surviving and winning in the low-carbon economy. Those early movers who manage them with immense skill and daring verve will create and build businesses and cities much better equipped to tackle the ecological and environmental challenges of the 21st century.

Companies – big and small – that fail to act now and in a meaningful way, however, could face significantly higher costs as they play catch up or risk making wrong long-term decisions without pricing in the costs of carbon. They risk facing oblivion while direct competitors and new entrants race away to create new technologies, services and products for the low-carbon economy. This book is also for you – before your competitors devour this book and your business along the way.

Finally, a word of warning. Acting individually, single countries, cities or companies are unlikely to have a significant effect on reducing the risks of extreme climate change. In order to achieve long-term emissions reductions on a scale that matches the significant and immediate threats outlined earlier and to move towards a low-carbon future, the planet's stakeholders – both governmental and private, both countries and cities, both businesses and individuals – will need to work together on a scale and method of cooperation in the low-carbon journey that has never been experienced before. This book, whilst of critical importance in your own low-carbon experience, is not one to be kept in a safe but to be shared with fellow colleagues and, dare I say it, even your competitors.

Cut Carbon, Grow Profits is split into eight broad sections. Section 1 deals with *Sustainability Perspectives* in four contrasting chapters – it presents a broad perspective on sustainability and the limits of the earth's biosphere and sets the overarching framework in looking at the world that we live in. It also addresses some of the corporate responsibility strategies and risk management strategies in the response of corporations to such limits.

Section 2 highlights *International Business Leadership* in four key chapters – it assesses how the world's top companies are addressing climate change from a corporate governance perspective. In addressing the coming market shift and carbon constraints, it raises the key question of whether carbon constraints present a threat or an opportunity, and assesses the strategies and strategies responses of international firms in Europe, USA and Asia Pacific.

Section 3 addresses, in five chapters, the *Corporate and Investment Opportunities* in clean technology and clean energy and looks at the new business model from the perspective of venture capital, hedge funds and corporations. It looks at the upside of climate change with a small case study of the auto sector. It also develops the business case for climate mitigation initiatives and assesses the technology imperative in the low-carbon era.

Section 4 assesses, in four wide-ranging chapters, *General Implementation Strategies,* as corporations begin the carbon journey. It assesses the change management strategies that need to be properly implemented to drive through tough initiatives. It also surveys the growing market for corporations to participate in the voluntary carbon credits market and addresses some of the key problems and issues in collaborating across organisational boundaries for ecological and environmental co-operation.

Section 5 takes an in-depth look at *Financial Strategies and Valuation* – how to value carbon and climate change. Two chapters – one looking at the basics of valuation and the other at valuation applications in a carbon-constrained world – are presented in this section.

Section 6 addresses, in three fascinating chapters, the climate change issue from the perspectives of *Consumers and Employees,* including how the impact of public opinion shapes the strategies of companies in producing carbon-friendly products and services; engaging customers through corporate and PR programmes, and engaging employees to drive climate change initiatives.

Section 7 offers some *Current Sector Perspectives* with live experiences and contributions from leading global companies from four different sectors of insurance, power generation, automobiles and communications writing in their own words, and assesses developments within sectors of industry that are likely to play an important role in future climate policies.

Section 8 on *Cities and Businesses* is a unique perspective of how cities are formulating strategies and initiatives to address climate change and sustainability. One chapter focuses on the role of local authorities supplemented by two in-depth case studies: one on a climate change agency in a major city while the other focuses on the building of a future eco-city.

Finally, there are numerous mini cases that discuss bottom-up initiatives to combat climate change throughout the book.

Acknowledgements

We offer our sincere thanks to Celia Cozens, managing editor at Middlesex University Press, for her support and encouragement throughout this book. Paul Jervis and Marion Locke provided invaluable support.

Thanks must also go to Rt Hon Tony Blair, UK Prime Minister, Dato' Seri Abdullah Haji Ahmad Badawi, Prime Minister of Malaysia, Rt Hon Margaret Beckett, UK Foreign Secretary, Rt Hon David Cameron MP, UK Leader of the Opposition, Tim Draper of Draper Fisher Jurvetson, Sir Martin Laing, Sir Richard Branson, founder and Chairman of the Virgin Group and Tan Sri Dr Francis Yeoh CBE of YTL Corporation for contributing forewords, post-words and quotes to this book and associated publicity materials. A venture like this could not proceed without financial support from a number of key parties – In particular, we should like to mention Arup, Ecofys, Ernst & Young, Lloyd's, Siemens, URS Corporation and YTL Corporation for their generous support and assistance.

Finally our grateful thanks must go to all the chapter contributors, who have come from eight countries across three continents. Many thanks for your time, energy, dedication and the commitment to share your experiences in this book.[6]

Kenny Tang

Thanks to my co-editor Ruth Yeoh who has provided a fresh pair of eyes, always willing to challenge and not always accepting the status quo. Her fresh perspective from the developing countries of Asia is something I valued highly in the book. Special thanks to Tan Sri Dr Francis Yeoh CBE of YTL Corporation for his inspiration to come up with the idea for such a timely book – he is such an example to us all by his Christian testimony, wisdom, deportment, love, character and strength.

Thanks also to everyone connected at Oxbridge Capital, especially Sir Paul Judge (chairman), Gordon Young, Nigel Rich, Peter Pearson, Sir Geoffrey Pattie and Yap Hon Seeng for their continuing support. Grateful thanks go to Fred Nadler, Sir Martin Laing, Paul Smith, Nigel Sizer, Anthony Palmer and Peter Campbell. Special thanks to Pastor Dr Peter Masters and everyone at the Metropolitan Tabernacle for providing us with a spiritual home.

On a personal note, special thanks to my wife, Lorraine, for being such a supportive, cheerful and steadfast wife; my eldest son Joseph, who finds everything, especially cars, so exciting; my daughter Hannah, who is now expressing herself so beautifully; and my youngest son, Timothy, who is a fascinating little toddler. Having previously had the book and the courage to tell my parents-in-law, Brian and Christine to switch off unused lights, this book should now provide them with the know-how to start a green business!

Ruth Yeoh

This book would not have been possible without the guidance, wisdom, experience, support and friendship of those who helped in our journey towards its completion. I would like to acknowledge and thank deeply the following: God for blessing me with so much to be thankful for; I thank Him for his love and mercies each day.

Dr Kenny Tang, my co-editor and mentor. His guidance and encouragement was invaluable from the start, with his expertise and experience helping to deepen my understanding of climate change and its overwhelming intricacies. We make a good team and I thank him for his insightfulness; my colleagues at YTL and at Credit Suisse, and friends for enriching my life with great humour and company.

I thank my siblings Jacob, Joseph, Joshua and Rebekah, family and relatives for their tremendous support; my father, for his love, encouragement and prayers. He taught me that 'to whom much is given, much is expected' and is the main motivation for this book. His leadership, strength and incredible wisdom to do business in the right way, and always in a Christian way, are all qualities which I will always admire and further cultivate.

This book is dedicated to my mother, who went to join the Lord in Heaven on August 5, 2006. Her courage and strength has and will always be my inspiration.

Dr Kenny Tang CFA and Ruth Yeoh

Oxbridge Climate Capital and YTL Corporation

Notes

1   Kenny Tang 2005. 'The Finance of Climate Change – A Guide for Governments, Corporation and Investors' Risk Books www.riskbooks.com
2   See, for example, 'Achieving more with less: How to use innovation to create sensible sustainable consumption – 5 tests of Societally Responsible Innovation' Kenny Tang, Francis Yeoh, Ruth Yeoh, The Wall Street Journal 11 September 2006.
3   Sir Nicholas Stern 2006, 'Stern Review of the Economics of Climate Change' Executive Summary (HM Treasury, London)
4   Matthew Ch 9 verses 36–38.
5   Sir Nicholas Stern 2006, 'Stern Review of the Economics of Climate Change' Executive Summary (HM Treasury, London)
6   Responsibility for the contents of, and arguments advanced within, each individual chapter rests with its authors. We have sought to ensure consistency of style and clarity of expression while avoiding considerable overlap, which is unavoidable in many cases.

Sustainability Perspectives and Strategies

1

Sustainability and Capitalism as if the World Matters

Jonathon Porritt, Forum for the Future and
Kenny Tang[1], Oxbridge Climate Capital

Introduction – biological and political imperatives

At the start of the 21st century, our lives are bound by two very different and potentially irreconcilable imperatives. The first is a biological imperative: to learn to live sustainably on this planet. This is an *absolute* imperative in that it is determined by the laws of nature and, hence, is non-negotiable. The second is a political imperative: to aspire to improve our material standard of living year on year. This is a *relative* imperative in that it is politically determined, with a number of alternative economic paradigms available to us. These imperatives are therefore very different in both kind and degree.

The need to find some reconciliation between these imperatives has never been more urgent. The world has been completely transformed over the last 60 years, with a combination of rapid population growth and massively increased economic activity (driven by access to relatively cheap sources of coal, oil and gas), exacting a harsh and continuing toll on the physical environment.

Biophysical sustainability and social sustainability

If we can't secure our biophysical survival, then it is game over for every other noble aspiration or venal self-interest that we may entertain. With great respect to those who assert the so-called primacy of key social and economic goals (such as the elimination of poverty or the attainment of universal human rights), it must be said loud and clear that these are secondary goals: all else is conditional upon learning to live sustainably within the Earth's systems and limits. Not only is the pursuit of biophysical sustainability non-negotiable, it is pre-conditional.

Having said that, these are really two sides of the same coin. On the one hand, social sustainability is entirely dependent upon ecological sustainability. As we continue to undermine nature's capacity to provide humans with essential services (such as clean water, a stable climate and so on) and resources (such as food and raw materials), both individuals and nation states will be subjected to growing amounts of pressure. Conflict will grow, and threats to public health and personal safety will increase in the face of ecological degradation.

On the other hand, ecological sustainability has become dependent upon social sustainability. With a growing number of people living within social systems that systematically constrain their ability to meet their needs, it becomes increasingly difficult to protect the natural environment. Forests are cleared to make way for land-hungry farmers; grazing lands are over-stocked, aquifers depleted, rivers over-fished; and the rest of nature is driven back into ever smaller reserves and national parks. Regardless of where an individual organisation places the primary focus of interest in the sustainability debate – on the social or the ecological side – it should be emphasised that the social questions are the key leverage points for stopping these undesirable feedback loops. It is human behaviour and the resulting social dynamics that lie at the heart of today's social and ecological problems.

Fortunately, all species have a deep survival instinct. Ultimately they do everything they can to secure their own survival chances. We humans have now coined a term for our survival instinct: it is called 'sustainable development', which means, quite simply, living on this planet as if we intended to go on living here forever. It is starting to dawn on people that our survival instincts have somehow become buried in the pursuit of ever greater material prosperity. To generate that prosperity, we have been literally laying waste the planet, tearing down forests, damming rivers, polluting the air, eroding topsoil, warming the atmosphere, depleting fish stocks, and covering everything with concrete and tarmac. And as our numbers grow, by an additional 85 million or so people a year, the pressures on the planet and its life-support systems (upon which *all* species depend, including ourselves) continue to mount year by year. We can no longer go on ignoring the challenge of biophysical sustainability.

Economic prosperity

Even as we witness this unfolding in front of our eyes, it seems that we have no choice in the rich world but to go on getting richer, even though it will undoubtedly jar with some people to describe the continuing pursuit of greater prosperity as an 'imperative'. Historians will reflect upon the fact that the current model of progress, premised on year-on-year increases in material prosperity, can only be traced back a few centuries.

Environmentalists argue that the pursuit of increased prosperity is a second-order political aspiration rather than a first-order imperative, and should in no way be set alongside the pursuit of sustainability. Exponents of the art of 'voluntary simplicity' (maximising one's quality of life while minimising one's dependence upon a wasteful, energy-intensive standard of living) point to the falsehood that increased prosperity automatically leads to a higher quality of life. However, the vast majority of people alive today both want to be better off themselves and want their children (if they have them) to be better off than them. This would appear to be as true of citizens in the world's richest nations as those in the poorest.

In rich countries or poor, with different justifications, it is the pursuit of greater prosperity that drives the political process. Those who claim that many people, deep down, know that increased prosperity won't necessarily make them happier, may well be right. But that is not the way they vote.

Alternatives to capitalism

Nothing lasts forever, and there is little doubt that viable alternatives to capitalism (or, at least, a very different model of capitalism) will emerge over time. The question is 'when' not 'whether', and in which direction. In mapping out the kind of transformation that is now both necessary and desirable, we will be emphasising the potential of a 'soft landing' for contemporary capitalism, seizing hold of the wealth of opportunity entailed in fashioning genuinely sustainable livelihoods for the nine billion people with whom we will be sharing this planet by the middle of the century. Capitalism is a complex, adaptive system, and is clearly capable of profound and rapid shifts.

Even those who do not share the kind of analysis presented here, based upon an understanding of environmental limits, have good reason to be concerned about the durability of this particular model of capitalism. A combination of different factors – the deregulation of cross-border capital flows; the emergence of currency trading on an unprecedented scale in today's 'casino economy'; increased liberalisation exerting downward pressure on wages and prices; extraordinarily high levels of debt in many countries and particularly in the US; oil trading at US$60–70 a barrel – make the maintenance of our current global economy look like an extremely dangerous high-wire act, with the prospects of a vertiginous collapse seeming ever more likely. Indeed, many of today's most trenchant critics of global capitalism believe that the collapse of capitalism could be upon us far sooner than anyone anticipates, often summoning up the analogy of the dramatic collapse of communism in a manner and at a time that defied all of the prognostications of the world's smartest think tanks and academics.

Sustainable development for real

Sustainability may best be defined as the *capacity for continuance into the long-term future*. Anything that can go on being done on an indefinite basis is sustainable. Anything that cannot go on being done indefinitely is unsustainable. In that respect, sustainability is the end goal, or desired destination, for the human species as much as for any other species. By contrast, sustainable development is the process by which we move towards sustainability.

The usefulness of sustainable development depends on being absolutely clear about what sustainability itself means, principally by reference to the biophysical parameters within which all human activity must be constrained. So, how do we determine those parameters and then ensure that we stay within them? Contrary to popular opinion (which sees sustainability as something rather fuzzy and hard to pin down), biophysical sustainability is capable of scientific explanation, definition and measurement. It is now well understood that there are three sets of services provided by the natural world upon which we still totally depend:

- The provision of resources for human activities

- The absorption and recycling of wastes caused by those human activities (through a variety of different sinks)

- The provision of additional ecological services (such as climate regulation, pollination and enhancing soil fertility).

Sustainability simply means that human society can continue to exist because ecosystems are able to go on providing life-sustaining services (such as clean water, soil fertility, climate regulation, and so on) and that society is capable of organising itself so that people have the opportunity to fulfil their needs.

In the short term, however, if sustainability is the *destination* (the point of which we can genuinely claim to be living within those biophysical parameters), then sustainable development is the *process* or *journey* which we must undertake in order to get to that destination. For this reason, sustainable development as a concept remains less scientific, more imprecise and more politically determined. But that does not mean to say that sustainable development, in contrast to sustainability, is somehow a 'science-free' zone. Herman Daly[2] put forward four core principles to underpin the sustainable development journey:

- Limit the human scale (or economic throughput) to that which is within the Earth's current capacity.

- Ensure that technological progress is efficiency increasing rather than throughput increasing.

- For renewable resources, harvesting rates should not exceed regeneration rates (sustained yield); waste emissions should not exceed the assimilative capacities of the receiving environment.

- Non-renewable resources should be exploited no faster than the rate of creation of renewable substitutes.

Unfortunately, many aspects of today's economic orthodoxy remain as firmly off-limits as ever, in terms of public debate, particularly the notion that progress is best served by the uncomplicated pursuit of ever higher levels of economic growth and personal consumption. This has a huge impact upon the quality of debate about sustainable development, and what it really means in terms of transforming conventional economic policies and practice. There are many in government and business, across the world, who are only too happy to see the concept of sustainable development remain totally detached from the debate about economic growth. But that cannot be.

Limits to growth

At the heart of contemporary capitalism lies the concept of economic growth. So one can't assess the compatibility of sustainable development and capitalism without first getting to grips with growth. Today's critique of growth is no anti-growth or zero-growth diatribe: economic progress can still work wonders, and billions of people around the world still need a lot more of it. But what *kind* of growth? For *whom*? Within what *limits*? And measured against what kind of *benchmarks*?

Sustainable systems

At the heart of the growth conundrum is a misconception so gross that it makes a complete nonsense of the way in which a vast majority of economists and politicians think about economic growth. For them, the global economy is *the* system, within which all else (human society, the planet and all other species) can be subsumed as subsystems. And once the global economy is seen as the overarching, self-containing system, it can then define its own operational boundaries and, theoretically, expand both permanently and exponentially, with constant increases in the throughput of both matter and energy.

Unfortunately, this is as close to biological and thermodynamic illiteracy as it is possible to get. The economy is, in the first instance, a subsystem of human society, which is itself, in the second instance, a subsystem of the totality of life on Earth (the biosphere). *And no subsystem can expand beyond the capacity of the total system of which it is a part. (see figure 1).*

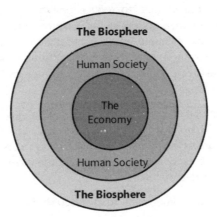

Figure 1: Sustainable Systems Source: Forum for the Future

That may sound so obvious as to insult the reader's intelligence. Yet, despite the re-uttering of it over the years by scores of 'maverick' economists and environmentalists, it remains steadfastly outside the canon of what passes for conventional neo-classical economics, with increasingly disturbing consequences.

It means that the majority of economists (and the politicians whom they advise) still do not appreciate that as an open subsystem of the much larger but essentially closed ecosystem, it is the physical limits of that ecosystem which will constrain the speed and scale at which the economic subsystem can expand. In the long run, it *cannot* grow beyond the capacity of the surrounding subsystem to sustain that growth – and the planet (or over-arching ecosystem) *cannot* grow. What we have is what we've got. Come what may, the scale of the economic subsystem will eventually be determined by the overall scale of the ecosystem, by its ability to provide high-grade resources and to absorb low-grade waste, and by the interdependency of all interlocking elements within that ecosystem. As eco-entrepreneur Paul Hawken put it:

> Contrary to what many people might believe, the rate and capacity of the Earth to create new material quality depends not upon human-driven activities, but upon the sun. Virtually all human activities remove or consume material quality. As ingenuous and important as industrial practices are, they also use material quality and order. Nature has the capacity to recycle wastes and reconstitute them into new resources of concentrated material quality. However its capacity is regulated by sunlight and photosynthesis, not by economic theory or politics. Today's extraction and processing of resources is overwhelming that capacity, while the waste from these processes systematically builds up in our water, air, soil, wildlife – and in ourselves.[3]

The dilemma of exponential growth

Optimists, however, point to the so-called 'invisible environmental hand', where economic growth can actually help to reduce pollution if it accelerates resource productivity at a faster rate than both resource consumption and population growth. The pessimists point to the 'rebound effect' (whereby any additional 'environmental space' created by resource efficiency is immediately offset by additional consumption), and simply invite people to re-examine the irrefutable empirical evidence of continuing and worsening ecological damage.

That situation is further worsened by the fact that we don't just continue to grow, but to grow exponentially. There is a crucial distinction between *linear* growth (when a quantity of something grows by the same amount over each time period, regardless of what is already there) and *exponential* growth (when the increase is not constant, but is proportional to what is already there).

This makes it all the more important to distinguish between different kinds of growth[4]:

- Growth in the economy's biophysical throughput (in a world bound by the laws of thermodynamics, indefinite growth of this kind is physically impossible)

- Growth in the economic value of that throughput (decoupled from the level of biophysical throughput itself)

- Growth in the economic welfare (which is much harder to calculate and very different from the growth in the economic value of biophysical throughput, although invariably treated as one and the same).

Growth in economic welfare is what matters most; growth in the economic value of biophysical throughput can, of course, generate precisely that (although it often does not), and certainly do so without any corresponding growth in biophysical throughput.

The roles of government and business

This poses a challenge for all of us: we can no longer expect to rely on the tried and tested mantra of 'increased economic growth': engineering the transition to a more sustainable world will require the best efforts of business people, professionals, religious and spiritual leaders, NGOs, educationists, the media and so on. But it is primarily politicians who have to make the most decisive interventions to enable others to play a fuller part in that transition. It is governments that win democratic mandates from electorates; it is governments that frame the legal and constitutional boundaries within which individual citizens and corporate entities must operate; it is governments that set the macro-economic framework through the use of fiscal and economic instruments; and it is governments (by and large) that set the tone for public debate and that can take the lead on controversial and potentially divisive issues.

But the truth of it is that governments have been extraordinarily dilatory in promoting sustainable forms of wealth creation. An increasingly convincing 'business case' for companies *voluntarily* to reduce their negative environmental and social externalities has come as manna from heaven to today's business-friendly, deregulation-inclined governments. If it can be shown that companies really do end up doing better (for example, by way of market share, performance and shareholder return) by championing corporate responsibility, why shouldn't governments just sit on the sidelines cheering them all on, doing a bit of 'naming and shaming' to encourage the others, and setting up catchy but invariably ineffective corporate social responsibility (CSR) initiatives? In an ideal world, *all* actions taken by a company to enhance its own commercial success should simultaneously generate benefits for society *over and above* those that come directly through the use of that company's products and services.

The power of markets

We are of course a long way from that kind of reciprocity, given the degree to which the interests of shareholders have been systematically prioritised by governments over the interests of all other stakeholders. Crude trade-off remains the name of the game in far too many instances.

As many commentators have pointed out, no less an authority than the redoubtable Joseph Schumpeter constantly reminded politicians that the real driving force behind capitalism is *disequilibrium*, based on the new combinations of technology, opportunity, information and shifting demand. He described this phenomenon as 'creative destruction', and urged governments not to intervene in markets to protect sectors or individual companies that were being overwhelmed by the transformative power of capitalism seeking out the next best way of generating better returns. As we know, this process of creative destruction can be very painful, especially as older industrialised economies (which are often very labour intensive) give way to different (more capital intensive) models of creating value.

As Stuart Hart has pointed out in *Capitalism at the Crossroads*,[5] this debate about creative destruction has a direct bearing on the way in which different companies are responding to the respective threats and opportunities caused by today's sustainability challenge. On the one hand, there is a cautious, modest process of continuous improvement underway (formalised in management systems such as ISO 140001), providing plenty of reassurance and comfort for those companies whose core business models evolved in an era of cheap energy, abundant raw materials and no sense of physical limits. On the other hand, one can now identify a growing number of new entrepreneurs more interested in bringing on 'disruptive' technologies or processes with a view to making those old business models entirely redundant – however much incremental 'greening' they may go in for. Hart draws an interesting analogy here:

> *'Just as nature enables some species to out-compete others through a process of natural selection and succession, so the sustainability revolution will enable those firms with more sustainable strategies to outperform – and ultimately, replace – those with outmoded strategies and damaging technologies. No amount of greening will save firms from the gales of creative destruction that are likely to ensue in the coming decades. Greening perpetuates the current industry structure; it fosters continuous improvement rather than reinvention or fundamental innovation. Given the velocity of technological change and the growing significance of sustainability, this no longer appears to be a viable strategy: creative destruction appears to hold the key not only to the growth industries of the future, but to corporate survival.'[6]*

Engaging with the base of the pyramid

World class companies are increasingly aware of the way in which societal expectations are rising on issues of this kind. Ever since C.K. Prahalad and Stuart Hart published their influential article 'The fortune at the bottom of the pyramid'[7] in 2002, growing attention has been paid to the challenge of addressing the needs of the poorest four billion people in the world today. This strategic thrust has been championed by the World Business Council on Sustainable Development (WBCSD which brought out an excellent booklet in 2004, *Doing Business with the Poor: A Field Guide*)[8] demonstrating the different ways in which companies are trying to 'blend financial and social value'. It is clear that a number of global trends are now encouraging companies to start thinking far more proactively about engaging with 'the base of the pyramid' to help promote sustainable livelihoods.

One of the most interesting aspects of the whole approach is that the base of the pyramid is likely to prove a far more welcoming test bed for some of the bolder, disruptive technologies upon which our sustainable future depends. Mature OECD economies are often so fixed in their ways, so deeply trapped in fixed infrastructures and decades' worth of sunk capital investments, that the prospective losers in any 'disruptive transition' towards a more sustainable economy fight like fury to protect their own (and their shareholders') vested interests. In many base-of-the-pyramid contexts, such vested interests do not command such blocking rights, opening up opportunities for far more radical market transformation strategies.

One particularly important example of this relates to the emergence of a host of new technologies designed to generate electricity at the point of use – the home, the office, the hospital, school or factory. These so-called 'distributed generation' or micro-generation technologies (including mini-wind turbines, mini-CHP (combined heat and power) plants, photovoltaic (PV) fuel cells, biomass boilers and biogas digesters) are not dependent upon grid connection, and could make a huge difference in terms of securing reliable and low-carbon supplies of energy. Indeed, in Schumpeterian terms, it is hard to imagine a more necessary process of 'creative destruction' than this one. Not surprisingly, the principal power-brokers in today's energy industries have been less than enthusiastic about investing in the research and development required to bring these alternatives to market. Obstacles confront pioneers of distributed energy systems at every turn. So why not look elsewhere, suggests Stuart Hart:

> Distributed generation faces few of these obstacles among the rural poor in the developing world. It may be decades before the electrical grid system is extended to provide service to those who currently lack access to dependable electric power. As a consequence, the rural poor spend a significant portion of their income – as much as US$10 per month – on candles, kerosene and batteries to have access to lighting at night and periodic electrical service. Furthermore generating electricity using kerosene and batteries is expensive, costing US$5 to US$10 or more per kilowatt hour. If offered a viable substitute, these people might abandon these dangerous, polluting and expensive technologies in favour of clean, efficient and renewable electric power. Yet few producers of distributed generation have targeted the rural poor at the base of the pyramid as their early market for these technologies, despite the fact that the market is potentially huge and is populated by people who would be delighted with technologies that cannot compete along the metrics used in developed markets.[9]

A glimpse into a sustainable future

However, there's a long way to go before we begin to see the fruits of this kind of market transformation. And the problem is that we just don't have that much time, especially as we still have a massive persuasion task on our hands.

The fact that something is necessary doesn't necessarily make it desirable. And desirability is something that advocates of sustainable development are not very good at. They are often hampered by the fact that the origins of much of what they stand for today were cast in the crucible of radical opposition to the established economic and political order back in the 1970s and 1980s. Like all opposition movements, environmental campaigners became better known for what they stood *against* rather than what they stood *for*, and to a certain extent that is still true today. Sustainable development embraces a far wider range of concerns than environmentalism per se, but it still suffers from the same problem as far as the general public is concerned: we know what you don't want to see happen, and we know that you are broadly in favour of environmental protection and helping the developing world, but what would our lives actually be like if everything suddenly went sustainable?

At one level, it is tempting to say that things probably wouldn't look very different – on the surface, at least. A sustainable society will still need a highly sophisticated infrastructure, and a mix of housing, industry, offices, recreational facilities, open spaces, and so on. But construction techniques will be radically different, with energy efficiency and renewables pushed to the absolute maximum, and carbon and other polluting emissions to the absolute minimum. There will still be roads – but fewer of them, and carrying cars that are four or five times as efficient as today's models. People will, indeed, be walking and cycling a lot more than they do today! And there will still be airports – though the numbers of people flying will be substantially reduced as the costs of flying gradually rise to reflect the impacts of aviation upon the environment, and upon climate change in particular.

In terms of the kinds of aspirations that most people have today, I very much doubt that these will be very different either. We all want the best schools and hospitals, the safest streets, the highest physical quality of life, and the fairest and most effective democratic process. And we will go on seeking them just as keenly in a sustainable society as we do today. The likelihood that things will, in all probability, be much more decentralised, with a lot more going on at the human scale and the community level, won't actually change any of that. There will also be a lot less international trade. A watchword of sustainable economics is self-reliance – not self-sufficiency, which I believe holds very few attractions. Self-reliance entails combining judicious and necessary trade with other countries with an unapologetic emphasis on each country maintaining security of supply in terms of energy, food and even manufacturing. The idea that today's neo-liberal, no-holds-barred model of globalisation will last much longer seems fantastical anyway, as nation after nation feels the pain of China and other lowest-cost economies making it all but impossible to compete in any serious sense.

With oil trading at well over US$100 per barrel, some of the most absurd anomalies of international trade and travel (apples from New Zealand, £10 flights to dozens of destinations and so on) will have rapidly disappeared. As part of our efforts to mitigate the worst threats of climate change, each individual will have his/her own carbon allowance allocated on an annual basis, and finding ways of living elegant, low-carbon lives will be both fashionable and profitable. This should usher in the first moment in modern history where cyclists have the edge over the owners of the next generation of gas-guzzling SUVs!

And there is no point in beating around the bush on one other thing: people who are better off will almost certainly be paying higher taxes than they do today. Two of the cornerstones of a sustainable economy are increased efficiency (in terms of resources, energy, raw materials, value for money, capital allocation and so on) and social justice. No serious definition of the word 'sustainable' could possibly allow for a continuation of the grotesque disparities in wealth that we see today, both within countries and between countries. This is not egalitarianism, but an uncompromising commitment to greater equity and to the elimination of the kind of poverty that still blights the lives of so many hundreds of millions of people.

Conclusion: programmed for sustainability?

As the chapter has argued, sustainability and capitalism do not automatically make natural bedfellows. Sustainability is all about the long term, about working within limits, about making more from less, about accommodation with others to secure equilibrium – and it demands a deep and often disconcerting re-engagement with the natural world. Contemporary capitalism responds to the shortest of short terms, abominates the very notion of limits, celebrates excess, accepts that its 'invisible hand' will fashion as many losers as winners – and has no connectedness with the natural world other than as a dumping ground and a store of raw materials. In a 'radical reform' of this kind, it should be clear that we are *not* talking about some revolutionary taking to the barricades. The notion of 'capitalism as if the world matters' demands a *reform* agenda, however radical it may appear to some, not a *revolutionary* agenda. But it does require a different level of engagement, both as citizens and as consumers, and a much greater readiness to confront denial at every point, to challenge the slow, soul-destroying descent into displacement consumerism, and to take on today's all too dominant 'I consume therefore I am' mindsets and lifestyles.

Societal response?

As the threat of ecological meltdown seems to become greater year by year, so, too, does our awareness of our interdependence and the need for unprecedented solidarity if we are to secure any kind of sustainable future. There is no other planet to which we can turn for help or to which we can export our problem.

If the Greenland ice sheet starts to melt at an accelerating rate (as many scientists believe is all but inevitable), and sea level rises of several metres become a reality in the next few decades, the consequences will be severe. Who knows what kind of backlash we might witness in our own European backyards when some of the worst effects of extreme weather events and climate change converge with the already severe impacts of chronic poverty in Africa and elsewhere?

This goes to the heart of just how resilient our societies are likely to be in the event not just of the occasional disruption but of cataclysmic shocks. There is now growing interest in planning for and funding a wide range of what we called 'adaptation strategies' regarding some of the likely impacts of climate change. But the adaptations pursued are almost invariably *physical*: higher flood defences or levees, 'climate-proofed' buildings, transport infrastructure built to higher engineering specifications, and so on. There would appear to be little interest in what might be described as 'psychological adaptation', either at the level of the individual or of whole communities.

Yet Hurricane Katrina offered a deeply disturbing insight into how people might behave in the event of similar disasters. The outbreak of widespread looting, violence and something resembling general anarchy can, on the one hand, be interpreted as specific to the city of New Orleans, a city fractured for many years by some of the highest levels of murder, gun crime and drug abuse anywhere in the US. On the other hand, it can be seen as a more chilling reflection of how the majority of people are likely to behave in circumstances where law and order have so clearly broken down. There are many potential shocks to our all too vulnerable systems that might trigger such reaction – not just climate change, though the increasing likelihood of some kind of 'runaway' climate change effect may in retrospect make Hurricane Katrina look like a gentle wake-up call!

It is not as if we don't know that these dilemmas will be upon us in the not too distant future. We have emphasised the *inevitability* of change, the *necessity* of adapting our political, economic, business and consumer systems to cope with that change. Even if we have not yet internalised the degree to which things must change on account of this broader limits-to-growth analysis (looking at the relationship between humankind and the natural world from a systems perspective), most have now started to internalise the implications of having to cope with climate change – treated in this case as a symptom of the inherent unsustainability of the broader system. But the degree of internalisation remains remarkably shallow. Whichever way you look at it, managing climate change, declining resources and collapsing ecosystem services is going to be a great deal harder for nine billion people than it would be for eight billion people, seven billion people or even six billion people.

Consumers and businesses

Proof of the necessity of change, however incontrovertible it may be, is a necessary but not sufficient condition for change to actually happen. It is not sufficient because at the moment it doesn't come up with any compelling explanation of how to make that necessary change *desirable* to the people who are going to have to change! In this respect, our contemporary model of consumer capitalism sets a very stiff challenge indeed. Ideas have to be *sold*; our citizenry (or 'consumertariat', as it more accurately defines the body politic today) has to be *seduced* into seeing the world in a different way. Is it any wonder that politicians and governments are struggling to find either the language or the incentives to start bringing people into a shared sense of the need for radical change?

It is not that people haven't tried to come up with one or two bridging devices to achieve this 'desirability element'. From time to time, for instance, there are great flurries of excitement about the potential for 'green consumerism' to become a significant force to bring about substantial market shifts. This remains an important element in the mix and continues to grow from year to year. But as a genuinely transformative influence, this kind of approach has always been constrained by the rather dowdy 'niche psychology' that seems to go with it. Efforts to convert that niche into a dynamic, mainstream consumer movement have had, until now, very limited success.

Others are out there cranking away at a much more technocratic approach to demonstrating desirability, emphasising the potential for a 'green industrial revolution' in terms of massive efficiency gains, reduced material throughput, strict carbon neutrality, industrial symbiosis and so on. This is very much part of the 'opportunity agenda' which is emphasised in this chapter. It is what gets many individual business leaders really fired up, positioning sustainable development in the zone of innovation, creativity and making money, rather than in the zone of constraint or regulated burden.

Opportunity is thus a key element in the case made for a rapid transition to a very different sort of capitalism: capitalism as if the world matters. We really do have a choice in finding better ways of improving people's lives than those we are currently relying upon. Responding to these challenges will generate extraordinary business opportunities for the wealth creators of the future.

The case made here is that the bipolar challenges of, on the one hand, the biophysical limits to growth and, on the other, of the terrible damage being done to the human spirit through the pursuit of unbridled materialism, (with all its attendant impact on natural resources, energy usage, air pollution, carbon emissions and so on), will compel a profound transformation of contemporary capitalism – and sooner rather than later if we want to avoid dramatic social, economic, political and physical disruption. This chapter has therefore advocated the idea of sustainability and capitalism as if the world matters: an evolved, intelligent, compassionate and elegant form of capitalism that puts the Earth as its very centre (as our one and only world) and ensures that *all* people become its beneficiaries in recognition of our unavoidable interdependence. And coping with climate change – treated in this case as a symptom of the inherent unsustainability of the broader system – is a test case of how we can begin to address this challenge.

Postscript: The Five Capitals Framework

Behind the notion of capitalism lies the notion of capital – which economists use to describe a stock of anything (physical or virtual) from which anyone can extract a revenue or yield. Capitalism has a number of important characteristics that distinguish it from other economic systems: private ownership of the means of production, reliance upon the market to allocate goods and services, the drive to accumulate capital, and so on. But the core concept of capitalism, from which it derives its very name, is the economic concept of capital.

Capital is a stock of anything that has the capacity to generate a flow of benefits which are valued by humans. It is this flow – normally of goods and services of benefit to people – that makes the capital stock an asset, and the value of the asset is derived entirely from the lifetime value of the flows to which it gives rise.

When people think of capital in this sense, they usually think of some of the more familiar 'stocks' of capital: land, machines and money. But in the description of the Five Capitals Framework that follows, this basic concept of capital (as in any stock capable of generating a flow) has been elaborated upon to arrive at a hypothetical model of sustainable capitalism. It entails five separate 'stocks': natural, human, social, manufactured and financial.

Natural capital

Natural capital (also referred to as environmental or ecological capital) is that part of the natural world which we humans make some use of or derive some benefit from – hence, its definition (in economists' jargon) as any stock or flow of energy and matter that yields valuable goods and services. There are different kinds of natural capital:

- *resources,* some of which are renewable (timber, grain, fish and water), while others are not (fossil fuels)

- *sinks* that absorb, neutralise or recycle waste

- *services* such as climate regulation.

Natural capital is therefore not the same as nature, but it is the basis of all production in the human economy and the provider of services without which human society could not sustain itself.

At the heart of the current environmental crisis is the way in which current patterns of consumption and production are unsustainably depleting our natural capital so that its ability to support the projected levels of the human population (let alone at the standard of living of most people in the affluent industrialised countries) is seriously brought into question.

The relationship between ourselves and the natural world works at many different levels; but the essence of our success as a species has been our ability to transform our natural capital into goods and services that satisfy our needs and improve our wellbeing. This natural capital provides a number of environmental functions which we make use of either directly or indirectly, particularly the flow of natural resources as inputs into our economy, the absorption of the by-products of that economy as wastes, and the provision of a number of critical 'environmental services' that underpin not just the human economy, but the whole of life on earth. From that perspective, biophysical sustainability has been defined as the maintenance of these key environmental functions, which, in turn, depends upon their resilience and renewability.

Over time, that process of transformation has accelerated dramatically as human numbers and technological productivity have grown, fundamentally altering the relationship between the overall system (the biosphere) and the subsystem of the human economy.

Human capital

The definition of human capital in our Five Capitals Framework is a simple one: 'the physical, intellectual, emotional and spiritual capacities of any individual'. Human capital consists of our health, knowledge, skills and motivation, all of which are required for productive work. Enhancing human capital – for instance, through investing in education and training – is vital for a flourishing economy. Poverty is both morally indefensible and socially inefficient in that it prevents millions of people from fulfilling their potential.

Social capital

Social capital is the value added to any activity or economic process by human relationships and co-operation. Social capital takes the form of structures or institutions which enable individuals to maintain and develop their human capital in partnership with others and includes families, communities, businesses, trade unions, schools, and voluntary organisations.

Manufactured capital

These two remaining stocks of capital (manufactured and financial) are probably most familiar to people. However, manufactured capital is not quite as simple a concept as it sounds. It is made up of material goods that contribute to the production process, but do not become embodied in the output of that process. The main components of manufactured capital include:

- *buildings* – the build environment of villages, towns and cities

- *infrastructure* – the physical fabric supporting social and economic life, including transport networks; schools; hospitals; media and communications; energy; and sewerage and water systems

- *technologies* – the means by which goods and services are produced, from simple tools and machines to information technology, biotechnology and engineering.

This list of components also includes software and chemical formulae, blueprints, instruction manuals and so on. But the underlying 'story' is much easier to grasp. Children the world over are brought up on the same account: that it was humankind's capacity to use tools that first helped us to establish our ecological niche, and that this slowly evolved into an increasingly powerful ability to assemble raw materials extracted from nature into objects, machines, buildings and so on. For most of our short history, this conversion process (from natural capital to manufactured capital) was relatively modest, localised and mostly low impact as far as the environment was concerned. But from the middle of the 18th century onwards, the Industrial Revolution transformed the balance of that relationship between the biosphere and the technosphere. The availability of cheap fossil fuels from the middle of the 20th century onwards has further increased the dependence of human beings upon countless different sources of manufactured capital.

Financial capital

The role of financial capital is perhaps the least understood of all the categories of capital now seen as essential to a sustainable economic system. Indeed, it is usually excluded from such models on the grounds that financial capital has no intrinsic value, is not essential for the production of goods and services, and simply provides a means of exchange for the fruits of other categories of capital. Paper assets that make up the stocks of money, bonds and equities have no value in themselves, but are simply derivatives of the underlying manufactured, natural, social or human capital stocks. In that fundamental sense, financial capital is not a separate category to the other capital stocks, but an aspect of social capital.

Our wealth depends on maintaining an adequate stock of each of these types of capital. If we consume more than we invest, then our opportunities to generate wealth in the future will inevitably be reduced. Sustainability can be achieved only if the stocks of capital are kept intact or increased over time.

At the heart of the current environmental crisis is the way in which present patterns of consumption and production are unsustainably depleting natural capital, such that its ability to support the projected levels of human population in the next century at any level, let alone at the standard of living we in the industrialised world enjoy, is seriously brought into question. As Paul Hawken and Amory Lovins argue in their book *Natural Capitalism:*[10]

> What might be called 'industrial capitalism' does not fully conform to its own accounting principles. It liquidates its capital and calls it income. It neglects to assign any value to the largest stocks of capital it employs – the natural resources and living systems, as well as the social and cultural systems that are the basis of human capital.

Many people now advocate a model of sustainable capitalism, based around maintaining and where possible increasing our stocks of these different capital assets, so that we succeed in living off the income without depleting the capital. They are the capital stocks from which we have to derive all our goods and services, and produce improvements in human welfare and quality of life. If consumption is at the expense of investments, then such consumption is not sustainable and will inevitably be reduced in the future.

However, it is worth bearing in mind that all such categorisations are more than a little arbitrary. In reality, there are only two sources of wealth in the world today: the wealth that flows from our use of the earth's resources and ecosystems, all powered by incoming solar radiation (our natural capital); and the wealth that flows from the use of our hands, brains and spirits (our human capital). All else – money, machines, institutions, etc. – is derivative of these two primary sources of wealth.

Notes

1   Material for this chapter was drawn from *Capitalism as if the World Matters*, Jonathon Porritt, Earthscan, London, 2006.
2   Daly H. *Beyond Growth*, Beacon Press, Boston MA, 1990.
3   Hawken P. *The Ecology of Commerce*, Weidenfield and Nicholson, London, 1993.
4   Ekins P. *Economic Growth and Environmental Sustainability*, Routledge, London, 2000.
5   Hart S. *Capitalism at the Crossroads*, Wharton School Publishing, University of Pennsylvania, Philadelphia PA, 2005.
6   Ibid.
7   Prahalad C.K. and Hart S. 'The fortune at the bottom of the pyramid', *Strategy and Business* No.26, 2002.
8   World Business Council for Sustainable Development (WBCSD) *Doing Business with the Poor: A Field Guide*, WBCSD, Geneva, 2004.
9   Hart S. *Capitalism at the Crossroads*, Wharton School Publishing, University of Pennsylvania, Philadelphia PA, 2005.
10   Hawken P., Lovins A. and Lovins L.H. *Natural Capitalism*, Earthscan, London, 1999.

Further References

Lovins A. *Winning the Oil Endgame: Innovation for Profits, Oil and Security*, Rocky Mountain Institute, Snowmass USA, 2005.
McDonough W. and Braungart M. *Cradle to Cradle*, North Point Press, New York, 2002.
Meadows D., Meadows D., Randers J. and Behrens III, W.W. *Limits to Growth*, Universe Books, New York, 1972.
Pearce D., Markandya A. and Barbier E.B. *Blueprint for a Green Economy*, Earthscan, London, 1989.

2

Climate Change and the Global Common Good: Emerging Corporate Responsibility Strategies in the Insurance Industry

Henri-Claude de Bettignies, INSEAD and CEIBS and François Lépineux, INSEAD

Introduction

The reality of climate change – already so visible – makes us more aware of the fact that we live in a fragile environment, and that the long term survival of humanity depends upon our capacity to deal with this challenge. A number of scientists exploring the future, some enlightened business leaders listening to scenarios, a small elite of international civil servants following the example of UN Secretary General, Kofi Annan, and a few politicians concerned with the destiny of future generations, advocate that the current dogmas of growth and competitiveness are leading us into a wall. They remind us of the profound message embodied in Hardin's 'Tragedy of the Commons'.

In this famous parable, Hardin[1] describes an open pasture in which each herdsman tries to raise as many cattle as possible, with the total number of animals grazing there being about what the pasture can well handle. This situation remains stable as long as wars, epidemics and other causes keep this number at a reasonable level. But when these causes vanish, the system is not stable anymore, and every herdsman has an incentive to include ever more cattle into the pasture – since if he does so, he will be able to capture all the resulting profits for himself, while distributing the costs (the effects of overgrazing) among all the other herdsmen. As Hardin rightfully comments:[2] 'this is the conclusion reached by each and every rational herdsman sharing a commons. Therein is the tragedy. Each man is locked into a system that compels him to increase his herd without limit – in a world that is limited. Ruin is the destination toward which all men rush, each pursuing his own best interest in a society that believes in the freedom of the commons. Freedom in a commons brings ruin to all.'

What can corporations and business leaders learn from such a parable, at a time when they are entangled in a competitive war of planetary dimension whose consequences are devastating for the environment? One would think that alarm signals regarding 'our common future',[3] now distributed by the global media, have percolated through the different layers of society around the world. Today, the corporate answer – still somewhat timid in its effectiveness – starts to be visible among pioneering leaders making use of concepts such as 'triple bottom line', 'corporate social responsibility', 'corporate citizenship', and the new mantra of 'sustainable development'. Beyond the forces that push them to short-term financial objectives, a growing number of multinationals are concerned about more complex issues of 'responsibilities', while the concept of *common good* starts to be heard if not yet really 'internalized'. The consequences of the globalization process contribute to stimulate such awareness.

But what is the common good? Does it have to do with 'basic needs' (such as water, security, or a healthy environment) or with higher aspirations (such as freedom, culture, or self-actualization)? How can it be defined on the global scale? We propose hereafter a possible characterization of the global common good: *being the supreme good of humanity as a whole, the global common good embraces those goods that are necessary for all of the peoples of the world, and for the citizens of all nations, to achieve their individual fulfillment. Although very general in its essence, the concept of the global common good can be approached through a variety of ways, material and immaterial: peace among nations, scientific knowledge, philosophical works, artistic heritage, biodiversity, a healthy climate, the quality of life, shared economic prosperity... all these elements represent as many conditions, aspects or partial expressions of the global common good, which exceeds and includes them in its universal perspective.*

Should multinational corporations, then, be concerned about the global common good? In a thought-provoking article published in 1992, Velasquez defended the view that in the case of non-repeated interactions and without signaling mechanisms, in the absence of a third-party authority that can enforce compliance with the principles of morality, individual agents – like corporations – have no moral obligations on the international level.[4] However, in the real world, MNCs do have repeated dealings with one another on the global scale; and signaling mechanisms can be available, notably through the channel of international networks such as the Global Compact, Business for Social Responsibility in the US and CSR Europe. In real life, nothing prevents MNCs from joining their forces in contributing to the global common good, should their leaders agree to change their mindset. Besides, the pursuit of the common good is not only a matter of abiding by the laws; it also and essentially consists in a personal attitude, in a voluntary commitment, in a freely chosen ethics. Therefore, it seems more appropriate to consider that multinational corporations can voluntarily contribute their fair share to the global common good. Several examples of enlightened corporate leaders, who pay attention to the demands of their multiple stakeholders, and behave in ways that protect the environment and foster social equity, arguably support this assumption.

For instance, in previous research on climate change, we have illustrated how – in the oil industry – different corporations (Exxon Mobil and BP Amoco) rely upon very different paradigms and strategies as far as global warming is concerned.[5]

Today illustrations are visible among financial institutions where we see more concern with responsibility issues. The sustainability benchmarking of European banks and financial services organizations conducted by Weber[6] confirms their rising interest regarding the environmental dimension. This chapter explores one sector in the financial services industry, selected (in particular) because of its centricity within the economic system: the insurance sector. In so far as insurance companies play such a fundamental role in society, contribute so much to enable us to cope with the risks of life, and make economic activity more possible, how do they define and internalize the concern for climate change, and thereby contribute to the search for the global common good? The results of an empirical research based on the study of a sample of ten companies are presented: Allianz, Aviva, AXA, IAG (Insurance Australia Group), ING Group, Lloyds TSB, Munich Re, Sompo Japan Insurance, Swiss Re and Zurich North America.[7] It seeks to analyze the corporate strategies adopted by this group of leading insurance companies confronted with the issue of climate change[8]. These strategies reflect their willingness to address mounting environmental challenges, and can also be viewed as an attempt to improve their negative image – a problem that has multiple causes.[9] The three main strategies developed by this group of companies will be examined in turn.

Designing innovative mechanisms to cover natural hazards

First of all, like any other organizations, insurance companies have an impact on the environment: they use large amounts of energy, consume paper, water and a number of goods, release CO_2 emissions, and produce waste. Most companies in our sample have chosen to handle this problem seriously so as to minimize their ecological footprint, and have now implemented an internal environmental management system (EMS), based on the conviction that effective management in this area reduces business risks, cuts costs and improves efficiency. As an example, Swiss Re has initiated a ten-year greenhouse neutral program in 2003, and is now continuously reducing its CO_2 emissions and its environmental impacts;[10] it applies best-practice standards of resource management to its properties and logistical operations. Likewise, ING keeps improving in-house energy efficiency, and has initiated a compensation program to offset CO_2 emissions related to business travel: it supports the rehabilitation of 300 hectares of tropical rainforest in Sabah, Malaysia. This program, associated with an increased purchase of green electricity and other kinds of renewable energy, is expected to curb the Group's carbon emissions by 30 per cent in 2008 compared to 2005.[11]

Within the Allianz Group, environmental management was launched in Germany in 1995, and extended to AGF, RAS and Cornhill in 2001. All big Allianz companies in Germany now comply with the requirements of the ISO 14001 standard and the European Eco Management & Audit Scheme (EMAS). When new administrative buildings are constructed, the Group is extremely attentive to ecological aspects. It has significantly reduced its CO_2 emissions per employee since 1996, by more than 20 per cent.[12] In Britain, Lloyds TSB has had a formal environmental policy since 1996, and targets specific buildings each year in order to improve energy efficiency.[13] Similarly, Sompo Japan had launched an internal energy-saving campaign in 1992; through a continuous effort, its CO_2 emissions have been sharply reduced. Environmental management is now implemented on a company-wide scale, and has been enhanced in 2005 through the 'Action Plan 60' which enables each facility to check its progress in 60 specific areas.[14]

These internal aspects are only a small part of the problem, and insurance companies are confronted with external environmental challenges of a much bigger importance. The biosphere itself is deteriorating at a rapid pace. For more than 15 years already, environmental experts from all around the world have worked together within the Intergovernmental Panel on Climate Change, and they have come to the conclusion that climate change is a reality and is caused by human activities. Global warming has many effects, including the rise of the sea level, the alteration of ecosystems, and the multiplication of extreme meteorological events, such as floods, mudslides, droughts, massive fires, storms, hurricanes and so on. International organizations such as the UNEP have already sounded the alarm on the seriousness of the global ecological crisis).[15]

In particular, tropical cyclones in the North Atlantic have increased both in frequency and intensity over the past two years, and generated enormous losses for the insurance industry.[16] The gigantic hurricane Katrina, followed by Rita a few weeks after, is certainly not the last catastrophe in relation to climate change; it should rather be considered as a forewarning sign of other catastrophes of various kinds, with even more severe potential consequences. There are strong indications that the increasing frequency and intensity of cyclones is due to the constant rise of the surface temperature of tropical oceans, caused by anthropogenic climate change).[17] Besides, these phenomena are not limited to the North Atlantic: the recent past has seen a spate of exceptional storms in other regions around the globe. And other meteorological hazards are also increasing in many countries. 'Economic losses due to natural disasters are doubling every ten years; should the current trends continue, they could reach almost US$150 billion per year in the next decade'.[18] This of course directly affects the insurance industry, which is confronted with a rise in the claims related to natural events. But there is a limit to the financial compensations companies can grant; to manage increases or uncertainty in risk, traditional insurance and reinsurance mechanisms can only extend until the point where they become inadequate to meet the needs of the victims.

That is why Munich Re speaks of 'unsettling developments'. Emerging risks resulting from environmental problems entail considerable hazard potential for the insurance business, and are a cause of concern for society as a whole. Methodologies that are currently used by the insurance industry are not adapted to the global warming threat that is looming ahead. The pricing of insurance products is traditionally driven by the risk profile of the policyholder, not by social or ecological factors. Besides, to maintain portfolios based on prudent risk management and meet their legal and regulatory obligations, insurance companies are led to reject certain risks, even though accepting them might benefit society. But 'innovative insurance mechanisms are urgently needed to face the increase in extreme meteorological phenomena and their destructive effects'.[19] These events suggest a systematic change in natural hazards, and call for a renewal of risk assessment models. The simple extrapolation from past experience is no longer a valid method to foresee the future. The insurance industry is now clearly confronted with the challenge of substantially adjusting its conditions, capacities and price structures to new risk patterns.

As financial institutions play an important role in shaping the future of the planet, they are called to devise new methodologies and create market solutions that try to keep it a livable place. In this regard, new instruments in the field of carbon finance represent promising strides, and insurance companies can also provide a significant impulse to promote the transition toward renewable energies. As a matter of fact, insurers and reinsurers alike have a strategic interest in developing appropriate responses to emerging risks linked to the rising pressure on natural resources and ecosystems, which may lead to higher insured losses and consequently to higher claims on insurers which will ultimately affect reinsurers. For example, Swiss Re is committed to constantly reviewing and adapting underwriting guidelines, supporting risk mitigation efforts, and providing new risk transfer solutions; it plays a leading role in the development of insurance-linked securities (ILS) and weather derivatives.

Likewise, Zurich North America uses state-of-the-art probabilistic models to quantify natural catastrophe risk regarding tornadoes, hail, windstorms, earthquakes and river floods; its list of monitored regions and perils, as well as the models themselves, are reviewed annually to improve estimates of risk exposure. Beyond natural catastrophes, Zurich also applies its expertise to monitor threats linked to terrorism. More generally, it has developed a holistic approach of risk management with the embedment of risk-based capital (RBC) modeling into its decision-making – RBC being defined as the capital needed to protect policyholders against losses occurring in worst-case scenarios (events with a one-in-2000 probability of happening in a given year). Through all these processes, Zurich remains at the forefront of risk modeling, always keeping abreast of new developments or improvements of simulation tools, especially with respect to the effects of climate change.[20]

Most companies in our sample are involved in the search for new approaches to cover natural hazards brought about by climate change, either from an adaptation viewpoint, whereby this phenomenon is seen as unavoidable and they can only respond to its impact as such; or from a mitigation viewpoint, which means devoting efforts to keep the impact of global warming to a minimum. Generally speaking, although the industry has managed to cope with the record losses of 2004 and 2005, its ability to handle extreme meteorological events in the future will depend on the development of adequate insurance solutions for catastrophe scenarios that have hitherto been considered inconceivable. In order to be able to face such scenarios, partnerships between the insurance industry, governmental bodies and civic constituencies will need to be established and/or strengthened. For instance, ING has joined the Global Roundtable on Climate Change, which brings together senior executives from the private sector, governmental bodies and NGOs; Zurich works with Earthwatch, a global nonprofit environmental organization, to rebuild mangrove forestation in exposed coastal areas in Sri Lanka, and to help mitigate the impact of future tsunamis. Additionally, 'more risk awareness, preventive measures, and an efficient crisis management system should be developed'.[21]

Integrating sustainability-related issues into asset management

Besides, some leading insurance companies have also started to incorporate sustainability-related issues into their investment decisions. In this regard, minds are changing at a relatively fast pace. For the past two decades, the movement of socially responsible investing (SRI) has kept continuously developing, in relation with the alarming visibility of global warming and other environmental threats, but also with some pressing societal issues such as the rise of social inequalities and exclusion, child labor, or human rights violations. These pioneering, sustainability-oriented insurance companies have understood that businesses which deliberately ignore the societal and environmental dimensions do so at their own peril (fear can be a powerful driver): they may experience lawsuits, tarnished reputations, and see their possibility to operate in important markets significantly reduced. A group of leading insurance companies has now adopted clear SRI strategies, and has undertaken to implement them in asset management practices.

Several companies in our sample are offering products in the area of sustainable investments. In Europe, Allianz and its subsidiary companies DIT and AGF Asset Management have built three mutual funds managed according to ethical and ecological criteria; their total value exceeded €200 million at the end of 2005.[22] ING aims to invest the premium income generated by its insurance business in a responsible manner; it offers a range of sustainable investment opportunities that are marketed through its business units in Europe and Australia under various names. For instance, the ING IM global sustainable equity funds had a total portfolio of €459 million at the end of 2005.[23] Likewise, Swiss Re invests in selected ecologically sound businesses and projects such as solar energy or integrated raw material production; at the end of 2004, the direct investments part of its eco portfolio amounted to CHF 31 million, and the indirect investments part of this same portfolio was essentially shared between the Storebrand Principle Global Fund and the Sustainable Performance Group (SPG), both of which use a 'best-in-class' approach and invest in sustainability leaders. In Japan, Sompo is currently marketing the eco-fund 'Beech Forest', launched in September 1999 with the purpose of purchasing equity shares of companies that are making proactive efforts to solve environmental problems; its assets amounted to ¥12 billion in May 2005.[24]

Furthermore, some companies are engaged in shareholder activism: Morley Fund Management, a division of Aviva in the UK, discusses with companies in which it has invested, to raise social, environmental, and ethical and governance issues with the management. It has exerted its shareholder voting rights in a number of cases in 2004, and is currently extending its voting policy to encompass all FTSE 350 companies.[25] Similarly, according to ING's Business Principles, ING has a global policy that promotes good corporate governance by voting for its proprietary assets in those companies in which it invests; in 2005, the use of these voting rights was further increased. Besides, Swiss Re has been actively involved in the Carbon Disclosure Project since its inception in 2000: this project is a combined effort by the world's largest institutional investors to collect information on the climate change policies of the FT 500 largest companies in the world in terms of market capitalization. The third request (CDP 3), signed by 143 institutional investors with assets of US$20 trillion, was sent out in 2005. The CDP currently brings together more than 200 institutional investors with more than US$30 trillion in assets.[26]

We also observe some insurance companies fostering the integration of sustainability-related issues into asset management through their participation in international initiatives spearheaded by the United Nations, such as the Global Compact's 'Who Cares Wins' Initiative and the UNEP Finance Initiative. The 'Who Cares Wins' initiative,[27] developed by the UN Global Compact in partnership with twenty of the world's largest investment companies representing US$6 trillion in assets worldwide,[28] seeks to make the consideration of social, environmental and governance issues part of mainstream investment analysis and decision-making.[29] The institutions involved also agree on the importance of bringing other actors in the financial world to join the program, including stock exchanges and pension funds, to reflect on how these dimensions could become standard components in the analysis of corporate performance. The signatories are committed to better integrate extra-financial considerations in value analysis, asset management and securities brokerage, and to tackle the challenge of changing the rules on the financial marketplace. What is at stake here is the achievement of a methodological breakthrough. The financial industry is expecting it, and leading institutions worldwide are now uniting their efforts to realize it.

Another international initiative that strives to fuel socially responsible investment worldwide is the UNEP Finance Initiative, launched in 2003 after the merger of previous separate initiatives. To date, more than 200 financial institutions from over 45 countries have signed the Statements, among which some 80 insurance companies from more than 20 countries. The purpose of the UNEP FI is to create a forum where insurance companies, as well as interested banks and asset management companies, can exchange experiences, stimulate each other in pursuing sustainable development, in applying the precautionary principle, and in striving to identify and assess environmental risks. Working groups have been set up to discuss and produce reports on a variety of subjects, including the impact of climate change (Aviva and Swiss Re participate in this working group), the development of renewable energies, the materiality of social, environmental and corporate governance issues to equity pricing, and the definition of best practices.[30]

Moreover, the UNEP FI plays an important role by fostering international dialogue on the regulation of global risk and environmental issues between the insurance industry, governmental bodies and financial regulators. Essential topics such as the effects of global warming, the risks associated with the transport of hazardous goods, or environmental reporting methods for the insurance industry, are debated through its interface. Eventually, the UNEP FI and the Global Compact have decided to work together in order to develop a set of Principles for Responsible Investment (PRI), with the participation of the world's largest pension funds. The UN PRI was officially launched on 27 April 2006 by Kofi Annan in New York, and international funds worth US$4 trillion have endorsed them after the European launch in Paris on 2 May 2006.[31]

Raising the awareness of all the industry's stakeholders

Besides, insurance companies can act as a lever for change in society by encouraging the incorporation of environmental issues by their customers and suppliers, and by all their stakeholders in general. Insurers can make their policyholders more aware of the impact of their practices on the environment, and share relevant information regarding corporate responsibility with them, thereby favoring the adoption of more responsible behaviors. As regards insurance for businesses, insurers educate employers to view risk management as a useful concern that improves safety and cuts costs. For instance IAG is especially active in the field of risk reduction and prevention: it has devised a self-assessment tool, named the 'Risk Radar', in order to help its business customers to rate themselves against safety and environmental standards. As regards building practices, IAG has sponsored a Cyclone Testing Station in Townsville, which advises industry and governments on how to minimize damage caused by severe wind events; it has also developed a 'Hail Gun' to test the vulnerability of building materials to the impact of hailstones.[32]

Furthermore, insurance companies can bring an essential contribution to raise the awareness of their suppliers on societal and environmental concerns, and to promote sound practices in these firms. For instance, in all its purchasing activities, ING strives to take into account environmental impacts; requirements regarding those issues are always part of ING's contract templates and thus concern the whole supply chain. In Germany, Allianz companies elaborated guidelines for environmental procurement in 2002; French and Italian subsidiaries AGF and RAS followed suit. Likewise, Lloyds TSB, one of the largest purchasers of products and services in the UK, has developed a process for assessing the environmental impacts and management of its suppliers. Sompo Japan has also adopted a purchase policy based on its 'Green Procurement' guidelines focusing on environmental considerations.

Globally considered, insurance companies have repeated interactions with almost all economic sectors, with all kinds of organizations, and with all the citizens of the countries in which they operate, through the myriads of insurance contracts that are signed every year. Therefore, they can enable all their business or societal stakeholders to reduce environmental risks and to adopt more sustainable practices. As an example, Swiss Re is committed to raising awareness about the pressing issue of climate change and its consequences through focused stakeholder dialogue, and shares its expertise with its partners and the general public to facilitate sustainable development; it has sponsored the TV documentary 'The Great Warming' in 2004. Swiss Re's technical publications are also important sources of information for interested stakeholders. Similarly, Zurich North America has set up a Hurricane Information Center on its website, providing various resources such as a 'Hurricane Preparedness Guide' elaborated by the National Oceanic and Atmospheric Administration in collaboration with the Federal Emergency Management Agency and the American Red Cross, as well as several disaster plans.

The centricity of the insurance industry within the economic system places it in a good position to influence the mindsets and behaviors of all actors in society regarding the global common good issue. We have explored elsewhere the three major determinants that are likely to induce multinational corporations to take the global common good into account: the deterioration of the biosphere, the rise of an anti-globalization sentiment, and the necessity to design new mechanisms of global governance.[33] In particular, insurance companies can be a driving force for the necessary adaptations of our modern societies confronted not only with climate change, but also with the 'peak oil' point that is looming ahead – two phenomena which will generate tremendous consequences for the way of life on our planet, much beyond Western countries.

The economic activities of man have already caused irreparable damage to the Earth. In many respects, thresholds of irreversibility have been crossed. Should these activities stop at this point or at least be markedly reduced, their enduring effects would continue to harm the environment for decades, and nobody knows what kind of equilibrium the climate would reach once the colossal amount of existing pollution and waste would have been cleared. But unfortunately, one can only notice that human economic activities, far from being reduced, are still increasing; quite logically, the negative ecological impact can't but worsen in proportion. If the current trends were to go on, a few extra planets would be needed to sustain these activities. Therefore the question of the very possibility for future generations to live on this planet in the long run is up for debate, and it will continue to be so, with a growing intensity as the twenty-first century passes by.

The uncertainty doesn't concern the existence of global warming but its magnitude: by the end of the twenty-first century, will the average temperature at the surface of the Earth have risen by 2°C, 6°C or 10°C? As for now, we don't know. But we know that major catastrophes are looming ahead if we don't change our relationship to the natural environment. A major UN report released in March 2005 on the state of ecosystems worldwide confirms these dark forecasts: 60 per cent of the world's ecosystems are being degraded by a variety of causes. Fresh water, clean air and the soil are being treated unsustainably, and human activities exert such a pressure on the natural functions of the Earth that the ability of ecosystems to support future generations is not guaranteed anymore.[34] Given the urgency of the problem, leading insurance companies and financial institutions worldwide, as well as other multinationals operating in various manufacturing and services industries, have understood that beyond embedding the concern for climate change in their own management, they need to induce a change in their stakeholders' behaviors.

Because of the very nature of their activity and their financial might, insurance companies have a tremendous lever on socio-economic change. Particularly by the huge financial investments they make (in managing the savings of their clients), they exert an impact on corporate behavior. Furthermore, through their significant lobbying efforts, they are able to influence governments and regulatory agencies, and hence, contribute to shape the rules of the game they play. With respect to climate change, the future of insurance will also gain from the development of risk reduction and prevention programs. For instance, as part of Sompo's adaptation approach, Sompo Japan Risk Management offers assessment of wind and water disaster risks to corporate customers, providing them with information so that they can avoid damage as much as possible. Through the education function they can and do play, insurers influence the individual conduct of their customers, suppliers and other stakeholders. Therefore, the insurance sector can play a decisive role for the education of the public regarding a number of important issues, and for the promotion of an environmentally friendly culture. It is also through these educational efforts that insurers will be able to contribute most effectively to the search for the global common good in the global era.

Conclusion

Over the past few years, most companies in our sample have identified sustainability as a central aspect of their activities, and have started to adopt strategies regarding the problem of climate change, striving to set the balance between their economic, social and environmental responsibilities. The idea of taking environmental issues into account has developed from being a vague concept to something concrete and valuable for the business. Some of these ten companies have devoted significant resources to define clear policies in this regard, and are committed to developing processes and practices that change the way they carry on their operations across all their businesses. They are now internalizing further the concern for global warming into many aspects of their management, raising the awareness of their stakeholders about that issue, and appear to make progress on the path to sustainability with respect to the best standards of conduct in the insurance sector.

For the financial services and insurance industry, it is only by demonstrating that it understands its responsibilities, embodies the concern for global challenges in corporate culture, anchors sustainability within core business and operates with integrity, that it will be able to rebuild the trust of all its stakeholders. Trust (lost recently), vital to the insurance business, represents its main asset. That is why the willingness of insurers to tackle climate change, as well as the implementation of transparent and ethical practices, is needed to restore the reputation of the industry. Enlightened leadership is essential to provide the impetus, to set the organizations in motion, and to follow up the internalization process. Beyond complying with external regulations, defining sets of values and elaborating codes of conduct, the challenge for insurance companies – as well as for other multinational firms – is to live the responsibility dimension in their daily operations, and to maintain a high ethical profile through all aspects of their activities. Well written CSR reports and professionally managed PR exercises will, in that case, not be substitutes for a genuine incorporation of environmental responsibility (at all levels) but its illustration.

In all the transactions with its many stakeholders, if the industry can rebuild, maintain and enhance trust, then its internalization of the concern for climate change will have its optimum impact (internally and externally). This will be possible only if – at the management level – insurance companies 'walk the talk' by the policies they define, the products they design, the methods they use to promote and sell them; by the way they manage and reward their employees, or by the level of transparency they practice. If they can introduce new methods of risk assessment and management that foster environmental protection, the enduring change necessary will be on track. A proactive attitude is essential to attain significant progress, which implies to create and market insurance products and services that encourage responsible organizational and individual behavior. Future generations may then have the possibility to cope better with the more risky world they will inherit from us.

Much scientific work has now confirmed Lovelock's Gaia hypothesis that the Earth functions as one great life-sustaining organism. According to Lovelock,[35] living matter is not passive in the face of threats to its existence; the atmosphere, the oceans, the land and all the species are components of a single complex system, wherein the biological processes of the Earth change environmental conditions in order to enable survival. Therefore, the damage human economic activities are causing to the integrity of the planet can't but entail defense reactions that will eventually backfire on humankind. This theory can be fruitfully compared with Daly and Cobb's suggestion that the biosphere should not be considered only as a resource for the human economy, but should be viewed as both ends and means (1994, p.201-203): 'Living things, individually and collectively, deserve consideration in their own right. [...] Their intrinsic value as well as their instrumental value must be considered. [...] If the health of the biosphere becomes an end in itself, the change in practical policies will be important.'

Given the current state of the planet and the existing trends, it seems that we are now close to the point when not only political leaders, but also business leaders, will widely acknowledge that the biosphere must be treated as an end in itself. Many signs suggest that the blind race for economic growth is not sustainable anymore, and the time is coming when drastic revisions will be unavoidable. Those corporations which keep doing business as usual in the name of the free market, being much more interested in their market shares and in their quarterly results than in the ecological impact of their operations, are likely to have no alternative than to veer off their course and to review their policies in the light of the preservation of the planet. The main response to the global warming issue and other environmental problems resides in a transformation of our energy-intensive way of life into an environmentally friendly lifestyle. In this regard, both corporations and consumers have a great role to play, should they agree to question their practices and to foster this change toward a more ecologically responsible economic model.

The pressure is growing. As public awareness of the state of our planet is gaining momentum, as civil society is making more explicit its concern about the environment, corporations will be compelled to take account of external voices, to review their priorities, and to adopt a multi-stakeholder approach. Like all other communities – the scientific community, the media community, the political community, the educational community – the business community bears its share of responsibility toward the global common good. Its responsibility is a specific one, and resides in the singular contribution that it can potentially offer, given the nature of its activities.[36] Multinationals are not condemned to the frozen logic of a competitive war for market share, obsessed by the financial analysts' pressure for earning per share. In line with this reflection, several attempts are made today to redefine the purpose of the corporation, indeed the corporation itself.[37]

A prospective vision suggests that the global common good concept will lead the twenty-first century. A paradigm shift is under way; the (still) dominant paradigm of shareholder value maximization might be replaced sooner than expected by another (rapidly) emerging paradigm, involving the co-operation of international institutions, governments, business organizations and civil society, in the search for the global common good. Forward-looking leaders and actors originating from these various spheres, having a vision of the future, and making use of their imagination, can accelerate the transition toward this new paradigm, and facilitate the advent of global governance schemes, now very much needed on the planetary scale. Corporate strategies that intend to tackle climate change are already giving illustrations of this perspective. Those companies – perhaps described as 'pioneers' – that are bold enough to devise and implement such strategies today are strengthening their license to operate, enhancing their long-term economic performance. They illustrate that the *common good* is not an abstract concept but the core element of a paradigm which does not condition our present but the possible one of the grandchildren of our grandchildren.

Notes

1   Hardin G. 'The Tragedy of the Commons', in B. Castro (ed.) *Business and Society*, Oxford: Oxford University Press, 1996, based on a presidential address presented before the meeting of the Pacific Division of the American Association for the Advancement of Science at Utah State University, Logan, 25 June 1968.

2   Ibid. p.220

3   Brundtland G. (ed.) *Our Common Future, Report of The World Commission on Environment and Development*, Oxford: Oxford University Press, 1987.

4   Velasquez M. 'International Business, Morality, and the Common Good', *Business Ethics Quarterly*, Vol.2, no.1, 1992, p.27–40.

5   Le Menestrel M., van den Hove S., de Bettignies H.C. 'Processes and Consequences in Business Ethical Dilemmas: the Oil Industry and Climate Change', *Journal of Business Ethics*, 2002, 41, 251–266.

6   Weber O. 'Sustainability Benchmarking of European Banks and Financial Service Organizations', *Corporate Social Responsibility and Environmental Management*, Vol.12, no.2, 2005, p.73–87.

7   The methodology used for the constitution of this sample rests on a selection process based on several criteria, including the publication of detailed sustainability-related information by the company in a dedicated report and/or on its website, the company's presence in specialized indices such as the DJSI World or the FTSE4Good, and its assessment by extra-financial rating agencies.

8   Information has been gathered not only through their Corporate Social Responsibility or Sustainability Reports, but also through company websites, specialized networks (such as the UNEP Finance Initiative), and press articles.

9   For an investigation of the factors of positive and negative perception of the insurance sector, see Bettignies H.-C. (de), Lépineux F. and Tan C.K. 'The Insurance Business and Its Image in Society: Traditional Issues and New Challenges', *INSEAD Working Paper Series*, 2005/79/ABCM, 2005.

10 Swiss Reinsurance Company, *Sustainability Report 2004*, 2005. (See also the company website, http://www.swissre.com). The group is committed to curb its CO_2 emissions by 15

per cent and invests in the World Bank Community Development Carbon Fund to offset the remaining emissions.

11 ING Group, *Corporate Responsibility Report 2005*, 2006.

12 Allianz Group, *Status Report 2005, Sustainability in the Allianz Group*, 2005.

13 Lloyds TSB, *Corporate Responsibility Report 2005*, 2006.

14 Sompo Japan Insurance, *Corporate Social Responsibility Report 2005*, 2005.

15 United Nations Environment Program, *2004 Annual report*, UNEP, 2005.

16 The North Atlantic tropical cyclones of 2004 already marked an all-time high since the recording of meteorological tracks began in 1851; but in 2005, hurricanes in the Atlantic broke again all meteorological and monetary records. According to Munich Re's estimates, insurance losses due to hurricane Katrina's devastation of the south of the United States amount to US$60 billion, which makes it the largest insured event on record. With Katrina, in addition to the devastating effect of the storm itself, water (inland flooding) became an additional loss factor, associated with the damage caused to the offshore industry (oil platforms, production facilities, pipelines), which has reached an unprecedented level (Munich Re, *Hurricanes – More Intense, More Frequent, More Expensive. Insurance in a Time of Changing Risks*, Knowledge Series, 2006).

17 Barnett T.P. et al., 'Penetration of Human-Induced Warming Into the World's Oceans', *Science*, 309, 2005, p.284–287; Emanuel K. 'Increasing Destructiveness of Tropical Cyclones Over the Past 30 Years', *Nature*, 436, 2005, p.686–688.

18 UNEP Finance Initiative, *The UNEP Sustainable Energy Finance Initiative*, Geneva, 2002.

19 Clements-Hunt P. 'The Challenge of Sustainability for Financial Institutions', in Seiler-Hausmann J.-D. et al. (eds) *Eco-Efficiency and Beyond. Towards the Sustainable Enterprise*, Sheffield (UK): Greenleaf Publishing, 2004, p.182–195.

20 Zurich Financial Services Group, *Annual Report 2005*, 2006. The website of Zurich North America is http://www.zurichna.com.

21 See ING Group, *Corporate Responsibility Report 2005*, 2006; Zurich Financial Services Group, *Annual Report 2005*, 2006; and Munich Re, *Hurricanes – More Intense, More Frequent, More Expensive. Insurance in a Time of Changing Risks*, Knowledge Series, 2006 respectively.

22 Allianz Group, *Status Report 2005, Sustainability in the Allianz Group*, 2005.

23 ING Group, *Corporate Responsibility Report 2005*, 2006.

24 Sompo Japan Insurance, *Corporate Social Responsibility Report 2005*, 2005.

25 Aviva, *Corporate Social Responsibility Report 2006*, 2006.

26 Reports published by the CDP and company responses are available on the website www.cdproject.net. The first information request (CDP 1), signed by 35 institutional investors, was sent out in May 2002; the second request (CDP 2), signed by 95 institutional investors with assets of US$10 trillion, was sent out in November 2003. Sompo Japan has joined the CDP initiative in February 2005 (Sompo Japan Insurance, *Corporate Social Responsibility Report 2005*, 2005.), and AXA supports the extension of the survey to all SBF 120 companies (French listed corporations) in 2006 (AXA, *2005 Annual Report. Activity and Sustainable Development*, 2006).

27 Global Compact, *Who Cares Wins: Connecting Financial Markets to a Changing World*, Global Compact Office, United Nations, New York, 2004.

28 Partner companies include major banking institutions such as ABN Amro, Credit Suisse Group, Deutsche Dank, Goldman Sachs, HSBC, Morgan Stanley, or UBS; and major insurers such as AXA, Aviva, or RCM (Allianz).

29 This initiative was launched in June 2004 at the Global Compact Leaders Summit in New York.

30 See UNEP Finance Initiative, *The UNEP Sustainable Energy Finance Initiative,* Geneva, 2002, and *The Materiality of Social, Environmental and Corporate Governance Issues to Equity Pricing,* Geneva, 2004.

31 The full text of the Principles for Responsible Investment, as well as an updated list of the asset owner signatories, is available on http://www.unpri.org.

32 Insurance Australia Group (IAG), *Sustainability Report 2005,* 2005.

33 Bettignies H.-C. (de) and F. Lépineux, 'Should Multinational Corporations Be Concerned with the Global Common Good? An Interdisciplinary Exploration', *INSEAD Working Paper Series,* 2005/31/ABCM, 2005.

34 Millennium Ecosystem Assessment, *Synthesis Report,* March 2005.

35 Lovelock J. *Gaia: A New Look at Life on Earth,* Oxford: Oxford University Press, 2000.

36 Porter M. 'CSR – A Religion With Too Many Priests?', Interview with M. Morsing, *European Business Forum,* 15, autumn 2003.

37 Post J., Preston L. and Sachs S. *Redefining the Corporation. Stakeholder Management and Organizational Wealth,* Stanford: Stanford University Press, 2002; Woot P. (de), *Should Prometheus Be Bound? Corporate Global Responsibility,* London: Palgrave MacMillan, 2005.

Further References

Aviva, *Corporate Social Responsibility Report 2005,* 2005.

Daly H. and Cobb J. *For the Common Good. Redirecting the Economy Toward Community, the Environment and a Sustainable Future,* Boston: Beacon Press, 1994.

ING Group, *Corporate Responsibility Report 2004,* 2005.

SAM Indices GmbH, *Industry Group Overviews – DJSI World,* Zurich, 2005.

Van den Hove S., Le Menestrel M., de Bettignies H.C. 'The Oil industry and climate Change: strategies and ethical dilemmas', *Climate Policy,* 2002, 2, 3–18.

3

Sustainability: a Risk Management Perspective

David Singleton, Arup

There are many good reasons why sustainability should be at the top of everyone's business agenda, not least because the continued survival of future generations depends on finding solutions to the combined issues of climate change, curing our dependency on fossil fuels for energy and transport needs, and ensuring widespread access to clean water. But above all, embracing sustainability is fundamental to managing a company's risk profile, and is essentially good business practice.

Sustainability and business

In so many different ways, businesses exert considerable influence on the world around them. No business operates in a vacuum. From physical roots in the community to the economic, social and psychological impacts through the activities of staff, customers and suppliers, firms have a role in society that cannot be ignored. Yet despite this influence on society, few companies are openly embracing strategies that have at their heart a sustainability agenda.

This does not come as a surprise. If we were to look at our own clients – as a firm, we have a global client base that influences most areas of the built environment – very few can be said to be motivated by altruism. For most, sustainability is at best a 'nice to have'; it is rarely a 'must have'.

This lends credence to the traditional economist's view about the place of sustainability in business which states that to do it meaningfully would cost too much, and would actually undermine a company's commercial position. The resulting rise in costs would lead to higher prices and drive customers away – a view most clearly expressed by David Vogel in a recent edition of the Harvard Business Review.[1] If pursuing a sustainable approach to business actively harms the bottom line, few companies will adopt it until forced to.

In fact privately, some in business and industry are even more suspicious. Sustainability has been seen as an enemy of business, as an expensive and flawed idea proposed by meddlesome 'greens' with an anti-business axe to grind.

Based upon our experience, the most potent driver towards sustainability will not come from a purely altruistic client base, as there simply isn't one yet. As a firm of experienced engineers helping clients solve technical problems across the world, we are a practical organisation that passionately believes engineering can make the world a better place, but is under no illusions about the realities of business. Making business sustainable, that is making a profit and developing a business without blighting the world for future generations, is becoming a business necessity based in cold, hard fact. Problems caused by scarce resources and climate change are here to stay and will probably get worse. Good businesses are spotting those problems, managing them like any other risk and then benefiting from the opportunities they throw up.

The traditional economist's view on the cost of sustainability ignores the unstoppable advance of nature. Rather than asking whether a company should undertake a sustainable approach to business in order to be able to boast about it in an annual report, or to use it as a tool to improve staff retention statistics, a better approach would be to acknowledge that all businesses exist in the earth's ecosystem.

Company boards and directors have an obligation to act in the best long-term interests of their firm and that includes addressing issues about how that business interacts with its surroundings. We've realised for a long time now that we have a significant impact – as engineers of the built environment – upon the world around us. Our approach to sustainability, which has a major influence on our corporate strategy, rests upon addressing three fundamental drivers that most affect society's future. Identified by conducting a series of scientific reviews of the major drivers of change affecting our world, these are climate change, energy resources and water.

Climate change

Having examined in detail the arguments of both sides of the climate change debate, we can find no fault in the claims of numerous scientific bodies that climate change is here; a manmade phenomenon caused by the emission of huge quantities of greenhouse gases – chiefly carbon dioxide. Scientific consensus indicates that climate change is inevitable. The question is no longer 'will it happen', but 'when?'. The effects of that change will be profound, and to deal with them it is imperative that we mentally, and physically, prepare for changes to nearly every aspect of society.

The Intergovernmental Panel on Climate Change estimates the world warmed by 0.6°C in the last century, and that the 1990s was the hottest decade since records began. Since the dawn of human civilisation, temperatures have fluctuated within a band of 1.0°C, but they are predicted to rise at least 1.4°C, and perhaps by as much as 5.8°C, in the next 100 years.

Among hundreds of forecast effects of this are: more unpredictable weather, changes to agriculture, and rising sea levels. Whilst a Mediterranean climate may seem attractive to those in the UK more used to cold drizzle, the effects of just a few degrees rise could actually be hugely disruptive to a country with an infrastructure and economy that has emerged from a cool, temperate climate.

In just one example, the worst-case predictions for rising sea levels in the Thames Estuary see the level of the river rising by up to four metres by 2100. That eventuality could see large parts of London – one of the world's business capitals – under water. Another example of what could be in store for low-lying communities is illustrated by the devastation wrought by Hurricane Katrina in the US, which left hundreds of people dead, and billions of dollars worth of damage.

BOX 1: DESIGNING FOR CLIMATE CHANGE

Designing building solutions to overcome these problems is a significant challenge, not simply from a technical perspective, but in convincing governments and developers to invest in the necessary research, and to accept the validity of taking action for dealing with climate change. While climate change is now a generally accepted phenomenon, the specific and localised effects are unknown and difficult – if not impossible – to foresee.

A key lesson from our experience is that tackling climate change in the built environment must embrace every aspect of design and planning. Planning or designing for climate change cannot be separated from other key considerations such as transport or energy. Successful planning in this area requires a holistic, sustainable approach, across all the different facets of a new development.

In projects like the Dongtan Eco-city, we have had the opportunity to fully integrate every aspect of planning into a sustainable masterplan. Transport, building design, social structure, energy, water, waste and economics all overlap, and feed into each other, to achieve sustainable goals including facing the issue of climate change.

Energy use

Sitting hand in hand with climate change is the second major driver for business this century – energy. The world is using more and more energy and the vast majority of that is fossil fuel. This, in turn, is creating greenhouse gases and contributing towards global warming. The world relies upon three main sources of energy: oil, gas and coal. All of these are finite resources and all must one day run out.

Estimates vary wildly as to when that day will arrive, but it is being hastened every day by the world's ever growing hunger for energy. In addition to the longstanding, vast consumption by the Western world, the burgeoning economies of India and China are making bigger and bigger demands on what is left. The International Energy Agency has estimated that the world will need 60 per cent more energy in 2030 than it needs now. Fossil fuel will still be called on to meet most of that demand, yet this will only make things worse for global warming.

In a vicious circle, as the climate warms up, the world is likely to use more energy, not less. The was illustrated in mid July 2006 when the UK experienced record temperatures; the increased demand for electricity from air conditioning units put severe demand on the country's national power grid.

Arguably our biggest dependency is on oil, which supplies 90 per cent of our energy needs for transport, food, and chemicals. The price and supply of this precious resource is also vulnerable to volatile international events, something set to become more of a problem as stocks run dry. But when will demand outstrip the supply of oil? Do we really know the true extent of the Middle East's oil reserve, or what lies hidden elsewhere? The general consensus is that the answer is an almost definite no. If this is true, how can we tell when to expect oil production to drop, leaving a void that needs filling? Will this lead to a global economic depression, as some predict, that challenges the widely held assumption of continued economic growth?

The energy debate is going to rage for quite a while. There are doom mongers, 'nay-sayers' and plenty who are sitting on the fence. What is clear however is that, at some point in the near future, there is going to be an energy gap between what is needed and what is left. Whether that is in 15 years or 50 years is difficult to predict, but if we are going to make a peaceful transition from fossil fuels to renewable energies, we – companies, governments and individuals – need to act now.

BOX 2: ENERGY IN THE BUILT ENVIRONMENT

The Beddington Zero Energy Development (BedZED) project in the UK is a significant example of increasing energy efficiency whilst facilitating a transition to renewable energy. The development meets all its energy needs with a combined heat and power (CHP) scheme fuelled by biomass from local urban tree waste, a renewable source. Energy needs were kept low by enhancing passive systems for heating and cooling so that active, energy-intensive mechanical systems could be omitted from the design. These passive systems include a wind cowl ventilation system, as well as strategic building orientation to take advantage of solar gain, with airtight construction and thermal insulation to retain heat.

Another renewable energy used on the site is solar, with photovoltaic cells installed on the roof. Other 'green' components of the development include low-energy lighting and appliances, on-site wastewater treatment and rainwater collection, as well as green roof areas and private gardens. Building materials were also sourced locally, some of which were recycled or reclaimed, therefore having a lower embodied energy.

Water demands

Unlike other energy resources, the Earth does not lack for water. On a global scale, there is enough water to satisfy current and future projections of the demands that mankind places on the water cycle. The particular feature of water that causes concern, however, is that it is fundamentally a local issue. While most of Europe can rely on a relatively plentiful supply of clean and usable water, continents such as Africa are facing a major crisis. There, every 15 seconds, someone dies because they don't have access to clean water. A billion people in the world struggle every day to find enough clean water with which to live. Water is vital for life and the support of society, but must be understood in its local context.

Water is also an issue that requires a fundamentally different engineering approach. Complex technological solutions will not provide a long-term sustainable answer in communities that don't have the technical experience to service such solutions. Arup is teaming up with the charity WaterAid to provide practical assistance throughout both the developed and developing world, enabling our engineers to learn first hand about local issues relating to water.

BOX 3: WATER AND FLOODING

The devastation major flooding can wreak on society has been dramatically proven again and again in recent years. From New Orleans in the US, to Boscastle in the UK, the new millennium has seen shocking examples of the sudden, destructive force of water unleashed. When the waters recede, communities have been left with enormous clean-up bills and the dead and injured to deal with. It is a problem that is expected to get worse.

Since 1998 floods in Europe have caused some 700 deaths, displaced around half a million people, and caused at least £17bn in insured economic losses. The damage has led the EU to propose a new flood directive to: 'help Member States choose the right tools with which to reduce the likelihood of floods and limit their impacts.'

THE FLOOD MANAGER'S QUANDARY

While flood defences can save lives and cut the frequency with which flooding happens, they can also mean that if flooding ever does take place, it can be more destructive than before. This can happen when conventional flood defences are built as they can give developers a false feeling of security and complacency. Land behind the defences and within the flood danger zone can then become subject to heavy and thoughtless building and development. If that does happen, and there ever is a flood, the result can be even more catastrophic than before.

Construction and maintenance of flood defence infrastructure, though frequently essential, is still only one part of the flood risk management equation. Planning, which takes full account of the components of flood risk – the sources, pathways and receptors – is an essential component of sustainable development.

What will change behaviour?

These three main environmental challenges to business are fact, even if their magnitude is open to debate. They are not scaremongering and they cannot be dismissed as irrelevant to business operations. Whilst they cannot be ignored, they should not, however, lead people into throwing their hands up in hopeless despair.

As we learn more and more about what lies in store; as projections and measurements become more sophisticated, and solutions and adaptations are suggested, business can now start to seriously plan for the challenges of a sustainable future. Leaders of businesses and directors of companies cannot deny what is happening; instead they need to be planning to address the effects. Essentially, it is good risk management protocol to be determining the likelihood of these effects and their implications.

The profound climate changes being predicted bring similarly profound physical risks to a company and its assets (see Box 3). The United Nations estimates that the cost of damage from natural disasters, much of it caused by freak weather that could be related to climate change, is doubling every decade.

As public opinion swings behind a need to take action there are significant risks to a company's reputation if it is seen dragging its feet or resisting a sustainable future. The rise of the ethical investor and growing interest in sustainable investments is another risk that has to be considered. However, it is the spectre of legislation and the market forces that could unleash the biggest risks to business, yet offer the biggest opportunities.

A legislative nirvana?

It seems increasingly clear that most of the challenges raised by these three global issues can, and will, be addressed by interventionist government regulation. Self-regulation is often called for, but it is debatable whether arguments made in favour of self-regulation are driven by self-interest, or by consideration of the greater good. Despite the increasing belief that there is a higher cost to business associated with compliance as opposed to integration of sustainability into business practices, self-regulation is unlikely to work.

The pace of government intervention varies from region to region, but cannot be ignored anywhere. That intervention will be aimed at making businesses and consumers aware of the true cost of valuable resources, particularly carbon, and introducing market forces to cut their use.

The first major impact of legislation in this area has been the burgeoning market in trading carbon emission credits. Several schemes are in operation, some global and some regional, some compulsory and some voluntary. All work from the basic premise that what is important is the overall level of carbon-based greenhouse gases in the atmosphere, not which individual companies or countries produce them. Carbon trading markets give businesses a choice. Invest to cut your own emissions, or continue as you are and pay someone else to cut their emissions. Already billions of pounds worth of emissions are traded each year. As schemes extend and grow to include new sectors and regions it will become a significant cost or opportunity in business.

Trading is just the early stage of regulation. New regulatory frameworks will be introduced that promote pricing based upon the true cost of the resources. The UK's water industry, for example, is operating under a regulatory regime that has price reduction for the consumer at its heart. This does not promote efficient use of the precious resource; governments will need to find a way to encourage them to do so. In the developed world, customers pay so little for water that the price for that asset would have to rise by significant multiples before water consumption would be influenced.

With some experts frustrated that carbon trading is not enough, there are growing calls for a common carbon tax to make the resource expensive. Only then, they argue, will business and consumers become serious about cutting their use of it. Different rates of tax have been suggested, varying from as low as US$16 a ton of CO_2 gas to the high rate of US$170. With a well known, stable and expensive rate of tax for carbon, it is argued that companies would face a clear pressure to cut emissions. That tax could replace other existing taxes on business. In addition to this, new ways to cut emissions, through developing cleaner energy, storing carbon or becoming more energy efficient, would be developed as a result of market pressure.

Legislation and regulation will not only provide pressure from above for business. Governments are going to realise that pressure will be needed from the bottom as well. They will legislate to make the worth of carbon emissions more transparent and thereby release the pressure of consumer choice. One mechanism being discussed in Britain to do this is the introduction of a personal carbon allowance. This idea is directly comparable to the far larger carbon emissions trading schemes involving large companies.

The scheme, which has been described as part reward-card scheme and part rationing, would see everyone given an identical personal carbon allowance for free. Every time someone wanted to do something involving a large carbon cost, whether it be filling up a car with petrol, taking a flight, or using a lot of gas to heat their home, it would cost carbon credits. More carbon-efficient activities, such as using public transport, would cost significantly less or nothing. Those using little carbon would be able to sell their surplus on the open market. Those wanting to use more than their allowance would have to buy extra on the open market or save up their allowance.

In addition, the scheme would be linked to long-term carbon emission targets and carbon allowances would reduce each year. Proponents of the idea say that overnight the elusive concept of carbon emissions would become visible to the public and have a direct impact on their pocket.

Change can be a good thing

The discontinuities that the inevitable changes to society bring will create considerable business opportunities. Pressures to cut emissions and preserve resources will mean existing business models will no doubt be modified. At the same time however, new services and new businesses will also be created to exploit the changes. Companies will have to get their own house in order, but will also have the chance to develop services to help other companies become sustainable and either mitigate the effects of the changes or adapt to them.

The International Energy Agency recently estimated that half of any cut in carbon emissions between now and 2050 would come from energy efficiency. With 40 per cent of the world's energy used in constructing or operating buildings, the opportunities for firms like us to help clients are immense. We have already found that developers in parts of Asia are willing to pay 50 per cent more on the construction of housing that includes energy conservation systems because there is a market for them, and they fetch a higher price. Other key technologies being developed to tackle the problem would be carbon capture and storage, renewable energy, nuclear energy and bio fuels. These are all technologies with a worldwide market.

The early mover could actually make a business out of these significant changes, but an approach that waits to see what those changes will bring will simply cost money in order to comply with regulations.

Green companies

There is no time to lose. There are companies already profiting from this approach, and those companies that lead in the field of sustainability are commercially outperforming those that lag behind. The Dow Jones Global Sustainability Index tracks companies in the Dow Jones Global Index that are in the top 10 per cent of sustainability performance. Since the index was created in 1999, it has consistently outperformed the Global Index.

In 2003, the Australian government commissioned a report looking at corporate sustainability from the point of view of investment. 'Corporate Sustainability – an Investor Perspective: The Mays Report'[2] assessed the sustainability of businesses in the listed property trust, resource, energy, insurance, agriculture and commercial industrial services sectors. It drew two general conclusions. Firstly, it found that behaving sustainably did add value to commercial endeavour. Case studies showed companies using sustainability to create new business, to improve established business or to lower their overall risk profile. Secondly, it found sustainability was a useful device for managing a company's intangible assets, such as its brand and its reputation.

Looking at the property sector, the report found three aspects of sustainability were particularly relevant: climate change, water and waste management, and community and customer pressure. This last factor is perhaps one of the most interesting. It concluded that as more and more companies start gauging their own performance against sustainability factors, property firms will be expected to follow suit. Large companies who themselves consider sustainability to be important will expect property firms in their supply chain to do the same.

It also confirmed our observation that sustainability is emerging as a driver of property value. As tenants increasingly decide they would prefer properties with sustainable features, rents for low-performing properties without these features will drop. As these rents drop, the underlying value of the asset will also fall. Conversely, landlords of properties with superior sustainability should be able to set higher rents and increase the value of their portfolio.

BOX 4: SUSTAINABILITY AT INVESTA

In 2003, Arup worked with Investa Property Group, one of the companies studied in 'The Mays Report'. Investa had positioned itself as a better manager of the resources that it used in its property portfolio. It saw the potential to develop a strategy that incorporated this position and use it to attract tenants with a particular interest in their own sustainability performance.

Investa developed a company-wide approach to sustainability, which it then used to drive its strategy and behaviour. Arup reviewed all of its systems, policies and activities, using a sustainability gap analysis. The gaps and opportunities identified were then prioritised and linked with the company's business goals. This prioritisation was used to draw up a sustainability framework and a detailed strategy for each individual business unit. The final stage of the project was to educate the group's staff, and to get them involved and enthusiastic about the sustainability strategy.

The results of the work were impressive. Not only did Investa save money by becoming more efficient, it also successfully differentiated itself from competitors.

On the back of the work, the group gained access to potentially large sums of socially responsible investment when, in 2004, it was rated Australia's leading real estate investment trust by Sustainable Asset Management (SAM) and included in the Dow Jones sustainability index. Its reputation was boosted when it won the 2004 Banksia Award for leadership in socially responsible investment and was named the 2004 Sustainable Company of the Year. Crucially, Investa was able to clearly position itself away from competitors and attract tenants looking for buildings with green credentials.

Conclusions

In the coming decades, problems caused by scarce resources and climate change represent a significant challenge to businesses. We believe the best approach to dealing with it is to manage it like any other risk. When companies look to advocate a sustainable business approach, it is possible to take a risk management view that is very aligned with a sustainability agenda. This is the precautionary principle in practice. Adopting a risk management framework makes good sense for the following reasons: companies will be better prepared for the inevitable; they will see that opportunities exist to provide new services or to refashion existing businesses; and firms will fulfil their obligation as members of society.

Few companies act altruistically and it does not make sense to undertake business activities unless they enable the continued development of a company. Climate change, high oil prices, and its diminishing supply, are all good reasons for a sustainable business approach. Above all though, embracing sustainability is essential to risk management, and it is the responsibility of each and every business to manage the risks it faces, on behalf of the business owners, employees and wider society. No business operates in a vacuum, and the sooner sustainability is embraced as good business practice, the better for us all.

Notes

1   David Vogel, 'The Low Value of Virtue', *Harvard Business Review*, June 2005.
2   *Department of the Environment and Heritage, Australian Government, 2003.*

4

Sustainable Computing: Sun Microsystems' Three-Step Eco Strategy of Innovate, Act and Share

Kenny Tang[1], Oxbridge Climate Capital

Introduction

The dramatic rise in economic productivity in the West in the late 20th and early 21st Centuries can be attributed in no small part to computer and networking technologies. As recently as the mid-1990s, the world of computers, mobile phones and the Internet held a potential for significant economic and environmental benefits, including reduced consumer travel through online shopping and e-commerce; reduced business travel through the use of teleconferencing and telecommuting; and lightened impact on global business resources through reduced paper use and computer-aided design. Computers and networks, it seemed, had arrived in order to help solve some of contemporary society's most dire environmental problems: increased energy consumption, depletion of natural resources, increased carbon emissions and other kinds of pollution. At multiple levels, that is happening.

Computer and networking technologies now power a range of daily applications we now take for granted – applications including online cash machines, search engines, auctions, emails, video conferencing, shopping and the like. Yet our reliance on such devices and their applications, the ever-increasing volume of energy necessary to power them, and even their disposable nature calls into question whether their many benefits will continue to outweigh their negative environmental impacts. Is the current level of consumption sustainable?

This chapter assesses one US-based company, Sun Microsystems, Inc., and the ways in which it answers this question while addressing sustainability issues through a number of successful initiatives. It investigates Sun's approach to the common problem of the massive amounts of energy needed to run a networked datacenter, and studies the knotty predicament of what to do with electronic waste, or e-waste. Finally, it evaluates Sun's three-pronged eco responsibility strategy – Innovate, Act and Share – and the effectiveness of such an approach in what could, if left unchecked, prove to be an unsustainable scenario.

Power-hungry datacenters

One of the key engines driving these recent productivity gains and daily conveniences is the datacenter. Datacenters are often very large facilities comprising a vast array of computers, communications and other networking equipment, as well as data storage devices. Many large companies own and maintain their own, while many smaller companies may use shared datacenter resources provided by third parties. Every financial transaction, whether online e-commerce or credit card transactions, runs through one of these datacenters.

Because of the growing population worldwide and its consequent impact on financial transactions, datacenters are increasing both in number and size. Unfortunately, such growth contributes to a surging global thirst for energy: a medium-sized corporate datacenter of 50,000 square feet and 4 megawatts of power can burn through the equivalent of more than 50 barrels of crude oil per day, averaging almost 2.5 barrels of oil per hour. While these numbers look large to start with, they do not even reflect our largest datacenters today. Overall, the energy consumption of many datacenters is increasing to capture the surge in online activity described above.

According to Adam Braunstein, a senior research analyst for the Robert Frances Group, the amount of electricity needed to run one large datacenter is equivalent to the needs of a city of 40,000 people.[2] Today, the energy needed to power a company's entire IT infrastructure accounts for an estimated 25 per cent of its total IT budget. And some analysts feel that the estimate could rise to as much as 40 per cent. For heavy tech users, this can mean millions of dollars every year. IDC, the global technology research firm, predicts that by 2009, technology operations in the US will spend twice as much for powering and cooling its datacenter as it did to purchase the server hardware itself.[3]

Founded in 1982, Sun Microsystems, Inc. spends US$2 billion annually on research and development of systems innovations that lower power consumption, increase datacenter efficiency, and drive capital and human productivity, according to David Douglas, Sun's vice president of eco responsibility. Douglas notes that electricity consumed by the world's datacenters produces nearly 200 million tons of CO_2 per year – more than the total carbon output of all automobiles in China.

In November 2005, Sun introduced the first eco-responsible computer processor, the UltraSPARC® T1 with CoolThreads™ technology. In an era when most processors required 150 watts, Sun's UltraSPARC T1 processor used just 70 – about the same amount of energy as a single incandescent light bulb. In addition to the environmental benefit of greatly reduced energy use, Sun's customers stood to realize significant cost savings on power, cooling and real estate. Powered by the UltraSPARC T1 processor, Sun's servers tucked the performance of a rack of servers into a single, 32-thread chip that consumed less energy, generated less heat and took up less space in the datacenter. Today, companies using the UltraSPARC save an estimated US$1,000 per server annually.

'There's a hidden price we're paying for the global Internet build-out, and for the impact millions of computers are having on the environment,' Douglas says, 'and Sun is on a mission to change this.' His company's products and policies, he explains, are good for Sun's shareholders, good for Sun's customers, and good for the planet.

E-waste strategies

Yet energy consumption and carbon reduction are only one piece of the environmental puzzle. On the opposite end is output – what happens when a server no longer serves? Innovation and demand for more capacious and faster computing have also increased the rate at which computing equipment of all kinds become obsolete, and the subsequent disposal and mushrooming mountain of e-waste is quietly becoming a critical issue in the industry.

In the US, where disposal laws vary from state to state, the Environmental Protection Agency (EPA) estimates more than 4,000,000 tons of e-waste hit the country's landfills each year, and physical space is only a part of the problem: the toxic ingredients in obsolete electronic goods pose additional threats to human health and the environment. While Congress is starting to respond, US oversight is still relatively weak compared to that of Europe, where many continent-wide regulations regarding the manufacture and disposal of e-waste were enacted more than a decade ago.

In response to e-waste legislation such as the European Waste Electrical and Electronic Equipment (WEEE) and Restriction of Hazardous Substances (RoHS) Directives, Sun Microsystems, Inc., has committed to a goal of having less than five per cent of its products end up in a waste stream. To this end, the company has instituted a program that attempts to eliminate regulated hazardous substances from its products by augmenting a global product take-back program in which customers can easily return Sun products for recycling or reuse. While the WEEE directive allows for no more than 35 per cent of a company's obsolete IT, telecommunications and consumer equipment products to enter the waste stream, Sun has gone well beyond it – the company successfully recycles, reuses or remanufactures more than 95 per cent of its products.

Sun also reduces e-waste by engineering products with dramatically longer life spans. While a typical PC may require some 300 watts of power and last between two and three years, the company's Sun Ray thin client (a desktop computer built without a hard disk drive that relies on a shared server) uses no moving parts and no fan, runs on four watts – the energy of a night light – and lasts on average 15 to 20 years: five to ten times that of an average PC.

Finally, Sun also invests in designing products that are easy to disassemble, reuse or recycle. The company's enclosures for its workstations and other products are designed with snap-fits, separable shielding materials and other features that make recycling the product more feasible. It manufactures and repurposes older Sun equipment for reuse to limited secondary markets, and successfully operates an asset recovery program to separate component commodities for re-sale and recycling. And Sun's design process includes assurances that restricted hazardous materials are not used, thus ensuring their absence from the waste/recovery stream. All these programs help Sun efficiently manage its resources through extended life and use.

Sustainable computing

Given how energy consumption, disposal, resource allocation and other pressing issues stand to shape society's ecology as well as its economies, certain leaders within the computing industry have chosen to address them with a variety of approaches. Balancing environmental and CSR issues with profitability remains an untested space, yet a few examples are proving that a company's concern for green issues can actually boost profits. Here we assess the initiatives taken by Sun, based on the three central commitments of its eco responsibility: Innovate, Act, Share.

The company's online 'Eco Center' explains it clearly: 'Sun innovates by making products and services that are both good for the environment and good for business. Sun acts by operating in an open, eco-conscious way on a day-to-day basis. And finally, Sun shares by making information and technology available to others so we can all move forward and participate in an increasingly sustainable way.' Let's look more closely at some examples of each component of Sun's three-pronged strategy.

1. Innovate

The computer industry is finally facing the challenge of lowering energy usage in datacenters through significant R&D investment in low-power servers and processors. For Sun, a recent innovation in this space is its highly successful CoolThreads™ technology. CoolThreads is the basis for the company's high-performance, energy-efficient Sun Fire™ T1000 and T2000 servers – servers that are gaining significant momentum in the market. CoolThreads feature the multithreaded (and thus energy-efficient) UltraSPARC T1 processor, designed with the intent of helping companies reduce energy consumption while still managing large volumes of data. Systems equipped with this processor run at lightning speed, setting numerous records and benchmarks for efficiency, and routinely outperforming Sun's competitors' systems.

In taking a holistic systems approach to the critical elements that customers require from Sun – namely software, systems, storage and services – Sun's products are designed to deliver real customer and environmental value though an energy-efficient design, a design that yields better performance while maintaining lower energy costs.

BOX 1 : PROJECT BLACKBOX: THE FIRST VISUALIZED DATACENTER

In October 2006, Sun unveiled Project Blackbox, a radical new concept for the future of network infrastructure. A scalable datacenter built into a standard shipping container, Project Blackbox uses state-of-the-art cooling, monitoring and power distribution systems and requires significantly less space than a traditional datacenter. These features allow

Sun's customers to realize significant cost and environmental savings associated with datacenter operations, as well as enhanced computing performance.

According to Sun's 2006 CSR report, aside from the business benefits of rapidly building or enabling increased datacenter capacity without building a new facility, Project Blackbox also offers important potential for use in developing or disaster regions. Governments and global relief organizations could leverage the project's easy management and support for up to 10,000 simultaneous thin-client users to bring computing to remote or impacted regions.

Customers who select a configuration with the Sun Fire CoolThreads technology-based servers will save about $1,000 a year per server, in addition to cost savings provided by the container's cooling advantage over existing datacenter implementations. Project Blackbox can accommodate up to 250 of these Sun Fire servers. Sun will extend its electronic waste and hazardous material leadership by taking back Project Blackbox containers and their systems for upgrading, reuse, recycling, or responsible disposal.

2. Act

Many forward-thinking employers have been applying computing and network technologies in order to provide a more eco-friendly work environment. This allows employees to work in flexible offices at any employer site or at home. Such flexwork programs may result in a dramatic reduction in CO_2 emissions in telework-friendly cities and significant savings in real estate and energy-related costs for the employer. Sun recognizes the impacts its corporate campuses have on the environment, and is taking steps to reduce these impacts. For them, this means a comprehensive flexwork program that allows the company's employees to work remotely from home or on the road (see 'Sun's Carbon-Smart Open Work Program' below).

When developing products, Sun strives for high standards of performance, reliability, energy efficiency and availability while minimizing harmful environmental impacts throughout the manufacturing of its products. And acting in eco-friendly ways often has contributed positively to Sun's bottom line: increasingly, Sun's customers seem to appreciate – even expect – a carbon-conscious business view.

BOX 2: SUN'S CARBON-SMART OPEN WORK PROGRAM

Like many progressive companies, Sun allows its employees to work wherever it is most convenient for them. For employees who choose to work from home, whether a few days a month or five days a week, Sun provides provisioning and support, including office equipment, broadband access, technical support, a formal registration process and established working agreements between employees and managers.

As part of the EPA's 'Climate Leaders' program, Sun has publicly committed to reducing greenhouse gas emissions related to its business operations by 20 per cent over 2002 levels by 2012. Five years into the program, more than half of Sun's 35,000 employees elected to work regularly outside the company's offices, saving them hundreds of dollars in gasoline each month and – between commuting, real estate and energy use – an estimated 30,000 tons of CO_2 released into the atmosphere.

In 2005, the EPA named Sun as one of the top 20 best employers for commuters.

3. Share

Unlike the Innovate and Act strands of Sun's eco strategy, Share reflects challenges and opportunities that cannot be addressed by a single organization. Instead, these situations necessitate co-operation and sharing among a range of organizations, including companies, research institutions and governments. This strand of Sun's eco strategy nods to the company's long history of working with open source communities and passion for transparency. Source code, documentation, and tools based on many Sun products, including its 64-bit, multithreaded UltraSPARC T1 processor, for example, are fully available to researchers, users, peers, partners and manufacturers to study, utilize and improve upon.

BOX 3: CHALLENGES, CHOICES AND COLLABORATIONS

Since November 2006, Sun – along with the EPA, Lawrence Berkeley National Laboratory and other environmental and information technology leaders – has focused on how eco responsibility can minimize harm to the planet while maximizing the benefits to business. One of the group's early goals was to establish an Energy Star-like industry standard for comparing the power usage of various servers in a datacenter. Like a sticker on a product in a vendor's showroom, such a clear public standard would allow datacenter managers to make smart purchasing decisions, and provide an industry-wide basis upon which to build other forms of accreditation.

Sun also collaborates with Lawrence Berkeley National Laboratory, the California Energy Commission and Silicon Valley companies such as Intel, Hewlett-Packard and others, on a program that examines energy efficiencies in the datacenter. Sun is currently looking at a wide range of options to tackle the inefficiencies of today's power distribution systems.

'Good for business and the environment'

Addressing the computing industry's sustainability challenges has several benefits. First, it benefits computing and networking consumers through significant savings in energy consumption and operating expenses. Equipment vendors benefit, too, since a strong pro-environmental stance acts as a differentiator, connecting the green-leaning company with a reputation of caring for the environment and for its customers through reduced energy usage, cost savings and reduced carbon emissions.

Sun's eco strategy is already producing results. David Douglas explains it like this: 'Through our eco-friendly products, workplace and e-waste initiatives, Sun has a truly unique and comprehensive value proposition for our customers. Sun's products today are consuming less energy, generating less waste, and enabling new, eco-responsible business practices. These innovations are changing the conversation with our customers by showing that eco responsibility can benefit the bottom line as well as the earth we share. Sun is working together with customers around the world to help reduce datacenter and desktop energy consumption without sacrificing performance or business results.'[4]

In producing eco-responsible computing systems designed to reduce energy and carbon production, manufacturers are delivering a carbon-neutral or a sustainable computing infrastructure. In Sun, the ability to do it all – to offer an alternative to power-hungry desktop and laptop computers; to help reduce the maintenance, upgrading, and operational costs associated with most PC client environments; to reduce power consumption and use of raw materials – helps pave a path to truly sustainable computing.

BOX 4: REDUCING COSTS, REDUCING CARBON

Here are three steps Sun recommends to its customers to lower their energy bills and begin reducing their carbon emissions.

First, understand where your datacenter electricity comes from and where it all goes. Your power bill will tell you how much power you use, and your utility can usually tell you how much CO_2 is emitted per kilowatt-hour.

Next, figure out what the energy is being used for. Many people are surprised when they learn that less than half the power is actually getting to the computers; it is common for air conditioning and power distribution losses to be responsible for significant electricity consumption. Once you understand where your power is going, it will be clear where to start your efforts.

One of the simplest tools for lowering server power is to upgrade older servers. Beyond upgrades, server consolidation and technologies such as virtualization are proving to be useful tools in getting more work out of existing systems. Alternative energy can also replace or complement standard grid electricity and result in reduced emissions.

It is important to note that these steps, while reducing emissions, will also lower your power bill. While these steps will not eliminate your electricity usage and resulting greenhouse gas emissions, you will have a much better handle on where you are, you will have experience with reduction programs and you can save yourself some money in the process.

Source: Sun Microsystems, Inc.

Concluding remarks

Between increased energy demands at datacenters and the perils associated with high volumes of potentially toxic e-waste, it is clear that the computing world faces serious challenges for an environmentally and economically sustainable future. The nature of the industry is such that developers and customers alike place high value on the newest, fastest products, but at what cost? Can such standards continue apace? Fortunately, like a few other manufacturers, Sun is imbued with a strong sense of corporate responsibility for both innovative products and a sustainable natural world. The computing field is finally facing these sustainability challenges, and Sun Microsystems, Inc. is one of its leaders.

This chapter assesses Sun's response to these sustainability challenges. It considers the company's role as an eco-responsible leader. Through innovation, Sun seeks to reduce the energy demands of computing and the environmental impact of network computing from server to thin-client desktop and grid computing. It acts by implementing a global take-back program, a 95 per cent product recycling program, and a company-wide flexwork policy for its employees. Building on its long heritage of transparency and open source sharing, Sun works to address problems and opportunities that require co-operation and sharing among a wide range of organizations, companies, research institutions and governments.

Writing in *Sustainable Industries Journal*, David Douglas, Sun's vice president of eco responsibility, said: 'Alone, no single product, service, change in behavior, or even company, will get us over the hurdles that stand between today and a truly sustainable computing infrastructure of tomorrow.' By acknowledging each of Sun's three tenets – Innovate, Act, Share – the company's eco strategy unfolds as a roadmap to ensure that its products and strategies do their part to bring a sustainable computing infrastructure a step closer to reality.

Notes

For more information: www.sun.com/eco.
1   My thanks to the various people who have provided informal comments and feedback.
2   From 'The Greening of the CIO', CIO Insights, July 2006.
3   IDC press release, 13 June 2006, http://www.idc.com/getdoc.jsp?containerId=prUS202105 06
4   Sun Press Release, 10 November 2006, http://www.sun.com/eco http://www. greenprogress.com/environment_article.php?id=360

Corporate Governance and International Business Leadership

5

Global Climate Governance: How the World's Largest Companies are Responding to Global Warming

Douglas G Cogan,
Institutional Shareholder Services

Institutional shareholder services

This chapter examines how 100 of the world's largest corporations are positioning themselves to compete in a carbon-constrained world. With the launch of the Kyoto Protocol in 2005, managing greenhouse gas (GHG) emissions is now part of doing business in key global trading markets. As leading companies move to join the international effort to combat global warming, climate governance practices will assume an increasingly central role in corporate and investment planning. Eventually, nothing short of an energy and technology revolution will be needed to stem rising greenhouse gas emissions across the globe.

Faced with record warmth, unprecedented hurricane activity and rapid shrinking of polar ice caps, industry opposition to confronting climate change is diminishing. Sceptics no longer question whether human activity is warming the globe but, instead, how fast. Similarly, companies at the vanguard no longer question how much it will cost to reduce greenhouse gas emissions, but how much money they can make doing it. Financial markets are starting to reward companies that are moving ahead on climate change, whilst those lagging behind are being assigned more risk.

Ultimately, effective corporate responses to climate change must be built on well functioning environmental management systems and properly focused governance practices. Shareholders and financial analysts will increasingly assign value to companies that prepare for and capitalize on business opportunities posed by climate change – whether from greenhouse gas regulations, direct physical impacts or changes in corporate reputation.

This chapter is designed as a benchmarking tool for institutional investors and corporations that are ready to seize on these trends. It employs a 'Climate Change Governance Checklist' to evaluate how 76 US companies and 24 non-US companies are addressing climate change through board oversight, management execution, public disclosure, emissions accounting and strategic planning. Information was gathered and synthesized in 2005 from securities filings, company reports, company websites and third-party questionnaires. Each of the 100 companies in this report was given an opportunity to comment on the draft profiles, out of which 84 companies offered comments.

Selection and scoring of companies

This chapter analyzes 100 companies in the ten most carbon-intensive sector industries: electric power; oil and gas; autos; chemicals; industrial equipment; metals and mining; coal; food products; forest products; and air transport.[1] Profiled companies have major operations in the United States and most operate as multinationals. They rank among the largest in their industries, based on market capitalization or revenues.

Companies were evaluated according to a Climate Change Governance Checklist. The checklist consists of 14 governance steps that companies can take to proactively address climate change. The checklist is used to rank companies on a 100-point scale. Each of the five governance categories carries a different number of maximum points, to reflect the number of actions available and their relative importance to the overall score.

Climate Change Governance Checklist: 100 Point System		
Board oversight		*Points*
1	Board committee has explicit oversight responsibility for environmental affairs.	
2	Board conducts periodic review of climate change and monitors progress in implementing strategies.	Up to 12
Management execution		
3	Chairman/CEO clearly articulates company's views on climate change and GHG control measures.	
4	Executive officers are in key positions to monitor climate change and co-ordinate response strategies.	Up to 18
5	Executive officers' compensation is linked to attainment of environmental goals and GHG targets.	
Public disclosure		
6	Securities filings identify material risks, opportunities posed by climate change.	
7	Sustainability report offers comprehensive, transparent presentation of company response measures.	Up to 14

Climate Change Governance Checklist: 100 Point System		
Emissions accounting		
8	Company calculates and registers GHG emissions savings and offsets from projects.	Up to 24
9	Company conducts annual inventory of GHG emissions from operations and publicly reports results.	
10	Company has set an emissions baseline by which to gauge future GHG emissions trends.	
11	Company has third party verification process for GHG emissions data.	
Emissions management and strategic opportunities		
12	Company sets absolute GHG emission reduction targets for facilities and products.	Up to 32
13	Company participates in GHG trading programs to gain experience and maximize credits.	
14	Company pursues business strategies to reduce GHG emissions, minimize exposure to regulatory and physical risks, and maximize opportunities from changing market forces and emerging controls.	

Source: *Institutional Shareholder Services*

Climate leaders: international competitors are still pacesetters

Whilst American companies are taking positive steps to address climate change at the governance level, most are still playing catch up with their international competitors – companies such as BP, Toyota, Alcan, Rio Tinto and Unilever. Based on the Climate Change Governance Checklist and the scoring system used, foreign companies lead in their governance responses to climate change in five of the nine industries that included both US and non-US companies (In the electric power sector, foreign companies were not analyzed.)

Such international leadership is partly because non-US companies are based in countries that have ratified the Kyoto Protocol and are moving forward with GHG emission controls. However, because the US firms also have operations in these markets and are subject to the same regulations, geography alone does not account for all of the difference. Other company-specific factors such as the integration of board and management environmental roles, long-term planning cycles and a commitment to sustainable development reporting, typically contribute to the leadership positions of many non-US companies.

Our research also identifies a handful of industry groups – coal, food product and airline companies in particular – where climate change continues to be widely unrecognized as a governance priority, despite the fact that it could have a tremendous impact on their businesses. Many coal companies (especially in the US), for example, have done little to mitigate the financial impacts of carbon regulations, despite managing the world's most carbon-intensive fuel source. Similarly, food product companies recognize that food-based raw materials and water resources are being put at risk, but few have articulated a strategy to address this mounting concern. Airline companies also fall into this category; among the world's fastest growing sources of CO_2 emissions they have the lowest average governance scores among all ten sectors examined, in part because they have looked to other industries to achieve emissions improvements.

Common themes of leadership companies

Whilst climate change should be a governance focus of all companies and major industry groups, the risks and opportunities presented by this issue are not distributed evenly. Some companies and industries – by virtue of the types and amount of energy they use – will be better positioned to respond than others. Alternatively, some companies and industries – by virtue of the types and location of their physical assets – will be more vulnerable to changing climatic conditions.

Among leadership companies, however, three governance practices are much in evidence that should serve as a model for all firms, regardless of the risk-reward ratio that climate change presents to their particular circumstances. At these leadership firms:

- **Boards of directors and senior executives are working together to address climate change and other sustainability issues.** A key challenge for all firms is ensuring that boards are adequately prepared to focus on GHG reduction and climate mitigation strategies.

- **CEOs have embraced climate change as a top priority for their firms.** True leaders are stepping up and speaking out, rather than leaving this issue to their successors.

- **Management teams are pursuing practical solutions to climate change.**[2] Rather than waiting for breakthrough technologies to address systemic challenges of reducing GHG emissions, they are working together to find cost-effective, near-term solutions, starting with conservation of energy and more efficient production processes. Some are also laying building blocks towards a carbon-neutral economy, with projects focused on renewable energy, carbon sequestration and infrastructure for hydrogen fuels.

Climate Leaders in 10 Major Industries: Based on 100-point Scoring System						
Company	Board	Management	Disclosure	GHG Data	Strategies	Total
Maximum	12	18	14	24	32	100
BP	9	16	13	23	29	90

Climate Leaders in 10 Major Industries: Based on 100-point Scoring System						
Company	Board	Management	Disclosure	GHG Data	Strategies	Total
DuPont	8	16	12	21	28	85
Alcan	9	15	11	20	22	77
AEP	10	11	12	19	21	73*
Toyota	9	14	10	14	18	65
GE	5	12	9	12	20	58
Rio Tinto	7	11	10	16	14	58
Int'l Paper	6	11	6	12	16	51
Unilever	6	8	8	13	12	47
UPS	3	4	6	10	7	30

*Cinergy also scored 73 points in the electric power sector.

Source: *Corporate Governance and Climate Change: Making the Connection*, Ceres, 2006.

Following is a summary of governance actions taken by leading companies in each of the ten industries examined:

BP (oil & gas): BP was the first major oil company to state publicly, in 1997, that the risks of climate change are serious and that precautionary action is justified. BP has cut its operational GHG emissions to 10 per cent below 1990 levels, and now aims to hold its emissions steady through to 2012. Due to the fact that use of petroleum products emits eight times more CO_2 than the processes that produce them, BP is focused on reducing its carbon emissions footprint. In 2005, BP established an Alternative Energy business unit that plans to invest US$8 billion in solar, wind, hydrogen and combined-cycle power generation technologies over the next decade. In partnership with General Electric, BP is developing carbon sequestration technologies.

DuPont (chemicals): DuPont's board of directors has overseen the company's climate change activities since 1994. The company is committed to reducing its GHG emissions by 65 per cent between 1990 and 2010. It also plans to increase energy use from renewables to ten per cent by 2010. It is actively engaged in GHG emissions trading and is involved in the development of next-generation refrigeration systems, fuel cells, biomaterials, lightweight materials and energy-saving insulation.

Alcan (metals): Alcan created an executive-level steering team in 2001 to embed energy efficiency and GHG emissions reduction goals throughout the company. It achieved 2.9 million tonnes of GHG reductions in 2001–2004, and is evaluating new targets for 2006. Through recycling programs and continued improvements in developing energy efficient products, Alcan believes the aluminum industry can become carbon neutral by 2020 on a life-cycle basis.

AEP and Cinergy (electric power): In response to shareholder requests, the board of directors at each of these electric utilities agreed to produce detailed reports in 2004 on their climate risk mitigation strategies. Both companies have established targets through 2010 to reduce their GHG emissions below historical levels and are pursuing development of integrated gasification combined cycle (IGCC) power plants. By gasifying coal to generate electricity and disposing of CO_2 emissions underground, these companies believe it is possible to make coal an emissions-free generating source. (This report analyzed only US companies in the electric power sector.)

Toyota (autos): Toyota formed a company-wide Global Warming Prevention Council in 1998 to meet the CO_2 emission targets set by the Kyoto Protocol. That same year, it introduced the Prius hybrid passenger car, now the best-selling gasoline-electric hybrid vehicle in the world. By 2010 Toyota plans to offer hybrid options across all of its major model lines. With regard to its facilities, it has set a goal to reduce its emissions by 20 per cent on a sales-weighted basis in 2001-2010. Toyota had achieved a 12 per cent reduction as of 2004.

General Electric (industrial equipment): As part of the 'Ecomagination' initiative announced by Chairman and CEO Jeffrey Immelt in 2005, GE has pledged by 2012 to achieve a one per cent reduction in its GHG emissions relative to 2004 levels. It also intends to cut the GHG intensity rate of its operations by 30 per cent by 2008. GE plans to double its investments in climate-friendly technologies such as wind turbines, highly efficient gas turbines, IGCC power plants, hybrid diesel-electric locomotives and water purification systems, to US$1.5 billion a year by 2010.

Rio Tinto (coal and minerals): Rio Tinto has a Climate Change Leadership Panel and a group Climate Change Executive to help co-ordinate GHG reduction efforts among its business groups. The company is developing 'low emissions pathways' for its products to reduce the GHG emissions intensity in coal combustion, metals smelting and electricity use. It has set five-year targets to reduce its GHG intensity rates and has also calculated its overall carbon emissions footprint.

International Paper (forest products): International Paper has an internal committee comprised of senior executives that reviews its polices on climate change and other environmental issues; this work is overseen at board level by its Public Policy and Environment Committee. The company plans to reduce its absolute GHG emissions by 15 per cent in 2000–2010. It was the first forest products company to join the Chicago Climate Exchange.

Unilever (food products): Unilever's Corporate Responsibility Council oversees the company's environmental and sustainability policies and performance. The company sets one and five-year targets for energy efficiency improvements and reductions in GHG emissions in manufacturing operations. Unilever is placing particular emphasis on the use of refrigeration equipment that either reduces, or eliminates, the use of coolants that contribute to global warming and ozone depletion. It makes a life-cycle assessment of the GHG emissions from its products.

UPS (air carrier): UPS's Corporate Environmental Affairs Group co-ordinates the company's GHG emissions reduction strategies. Strategies include increasing the fuel efficiency of its aircraft and vehicles, testing new technologies for its facilities and taking advantage of its integrated network and inter-modal capabilities to improve operating efficiency and reduce miles driven. UPS maintains a large fleet of alternative fuel vehicles and is deploying hybrid technologies.

Average Industry Scores						
Industry	Board	Management	Disclosure	GHG Data	Strategies	Total
Maximum	12	18	14	24	32	100
Chemicals	5.9	9.0	7.7	13.8	15.5	51.9
Electricity	5.5	8.8	8.7	13.7	11.9	48.5
Autos	6.5	9.0	7.9	12.9	11.6	47.9
Equipment	3.0	7.5	5.1	11.2	15.5	42.3
Mining	4.7	8.1	6.2	10.5	12.7	42.2
Forests	4.0	7.8	5.4	9.4	11.0	37.6
Oil & Gas	4.1	6.1	4.9	10.3	9.5	34.8
Coal	1.6	3.6	5.4	5.2	5.6	21.4
Food	1.6	3.2	2.5	5.4	4.9	17.6
Airlines	0.9	3.0	3.7	4.6	4.4	16.6
Average	3.8	6.6	5.8	9.7	10.2	36.1

Source: Corporate Governance and Climate Change: Making the Connection, Ceres, 2006.

US companies: progress since 2003

Our research, first published in 2003, introduced the Climate Change Governance Checklist. Twenty global companies were scored on 14 governance actions to proactively address climate change. A key finding of that report was that major American companies and industries were largely ignoring or discounting climate change in their governance practices and strategic planning.

This is no longer the case. Corporate leaders in many US industries have begun to meet the climate challenge as the following examples illustrate:

- In 2003, US-based petroleum companies virtually had a single-minded focus on oil and gas development. *In 2004, Chevron formally integrated renewable technologies into its energy portfolio and now invests more than $100 million per year in low-carbon and carbon-free energy alternatives.*

- In 2003, US auto companies relied on sales of big sport utility vehicles (SUV), with low gas mileage, as their main source of profits. *In 2004, Ford introduced the first American-built hybrid SUV and now plans to increase hybrid vehicle production tenfold, to 250,000 a year, by 2010.*

- In 2003, few US power companies acknowledged the risks related to climate change. *In 2004, American Electric Power announced plans to build the first commercial scale plant using coal gasification technology, calling it the 'right investment' given foreseeable GHG regulations. Cinergy and other power companies are now advocating for a national climate policy with mandatory emission controls.*

- In 2003, US equipment manufacturers were largely silent about their plans to develop GHG-saving technologies. *In 2005, General Electric launched its 'Ecomagination' campaign, a plan to double investments in climate-friendly technologies and reach US$20 billion in annual sales by 2010.*

The US companies, covering ten different industries, provide many positive examples of actions that companies are taking to integrate climate change into their governance practices and strategic planning. In profiles available at the Ceres website, we examine five such topics in detail.[3]

- **Board oversight:** Companies like Anadarko Petroleum, Cinergy and Dow Chemical, have created climate change task forces to integrate board oversight with executive-level actions to manage GHG emissions.

- **Management execution:** The CEOs of companies like Alcoa, Duke Power and United Technologies, have become leaders in their industries by articulating the business case for GHG controls and a supportive government regulatory framework.

- **Public disclosure:** Companies like DuPont, Ford and Entergy, have disclosed their climate risks and opportunities in their securities filings and other public documents.

- **Emissions accounting:** Companies like General Motors (GM), Southern and Sunoco have provided detailed public accounts of their GHG emissions, which include historical baselines, tracking of emissions savings and projections of future trends.

- **Strategic planning:** Companies like Air Products & Chemicals, Edison International and Weyerhaeuser, have created business management and product development plans that are poised to seize new opportunities presented by climate change.

Analysis of industries (as of 2005)

High scoring industries:

Chemical industry *(average score: 51.9 points)*

Among the ten industries evaluated, the chemical sector had the highest overall scores and tied with two other industries for the highest management and strategies scores. Chemical companies also scored strongly on board oversight.

- *Top strategies scores:* Chemical companies are focused on new products that promote energy efficiency and growing demand for climate-friendly technologies. DuPont, for example, is developing next generation refrigerants with low or no global warming potential and is leading an effort to build the world's first pilot-scale 'bio-refinery', using the entire corn plant to produce ethanol fuel. Air Products and Praxair are both involved in developing hydrogen and carbon sequestration technologies.

- *High board and management scores:* Most chemical companies have good management and/or board governance systems in place for handling climate change. These high scores are partly the result of the industry's long experience with the 1987 Montreal Protocol, which required a phase-out of chemicals that deplete the Earth's ozone layer. DuPont's board has been overseeing climate change activities since 1994.

- *High emissions accounting scores:* As leading industrial energy consumers many chemical companies have invested in more efficient energy systems and other changes in manufacturing processes that have reduced GHG emissions considerably. Whilst some companies have set GHG 'intensity' reduction targets, DuPont and Bayer have set targets for 2010 to reduce overall emissions by 65 per cent and 50 per cent respectively, relative to 1990 levels. Several companies conduct life-cycle assessments that measure product end-use GHG emissions.

Electric utility industry *(average score: 48.5 points)*

The electric utility sector had the highest average disclosure score, second-highest emissions accounting score and the second highest average score of the ten industries examined.

- *Top disclosure scores:* Accounting for nearly two-fifths of the nation's CO_2 emissions, electric utilities face considerable risks from climate change regulations. Six of the 19 companies profiled have published climate risk reports. Nine have expressed varying degrees of support for mandatory curbs on CO_2 emissions.

- *High emissions accounting scores:* Power companies have been required since 1990 to monitor and report CO_2 emissions. Many companies have also taken advantage of the 1992 Energy Policy Act to register CO_2 emissions savings under the Section 1605(b) program.

- **Above-average strategies scores:** High-scoring companies are pursuing low-carbon and non-carbon energy options – renewables, natural gas and clean coal – to generate electricity. Noteworthy examples include AEP and Cinergy, which are moving forward with plans to build commercial-scale integrated gasification combined cycle (IGCC) power plants, and Edison International, which is partnering with BP to build the nation's first hydrogen fueled power plant, with most of the CO_2 being captured and stored underground. Lower scoring utilities remain committed to traditional forms of coal-fired generation and are less focused on demand-side management programs.

Auto industry *(average score: 47.9 points)*

Auto companies had the highest average board score and tied with the chemical industry for the highest average management score. It had the third highest disclosure score.

- **Top board and management scores:** Automakers recognize that policies to address climate change pose risks to the industry, which remains almost entirely dependent on petroleum and is one of the fastest growing sources of CO_2 emissions. Many companies have task forces to co-ordinate board and executive level actions, and include climate change in strategic planning. Ford recently issued the industry's first stand-alone report examining the business impacts of the climate issue.

- **High emissions accounting scores:** Auto companies have developed reliable and consistent systems to measure emissions from their operations. GM has been tracking its GHG emissions since 1990 and has been a leader in setting targets and recording savings from its global facilities. GM, Ford and other auto companies, however, have backed away from estimating carbon emissions resulting from operation of their products, which are a far greater source of emissions.

- **Above-average strategies scores:** Japanese automakers have long held the lead in developing fuel-saving technologies. Honda's product line has the highest fleet fuel economy average, while Toyota has established itself as the leader in gasoline-electric hybrids. Ford is developing multiple advance fuel technologies and has two hybrid models on the market GM has spent more than $1 billion on fuel cell research and recently expanded its offerings of flexible fuel vehicles that run on E85 ethanol. European automakers lead in diesel engine technology, which offers fuel economy advantages over gasoline-powered engines.

Middle scoring industries:

Industrial equipment industry *(average score: 42.3 points)*

Industrial equipment companies tied with chemical companies for the highest average strategies score, but had weak board scores.

- *Top strategies scores:* Industrial equipment manufacturers are in a strong position to reduce GHG emissions with technologies that are energy efficient and use alternative energy sources. The highest scores were posted by General Electric, ABB and United Technologies, which are major providers of efficient power plants and distributed energy systems.

- *Above-average management scores:* Environmental and sustainable development issues are becoming a higher management priority at these companies, since most of the products they produce are very energy intensive and a major source of emissions.

- *Below-average board scores:* Equipment manufacturers serve many 'smokestack industries' that until recently have placed relatively little emphasis on reducing GHG emissions. Limited board action may reflect the involvement of these other industries as board members and primary customers.

Metals and mining industry *(average score: 42.2 points)*

This industry had above average overall scores, led by aluminum producers Alcan and Alcoa. US steel companies had among the lowest average industry scores.

- *Above-average board and management scores:* Metals and mining companies face a constant sustainable development challenge of producing affordably priced products as natural resources are depleted. Alcan created an executive-level team in 2001 to incorporate energy efficiency and GHG reduction goals throughout the company.

- *Above-average emissions accounting and strategies scores:* Changes in manufacturing processes, more efficient energy use and expanded resource recovery programs have enabled many companies to reduce GHG emissions considerably, including a 25 per cent reduction at Alcoa facilities since 1990.

- *High scores for aluminum producers:* Aluminum producers believe that the use of primary aluminum in transportation and recycling can have substantial positive impacts in reducing GHG emissions. Alcoa has set a goal to make 50 per cent of its products from recycled aluminum by 2020. Alcan and Alcoa believe the aluminum industry can become carbon neutral by 2020.

Forest products industry *(average score: 37.6 points)*

Forest products companies had relatively strong board, management and strategies scores but weak disclosure scores.

- *Above-average strategies scores:* Forest product companies manage vast terrestrial carbon 'sinks' through the forests they grow, putting them in an advantageous position if they can manage their resources sustainably. Biomass energy, which is carbon neutral, is the primary power source for most forest products companies. International Paper was the first company in this industry to join the Chicago Climate Exchange, a voluntary GHG trading market.

- *Average board and management scores:* Company leadership has focused on energy efficiency and fuel-switching to reduce GHG emissions, but less attention has been devoted to climate-related product opportunities and physical risks.

- *Below-average disclosure scores:* Forest products companies face comparatively high risks from the physical effects of climate change, such as potential increases in wildfires, windstorms and pest infiltrations, as well as possible migration of tree species away from the forests they own or manage. Company disclosure on these potential risks is very weak.

Oil and gas industry *(average score: 34.8 points)*

Oil and gas companies had the widest disparity of responses, with European companies showing strong leadership and many US companies lagging behind, especially those focused primarily on US oil refining and distribution of natural gas.

- *Wide variations on board, management and emissions accounting scores:* The three highest scoring companies – BP, Royal Dutch Shell and Statoil – distinguish themselves with strong board and management involvement on climate issues. BP and Royal Dutch Shell are the only two companies that have set long-term GHG reductions goals and measure emissions from customer use of products. Statoil stands out for emitting only 40 kilograms of CO_2 per unit of production, compared to the industry average of 130 kilograms, and for its efforts (along with BP and Royal Dutch Shell) to demonstrate carbon sequestration to enhance oil recovery.

- *Wide variations on strategies scores:* BP and Royal Dutch Shell have made major financial commitments to alternative energy sources, such as solar, wind and hydrogen. Among US firms, Chevron is investing over $100 million a year in low-carbon technologies, while ExxonMobil has dismissed wind and solar power as being 'inconsequential.'

- *Low scores for US natural gas producers:* Natural gas-focused firms such as Burlington Resources, El Paso and Williams, have done little to examine the climate issue. Such companies stand to benefit from CO_2 regulations that favor clean-burning, lower-carbon domestic energy sources.

Low scoring industries:

Coal industry *(average score: 21.4 points)*

- *Well below- average scores in four out of five governance areas:* Coal is the most carbon-intensive fuel source, accounting for 36% of the nation's CO_2 emissions (including coal burned to generate electricity). Arguably, the coal industry has more at stake in addressing climate change than any other industry, yet many companies' governance response has been limited or nonexistent.

- *Near-average disclosure score:* As with domestic natural gas suppliers, domestic coal producers have a narrow geographic focus and one main delivery option. Unlike gas producers, however, coal companies stand to lose much more as a result of carbon emission constraints. Most companies acknowledge that GHG regulations could adversely affect power-sector demand for coal, but otherwise choose to downplay or ignore the issue.

- *Well-below strategies score:* The primary strategy being pursued (especially by larger coal companies) is the support of research into technologies to gasify coal and store CO_2 emissions underground. This research is being done in conjunction with government energy agencies and electric utilities. Carbon sequestration technologies, however, have yet to be proven technologically and commercially. Coal-bed methane recovery is another important, but more limited, commercial option.

Food products industry *(average score: 17.6 points)*

- *Lowest disclosure score:* Although several leading food products companies acknowledge the threat posed by climate change to food-based raw materials and water resources, few companies have articulated a strategy to address this threat. Leading companies like Unilever are at least focused on the issue.

- *Low emissions accounting score:* While food products are not GHG-intensive, food processing is relatively energy intensive. Many food products companies have taken steps to make their operations more energy efficient. Leading companies like Unilever and Nestlé have also focused on GHG emissions from product packaging and refrigeration systems.

- *Low strategies score:* Some food products companies like Archer Daniels Midland (ADM) and Bunge develop feedstocks for ethanol-based transportation fuels. Biomass fuels could be a boon to the agricultural industry, however, CO_2 benefits will come mainly from cellulosic sources (like grasses) that are nearly carbon neutral, rather than corn-based ethanol, which provides about a 20 per cent savings in GHG emissions relative to gasoline.

Airline industry *(average score: 16.6 points)*

- *Lowest average score in four out of five governance areas:* Aircraft are among the fastest growing sources of CO_2 emissions in the world, expected to reach five per cent of global CO_2 emissions by 2020. Emissions improvements are largely outside of the companies' control, however, as they are dependent on advances in engine and airframe design and improvements in airport and air traffic management systems.

- *Low management scores:* Airline profitability is largely dependent on managing fuel costs, therefore giving these companies a built-in incentive to improve the fuel efficiency of their operations. This suggests that management has an indirect focus on reducing GHG emissions that may not be reflected in these scores.

- *Higher scores for freight carriers:* Freight carriers have large ground delivery fleets with GHG management options available through logistics and fuel alternatives. Passenger carriers are more dependent on GHG reductions available through logistical changes in government-controlled air traffic management systems.

	Electric Power	Manu-facture	Auto & Trans	Oil & Gas	Forestry	Agricul-ture	Fisheries	Healthcare	Real Estate	Tourism	Water
Regulatory Risk	■	■	■	■	■	■					
Physical Risk (dependent on location)	■	■	■	■	■	■	■	■	■	■	■
Competitive Reputational Risk	■	■	■	■	■	■	■	■	■	■	■
Regulatory Opportunity	■	■	■	■	■						■
Technological Opportunity	■	■	■	■	■	■					■
Competitive Reputational Opportunity	■	■	■	■	■	■	■	■	■	■	■

Climate risk & opportunities in selected industries
Source: Ceres report – Managing the Risk and Opportunities of Climate Change: A Toolkit for Corporate Leaders

Why companies must act now

Given the sweeping global nature of climate change, climate risk has become embedded, to a greater or lesser extent, in every business and investment portfolio. Companies with significant GHG emissions or energy-intensive operations face risks from new regulations. Climate change also poses direct physical risks to a wide array of firms and industries. Climate change deserves discussion in securities filing in the many instances in which direct financial risks or opportunities can be identified.

Physical risks: Businesses are at risk from the physical impacts of climate change, including the increased intensity and frequency of weather events, droughts, floods, storms and sea level rise. Changes in consumer habits that accompany changing weather patterns will also affect profitability in a number of sectors.

- Following Hurricane Katrina, one of the strongest hurricanes on record, the US city of New Orleans remains a city in disrepair. Businesses along the Gulf Coast suffered billions of dollars worth of infrastructure damage, with particularly costly effects to oil and gas rigs and refineries. Forecasters are predicting very active hurricane seasons in the years to come.

- Long-term capital investment plans may not properly account for climatic alterations. A proposed US$7 billion pipeline in Canada's Mackenzie Valley, for example, is dependent on permafrost or frozen ground as a supportive structure. When permafrost thaws, a process that has already begun, long-term investments in the pipeline will be at risk.

- All told, trillions of dollars of property on, or near coastlines now, stand in harm's way. Inland, drought and more frequent heat waves could lead to the collapse of local food systems. According to the World Meteorological Organization, the percentage of the Earth's land area stricken by severe drought has already more than doubled over the last quarter century.[4]

Regulatory risk: State, national, and international regulations are putting increasing pressure on companies with emissions from operations or products to invest in emissions controls, purchase carbon credits, or face clean-up costs.

- In the United Kingdom and throughout Europe, as well as in Canada and Japan, the Kyoto Protocol has come into effect. Developing countries like China also have emission reduction laws in place. Compliance with global emission reduction requirements is likely to be significantly more costly for companies with the poorest climate governance.

- Nationally, it is only a matter of time before Congress enacts federal carbon constraints. A growing number of Wall Street firms, industry CEOs and evangelical leaders are questioning the US government's voluntary approach to climate change and are calling for greater measures to reduce regulatory uncertainty.

- In the face of federal inaction, regulatory activity is picking up at the state and regional level. California and ten other states are moving to limit CO_2 emissions from automobiles. This would impact at least 33 per cent of all new cars and light trucks sold in the US. Likewise, four states are already regulating CO_2 from electric utilities, and others are considering doing so. Seven northeastern states have agreed to a cap-and-trade emissions reduction program for the electric power sector, and California, Oregon, and Washington are working on a similar region-wide approach to limit greenhouse gases.

Competitive risk: Tightly linked to regulatory risk in the global and domestic marketplaces, climate risk preparedness will be a key driver in a company's ability to compete.

- At present, Ford and General Motors are engaged in a high-stakes struggle to remain competitive as customers turn away from gas-guzzling SUVs in favor of hybrids and other vehicles from Japanese competitors. In China, auto sales are surging well beyond the growth rates that the US market has seen in recent decades. Only 19 per cent of current US passenger cars and 14 per cent of light-duty trucks, however, meet China's 2008 emission standards.[5] Both Toyota and Honda have decided to introduce their highly fuel-efficient hybrid models in the burgeoning Chinese market.

- By some estimates, companies in the electric power sector that have not prepared for the inevitable future costs of carbon emissions could see losses in EBITDA (Earnings Before Interest, Taxes, Depreciation, and Amortization) of 24 per cent to 83 per cent.[6] Some public utility commissions now require utilities to include a cost for their carbon emissions, which will accelerate demand for cost-effective energy from providers of 'clean' power such as wind, solar, hydro and possibly nuclear power.

Technological and competitive risks and opportunities: Companies in many sectors can increase profitability by implementing energy efficiency strategies and developing emission-reducing technologies, or new products that meet changing corporate and consumer demands.

- Fossil fuels have been the driver of economic growth for more than two centuries, but change is clearly afoot. Global investments in renewable energy hit a record US$30 billion in 2004, providing 1.7 million jobs worldwide. Far larger investments are expected in the years ahead, as Europe, the US, China and Japan aggressively embrace solar, wind and other climate-friendly options over increasingly costly fuels like oil and natural gas.[7]

- Two remaining wildcards in this energy transition are coal and nuclear power, both of which face huge questions regarding waste disposal. In the case of coal, it is CO_2 disposal in the atmosphere that is the problem. If means are not found to capture and store CO_2 economically underground, coal, as the most carbon-intensive fossil fuel, will have to relinquish its role as the leading provider of electricity in a carbon-constrained world. Nuclear power could serve as a carbon-free alternative to coal. However, permanent disposal of high-level radioactive waste remains a vexing challenge, as do concerns over the safety of nuclear plants and proliferation of uranium fuel at a time of heightened global security risks.

- To halve the projected rate of CO_2 emissions from energy by 2050, and stabilize atmospheric concentrations at twice pre-industrial levels, 25 billion tons of CO_2 emissions savings must be found. BP and Ford have supported research at Princeton University to explore ways in which energy demand could double over the next five decades (as is now projected), without increasing CO_2 emission rates above current levels. Princeton has identified seven strategies that could achieve this goal, each of which would supplant 3.5 billion tons of CO_2 emissions from other sources by 2050. For each of the strategies, US businesses have an opportunity to capitalize on technological innovation:[8]

1. Use existing energy efficiency methods to cut carbon emissions from buildings by 25 per cent

2. Increase fuel economy in cars so that two billion vehicles run at an average of 60 miles per gallon

3. Use natural gas in place of coal at 1,400 one gigawatt (1,000 megawatt) generating plants

4. Capture and store the CO_2 generated at 1,600 gas-fired generating plants

5. Achieve a 50-fold increase in wind power

6. Achieve a 700-fold increase in the use of solar photovoltaics

7. Produce 34 million barrels of bio-fuels a day, using roughly 250 million hectares of arable land (approximately 16.5 per cent of the world's available resources).

In short, the stakes could not be higher for global companies and investors. The greatest investment opportunities as this new era takes hold will lie with companies that capitalize on this emerging shift in global energy use and production methods. The greatest risks will be with those that choose to ignore these trends and try to carry on with business as usual.

What companies should do

Companies that are successful in facing this challenge must have comprehensive climate change strategies, with the following four key elements:

1. Companies must assess the deepening financial connections between climate change and their businesses. Companies with significant GHG emissions, or high-energy use, need to assess their exposure from new regulations and develop strategies for mitigating those risks. Companies vulnerable to the direct physical risks also need to take stock of their assets and supply chains. All of these assessments must be evaluated and managed at the highest corporate levels, including by CEOs and boards of directors.

2. Companies must develop and implement action plans to manage climate risks and seize new market opportunities. These plans should include new corporate policies and procedures for reducing and mitigating risk, setting absolute GHG reduction targets and energy efficiency goals, and developing or purchasing new clean energy technologies. Companies should also participate in climate policy dialogues that will reduce financial risks and enhance competitiveness opportunities.

3.   Companies must share and discuss their climate strategies with investors, analysts and other stakeholders. Companies should disclose their assessments and implementation plans in annual financial reports and corporate responsibility reports. Further, they should engage with shareholders, Wall Street analysts and public interest groups to obtain feedback in developing effective, proactive responses to climate change.

4.   Most importantly, corporate leaders must overcome a tendency toward short-term thinking to implement these climate strategies successfully, emphasizing long-term financial results and building long-term shareholder value. In essence, the gap between corporate decision-makers and the lasting effects of their decisions must be narrowed.[9]

This constitutes an enormous challenge. In almost every instance chief decision makers leave their companies long before the capital they deploy does. A typical corporate CEO may look three to five years ahead when making a capital investment. By comparison, the average term of service for a long-lived asset like a fossil fuel energy plant is more than 30 years, and CO_2 emissions from such a plant last an average of 100 years.

Increasingly, climate risk is embedded in every business and investment portfolio. The fundamental challenge ahead is to stabilize atmospheric concentrations of CO_2 as world energy use may double by 2050. Investors must continue to engage corporate boards and managers to ensure that comprehensive climate governance strategies are put in place.

The Climate Change Governance Checklist discussed in this chapter is a tool to help this to be achieved.[10] It rewards companies that are reporting their GHG emissions and are seizing new business opportunities from growing demand for climate-friendly products and services. Such companies typically have a long-term perspective that matches the investment horizons of retirement systems and endowment plans, which must look to the future well being of their beneficiaries as part of their fiduciary duties. Working together – and with the help of such tools – investors and companies will rise to the challenge posed by global warming.

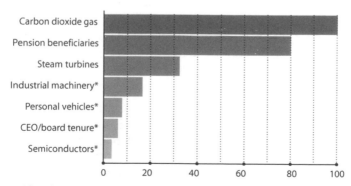

Average life cycles vs. natural life cycles

*Source for capital cydes: U.S.Department of Commerce, Bureau of Economic Analysis

100 company scores by sector – maximum score 100

TOP SCORING SECTORS		MID SCORING SECTORS		LOW SCORING SECTORS	
Chemical industry	**51.9**	**Industrial equip**	**42.5**	**Oil and Gas**	**34.8**
Company	score	GE	58	BP	90
DuPont	85	ABB	54	Royal Dutch	79
Bayer	71	UTC	52	Statoil	72
ICI	60	Hitachi	51	Total	62
BASF	59	Mitsubishi	45	Chevron	57
Dow Chemical	59	Siemens	40	Anadarko	39
Air Products	49	Caterpillar	27	Sunoco	39
Praxair	43	Deere	14	Amerada Hess	35
Rohm & Haas	40			ConocoPhillips	35
Monsanto	32	**Metals and Mining**	**42.2**	ExxonMobil	35
PPG	21	Alcan	77	Marathon	26
		Akoa	74	Occidental	25
Electric power	**48.8**	Nippon Steel	67	Valero	24
AEP	73	BHP Billiton	63	Apache	22
Cinergy	73	Anglo Amer.	56	Tesoro	15
Entergy	65	Newmont	24	Burlington	13
Exelon	63	Nucor	21	Devon Energy	11
Calpine	55	U.S. Steel	20	El Paso	9
PG&E	54	Mittal Steel	14	Murphy Oil	6
Xcel Energy	53	Phelps Dodge	6	Williams	3
Edison Int'l	51				
Southern	51	**Forest Products**	**37.2**	**Coal industry**	**21.4**
TXU	51	Int'l Paper	49	Rio Tinto	57
DTE	50	Abitibi	45	Peabody	23
FirstEnergy	50	Weyerhaeuser	35	CONSOL	14
FPL Group	50	MeadWestvaco	31	Arch	8
Duke	47	Georgia-Pacific	26	Foundation	5
Progress	36				
AES	34	These charts show the 100		**Food Industry**	**17.6**
Sempra	24	company scores, listed by sector.		Unilever	49
Dominion	27	The chemical sector had the		Nestle	29
Constellation	23	highest average governance		General Mills	22
		scores, and the airline sector		ADM	12
Auto Industry	**47.9**	had the lowest average scores.		Altrla	11
Toyota	65	Average scores for each sector		PepsiCo	9
Honda	62	are shown in bold, followed by		Bunge	5
Ford	58	individual company scores.		ConAgra	4
GM	52				
Daimler	43			**Airline Industry**	**16.6**
Volkswagen	37			UPS	30
BMW	35			British Airways	27
Nissan	33			Air France	23
				FedEx	18
				AMR	9
				Southwest	6
				UAL	3

Appendix 1: How companies were scored

The scoring system used in this research is intended as a benchmarking tool for institutional investors and corporations ready to take action on climate change; it is *not* a simplistic ranking of 'best and worst' companies. The scoring system measures the degree to which companies perceive the risks and opportunities posed by climate change, and the governance actions they are taking in response.

No two companies are alike, and their possible response options to climate change vary. Because the choices, challenges, risks and opportunities that companies face in addressing climate change are not identical, companies should be judged individually, as well as in comparison to their industry groups and the overall survey sample. *Of particular interest to investors should be companies that rank high or low in relation to their industry peers.*

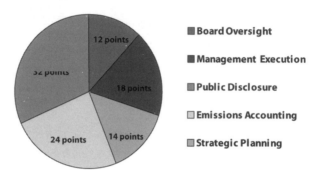

Climate Change Governance Weighting
Source: Institutional Shareholder Services

The scoring system used, rewards companies that have taken the following types of actions:

- **Public disclosure:** Our analysis is largely dependent on information companies have placed in the public domain for use by investors and other interested stakeholders. Companies with more available information on their governance responses to climate change – as presented in securities filings, sustainability reports, corporate websites, CEO presentations and responses to third-party questionnaires (like the Carbon Disclosure Project), generally score better than those with less publicly available information.[11]

- **Policy advocacy:** We also credit companies that have spoken publicly about climate change in a policy context. Though companies express near-universal support for market-based actions taken on a voluntary basis to control GHG emissions, such measures have done little to slow rising emissions. In addition, the absence of US government control targets has added to investor uncertainty and complicated corporate strategic planning. Accordingly, the scoring system rewards companies that support a government regulatory framework to address climate change and that are explicit in their own governance responses. It credits CEOs who have assumed advocacy roles in their industries, as well as boards of directors and executive committees that have taken active, clearly defined roles to incorporate climate policy considerations into their strategic planning and decision-making.

- **Early action:** Our scoring system reserves the most credit for companies that have taken early actions to address climate change and control GHGs. The Framework Convention on Climate Change (ratified by the US Congress in 1992) set 1990 as a baseline year to reduce GHG emissions. Consistent with the science backing the need for GHG reductions, the scoring system reserves the most points for companies that have achieved actual reductions below their 1990 levels. Whether these early movers reap long-term financial benefits from their actions will depend in part on how they are treated by regulators and the capital markets. In any case, we assume that companies with more experience with, and general preparedness for, carbon emission constraints, stand to gain the greatest competitive advantages.

- **Long-term planning:** Our scoring system rewards companies that take a long-term view of their enterprises and capital investment decisions. Climate change presents a 'governance gap' in decision-making, whereby the warming effects of GHGs in the atmosphere far outlast the tenure of corporate executives and the payback periods of their investments. Accordingly, the scoring system rewards companies that project their GHG emissions well into the future and that seek to reduce their carbon emission 'footprints' over the life-cycle of the products they sell. The scoring system also recognizes that because some products and capital equipment are more durable and carbon-intensive than others, some companies and industry groups have greater opportunities to address climate change in a long-term planning context.

Notes

1 These industries were selected based on emissions data included in the 'Annual Energy Review: 2004' issued by the US Energy Information Administration.
2 For more information, see 'Managing the Risks and Opportunities of Climate Change – A Toolkit for Corporate Leaders', Ceres, 2006.
3 To view profiles at the website, www.ceres.org, click on the table of contents of the full publication, 'Corporate Governance and Climate Change – Making the Connection'.
4 For a comprehensive review of the physical risks, see 'The Economics of Climate Change,' written by Sir Nicholas Stern. The report can be viewed at www.hm-treasury.gov.uk.
5 See 'Going Nowhere: Price Consumers Pay for Stalled Fuel Economy Policy,' US Public Interest Research Group, 2004.
6 'Renewables 2005: Global Status Report,' Renewable Energy Policy Network for the 21st Century, 2005.

7   See Hugh Wynne, 'As CO_2 Emission Limits Gain Traction, Utilities May Reap Windfall Profits', Sanford C. Bernstein and Company, February 2006.

8   See Robert Socolow, 'Stabilization Wedges: Mitigation Tools for the Next Half Century', Princeton University, 2005.

9   For more background, see James O'Laoughlin and Raj Thamotheram, 'Enhanced Analytics for a New Generation Investor: How the Investment Industry Can Use Extra-financial Factors in Investing,' Universities Superannuation Scheme, 2006.

10 For more information, contact the author at doug.cogan@issproxy.com

11 For more information on the Carbon Disclosure Project, visit their website at www.cdproject.net

Further References

Carbon Disclosure Project, company responses to annual questionnaire available at www.cdproject.net.

Ceres, 'Managing the Risks and Opportunities of Climate Change – A Toolkit for Corporate Leaders', 2006.

Cogan D.G. 'Corporate Governance and Climate Change – Making the Connection', Ceres, 2006.

O'Laoughlin J. and Thamotheram R. 'Enhanced Analytics for a New Generation Investor: How the Investment Industry Can Use Extra-financial Factors in Investing', Universities Superannuation Scheme, 2006.

Renewable Energy Policy Network for the 21st Century, 'Renewables 2005: Global Status Report', 2005.

Socolow R. 'Stabilization Wedges: Mitigation Tools for the Next Half Century', Princeton University, 2005.

Stern, N. 'Economics of Climate Change', UK Treasury Department, 2006.

US Energy Information Administration, 'Annual Energy Review: 2004', 2005.

US Public Interest Research Group, 'Going Nowhere: Price Consumers Pay for Stalled Fuel Economy Policy', 2004.

Wynne H. 'As CO_2 Emission Limits Gain Traction, Utilities May Reap Windfall Profits', Sanford C. Bernstein and Company, 2006.

6

The Growing Risk of Climate Change: Implications and Strategies for Asian Companies and Economies

Ruth Yeoh, YTL Corporation

'The greatest security threat we face as a global community won't be met by guns and tanks…It will be solved by investment in the emerging techniques of soft power – building avenues of opportunity that will lead to a low carbon economy.'

Margaret Beckett, UK Foreign Secretary, foreign policy address at the British Embassy in Berlin, October 2006.

Introduction to global warming: the hard facts

Mankind has historically had a voracious appetite for resources, brought on by the Industrial Revolution and ongoing civilisation, accelerated to this present day. The abysmal news is that the world recently went into ecological red on the 9 October 2006, meaning that for the rest of the year mankind will be living beyond its environmental means. Scientists explain that Ecological Debt Day or Overshoot Day, measures the point at which the consumption of resources exceeds the ability of the planet to replace them. In effect, 'from Oct 9 until the end of the year, humanity will be in ecological overshoot, building up ever greater ecological debt.'[1] What is alarming is that it gets earlier every year.

The National Energy Foundation (NEF) policy director Andrew Simms offers the following explanation, 'In a market economy, the only constraints on what we consume are what we may legally buy and what we can afford. The result is, as the great environmental economist Herman Daly warned, that we end up treating the planet as if it were a business in liquidation. If you were managing a business, you would be considered grossly negligent if you had no idea of your assets or cash flow. Yet this is how we manage our environmental resources.'[2]

So how does all this relate to global warming? Global warming is caused by the expanding emission of greenhouse gases (GHGs) caused by human activities – and a vast majority of GHGs are from carbon dioxide (CO_2: 83%; Methane: 8.8%; and Nitrous Oxide: 6%), according to Eurostat. CO_2 concentration in the atmosphere has shot up by 30% since 1800 and is expected to double within this century. The rich industrialised countries emit almost half of the world's carbon dioxide and the International Energy Agency (IEA) has forecasted that power generation and transport in developing economies could drive CO_2 emissions to 40 billion tons by 2030 if current consumption habits continue (see Figure 1). America is still the largest emitter of GHGs but China, India and other developing nations are closing in.

Most scientists agree that global temperatures are likely to rise between two and six degrees Celsius by the end of the century from the burning of fossil fuels for power generation (the biggest contributor of emissions at 24.5%, with coal being the biggest contributor among sources of power) and transport (13.5% of emissions) – and this would cause disasters such as floods and famines to worsen, putting millions at risk. Deforestation (18%) is the second biggest source of emissions.

In addition to the implications of a rise in global average temperatures, secondary effects will include rising sea levels and a rise in extreme weather patterns, which will eventually have consequent implications on our health. In some regions, damage from climate change has become grievously visible, with stronger hurricanes, floods and disintegrating ice sheets testament to its merciless severity. Other consequences will include a decline in overall biodiversity, with changes in mean global temperatures and consequent alterations in the hydrological cycle threatening various species of flora, fauna, and ecosystems. There are also implications for agriculture and food security, in which as little as one degree Celsius of global warming could produce a 161 kilometre shift in temperature zones, with a shift in agricultural belts decreasing food production where it is most needed and escalating food scarcity to record levels on this earth.[3] Loss of human lives, however, will be most significant in least developed nations.[4]

Global warming: a clear global risk

Climate change may well be the greatest threat and challenge of our generation, presenting tremendous challenges and strains to the environment, the world economy and to individual businesses. It will have both negative and positive implications for global economies, and businesses must regard climate change as a clear example of risk whereby long-term planning is one such solution to mitigate its potentially irreversible effects. According to a recent International Energy Agency (IEA) report, carbon dioxide emissions and oil demand will continue to grow rapidly over the next 25 years, and this worrisome trend is likely to worsen, extending this outlook beyond 2030 (see Figures 1 & 2).

Figure 1: Growing CO_2 emissions
The Energy Information Administration (EIA) estimates global CO_2 emissions will rise 75 per cent from 2003 to 2030. Emissions increased by 2.5 per cent per year from 2000 to 2002, mostly from developing nations.
Source: CDIAC, UNEP

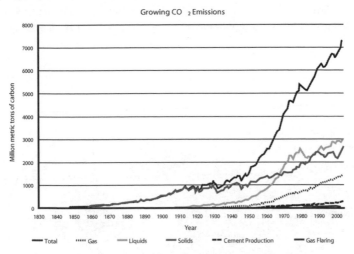

Figure 2: World primary energy consumption
World primary energy consumption by fuel type (Quadrillion British thermal units, Btu) is shown for the years 1979 to 2005, with demand forecasts up to 2015. Asia accounts for three-quarters of growth.
Source: IEA, EIA, International Energy Outlook 2006

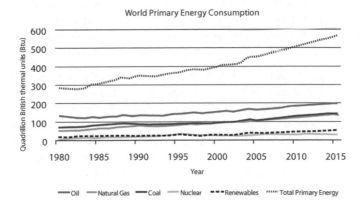

The *World Economic Forum* recently published its *Global Risks 2006 Report* which assesses today's global risk landscape. It identifies four key risk scenarios, drawn from an extensive list (available online at www.weforum.org) and illustrates the different forms that global risk will take in the decade ahead. Risks whose probabilities are high in the short term include oil price spikes and localised terrorist incidents, for which companies and governments are reasonably well-prepared. Climate change features as a long term environmental risk whose impact is potentially very severe, next to influenza pandemics and outbreaks. Organisational risks can be considered as a subset of the various global risks and these are highlighted in Figure 3. Here, we see the risks presented by climate change are interrelated with other key risks, from storms and environmental degradation to regulation and the future of long-term energy prices.

Figure 3: The risk spectrum
Source: H.F. Kloman, 'Rethinking Risk Management', Geneva Papers, July 1992; H.F. Kloman, Risk Management Reports, March 1998.

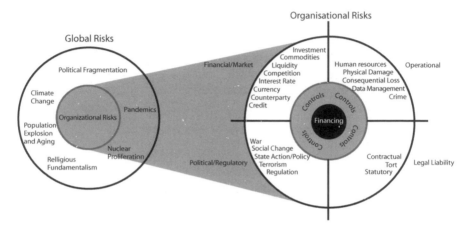

The Report admits there is still uncertainty as to how climate change risks will manifest though one thing is clear: 'rises in sea levels, gradual temperature shifts and intensifying weather patterns have the potential to impact heavily on both society and the global economy, and are increasingly well understood as risks to business.'[5]

However, a growing body of scientific evidence indicates the seriousness of the long-term challenge of climate change, as it may potentially become irreversible over the next ten to twenty years. British Foreign Secretary Margaret Beckett warned that climate change, with drastically diminishing resources in some of the most volatile parts of the world, has the potential to unleash a 'potentially catastrophic dynamic' in regions already at breaking point, regarding climate change as a growing threat to international security and the world economy.[6] Therefore, involvement and cooperation between sectors and governments will be a strong determining factor in reducing this risk.

Key energy and environmental challenges in Asia

Asia is currently at a crossroads when it comes to climate change. One need only travel to haze-filled Southeast Asia, be stuck in a gridlock in Jakarta, breathe in the polluted air in Beijing, and contract bronchitis in Hong Kong to experience the full furore of climate change. A Time Asia (2006) article summarises Asia's dilemma to be one where 'the forces damaging the environment are the same ones that drove the economic miracle that has lifted more than 270 million Asians out of poverty in the past 15 years.'[7] Rapid industrial expansion in many Asian countries – combined with rising affluence – has led to an increasing need for energy.

In an address to the OECD Forum, Resident Director General of ADB, Philippe Bénédic[8], states that energy demand in Asia has grown a staggering 230 per cent between 1973 and 2003, compared to an average worldwide increase of 75 per cent. In 2003, total primary energy supply (TPES) for Asia was 2,650 million tons of oil equivalent, representing 25 per cent of world total energy supply compared to only 13.3 per cent ten years ago.

By 2020, the region will require nearly 5.6 billion tons of oil equivalent per year – more than double what it consumed in 1997. This trend can be said to be neither economically nor environmentally sustainable (see Figure 2). This great demand for energy cannot be sufficiently met by conventional fossil-fuel sources such as oil, coal and gas, and the problem is further worsened by soaring oil prices (as most Asian countries are oil importers). This is driving governments to pursue more balance in the fuel mix – which will see growth in the renewable energy sector, natural-gas consumption, wind energy, nuclear power, and the advance of oil substitutes such as the biofuels, ethanol and biodiesel.

Figure 4 shows the constraints and possible solutions (through a combined strategy of leadership and co-operation) of renewable energy development in Asia:

Figure 4: Constraints and possible solutions of renewable energy development in Asia
Source: WCRE.

Constraints	Solutions
• Limited awareness on alternative energy options	Leadership with intention to:
• Lack of reliable data to undertake specific projects	• Gradually expand the share of renewable energy in overall consumption
• Poor or no research and development base	• Promote integrated use of various energy forms
• No commercial business models	• Developed decentralized renewable energy systems for use in rural areas
• Inadequate access to latest Renewable Energy technology	
• Limited financial resources	• Create a level playing field for renewable energy through various support mechanisms
• Lack of supporting policies and necessary regulations	• Overcome the inherent bias and distortions in energy policies favoring fossil fuels
• Limited institutional set-up	

Sustainability a priority

To make sustainability happen, Asia needs to balance the conflict between two competing goals of ensuring quality of life, and living within the limits of nature (keeping in mind the world is already in ecological red). In light of these major challenges, the ADB has identified the following strategies for developing Asia, urging regions to focus on the areas of energy efficiency, renewable energy and low carbon technologies (see Figure 5):

Figure 5: Three strategies for sustainable development in Asia

Source: 'Key Energy Trends and Challenges in Asia', Statement of the Asian Development Bank, (Philippe Bénédic, Resident Director General, European Representative Office), OECD Forum 2006: Balancing Globalisation, 22–23 May 2006, Paris.

- **Energy efficiency:** Huge prospects remain to improve energy efficiency which is notoriously low in many Asian countries. In China, for example, GDP is expected to quadruple by 2020 whereas commercial energy supply will only double. Energy intensity will, therefore, need to be halved over the next 15 years.

- **Energy diversification:** Alternative and renewable energy sources will probably double in the next 20 years from an average 8–10 per cent today to almost 18–20 per cent. This will, however, depend on the implementation of conducive policies, reduction of fuel and coal subsidies, and stronger incentives for renewable and clean energy to tap large hydropower, biomass, solar and wind energy sources.

- **Climate change:** According to the International Energy Agency (IEA), US$16 trillion of energy investments will be needed through 2030, including US$4–5 trillion in Asia over the next 15 years, to be mostly financed through capital market resources and public private partnerships. More emphasis on low carbon technologies is clearly needed to mitigate the possible negative impact of these investments on the world climate. Since the 1980s, Asia's share of GHG emissions already soared from less than one-tenth of global emissions to nearly one-quarter of the world's total.

It is imperative that Asia's energy production and consumption needs move to a more sustainable path to ensure not only the security of Asia's oil and gas supplies but also its environment too. True, economic growth will provide more jobs and benefit economies. However, more production and consumption will also bring about damaging consequences for the environment. Increased logging activities, sprouting factories, power plants and the increasing frequency of dumping chemicals in rivers are contributing to the region's environmental woes. The conflict between economic growth and environmental protection is intensifying at a frighteningly exponential growth rate.

However, this is not to say that the journey to sustainability will be impossible. The argument here is that economic growth, which is responsible for much of Asia's environmental disaster, can also bring about its recovery. At one stage, Japan was one of the worst polluters the world has ever seen – today, Japan has cleaned up its act and Tokyo has become one of the world's cleanest megacities, thanks to stricter laws, tougher enforcement and growing environmental consciousness, especially amongst the younger generation.

Growth, policies and improved environmental technology (together with innovation) that are both sustainable and green will help developing Asia become efficient in cleaning up its pollution and certainly help in its environmental management.

The excellent news is that energy-efficient technologies used today are now far more superior than previous technologies used in the West's first clean-ups. However, Asia must seriously commit to investing in environmentally friendly policies and technologies in order to instigate positive change.

The policy arena in Asia

It seems the only logical solution to balance the budget and end ecological overshoot would be to demand less of the planet. A lot will depend largely on global initiatives and international policies. Renewable energy policies can play a role by:

- redirecting resources

- increasing the speed of innovation and research development,

- and increasing public awareness

Figure 6 gives a summary of key milestones in climate change policy.

Figure 6: Timeline of key milestones in climate policy, 1979–2005
Source: UNFCCC, AIP

1979	First World Climate Conference
1980	First Assessment Report of the IPCC; initial evidence that human activities might be affecting climate, but significant uncertainty
	Second World Climate Conference; agreement to negotiate a 'framework treaty'
1992	UNFCCC established at the UNCED (also known as the Earth Summit) in Rio de Janeiro, Brazil
	Annex 1 developed countries pledge to return emissions to 1990 levels by 2000
	United States ratifies UNFCCC later in the year

1993	Clinton administration publishes its climate Change Action Plan, a collection of largely voluntary emission-reduction programs
	IPCC Second Assessment Report completed (published in 1996); stronger conviction expressed that human activities could be adversely affecting climate
1995	Berlin Mandate developed at the first COP (COP 1) to the UNFCC
	Agreement to negotiate *legally binding* targets and timetables to limit emissions in Annex 1 countries
1997	COP 3 held in Kyoto, Japan, leading to the Kyoto Protocol
	Annex 1/Annex B countries agree to binding emission reductions averaging 5% below 1990 levels by 2008–12, with 'flexibility mechanisms' (including emissions trading) for compliance; no commitments for emission limitation by developing countries
	US Senate passes Byrd-Hagel resolution, 95 to 0, stating that the United States should accept no climate agreement that did not demand comparable sacrifices of all participants and calling for the administration to justify any proposed ratification of the Kyoto Protocol with analysis of benefits and costs
1998	COP 4 held in Buenos Aires, Argentina; emphasis on operationalising the 'flexibility mechanisms' of the Kyoto Protocol
	IPCC Third Assessment begins
1999	COP5 held in Bonn, Germany, continued emphasis on operationalising the flexibility mechanisms
2000	Global Climate Coalition dissolves as many corporations grapple with threat of warming, but oil lobby convinces US administration to deny problem
2001	Third IPCC report states badly that global warming, unprecedented since end of last ice age, is 'very likely' with possible severe surprises
	Bonn Meeting, with participation of most countries but not US, develops mechanism for working towards Kyoto targets
2003	Deadly summer heatwave in Europe accelerates divergence between European and US public opinion
2005	Kyoto Treaty goes into effect, signed by major industrial nations except US. Japan, Western Europe, regional US entities accelerate work to impede emissions
	Hurricane Katrina and other major tropical storms spur worldwide debate over impact of global warming on storm intensity

IPCC = Intergovernmental Panel on Climate Change
UNFCCC = United Nations Framework Convention on Climate Change
UNCED = United Nations Conference on Environment and Development
COP = Conference of Parties

Experience in Europe and the US has shown that favourable government policies can be a strong catalyst for the development of alternative energy. Thus, governments in Asia are implementing policies by encouraging or mandating alternative energy investment. Coupled with strong economic growth and growing Asian environmental issues, the prospects for meaningful growth in alternative energy investment and manufacturing in the region are good. China and India, already among the world's top ten countries for wind turbine installation, seem to have significant growth potential, and in most other places the outlook is promising–Korea stands out with its aggressive plans for photovoltaic (PV) cells. The *Clean Development Mechanism* (CDM) of the *Kyoto Protocol* for reducing GHG emissions, together with non-binding international partnerships like the *Asia-Pacific Partnership for Clean Development and Climate* (US, Australia, China, India, Japan and Korea) could also fuel investments in Asia by providing an additional potential revenue stream to further enhance project economics (see Figure 7).

Figure 7: How the CDM can help developing countries in Asia
Source: 'Establishing National Authorities for the CDM: A Guide for Developing Countries', 2002.

For developing countries in Asia, the CDM offers the following opportunities:

- it can attract capital for projects that assist in the shift to a more prosperous, but less carbon-intensive economy

- it encourages and permits the active participation of private and public sectors

- it can be an effective tool of technology transfer if investment is channeled into projects that replace old and inefficient fossil fuel technology or create new industries in environmentally sustainable technologies; and

- it can help developing countries define investment priorities in projects that meet their sustainability goals.

In 2002, Japan adopted a *Special Measures Law Concerning the Use of New Energy by Electric Utilities* covering new energies including wind, solar, biomass, small hydro and geothermal. It can be observed that many Asian governments are starting to provide incentives for alternative energy (see Table 1).

Table 1: Clean energy incentives by country

Conventional power generation using coal or gas is often more cost-competitive than alternative energy, hence the latter needs to be either financially supported or mandated to stimulate installation.

Country	Feed-in tariff	Renewable portfolio standard	Tax reductions or credits	Public loans/ financing
China	•		•	•
Hong Kong				
India	• (1)	• (1)	•	•
Indonesia	•			
Korea	•		•	
Malaysia	•		•	
Philippines			•	•
Singapore			•	•
Taiwan	• (2)		•	•
Thailand	•	•		

Note (1): Many states have policies, but there is no overall national policy.
Note (2): Currently drafting legislation
Source: Goldman Sachs, Renewables 2005: Global Status Report, Industrial Technology Research Institute (Taiwan), Energy Commission (Malaysia).

Why invest in solutions to climate change?

Renewable energy is the fastest growing energy sector in terms of per cent annual increase, and has potential in terms of responding to global environmental, economic, safety, social and sustainability goals. Factors such as new markets opening up, growing environmental concerns, company savings via carbon credits, and less resistance from environmental lobby groups towards nuclear power and uranium mining have fueled popularity in alternative energy. According to a report released by the *Renewable Energy Policy Network for the 21st century* (REN21), global investment in the clean energy sector (excluding large hydropower) reached a record of US$30 billion in 2004, pushing renewable energy capacity to 160GW; representing 4 per cent of global capacity.

It is becoming a big business, attracting some of the world's largest companies including Sharp, Siemens, General Electric and Royal Dutch Shell. Market leaders championing renewable energy in 2004 included China in solar hot water, Germany in solar electricity, Brazil in biofuels and Spain in wind power. The fastest growing energy technology is grid-connected solar photovoltaic (PV) which grew in existing capacity by 60 per cent, per year from 2000–2004. Other renewable energy power generation technologies include biomass, geothermal, and small hydro, which are mature and growing by more traditional rates of 2 per cent to 4 per cent, per year.

The costs of renewable energy technology have been shown to fall with increased investment and capacity expansion, therefore it can be anticipated that the cost of renewable energy will drop below that of fossil fuel costs (see Table 2).

Table 2: Costs of renewable energy compared with fossil fuels and nuclear power
Source: ICCEPT 2002

Technology	Current cost (US cents/ kWh)	Projected future costs beyond 2020 as the technology matures (US cents/kWh)
Biomass Energy:		
• Electricity	5–15	4–10
• Heat	1–5	1–5
Wind Electricity:		
• Onshore	3–5	2–3
• Offshore	6–10	2–5
Solar Thermal Electricity (insolation of 2,500kWh/m² per year)	12–18	4–10
Hydro-electricity:		
• Large scale	2–8	2–8
• Small scale	4–10	3–10
Geothermal Energy:		
• Electricity	2–10	1–8
• Heat	0.5–5.0	0.5–5.0
Marine Energy:		
• Tidal Barrage	12	12
• Tidal Stream	8–15	8–15
• Wave	8–20	5–7

Grid-connected photovoltaics, according to incident solar energy (insolation):		
• 1,000 kWh/ m² per year (e.g. UK)	50–80	~8
• 1,500 kWh/ m² per year (e.g. Southern Europe)	30–50	~5
• 2,500 kWh/ m² per year (most developing countries)	20–40	~4
Stand-alone systems (incl. batteries), 2,500 kWh/ m² per year.	40–60	~10
Nuclear Power	4–6	3–5
Electricity grid supplies from fossil fuels (inc. T &D)		Capital costs will come down with technical progress, but many technologies largely mature and may be offset by rising fuel costs.
• Off–peak		
• Peak	2–3	
• Average	15–25	
Rural electrification	8–10	
	25–80	
Costs of central grid supplies, excl. transmission and distribution:		Capital costs will come down with technical progress, but many technologies already mature and may be offset by rising fuel costs.
• Natural Gas	2–4	
• Coal	3–5	

The renewable energy investment potential in Asia

There is huge growth potential for renewable energy in Asia. Renewable energy investment comes from a wide range of public and private sources, and there is a growing belief in the investment community that renewable energy is a serious business opportunity. Multilateral lending agencies such as the Asian Development Bank, as well as a number of countries like Germany and Japan, are pouring expenditure into renewable energy projects in Asia.

Investment flows are being aided by two things: technology standardisation, and growing acceptance and knowledge by financiers at all scales, from large wind farms to microfinancing.[9] More and more Asian countries are emphasising alternative energy sources and introducing new regulations to promote them, with companies in these areas needing more capital requirements. Hedge funds are also eyeing opportunities in the sector and UK-based environmental organisation Trucost and the Association for Sustainable and Responsible Investment in Asia (ASrIA) have released a major Asia-oriented report investigating the carbon emissions of major regional corporations, to encourage institutional investors to take into account the environmental impacts of the companies in which they invest.[10]

Major investments have already taken place – in August 2006, the World Bank brokered the largest ever GHG contract, which will see Asian and European organisations paying two Chinese chemical firms US$1 billion to reduce CO_2 emissions by 19 million tons a year.[11]

Another interesting phenomenon is the listing and acquiring of companies. Seven renewable energy companies in Asia-Pacific have conducted public equity issues in the past two years. Suzlon Energy of India, which develops turbines and blades for wind-power generators, conducted its US$344 million IPO in October and SunTech Power Holdings of China priced its successful US$455 million IPO in December 2005.[12] The *Renewable Energy Exchange Asia* was also recently launched in Singapore, sponsored by a UK-sponsored non-governmental organisation called the *Renewable Energy and Energy Efficiency Partnership* (REEEP). The REEEP focuses on the development and support of legislative and regulatory frameworks that accelerate the marketplace for renewable energy and energy efficiency, with the purpose of the Exchange to act as a 'matchmaker': investors who cannot find bankable projects and developers who cannot find cash for their ventures. Since its launch in June 2006, it has arranged meetings between proponents, interested parties and potential investors for more than 20 projects, from biodiesel plants to small hydroelectric projects in Southeast Asia.

Government cars in Malaysia are now running on bio-fuels made from palm oil, the Philippines uses sugar cane waste to produce power and more than 30 million people in China get their hot water from solar heaters.[13] Furthermore, India is currently Asia's leading user of wind energy, with India and China recognised as major forces at major conferences such as the *Renewable Energy Finance Forum*. Paul Fernando Soares, Chief Representative Officer in Beijing for Indian wind firm Suzlon, explains the rationale as such: '...of the 10 most polluted cities in the world, eight are in China. Over the past five years, China has become increasingly worried about its image abroad. China wants to be seen as a serious country that cares about the environment and the well-being of its citizens. Similarly, in India, the targets and policies for backing renewables are as good, if not better, than in China.'[14] India plans to create 10 per cent of its power supply though renewable energy by 2012. Several other Asian countries have also set ambitious policy targets for renewable sources (see Table 3).

Table 3: Asian government renewable energy targets

Country	Stated Targets
Australia	9500 gigawatt-hours (roughly extra 2 per cent of total energy) to be sourced from renewable energy annually by 2010.
China	Rmb1.5 trillion (US$184 billion) to be invested in renewable energy sources by 2020, under the 11th Five Year Plan (FYP). Renewable energy to be 10 per cent of electric power capacity by 2010 (expected 60GW); 5 per cent of primary energy by 2010 and 10 per cent of primary energy by 2020. Wind power to comprise 5,000MW by 2010 and 30,000MW by 2020.

Hong Kong	1 per cent and 2 per cent of electricity to be supplied from renewable energy by 2012.
India	Renewable energy to be 10 per cent of added electric power capacity during 2003–2010 (expected 10GW). Wind Power to generate 5,000MW by 2012 (likely to be reached before 2009). 12 per cent of overall energy to be sources from renewables by 2012.
Japan	Utilities to source 1.35 per cent of total electricity from renewables by 2010, excluding geothermal and large hydro (RPS). 3,000 megawatts (MW) from wind by 2010.
Korea	Renewable energy to be 5 per cent of total energy by 2010 and 8.5 per cent by 2012 from 2 per cent in 2004.
Malaysia	Renewable energy to provide 5 per cent of electricity generation by 2005, equal to between 500MW and 600MW of installed capacity, backed by Fuel Diversification Policy (2001) and Small Renewable Energy Program (SREP). Under the Ninth Malaysia Plan (9MP), this was modified in 2006, with new targets to achieve 350MW of installed capacity by 2010 (30MW on peninsular Malaysia, and 50MW on Sabah).
Philippines	Renewable energy to provide 4.7GW total existing capacity by 2013.
Singapore	50,000m2 (~35 MWth) of solar thermal systems to be set in place by 2012.
Thailand	Renewable energy to contribute 8 per cent of total primary energy by 2011 (excluding traditional rural biomass).

Source: Macquarie Securities, Goldman Sachs, BCSE, Earthscan, Asia Money.

Hence, it is most encouraging to witness this interesting trend in Asia – not only is there a shift in renewable policy, there is now an intertwining shift in investments too.

Strategies for Asian companies

Businesses nowadays are becoming more environmentally conscious, spurred by the government to adopt measures to practice sustainability and driven by the possibility of saving money. Being green has most certainly become a moral issue and most companies are on a quest to improve their images by looking good environmentally. However, it must be noted that tackling carbon exposure is more than good environmental stewardship – it can also safeguard a company's share price in the near term and create a long-term competitive advantage for those companies willing to take it seriously.

There is evidence that managers and companies are now being rewarded for being green, with banking analysts rewarding 'brownie points' in the form of good ratings to shining examples in the industry. Regulatory compliance under the *Kyoto Protocol* is the primary motivation for emission reductions in Europe and Japan, and it could impact on developing economies in Asia sooner rather than later.

So what can Asian companies do to capture low carbon opportunities and profit at the same time? Figure 8 illustrates the cycle of strategic vision for a low carbon and biodiverse future.

What must be done 'now' is that companies must be ready to:

- endure one-off failures and increase its level of engagement with investors.
- Face low incremental return on investments
- Reduce costs by reducing energy and water use
- Implement effective penalties for not spending or managing discharges and wastes
- Reduce GHG emissions

Future drivers will include:

- Using environmental threat as an opportunity
- Superior management which will help access and operate best new resources
- Increased research and development spend (which is anticipated to drive competitive positioning between the next 5–15 years)
- Government tax incentives to enhance project economics

Figure 8: Drivers of strategic vision towards a low carbon future.
Source: Sir David King, Chief Scientific Adviser to HM Government, London, UBS Conference: 'Global Action to Control Global Warming', February 2006.

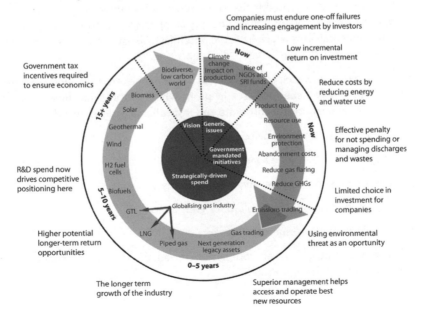

Over the next 5 to 15 years, the way a company manages its carbon exposure could create or destroy shareholder value. Managers who fail to respond to calls for more transparency and better planning will face greater public censure and charges of breach of duty. They may even find the share price of their companies discounted in capital markets. It is thus interesting to see that since 2005, leading American corporations like General Electric and Wal-Mart have pledged strong efforts to limit their emissions. Executives are now not only hoping to improve public relations but fear future lawsuits for causing damage, not wanting their companies to be caught off guard by emission regulations, and suspecting their profits could tumble from a loss in competitive advantage due to the effects of climate change. Powerful investors, from state pension funds to Wall Street firms like Goldman Sachs are also weighing in on global warming risks before investing in a company.

To analyse the strategies Asian companies must adopt, a good starting point will be to assess the various industries and their sensitivity to carbon limits:

- Potential 'losing' companies will be those whose production generates lots of GHGs, particularly carbon dioxide. Coal and petroleum industries, the airline industry, auto manufacturers and logistics companies that make or rely on products that generate CO_2 will need to be wary. Electric utilities industries are also facing the pressure, as most rely heavily on coal-fired generation. However, some utility companies are expressing increased interest in GHG trading and other market-based mechanisms, believing the blow of emissions limits could be softened by using economic mechanisms instead of a rigid regulatory regime.[15]

- Potential 'winning' companies, on the other hand, are a diverse group. Beneficiaries of emissions limits will be renewable energy companies, the biofuels industry, diversified technology companies, and engineering and environmental firms which have the potential to assist companies with liabilities to reduce their CO_2 emissions.

Regardless of sector, however, companies that implement energy efficiency and energy saving programmes will see increases in profit whilst at the same time, meet their climate targets. Motivations for corporate and institutional actions include[16]:

- Reducing costs and improving profitability
- Risk mitigation to hedge against uncertainty
- Developing a competitive advantage via early action
- Regulatory positioning via voluntary 'early action'
- Developing new products and markets

In particular, the strategies Asian companies can adopt on climate change through incorporating these measures include:

- Emission reductions such as energy efficiency improvements, cogeneration (generation of heat and power) projects and fuel-switching. It is noteworthy that early action in this area can enable companies to implement such projects effectively through testing, evaluating and improving the technologies and practices being used.

- Emission accounting, auditing and reporting

- Development of an internal base line

- Market screening of carbon offset markets: Internal/external carbon trading and hedging

- Enabling new technologies

- Creating new low-carbon products and services for the ever discerning consumer

Corporate environmental reporting

Accounting, corporate environmental reporting, carbon footprints and tracking systems are rising areas of development, whereby companies must learn to account for the carbon dioxide emitted from or consumed by its business. They are also good ways to involve and educate staff on the risks and options related to climate change, and to gain significant competitive advantage. Larger companies can, for example, establish an internal GHG programme to help meet their CO_2 emissions targets. Management consulting firm McKinsey is further helping financial analysts to develop global reporting standards to facilitate rating of companies. For example, in Europe's utility sector, several new variables make it possible to measure carbon emissions against production or revenue – two that are gaining exposure are the carbon factor of the production portfolio and the revenue/profit exposure per carbon profile.[17]

Furthermore, companies should engage in corporate environmental reporting for the following motives, as outlined by the ACCA (2002):

- Risk management – mitigating risks in terms of financial, legal and reputation implications

- Marketing strategy – public image and brand enhancement such as through receiving environmental and sustainability awards

- Legal needs – to keep in pace with or anticipate regulations

- Competition – to get ahead of or stay with competitors

- Ethics – individual commitment; commitment to accountability and transparency

- Accounting requirements – in compliance with financial reporting requirements and providing a link between financial and environmental performance/reporting

- Investors' interests – demands of green (ethical) investors

- Employees' interests – attracts right staff from the labour market

- Value-added reporting – to add value to corporate reports and communicate to wider range of stakeholders, addressing their environmental concerns

- Certifications needs – to indicate compliance with ISO14000 and other environmental regulatory guidelines

Companies must, however, note that uncertainty about future regulations is the biggest risk in the carbon equation as executives often need long-term assurances on credits and emission levels to encourage them to plan for expensive capital investments. Both the Kyoto Protocol and EU ETS have set initial goals but it is uncertain what will happen thereafter.

Having said that, what is certain is that management leadership is necessary to steer Asian firms towards a brighter and cleaner future, with well-managed firms in all sectors and industries ideally using the challenge of global climate change to stimulate innovation and improve business activities through unifying their business performance, as well as environmental goals. It will be the quality of a firm's management and its strategy to adapt to future carbon limits that will determine its success, helping to make it a 'winner' and deliver shareholder value while at it. Asia can most certainly lead the way, as we have seen with the example of Japan and its positive transformation to a clean energy zone.

A case study on greening our growing company in Asia: YTL Corporation, Malaysia

'It is imperative that developments are sustainable for our own economic welfare otherwise we are cursing future generations with our negligence as we are now cursed by previous generations of political and business leaders that did not pay attention to sustainability...' Tan Sri Dato' (Dr) Francis Yeoh, Managing Director, YTL Corporation.

The YTL Corporation is one of the largest companies in Malaysia listed on the Kuala Lumpur Stock Exchange and together with its four listed subsidiaries has a combined Market Capitalisation of almost RM19 billion (US$5 billion). The company, listed in 1985, has also had a secondary listing on the Tokyo Stock Exchange since 1996.[18]

YTL is one of the largest independent power producers in Southeast Asia. As one of Malaysia's leading integrated infrastructure conglomerates, it owns and manages regulated assets with long term concessions globally, employs over 6,200 people around the world and currently serves over ten million customers worldwide. Its key businesses include: utilities, high speed rail, cement manufacturing, construction contracting, property development, hotels and resorts, and technology incubation.

YTL's strategy of providing World Class services at very competitive prices, together with its innovation vision, has led directly to it recording a compounded annual growth rate in pre-tax profits of 55 per cent over the last fifteen years, and an enviable track record of creating shareholder value. The company's strategy has also resulted in it and its subsidiaries accumulating numerous International Awards in the process.

In 2006, YTL and its subsidiaries ('YTL Group') reported on sustainability measures and addressed climate change, published in their Corporate Social Responsibility 2006 Report. The company is one of only a handful of companies who have taken initiatives to pioneer corporate environmental reporting (CER) and CSR in its home country, Malaysia – the rationale being that there is conventional wisdom in businesses that companies can no longer afford to be socially and environmentally irresponsible. A recent study showed that companies will benefit not only from being socially responsible but also from being able to demonstrate convincingly that they are socially responsible through communicating to stakeholders their commitment to, and record on, CSR.[19] YTL believes that effective corporate social responsibility can deliver benefits to its businesses and, in turn, to its shareholders.

YTL Corp's statements on corporate governance and internal control are also included in a separate section of their Annual Report. In this chapter, the various company subsidiaries will be examined, through observing the individual and collective activities of the Group, outlined in the environmental responsibility section of the company's CSR Report (see Figure 9):

Figure 9: Environmental Responsibility of YTL Corporation – selected excerpts adapted from YTL Corporation Bhd, Corporate Social Responsibility Report 2006.

ENVIRONMENTAL RESPONSIBILITY

The YTL Group's environmental vision

We are fully committed to being a responsible corporate citizen. Energy plays an essential role in ensuring quality of life for people everywhere, for us and for future generations. Supplying energy reliably is critical to helping people maintain and improve their standard of living. However, this brings with it significant challenges – for example, the very real threat of climate change means that we need to continue to provide and deliver energy in a way that minimises the impact our emissions have on the environment. We recognise the importance of sustainable development, taking account of the impact of our operations on society and understanding the dire consequences of global warming.

Energy saving and resource conservation

Water & sewerage services

Wessex Water, our subsidiary in the UK, operates under a stringent set of environmental directives and regulations with a key long-term goal of becoming a sustainable water company. Wessex Water's comprehensive programme to achieve this goal has ensured that all compliance rates for drinking water, sewage treatment and bathing water have not only been met but are amongst the best in the United Kingdom.

Wessex Water is currently recognised by the water industry regulator, Ofwat, as the most efficient operator in England and Wales. Advanced treatment techniques, automation, state-of-the-art control and monitoring systems ensure consistently high standards at a low cost. The company has a high 99.93 per cent compliance rate in accordance with EU standards and has adopted the ISO 9000 quality assurance for its water production and control systems. In terms of sewage treatment standards, the company has obtained greater than 99 per cent compliance with discharge standards and almost 100 per cent compliance with bathing water standards, as well as maintaining some of the best rivers and bathing waters in the country.

Issues to Incorporate in Sustainable Development

Source: Wessex Water; Striking the Balance Report: Introduction.

Wessex Water publishes a yearly sustainability report reporting on environmental indicators and sustainability issues. The water company's 'Striking the Balance' 2006 report, which provides a wealth of information on these important areas, can be accessed at its website: http://www.wessexwater. co.uk/strikingthebalance2006/

Power generation & transmission

YTL Power has been instrumental in changing the Malaysian Government's policy to use clean fuel like natural gas instead of sticking to a four fuel policy which includes abundant use of coal and crude oil.

YTL Power was the first Independent Power Producer in Malaysia and we were very careful from the outset that our gas fuelled combined cycle power plants would not cause environmental damage. The potential damage involves the emissions of nitrogen dioxide (NOx) into the atmosphere and the discharge of hot water back into the sea. The Paka and Pasir Gudang Power Stations in Malaysia are designed to minimise these emissions.

Another specific design feature is the burners of the gas turbines. These gas burners produce very low NOx levels during operation and thus help to mitigate the amount of emissions into the atmosphere. The NOx emission levels achieved are within the allowable limits of the present Malaysian environmental quality regulations and well within World Bank standards, with emissions of CO_2 and NOx monitored continuously using automated equipment.

YTL Power's ElectraNet operation in Australia operates in line with a Code of Sustainable Practice. Their procedures and systems for the management of potential environmental impacts are incorporated in the company's guide, accessible on their website (http://www.electranet.co.au).

Property development

In our Sentul project, we made the decision to maintain a 35-acre green lung in the heart of Kuala Lumpur as a park for the use of our residents because we believe that this will enhance the quality of life of the people who buy our properties. We have adopted this philosophy throughout all our current residential property developments, such as Lake Edge in Puchong, Lake Fields in Sungei Besi and Pantai Hillpark. We have placed the focus on reducing the number of units in favour of maintaining a balance between nature and development, and have adopted building and design techniques that make the most of natural sunlight and improve airflow to reduce the need for artificial light and air-conditioners.

Express rail link

The YTL Corporation is a major shareholder of Express Rail Link Sdn Bhd – a railway development company which was awarded a concession on 25 August 1997 to finance, design, construct, operate and maintain the KLIA Ekspres, KLIA Transit and other ancillary activities related to railway services.

The fleet consists of twelve state-of-the-art, high-speed trains which have no direct emissions of pollutants and have 'built in' energy savings by design. We acknowledge that environment friendliness does not end with the trains. There is an energy saving programme for trains that was implemented in 2003. Drivers were trained to operate the trains using energy saving techniques, which ERL Maintenance Support Sdn Bhd (E-MAS) named the 'MAKAN' principle:

- **M**ake sure that trains are switched off during stabling
- **A**s much driving as possible in coasting mode
- **K**now to brake early and with not more than 40 per cent braking force
- **A**s much as possible using the electrical brake
- **N**o traction effort more than 80 per cent

With this programme, E-MAS was able to reduce the energy cost per trip from RM65.59 in 2003 to RM62.11 in 2005, translating into a total saving of approximately RM300,000 for the year 2005. In 2006, E-MAS's target is to reach an energy cost per trip of RM67, despite the 12 per cent increase of electricity cost in June 2006. E-MAS also recently launched the Building Facilities Energy Saving Programme, with targets to achieve savings of energy costs of RM100,000 per year by modifying the existing installations.

Climate change

We recognise the impact of global warming and climate change on our community, not just locally, but globally. We regard climate change as a clear risk and have taken measures to reduce green house gas (GHG) and noxious emissions in all our activities, from our utilities and cement manufacturing plants to property and hotel operations.

Our Managing Director, Tan Sri Dato' (Dr) Francis Yeoh Sock Ping attended the 2006 Clinton Global Initiative (CGI) in New York, an annual meeting where top leaders meet to focus on issues such as energy and climate change. He was further invited by CNBC to discuss the effects, solutions and business of climate change, alongside a top panel of experts on their 'Global Players' special, a follow up programme of the CGI. The panel included top academics and business personalities such as Jeffrey D Sachs (Dean of the Earth Institute, Columbia University), Jim Hansen (Head of the Goddard Institute), Jeremy Leggett (CEO Solarcentury) and Fred Smith (President of the Competitive Enterprise Institute). Tan Sri Francis was the only Asian businessman chosen to represent Asian perspectives on climate change.

The YTL Group is constantly searching for innovative ways to encourage energy saving and to minimise the risk and glaringly visible effects of climate change. We, therefore, anticipate our future projects to integrate technology, policy and positive action to steer our company towards being not only clean and green, but also secure, in trust for future generations.

Water & sewerage services

Climate change awareness and carbon management have been at the forefront of Wessex Water's developments. Its environmental impacts – for example, quantities of water taken from the environment, effluent released into rivers, reuse of sludge and greenhouse gas emissions (mainly carbon dioxide and methane) – are closely monitored through environmental regulation. It is important to note that tighter environmental regulation has consequently benefited the water environment more. Wessex's carbon dioxide emissions are now lower than in 1990 because of technological advancements enabling the carbon content of an average kWh of electricity from the national grid to be lower.

However, its energy consumption has climbed through increase of sewage treatment to meet environmental regulation. The company's carbon dioxide emissions, 95 per cent of which came from consuming energy, have increased significantly in the last few years and plans are now underway to reduce these emissions. The Royal Commission of Environmental Pollution published a report in 2001 that lobbied for a 60 per cent decrease in carbon dioxide emissions from energy use by 2050 to avoid escalating damage to the earth's environment.

Climate change and carbon management at Wessex Water
Source: Wessex Water; Striking the Balance Report; 'Climate change and carbon management'.
Source: Environmental Responsibility of YTL Corporation, selected excerpts adapted from YTL Corporation Bhd, Corporate Social Responsibility Report 2006.

	Reduction of Emissions	
	Carbon Dioxide	Carbon Dioxide and Methane Combined
What we emitted in 1997	101,108 tonnes	168,224 tonnes
What we would need to emit in 2050 (60% less than 1997)	40,423 tonnes	67,312 tonnes
Annual reduction needed from 1997 levels	1,145 tonnes	1,904 tonnes

Conclusion

The research presented in this chapter has shown a remarkable picture of the accelerating momentum, commercial viability and policy initiative of sustainability and renewable energy in Asia. The goal will be sustainable development whereby society should adopt a policy of sustainable development that allows society to meet its present needs whilst preserving the ability of future generations to meet their own needs.[20] It is concerned about the rights of future generations and the 'triple bottom line' of economic prosperity, social equity and environmental protection.[21]

From a business perspective, the focus will be the creation of long-term shareholder value by recognising that corporations are dependent on licenses provided by society to do business. If businesses choose not to comply with sustainable development policies, society can enforce compliance through imposing additional government regulation and control.[22]

Overall, the time has come now to think beyond traditional precepts of power politics and beyond positions dictated by short-term interests – a new era of Green Power has arrived bringing with it a surge of entrepreneurs, innovators and new entrants. Asian companies and economies will need to adapt fast and innovate quickly in the new low carbon environment, for the sake of Asia's security in energy, food production, water and health if it is to survive the extreme effects of climate change.

Four key strategic imperatives for Asian companies

Adaptation is necessary and unavoidable

So why adaptation? There are six reasons why adaptation is necessary;

- Climate change cannot be avoided

- Anticipatory and precautionary adaptation is more effective and less costly than forced last-minute fixes

- Climate change may be more rapid and pronounced than current estimates suggest and unexpected events, as already witnessed globally, are more than just possible

- Immediate benefits can be gained from better adaptation to climate variability and extreme atmospheric events (for example, with the hurricane risk, strict building laws and better evacuation practices will need to be executed)

- Immediate benefits can be gained by removing maladaptive policies and practices (for example, building on flood plains and vulnerable coastlines)

- Climate change brings opportunities as well as threats

Embrace renewable energy

The case for renewable energy is on the rise. Ideally, a combination of improved energy efficiency and alternative energy is a solution to global warming. It must be noted, however, that from the environmental and safety perspective, carbon capture methods (the storage of CO_2 either underground or in the ocean) is not technically proven to be secure, however helpful this would appear to be in the short-term.

Change energy use and mix through innovation

It is now not a question of whether we will use oil, coal and gas, but rather *how* we will use them less – and through cleaner and greener methods, of course! Replacing our energy infrastructure over the next 50 years is expensive but not prohibitive. Power generation through renewable sources at the point of use should be an imperative!

Remember the 3 'I's

The 3 'I's that Asian firms and economies should keep in mind are:

- **Implementation** – because without effective policies at the national, regional, and local level, the *Kyoto Protocol* and other such policies will fail.

- **Improvement** – because companies and governments have the necessary means to adapt and evolve to changes which will involve new insights, developments and circumstances.

- **Innovation** – because this will require substantial inputs in terms of money, time, energy and creativity.

Notes

1   Simms A. 'World living beyond environmental means', *Singapore Business Times*, 9 October 2006.

2   Simms A. 'The human race is living beyond its means', *The Independent*, 9 October 2006.

3   Figueres C. (ed.) 'Establishing National Authorities for the CDM: A Guide for Developing Countries', 2002.

4   Stern N. 'Economics of Climate Change', HM Treasury, 30 October 2006.

5   'Global Risks 2006', A World Economic Forum Report, 2006.

6   Beckett M. (UK Foreign Secretary) foreign policy address at the British Embassy in Berlin, *The Straits Times* Interactive, 25 October 2006.

7   Walsh B. 'Visions of Green', *Time Asia* Magazine, 9 October 2006.

8   Bénédic P. (Resident Director General, ADB) 'Key Energy Trends and Challenges in Asia', OECD Forum 2006, Paris, 22–23 May 2006.

9   Martinot E. *Global Revolution: A status report on renewable energy worldwide*, Earthscan, James & James, 2 November 2006.

10 *Asia Money*, September 2006.

11 Walsh B. 'Visions of Green', *Time Asia* Magazine, 9 October 2006.

12 *Op.cit.*, Morrow R. 2006.

13 Blume C. 'Asia Increasingly Turning to Renewable Energy', *VOA* News, Hong Kong, 3 April 2006.

14 Hopkins D. 'India and China recognised as major forces at the Renewable Energy Finance Forum', *Carbon International*, 29 July 2006. See http://www.carboninternational.com/newsite/

15 Wilkinson A. 'Carbon Management: Strategic implications of climate change', CLSA U: Blue Books, October 2005.

16 Ibid.

17 Grobbel C., Maley J. and Molitor M., 'Preparing for a low-carbon future', *The McKinsey Quarterly*, No.4, 2004.

18 The company's corporate website can be accessed on: http://www.ytl.com.my/

19 Thompson P. and Zakaria Z. 'Corporate Social Responsibility Reporting in Malaysia: Progress and Prospects', Nottingham University Business School, Malaysia Campus; and University of Malaya, Malaysia, 2004.

20 Brundlandt G. (WCED) *Our Common Future*, Oxford University Press, 1987.

21 Whittaker M. 'Emerging "triple bottom line" model for industry weighs environmental, economic and social considerations', *Oil and Gas Journal*, 20 December, 1999.

22 Fanchi J.R. 'Energy in the 21st Century', *World Scientific*, January 2005.

7

The Coming Market Shift: Business Strategy and Climate Change*

Andrew J Hoffman, University of Michigan

*This chapter was supported by the Frederick A and Barbara M Erb Institute for Global Sustainable Enterprise at the University of Michigan and the Pew Center on Global Climate Change

Introduction

In many respects, the scientific debate is irrelevant. For the business community, climate change represents an impending market shift – one that will both alter existing markets and create new ones. It will not be unlike shifts that have occurred in the past, when consumer needs changed, or technology advanced, and some companies declined while others rose to take their place. In the 1980s alone, computers eliminated the typewriter industry, compact discs replaced phonograph records, and the Bell System's demise wrought structural changes in telecommunications.[1] New competitive environments produce both risks and opportunities, as well as winners and losers.

This market shift will create new supply and demand for emission-reducing technologies, new financial instruments for emissions trading, new mechanisms for transferring technologies globally (i.e. Joint Implementation and the Clean Development Mechanism), and new pressures to retire historic sources of greenhouse gases (GHG). The shift will affect all companies to varying degrees, and all have a managerial and fiduciary obligation to assess their business exposure and decide whether action is prudent.[2] In short, as the market shift of climate change looms on the business horizon, the argument against action is increasingly harder to make.

For many within the business community, the future is a carbon-constrained world and the time for action is now.[3] Companies with this perspective already have engaged in GHG reductions. Yet other companies (particularly in the United States) continue to resist and deride their proactive competitors with labels such as 'carbon cartel' or 'Kyoto capitalists.'[4] Such resistance is a very risky strategy, however, in the face of the coming market shift.

The debate is thus strategic (not scientific) and companies taking voluntary climate action are not practicing philanthropy or pure social responsibility (although many couch their activities in the language of 'doing the right thing'). In fact, many companies are agnostic about the science of climate change. They engage the climate-change issue as a way to protect their strategic investments and to search for business opportunities in a changing market landscape.

This chapter seeks to explain the current business phenomenon at three different yet closely related levels of response. First, we look at the early warning signs that suggest a market shift is coming. Second, we identify the various business frameworks that can be and are being used to link climate change to business interests. Third, we describe some specific ways in which companies synergistically integrate climate change and business strategy to contribute to the bottom line.

Emergent early warnings: the growing case for climate action

Climate change and consequent policies to reduce GHG emissions create systematic risk across the entire economy, affecting energy prices, national income, health and agriculture. Climate change also creates regulatory, physical and reputational risks at the sector, industry and company levels.[5] As the competitive environment alters, certain companies, industries and sectors will be more at risk than others. Some see the electric utility, steel and aluminum industries as particularly vulnerable.[6] Others warn of impacts to oil and gas,[7] or to automakers.[8] Some see American companies overall as less prepared than their European and Asian counterparts to handle climate-related policy.[9] Regardless of specific vulnerability, very few business sectors are immune to climate change and the inevitable market shift. All of which leads us to ask: Where are the market signals coming from? How are they promoting the business case for action?

The first place to look is the public policy arena, where there are signs that the enactment of a US national climate policy is very near. In much the same way the US Environmental Protection Agency (EPA) was formed in 1970,[10] individual states are increasingly enacting climate-related legislation, creating a spreading patchwork quilt of state and regional regulation. This motivates some corporations to support the idea of a national policy.

The US Senate took a significant step forward in the summer of 2005 when a solid majority supported a resolution that stated, 'Congress should enact a national mandatory, market-based programme to slow, stop, and reverse growth of these [GHG] emissions.' The resolution was followed by Energy Committee hearings on a cap-and-trade bill authored by Senator Bingaman (D-NM) and based on the recommendations of the National Committee on Energy Policy (NCEP). In April 2006, the Energy Committee held a full-day climate conference to discuss design elements of potential legislation, a process to which dozens of corporations submitted comments. Finally, a new version of the McCain-Lieberman climate bill will likely be released in 2006, and will share the stage with proposed legislation from several other senators, including Bingaman and Feinstein (D-CA).

In a recent survey by the Pew Center on Global Climate Change,[11] some 31 companies reported that US government policy on climate change is coming. The majority of this sample forecast that a national policy will be established sometime between 2010 and 2015, and that it will set the needed price signals for companies to begin reducing their climate impact.

Policy is not the only arena in which movement toward a carbon-constrained world can be observed. On the financial front, mainstream investors are beginning to take notice of climate change.[12] Financial services companies like Goldman-Sachs, Bank of America, JP Morgan, Chase, and Citigroup have adopted guidelines for lending and for asset management aimed at promoting clean energy technologies.[13] The Carbon Disclosure Project is another barometer of this development. When the project began in 2002, 35 institutional investors endorsed a letter requesting disclosure of information on GHG emissions through a questionnaire that was distributed to *Fortune* 500 companies. In 2003, 95 institutional investors with $10 trillion in assets endorsed the letter. By 2006, those numbers had climbed to 211 institutional investors with $31 trillion in assets.[14]

On the corporate side, the intersection of fiduciary responsibility and climate strategy is coming into focus, particularly around the 'materiality' of GHG emissions under the Sarbanes-Oxley Act of 2002.[15] Some companies (and their directors) could face lawsuits based on their carbon emissions. Some already do. Eight states and New York City have filed an unprecedented lawsuit against five of America's largest power companies, demanding that they cut CO_2 emissions.[16] Such developments have led some major insurers to express concerns about Directors' and Officers' exposure to liability if climate risk is not properly disclosed. Company shareholders are equally concerned. The number of shareholder resolutions requesting financial risk disclosure and plans to reduce GHG emissions increased from 20 in 2004 to 30 in 2005.

Energy prices continue to rise, affecting all areas of the economy. This only strengthens the business case for energy efficiency and associated GHG reductions. In 2003, the Pew Center on Global Climate Change conducted a scenario planning exercise involving top global industry, academic, and government experts. In the published results, the worst-case energy price inputs projected out to 2035 were all surpassed by 2006.[17] In the marketplace, consumers are feeling the pinch of rising energy and fuel prices and are searching for new products to lower costs, such as hybrid vehicles and energy-efficient appliances. The Carbon Trust forecasts that climate change could become a mainstream consumer issue by 2010, placing existing corporate brands at risk.[18]

National energy concerns are pushing the frontiers of technology, and US President Bush laid out new priorities for energy research in his 2006 State of the Union address. Future planning for domestic and foreign energy supply increasingly draws attention to the development of various high-efficiency coal combustion options.[19] Beyond coal, clean-energy markets continue to exhibit dramatic growth. Global wind and solar markets reached US$11.8 billion and US$11.2 billion, respectively, in 2005. This was an increase of 47 per cent and 55 per cent over 2004.[20] Kleiner Perkins Caulfield & Byers, a leading venture capital firm, has announced a set-aside fund of US$100 million for investments in technologies that provide cleaner energy, transportation, air and water. Partner John Doer states, 'This field of greentech could be the largest economic opportunity of the 21st century. There's never been a better time than now to start or accelerate a greentech venture.'[21]

Also coming into focus are the physical risks of climate change, especially in the wake of recent natural disasters. The insurance industry is understandably concerned about the US$46 billion in losses related to natural catastrophes in 2004. Additionally, Swiss Re estimates that total insured natural catastrophe property and business-interruption losses reached US$83 billion for the industry in 2005. Future events will disproportionately affect vulnerable industry sectors, such as agriculture, fisheries, forestry, health care, insurance, real estate, tourism and offshore energy infrastructure (oil rigs and pipelines).[22] Informing all these concerns, the scientific community continues to develop research and data around issues of glacial melts, sea level rise, ocean acidification, and associated impacts on global water currents.[23] In fact, for the vast majority of the scientific community, the issue is not whether climate change is happening, but what can be done to slow its progress and mitigate its effects.[24]

All of these signals present a compelling case for companies to pay attention to climate change. The number of American companies addressing the issue has risen notably since 2003.[25] Indeed, a changing competitive environment is creating the most compelling reasons to address climate change. It impacts companies through partners in the supply chain. (Wal-Mart has recently announced that it will initiate a programme to show preference to suppliers who set goals for aggressively reducing GHG emissions.[26]) It impacts companies through competitors in the marketplace. (Toyota has been able to take market share from other automakers in part through its expansion into hybrid drive trains.[27]) In sum, all the signals warn: 'Businesses that ignore the debate over climate change do so at their peril.'[28]

Linking climate change to business interests

While the strategic benefits of adopting voluntary GHG reductions are as varied as the companies undertaking them (see Table 1), the universal key to financial success is a company's assessment of its strategic positioning vis-à-vis GHG emissions. As a baseline model, companies have sought strategic benefits from voluntary GHG reductions within seven general frameworks: (1) operational improvement; (2) anticipating and influencing regulations; (3) accessing new sources of capital; (4) improving risk management; (5) elevating corporate reputation; (6) identifying new market opportunities; and (7) enhancing human resource management.[29] Each presents new kinds of questions to help companies ascertain their vulnerability under a climate change protocol.

Table 1 A Select List of Companies Taking Voluntary Action to Reduce GHG Emissions

ABB	DuPont	Manitoba Hydro	SC Johnson
Air Products	Entergy	Maytag	St Lawrence Cement Inc
Alcan Aluminum	Equity Office Properties Trust	MeadWestvaco Corporation	STMicroelectronics
Alcoa	Ford Motor Company	Miller Brewing Company	Stora Enso
American Electric Power	General Motors Corporation	Motorola	Suncor Energy
Baxter International	Georgia-Pacific	National Renewable Energy Laboratory	Sunoco
Boeing	Hewlett-Packard Company	Norm Thompson Outfitters	Temple-Inland Inc
BP	Holcim	Novartis	Toyota
California Portland Cement	Holcim (US) Inc	Ontario Power Generation	TransAlta
CH2M Hill	IBM	Pechiney	United Technologies
Cinergy Corporation	Intel	Pfizer Inc	Waste Management Inc
the City of Chicago	Interface Inc	PG&E Corporation	Weyerhaeuser
Cummins Inc	International Paper	Rio Tinto	Whirlpool
Deutsche Telekom	John Hancock Financial	Rohm and Haas	Wisconsin Energy Corporation
DTE Energy	Lockheed Martin	Royal Dutch/Shell	

Operational improvement

In this framework, the links between climate change and business interests are forged when reductions in GHG emissions expose opportunities for process optimization (such as lower energy costs, reduced material utilization rates, minimized emissions, and decreased costs of transportation.[30] Energy efficiency is the first and central issue for any assessment of the economics of GHG reductions. In conjunction with their GHG reduction programmes, some companies have begun to ask, 'How energy efficient are our operations? Is our company at the limits of efficiency?' These companies have found economic gains waiting in energy-use reductions both as complex as plant alterations and as simple as lighting upgrades.

Going further, an assessment of GHG emissions and reduction opportunities often reveals new insights into taken-for-granted or under-studied operational parameters. Not all operational improvements lie within the operating plant. Some companies have found more benefit in focusing on improvements in transportation or distribution.

Anticipating and influencing climate change regulations

While regulatory compliance is typically viewed as a cost of doing business, the regulatory terrain of climate change is complex and emerging on many levels. In order to think strategically about climate change regulations, business managers must adopt a multi-pronged approach. Managers must be aware of developments in policy standards at the international, national and regional levels. They must be prepared to respond, if and when those standards emerge. And, they must be able to assess whether they can have an influence on the shape those standards will take. If a company can influence the final form of climate programmes to align with their own internal plan, they will deflect the need for operational change in order to comply. Their competitors, on the other hand, will have to adapt existing operations. Companies that can anticipate and influence regulations are, in effect, setting their own programmes as the regulatory standard. For example, BP's expertise in cap-and-trade earned the company an advisory role in designing the United Kingdom GHG Emissions Trading System.[31] Similarly, Shell's experience with their own emissions trading desk won them an advisory role in developing the European Union's (EU) Trading Directive. These national and international programmes incorporate distinct elements reflecting the companies' special experience and expertise in GHG trading.

Accessing new sources of capital

The availability of capital is directly related to the issue of GHG trading. In many cases, governments are introducing financial incentives to reduce GHGs. At the outset, the dividends are likely to come from government subsidies. Going forward, they will come more and more from inter-firm trading as trading directives (like that in the EU and UK) go into effect. How much money is at stake? Richard Sandor, chairman of the Chicago Climate Exchange, estimates the market could be as large as the existing US$5 billion annual market for sulphur dioxide.[32] The World Bank foresees a US$10 billion market in GHG emissions by 2006.[33] CO2e.com estimates the range from US$10 billion to US$3 trillion by 2010.[34] Others estimate it could be as large as US$100 billion per year after the Kyoto Treaty goes into effect.[35]

Of course, these estimates include contingencies that must be weighed into the calculation of any climate change strategy. One such contingency is the inclusion of carbon sinks and the exclusion of trade ceilings, which sends conflicting signals through the market. Other contingencies depend on who participates. According to the research group Climate Strategies, the market will be about US$9 billion if the EU, Japan, Canada, Australia and New Zealand are potential buyers. This market figure would increase substantially if the United States were to join the group.

Improving risk management

In the strategic framework of risk management, greenhouse gas reductions can reduce financial risks. According to the Coalition for Environmentally Responsible Economies (CERES), US$7.4 trillion in corporate assets today potentially are threatened by climate change.[36] This leads the Coalition to conclude that corporate board members, senior executives, and institutional investors can no longer ignore such costs, and would be negligent in their fiscal responsibilities should they do so. The risks are enormous. They are both physical (the results of droughts, floods and hurricanes) and financial (the effects of GHG liabilities on share price and asset valuation).

Elevating corporate reputation

Greenhouse gas reductions also present an opportunity to enhance a corporation's reputation. This can have an impact on a variety of important constituencies, including, but not limited to, voters who influence future policy, jurors who sit in judgment on legal cases, investors who consider environmental investment strategies, communities that influence corporate expansion and new construction, reporters who write about a company's initiatives, activists who protest a company's operations, employees who produce goods and services, and the consumers who purchase those goods and services.

Identifying new market opportunities

Greenhouse gas reductions can expose important information and insights for guiding new strategic directions. Companies can exit increasingly risky business areas in favor of more secure options by measuring environmental costs and risks associated with product or process lines. New market opportunities also emerge when a company remains alert to changes in consumer preference, media attention, community concerns, and regulatory programme trends.

Enhancing human resource management

At the core of all these strategies lies an often overlooked and under-rated initiative: the engagement of the workforce. Technological and economic activity may be direct causes of climate change, but it is the culture of an organization that guides the development of solutions.

The organizational implications of climate change involve both quantifiable and non-quantifiable benefits. First, implementing strategies for GHG reductions requires substantive changes, in both the structure and the culture of an organization. Such changes include, among others, reward systems, training programmes, management philosophy, employee involvement, reporting requirements, data collection, and analysis. In all of these and more, companies must engage workers as partners in identifying and enacting strategies for – and reaping the benefits of – reducing GHG emissions.

Second, the adoption of greenhouse emissions strategies can improve a company's morale and consequently increase the retention rates of its skilled workers. Lower recruiting and training costs notwithstanding, a strong company morale contributes significantly to the attraction and retention of a high calibre workforce. Such organizational benefits may be difficult to quantify, but they are real.

We mentioned at the beginning of this section that addressing climate change and the coming market shift require a company to ask new types of questions about new types of issues. Table 2, below, offers a snapshot of the key questions that require attention within the frameworks outlined above.

Table 2 Questions for Exploring the Strategic Benefits of Voluntary Greenhouse Gas Reductions[37]

Operational improvement

- What is the energy efficiency of your operations, and can you improve it?

- Do you know how to measure your company's production of carbon dioxide and other greenhouse gases (methane, nitrous oxide, hydrofluorocarbons, perfluorcarbons, and sulphur hexafluoride)?

- Do you know the available technologies or alternatives for reducing emissions and the cost/benefit trade-offs associated with each?

Anticipating and influencing climate change regulations

- Do you know how to monitor and forecast the development of GHG regulations at the state, federal and international levels?

- Can you influence the form of those regulations?

Accessing new sources of capital

- Do you know how to conduct commodity trading of GHG emissions and are you aware of government subsidies for efforts to reduce GHG emissions?

Improving risk management

- Are any of your operations at risk due to the natural consequences of climate change and do you know the financial implications of that exposure?

- Do you know how to quantify your emissions and the financial liabilities that may incur should a GHG disclosure scheme go into force?

Elevating corporate reputation

- How is your company's market reputation improved or harmed by its posture towards GHG reductions?

- Do you have good relations with key constituencies that care about that posture?

Identifying new market opportunities

- Are there alternative product or process lines that you could be exploring that will become more attractive as GHG reduction programmes proliferate?

- Are there products or services (including GHG credits) that your company can sell to other companies who have decided to embark on voluntary GHG reduction programmes?

Enhancing human resource management

- Are your employees concerned about GHG emissions?

- Would voluntary reduction initiatives improve morale, increase the retention rates of skilled workers, lower the costs of recruiting and training new ones, or attract and retain higher calibre applicants?

Integrating climate change and business strategy

In today's business world, several companies already have a history of experience in working with climate-change issues. These are the companies now trying to shift their climate-related strategy from one focused on risk management and bottom-line protection to one that emphasizes business opportunity and top-line enhancements. While this does not mean that all such initiatives are singularly driven by the issue of climate change, nonetheless, climate change is a market shift that further enhances the value proposition of the initiative. Goldman Sachs, for example, identifies three climate-related ways to add value to the company portfolio: protect reputation, enhance competitive position, and develop new products.[38]

Some companies have focused their efforts on fundamental technology shifts. DuPont, for example, has identified the most promising growth markets in the use of biomass feedstocks. These can be used to create new bio-based materials such as polymers, fuels and chemicals, applied biosurfaces, and biomedical materials. The company's goal is to have 25 per cent of its revenue come from such non-depletable resources, and today is two-thirds of the way toward meeting that goal. One promising development is the Sorona® polymer, a result of the joint venture between DuPont and Tate & Lyle plc. In 2006, DuPont will produce 1,3-propanediol, the key building block for the new polymer, using a proprietary fermentation and purification process based on corn sugar. This bio-based method consumes less energy, reduces emissions, and employs renewable resources instead of traditional petrochemical processes.

Another promising development is the 2006 creation of a partnership between DuPont and BP to develop, produce and market a next generation of biofuels. The two companies have been working together since 2003 to develop materials that will overcome the limitations of existing biofuels. The first product to market will be biobutanol, which is targeted for introduction in 2007 in the UK as a gasoline bio-component. This biofuel offers better fuel economy than gasoline-ethanol blends and has a higher tolerance of water contamination.[39] Both of these developments represent a significant change in product lines and research focus for DuPont, and one that dramatically reduces the company's environmental footprint. DuPont's R&D leadership predicts that over 60 per cent of DuPont's future business will come from the use of biology to reduce the use of fossil fuels.

Alcoa is another experienced corporation that believes future climate policies will create market opportunities, in their case by expanding aluminum recycling. Recognizing that aluminum produced from recycled materials requires only five per cent of the energy needed to make primary aluminum, and that energy prices probably will continue to rise, the company has pledged that 50 per cent of its products (excluding raw ingot sold to others) will come from recycled aluminum by 2020. Alcoa views increased recycling as one of the company's more significant long-term strategic opportunities. Another one is the expected boost in demand for aluminum as a material for lighter weight vehicles. Alcoa has developed 'Dura Bright' commercial truck wheels that are lower in mass than conventional wheels, and do not require polish or scrubbing. Current Alcoa data indicate that a ten per cent reduction in vehicle weight typically yields a seven per cent reduction in GHG emissions.

The insurance underwriter, Swiss Re, also is looking at ways in which to augment existing climate change activities and create new business opportunities. Insurance is perhaps the one industry most directly affected by the physical impacts of climate change because it underwrites natural catastrophes and property loss. Since climate change directly affects Swiss Re's core business, with or without regulation, the company is integrating related concerns into its underwriting practices. Notable in this regard are insurance packages for Directors & Officers (D&O) and Business Interruption (BI). Moreover, the company now channels considerable investments into a number of environmentally impacted sectors, including alternative energy, water, and waste management/recycling. Specifically, Swiss Re seeks opportunities representing medium to high risk-return investment profiles: infrastructure (wind farm, biomass, solar); publicly quoted, small- to medium-capitalized growth companies; and cleantech venture capital (the highest risk-return profile). Tightening policy frameworks increase the demand for such projects, and the company's investment strategy is beginning to pay off. The value of Swiss Re's market portfolio rose substantially in 2005, thanks to both a strong share performance and new investments.

Yet another example of climate change/business strategy integration is found among the oil companies. The Shell Group has discovered that their operations, and more importantly their products, are squarely in the middle of the climate controversy. This is an issue the company cannot ignore. In 2005, Shell's operations emitted 105 million metric tons of CO_2, while downstream combustion of its fossil fuels generated an additional 763 million metric tons. Together, these emissions account for some 3.6 per cent of global CO_2 emissions from fossil fuel combustion.

A primary source of GHG emissions is the flaring of methane gas in exploration and refining operations. Shell is working to end the flaring practice and now captures the gas, either pumping it back underground to enhance well production or feeding it to nearby facilities for power production. When the economics are right, methane can be converted into liquid natural gas (LNG), a major area for potential growth. Looking ahead, the 2005 edition of Shell's *Global Scenarios to 2025* articulates a vision of how worldwide forces may shape markets over the next two decades. The conclusion is that the world and its business enterprise eventually will face a price for carbon. This conclusion justifies Shell's efforts to increase natural gas production (especially LNG), and the company's investments in wind, solar, biofuel, coal gasification, and experimental hydrogen delivery systems – all of this while still working to make its core fossil fuel business succeed in a carbon-constrained world.

Conclusion

Early warning signals, identifiable business interests, and integrated business strategy all inform us that inaction is not a viable option with regard to the impending market shift caused by climate change. As a start, companies should understand their vulnerability by developing a clear understanding of their emissions profile and of the risks and opportunities this profile creates. Next, companies should understand the possible policy options of future regulation. Finally, companies that have experience with GHG reductions should try to influence policy formation so as to reduce the uncertainty of the market shift.

Companies that are now taking action view those that do nothing as not only missing out on a myriad of near-term financial opportunities, but also setting themselves up for long-term political and financial challenges. Advancing climate regulation, rising energy prices, and the investment community's increasing attention on climate change all bring a fluid business environment into stark relief. The rules of the game are changing in ways that cannot be ignored. In the near term, companies need to be prepared for a carbon-constrained world that will alter existing business models. In the long term, they need to be prepared for a carbon-constrained world in which they will be transformed.

In the end, sustainable climate-related strategies cannot be an add-on to business as usual. Instead, climate-related strategies must be integrated into a company's overall business strategy for success. Linda Fisher, DuPont's Vice President and Chief Sustainability Officer, has articulated this mandate for the entire business community: 'We need to understand, measure, and assess market opportunities. How do you know and communicate which products will be successful in a GHG-constrained world? How should we target our research? Can we find creative ways to use renewables? Can we change societal behavior through products and technologies? The company that answers these questions successfully will be the winner.'[40]

Postscript

The following abbreviated business cases, featuring Cinergy Corporation (now Duke Energy) and Whirlpool Corporation, illustrate in a real-life context the range of issues many companies face as they grapple with climate change and search for strategic solutions.

Cinergy Corporation[41]

Cinergy Corporation (now Duke Energy) is heavily reliant on coal combustion for the generation of electricity. This makes the company particularly vulnerable to carbon regulation. Yet, according to Chairman and CEO Jim Rogers, addressing GHG emissions is not only the ethically right thing to do, it is also a smart business decision. Rogers believes that US industry soon will face domestic carbon constraints, a prediction that presents Cinergy with a serious strategic challenge. While climate change is a long-term problem, many industries need short-term regulatory and market clarity to properly value potential investments. For power companies like Cinergy, the future of climate policy and carbon regulation will affect strategic decisions about investments in new capacity having an expected life of 40 or 50 years.

'The greatest risk we face is 'stroke of the pen' risk, the risk that a regulator or congressman signing a law can change the value of our assets overnight,' says Rogers. 'If there is a high probability that there will be regulation, you try to position yourself to influence the outcome.'[42] Cinergy is managing this regulatory risk through its voluntary GHG emission reduction programme and its aggressive leadership role within the utility industry. These actions make the company a legitimate participant in the national policy debate, creating the opportunity to work with government, trade associations, environmental organizations, and other stakeholder groups to help shape legislation on GHG emissions.

But, while Rogers leads Cinergy with a long-term focus, he does not feel that the company can take definitive action on climate change until there are both clear regulatory and market signals to do so. As Kevin Leahy, the company's General Manager of Environmental Economics and Finance, explains, 'The technologies will emerge when CO_2 has a price signal. All we need is a market signal to act, and that market signal will be created by regulation.'[43]

In September 2003, Cinergy formally announced its voluntary GHG emissions reduction programme, with the goal of reducing annual emissions for the years 2010 through 2012 to five per cent below the 2000 baseline. The company's decision to more aggressively embrace climate change is based on a long-term view of the strategic implications of the issue. According to Rogers, 'When your time horizon is short, you're thinking 'stonewall it and it won't happen on your watch.' If you are a steward, you make decisions on a longer time horizon, looking beyond your own tenure. When you think of it that way, your view changes. We look 20, 30, 50 years down the road.'[44]

Rogers identifies six 'signposts' indicating that climate change is an issue to be dealt with head on: (1) individual states are taking action; (2) an increasing number of US Senators are expressing concern about global warming; (3) the Kyoto Protocol was ratified and became law on February 16, 2005; (4) a growing number of shareholder groups are asking companies to quantify the risks associated with GHG emissions;

(5) CO_2 and GHG emissions trading markets are developing in Europe and the United States; and (6) global warming is becoming part of our everyday consciousness. Notably absent from this list is scientific research and analysis. According to Rogers, 'Our decisions are purely business based. The science is interesting, but not truly relevant for our purposes.'[45] Based on these trends, he believes it is his responsibility to prepare the company for the likelihood of operating in a carbon-constrained world.

Looking to the future, coal's abundance and low cost in the United States leads Cinergy to believe that coal will continue to be central to the country's longer term fuel mix. Cinergy's work with environmentalists gave the company an early indication of a potential to break the carbon-environmental impasse. Some environmentalists already were warming to the idea of coal being part of the solution.

The most promising means currently available for utilizing coal in a carbon-constrained world is through the implementation of Integrated Gasification Combined Cycle (IGCC) technology, together with Carbon Capture and Sequestration (CCS). Cinergy has been involved in IGCC research since the early 1990s when it built one of the first demonstration plants in the United States in partnership with the US Department of Energy (DOE) through the Clean Coal Technology Demonstration Programme. In 2004, Cinergy entered into an agreement with GE Energy and Bechtel Corporation to study the feasibility of a commercial scale (600 MW) IGCC generating station.

Ultimately, Cinergy believes that resolving the climate change issue will require a paradigm shift regarding the technologies employed to refine and use energy. All of the technologies being discussed today and deployed over the next 20 to 30 years will continue to utilize fossil fuel as their source of energy. Even hydrogen will likely come from fossil fuels. Although these technologies are more energy efficient and have the capability to capture CO_2, they are only stop-gap or bridging technologies to be used until low or zero carbon technologies are developed and deployed in the second half of this century.

Looking to that future, Rogers worries how climate change could alter the fundamentals of his industry. 'I worry that we are using 100 year-old technology. There will be a transformative technology. At what point will our generation and transmission lines become obsolete? There are a lot of things you might do, if you think there will be a new technology in 25 years. You need to hit your numbers with a short term view, but you need to run your company with a long term view.'[46]

Having a seat at the policy table and influencing the final legislation will help ensure that it fits with Cinergy's interests and future direction.

Whirlpool Corporation[47]

At the ninth meeting of the Conference of the Parties of the Kyoto Protocol in 2003, Whirlpool became the world's first appliance manufacturer to announce a GHG reduction strategy. But unlike many other companies that have made similar pledges, Whirlpool's approach to climate change involves neither dramatic changes to its operations nor significant bottom line costs. The company's strategy is laser focused on leveraging its current core competencies, and continuing down the same path it has been on for years, that is, bringing the most energy-efficient products to the market. In so doing, Whirlpool is reducing GHG emissions through its consumers. The mantra among the workforce is 'energy efficiency', plain and simple.

In 2003, Whirlpool announced a plan to – by 2008 – decrease total GHG emissions from global manufacturing, product use and end-of-life by three per cent from a 1998 baseline. The company projected increasing sales by 40 per cent over the same period.

Customers are the key to Whirlpool's efforts to address climate change. The company's internal studies conclude that of the nearly 30 tonnes of CO_2 emitted during the life of an average washing machine, over 93 per cent come from the use phase. Of the remaining amount, two per cent come from manufacturing and five per cent come from end-of-life disposal. This is corroborated by a 1992 United Kingdom-based PA Consulting Group study which also shows that over 93 per cent of washer emissions come from use.

The concentration of emissions in the use phase presents an opportunity for focused efforts to reduce those emissions. While the company still seeks energy reductions throughout the supply chain, it has determined that further improvements in the manufacturing process would be hard to find.

Driven by mandatory and voluntary programmes, as well as by competitor pressure and consumer demand, Whirlpool has been engaged in a constant search for energy efficiencies with its appliances. The company (and the industry) has achieved dramatic energy savings over the past 30 years. Compared to models from 1970, today's refrigerators use less than half as much energy and washing machines and dishwashers use approximately one-third as much. Since 1980, the overall percentage of the United States home energy use that is dedicated to appliances has dropped by two-thirds, to between 18 and 20 per cent.

These improvements have not always been easy. In the past, Whirlpool has felt that it was paddling upstream against consumer demand. For example, in 1993 the company was the winner of the Super Efficient Refrigerator Programme (SERP) competition sponsored by the Environmental Protection Agency, the Department of Energy, and 27 national utilities. Though the company received the US$30 million prize for winning the challenge, and enjoyed the accolades that came with it, some employees felt that the corporate investment far outweighed the reward. In the end, the prize money barely defrayed the development dollars and the company was forced to go to great lengths to generate consumer interest in the product. This experience planted concerns within the company that you cannot get too far ahead of the market. In other words, efficiency gains must not exceed manufacturing costs or consumer demand.

Over the past two years, Whirlpool executives have sensed a market shift as consumers have become increasingly interested in energy efficiency. This, the company believes, is driven by both increasing awareness of climate change and environmental issues, and by increasing energy costs. According to Casey Tubman, Brand Manager of Fabric Care Products, 'In the 1980s, energy efficiency was number ten, eleven or twelve in consumer priorities. In the last four or five years, it has come up to number three behind cost and performance, and we believe these concerns will continue to grow.'[48]

Energy efficiency still requires consumer education. The most efficient washers can cost up to US$500 more than traditional washers (absent any rebates). However, depending on utility rates, they can save between US$75 and US$100 per year, yielding a five-year payback. The educational challenge is making the payback as visible as the purchase price.

Today, the Whirlpool Duet® is a front loading washing machine that uses the horizontal axis orientation to yield efficiencies of 68 per cent less energy, 67 per cent less water, and 50 to 70 per cent less detergent than traditional top loading machines. Most importantly, the machine has been extremely successful in the marketplace and has served to counter the internal resistance that resulted from the SERP experience.

Going forward, Whirlpool believes that the focus on efficiency will have other long-term benefits for the company in terms of market share. According to Tubman, energy efficiency is becoming a source of competitive advantage through brand loyalty. 'Once someone buys a high efficiency device, they never go back to buying a traditional machine.'[49] Whirlpool's market research supports this conclusion. According to Steve Willis, Director of Global Environment, Health and Safety, Whirlpool surveys demonstrate that 'there is a strong correlation between a company's performance in appliance markets and their social response to issues such as energy efficiency and pollution.' While not uniform across products or regions, Whirlpool believes that environmental attributes (water and energy conservation) produce customer loyalty and repeat purchases.

As an added benefit, Whirlpool executives believe that the company's focus on energy efficiency, like its other responsibility efforts, helps to draw and retain employees who feel good about the company and perform better. In Tubman's words, 'The values stay here because the people stay here and the people stay here because the values stay here.'[50]

On the issue of climate-change policy, Whirlpool's primary focus on end-use emissions leads executives to feel strongly that any national policy aimed at addressing climate change must include credit for use-cycle reductions. 'Who gets the use credits?', asks JB Hoyt. 'Should the utility get it? The user? The manufacturer?'[51] End-use emissions is the number one issue, even though the company has been working on emissions reduction for a very long time.

All of this leads to the conclusion that a focus on GHG reductions through energy efficiency is central to Whirlpool's core strategy. A focus on energy efficiency gives the company a premium product well suited for a carbon-constrained future. Even though there is relative technological parity between the product offerings of domestic and European manufacturers, Whirlpool is concerned that Asian-based manufacturers could overrun the domestic market with cheap, less energy-efficient machines. Increased home energy prices resulting from efforts to reduce GHG emissions could be a windfall for Whirlpool as consumers place an even higher premium on energy efficiency. Banking on this future, Whirlpool has stayed the course and has continued to do what it does best –bring energy efficiency into the home.

Notes

1 Hoffman A. 'Examining the Rhetoric: The Strategic Implications of Climate Change Policy', *Corporate Environmental Strategy*, 9 (4), 2002, pp.329–337.

2 Hoffman A. 'Climate Change Strategy: The Business Logic Behind Voluntary Greenhouse Gas Reductions', *California Management Review*, 47(3), 2005, pp.21–46.

3 Margolick M. and Russell D. *Corporate Greenhouse Gas Reduction Targets*, Arlington, VA, Pew Center on Global Climate Change, 2001.

4 Hoffman A. 'The "Carbon Cartel" or Wise Capitalists: What is Going on with Voluntary Greenhouse Gas Reductions?' *American Bar Association Air Quality Newsletter*, 9 (1) (November) 2005, pp.3–7.

5 Wellington F. and Sauer A. *Framing Climate Risk in Portfolio Management*, Boston, MA, Ceres, 2005.

6 Karmali A. 'Best Practice in Strategies for Managing Carbon' in K. Tang (ed.) *The Finance of Climate Change: A Guide for Governments, Corporations and Investors*, London, Risk Books, 2006, pp.259–270.

7   Austin D. and Sauer A. *Changing Oil: Emerging Environmental Risks and Shareholder Value in the Oil and Gas Industry*, Washington DC, World Resources Institute, 2002.

8   DeCicco J., Fung F. and An F. *Automakers' Corporate Carbon Burdens: Update for 1990–2003*, New York, Environmental Defense, 2005.

9   Cogan D. *Corporate Governance and Climate Change: Making the Connection*, Boston, MA, Ceres Inc., 2006.

10 Hoffman A. *From Heresy to Dogma: An Institutional History of Corporate Environmentalism*, Stanford, CA, Stanford University Press, 2001.

11 Hoffman A. *Getting Ahead of the Curve: Corporate Strategies that Address Climate Change*, Arlington, VA, Pew Center on Global Climate Change, 2006.

12 *New York Times*, 'Investors Seek Climate Change Information', *New York Times*, 15 June 2006, C8.

13 Epstein P. and Mills E. *Climate Change Futures: Health, Ecological and Economic Dimensions*, Cambridge, MA, Center for Health and the Global Environment, Harvard Medical School, 2005.

14 See www.cdproject.net/, accessed 3 March 2006.

15 Smith J. 'The Implications of the Kyoto Protocol and the Global Warming Debate for Business Transactions', *NYU Journal of Law & Business*, 1(2): 511:550, 2005; Ewing K., Hutt J. and Petersen E. 'Corporate Environmental Disclosures: Old Complaints, New Expectations', *Business Law International*, 5(3), 2004, pp.459–515.

16 Semans T. and Juliani T. 'Succeeding in a Carbon-Constrained World', *Corporate Strategy Today*, July 2006, pp.21–37.

17 Mintzer I., Leonard J. and Schwartz P. *U.S. Energy Scenarios for the 21st Century*, Arlington, VA, Pew Center on Global Climate Change, 2003.

18 Carbon Trust, *Brand Value at Risk from Climate Change*, London, Carbon Trust, 2004.

19 Pacala S. and Socolow R. 'Stabilization Wedges: Solving the Climate Problem for the Next 50 Years with Current Technologies', *Science*, 305(5686), 2004, pp.968–972.

20 Makower J., Pernick R. and Wilder C. *Clean Energy Trends 2006*, San Francisco, Clean Edge Inc., 2006. www.cleanedge.com/reports/trends2006.pdf, accessed 3 March 2006.

21 Chea T. 'Doerr Firm Invests in "Green Technology"', *USA Today online*, 10 April 2006. www.usatoday.com/tech/news/2006-04-10-green-venture-capitalist_x.htm, accessed 22 June 2006.

22 Ceres, *Managing the Risks and Opportunities of Climate Change: A Practical Toolkit for Corporate Leaders*, Boston, MA, Ceres Inc., 2006.

23 Lemonick M. 'Has the Meltdown Begun?' *Time*, 27 February 2005, pp.58–59.

24 Eilperin J. 'Debate on Climate Change Shifts to Irreparable Harm', *Washington Post*, 29 January 2006, A01.

25 Deutsch C. 'Study Says U.S. Companies Lag on Global Warming', *New York Times*, 22 March 2006, C3.

26 Birchall J. 'Wal-Mart Sets Out Stall for a Greener Future', *The Financial Times*, 26 October 2005, p.27.

27 Bennett O. 'Healthy, Wealthy And Wise Inc. "Sustainability" Used To Be Just For Hippies. In America, It's Now Big Business.' *The Daily Telegraph*, 25 October 2006, p.8.

28 Crane D. 'Canada Needs to Develop a Clear Plan on Kyoto', *The Toronto Star*, 18 September 2004, D2.

29 Op. cit., Hoffman A. (2005), p.40.

30 CO2e.com, *Greenhouse Gas Market Overview*, Toronto, CO2e.com LLC, 2001.

31 Buchan D. 'Race to Acclimatize Companies to Scheme for Limiting Greenhouse Effect: The Government Hopes to Lead the way in Pollution Permit Trading', *The Financial Times*, 4 January 2002, p.4.

32 'Exchange in Pollution Credits Formed', *Chicago Sun-Times*, 17 January 2003, p.53.

33 'Trading in Greenhouse Gases', *Christian Science Monitor*, 24 October 2002, p.8.

34 Op. cit., CO2e.com, 2001.

35 Nesmith J. 'Rejection of Kyoto Treaty on Climate may Leave U.S. Companies out in Cold', *The Atlanta Journal*, 27 July 2002, 8G.

36 Innovest Strategic Value Advisors, *Value at Risk: Climate Change and the Future of Governance*, Boston, MA, Ceres, 2002.

37 Op. cit., Hoffman, A. *California Management Review*, 2005.

38 Moran M., Cohen A., Swem N. and Shaustyuk K. 'The Growing Interest in Environmental Issues is Important to Both Socially Responsible and Fundamental Investors', *Portfolio Strategy*, Goldman Sachs, 26 August 2005, p.5.

39 DuPont, *Press Release: DuPont and BP Announce Partnership to Develop Advanced Biofuels*, Wilmington, Del., DuPont, 2006.

40 Op. cit., Hoffman, A. 2006, p.7.

41 Material for this case study was drawn from Hoffman A. 'Cinergy: Managing "Stroke of the Pen" Risk', in *Getting Ahead of the Curve: Corporate Strategies that Address Climate Change*, Arlington, VA, Pew Center on Global Climate Change, 2006, pp.64–75.

42 Ibid. p.47

43 Ibid. p.64

44 Ibid. p.39

45 Ibid. p.66

46 Ibid. p.61

47 Material for this case study was drawn from Hoffman, A. 'Whirlpool: Don't Switch Tracks When the Train is Already Moving', in *Getting Ahead of the Curve: Corporate Strategies that Address Climate Change*, Arlington, VA, Pew Center on Global Climate Change, 2006, pp.121–128.

48 Ibid. p.6

49 Ibid. p.123

50 Ibid. p.124

51 Ibid. p.127

8

Carbon Constraints: Threat or Opportunity?

Karl Schultz, Energy Edge and
Peter Williamson, Energy Edge and INSEAD

Climate change: a strategic issue

Today businesses throughout the world may be exposed to climate change in up to three broad ways. First, governments are imposing limits on greenhouse gas emissions. Secondly, some of the effects of climate change will directly impact the business environment. Thirdly, public perceptions of corporate behaviour have the potential to impact the bottom line. Before turning to the impacts on corporate strategies and possible sources of competitive advantage, it is worth briefly elaborating each of these drivers of increased business exposure to climate change and associated carbon constraints in turn.

Regulatory exposure

The Kyoto Protocol, which was negotiated in 1997 and by July of 2006 had been ratified by 164 nations, invokes binding limits on emissions. With Russia's ratification, the treaty went into force in February 2005. Kyoto's limits are generally viewed as just a small step towards stabilizing atmospheric concentrations of greenhouse gases at a level that will have acceptably manageable consequences on the global environment, human health, natural resources and physical infrastructure.

The European Union (EU), former Soviet Union and Japan represent the majority of capped emissions, with the EU and Japan facing a clear shortage of allowances to comply. The EU Emissions Trading Scheme, started in 2005, has become the largest emissions market, but is only one of the measures that European nations are taking in order to comply with their targets under the Kyoto Protocol, with renewable energy requirements, efficiency standards, and other measures implemented to reach compliance levels.

Other nations facing caps under Kyoto are planning emissions trading schemes. Japan has created a voluntary emissions trading scheme, and Japanese companies are major purchasers of international emission reduction credits. Countries that have ratified Kyoto but that do not have binding limits on their emissions, such as Brazil and China, are becoming very active in promoting investments in projects that create emissions reduction credits, reducing emissions by an anticipated one billion tonnes by 2012. These countries are also undertaking to reduce emissions through policies such as efficiency standards.

Even Australia and the United States, the two major countries that did not ratify the Kyoto Protocol, are taking a number of steps at the federal and state levels to reduce emissions. Both Australia and the US are funding research into emissions reduction and sequestration technologies, and provide incentives for green energy projects. In Australia, the state governments are developing plans to impose a nationwide emissions trading scheme regardless of the involvement of the Federal government, and in the United States state and regional level emissions trading schemes are being planned.

But, while limits on greenhouse gas emissions set by Kyoto will have significant impacts on industry, they will not even come close to solving the problem of climate change. A drastic reduction in global emissions is necessary to stabilize concentrations in the atmosphere at what will be considered an acceptable level. Kyoto only limits industrialized nations' emissions at approximately 5.2 per cent below 1990 levels in the period 2008–2012. Worldwide cuts of between 15 and 50 per cent below 1990 levels are needed to stabilize concentrations at levels necessary to avert the risk of a climatic catastrophe.

Discussions are already underway to consider next steps beyond Kyoto's period of 2008–2012, and even the United States, despite its non participation in the Kyoto Protocol, is involved in this process. These discussions include a pathway for the developing countries to take on limits, and a longer-term framework to allow greater regulatory certainty when companies consider the carbon emissions implications of new investments. The momentum and vested interests of companies involved in emissions allowance and credit markets makes deeper and broader global carbon constraints practically inevitable.

Business exposures to climate change

The costs of climate change to industry will not all stem from regulations. The direct impacts of climate change on infrastructure, agricultural production, and human health on business will be varied but very real. Companies that operate in developing countries (or have supply chains that depend on them) are likely to be even more exposed, as many of the most severe impacts will face these nations. Businesses may even have to deal with a world in which global instability becomes the norm – the US Pentagon prepared a report on the impacts of climate change on international security that states: 'warfare may again come to define human life ... As the planet's carrying capacity shrinks, an ancient pattern re-emerges: the eruption of desperate, all-out wars over food, water, and energy supplies.'[1]

Moreover, the industries most exposed to climate change are not always the obvious, heavy energy users. In fact, one of the industries most likely to be affected is insurance. John Coomber, then CEO of re-insurer Swiss Re states: 'Climate change is a phenomenon that is starting to have a major impact on Swiss Re, its partners, and our clients. The question is no longer whether global warming is happening, but how it's going to affect our business.' A study by Swiss Re, estimated that the costs of claims to insurers from climate change related weather events will be between US$30 and US$40 billion per year in ten years.[2]

Depending on the industry and company, the exposure to climate change will be positive or negative, and may include:

- Access to water resources

- Price hikes and price volatility across different sources of energy

- Supply chain challenges caused by weather, infrastructure strains (shipping, inventory)

- Risks to assets from sea level rise and weather (infrastructure)

- Changes in customer needs (caused, for instance, by changes in economies, product demand related to weather, resource availability, etc)

- Country investment risk caused by changes in national political and security conditions.

Public perception exposure

A study of the effects of the oil giant ExxonMobil's stance on climate change – which generally is viewed as less interested in mitigating its greenhouse gas emissions than its peers, BP and Shell – indicated that the company may face a number of risks, including a hit on its brand value of between US$2 and US$3 billion, as well as problems with staff retention, recruitment, and political access amounting to between US$10 and $50 billion. In addition, its exposure to litigation risk from the damage of climate change could potentially exceed US$100 billion. Each year at ExxonMobil's annual shareholder meeting a resolution, most recently supported by 20 per cent of votes, is proposed that demands justification for the company's position.[3]

Different companies will face varying degrees of exposure to public perceptions. Some companies, such as renewable energy producers, will benefit by being seen as contributing to solving the climate problem, while others will face inherent criticism because of the product that they produce – however necessary it is for the economy. Also, those companies with strong brand names and a significant retail component to their sales will be more exposed than companies that sell to industry. As such, coal companies, whose principal customer base are electric power producers, will be less exposed (at least to public perceptions) than oil companies, that sell petrol to consumers directly.

Threat or opportunity?

The total costs of these impacts will differ markedly depending on whether a company's exposure derives from its direct emissions, indirect emissions (such as its purchase of electricity from a carbon emitting utility or from sale of a product that results in emissions, like coal or automobiles), or from the impacts of climate change on the business (as we saw above). The challenge for management lies in reducing the totality of these costs and the associated risks including handling the possibility of a shortage of emissions allowances, managing the risks to the company's credit rating, and re-thinking the optimal portfolio of energy sources in a carbon-constrained world. This means developing a broad and comprehensive strategy for managing the new environment. Perhaps most interesting of all, it means looking for new opportunities to gain competitive advantage in a carbon-constrained world. As we will see below, if handled correctly, climate change can be an opportunity to steal a march on rivals, not just an unwelcome problem to be dealt with.

But are businesses approaching the issue strategically? In Europe, where most large companies face direct caps on emissions, the issue is being addressed and companies in Japan have long been leaders in hedging their carbon exposure through acquiring international emission credits. Yet a parallel study of US electric utilities' exposure to greenhouse gas emissions constraints concluded that between 10 and 35 per cent of the total market capitalization was at risk.[4] This is in a country that has not ratified Kyoto, but where more states and local governments are taking action to reduce emissions, and companies are still exposed to the direct business risks of climate change

Companies in developing countries without caps, such as China, India and Brazil, are not facing the same likelihood of emissions caps, but in the medium term even these countries are likely to take on targets. Meanwhile, companies in developing countries may well find themselves in the 'front line' of direct business impacts of climate change. This level of exposure obviously demands top management attention. But from a competitive advantage standpoint, relative exposure counts more. Here the results look even more startling: another respected study found that the value at risk because of climate change varied between companies by a factor of nearly 60 times.[5]

Strategic opportunities in managing carbon constraints

While most businesses will face additional costs associated with carbon constraints, there are also three areas of opportunity to gain competitive advantage:

- Minimising the additional costs more effectively than competitors
- Differentiating the product by bundling carbon credits into the offering
- Turning the capacity to supply carbon credits into a profit centre

Each is worth consideration in turn.

Minimising the additional costs

While the market price of emissions constraints is dependent on many factors outside the control of most companies, such as weather and fuel prices, the strategic company will be able to both reduce its own costs and adapt to changes by taking a number of measures that may include:

- Diversifying fuel consumption to allow for flexibility to exploit divergent price trends that competitors locked in to one fuel source cannot enjoy

- Active carbon asset management to reduce potential exposure to carbon price fluctuations

- Public/shareholder public relations: enhance sales or share price.

Product differentiation through bundling

There are a number of opportunities for companies to gain competitive advantage by understanding the carbon constraints throughout their supply chain and customer base, thus anticipating and reacting strategically to these needs. For example, a fuel supplier might be able to secure low-cost carbon credits and offer electric utilities short on allowances a combination fuel and credit product that matches its customer's allowance needs. Likewise a bank or insurance company may, through its contacts with energy companies producing credits, be able to offer a package of finance/insurance and carbon credits to offset emissions from new build. A manufacturer with caps on its emissions who is able to choose different fuels to supply production would be able to track the energy and allowance prices to come up with the lowest production costs.

Turning carbon credit supply into a profit centre

Many companies will also be in a strong position to supply credits for what is likely to be a growing market. This is especially true for companies in developing countries that may benefit by reducing their own emissions or identifying other companies where low-cost emission reductions are possible, also gaining valuable hard currency finance from companies looking for emission reductions. Some companies with caps on their emissions will find that emissions reductions at their facilities are significantly less costly than the price of a traded allowance. Others will be in a position to source emissions credits from projects specifically designed to offer low cost reductions, in developing countries and economies in transition. For instance, a power generator with skills in producing power from methane that would otherwise be emitted to the atmosphere may be able to develop projects, create carbon credits, and then use these to either offset its own emissions or sell the credits – possibly to strategic partners or electricity customers who have a choice of power supplies.

The opportunities are not limited to heavy industry. Some traders speculate that the carbon credit market may become the largest traded commodity in the world. Investors, traders, insurance companies and of course consultants all may benefit from the creation, supply and transaction of emissions credits.

From strategy to action

To turn these strategic ideas into an action plan, companies will need to follow the rigorous, five-step process outlined below.

Strategy Building
Steps

Assess Carbon Exposure

Compare Exposure with
Competition's

Assess Mitigation Options

Assess Strategies to Gain
Competitive Advantage

Develop a Strategic Plan

Source: Authors' own

Assess your carbon exposure

For those companies with caps placed on their emissions, this may at first glance seem to be a simple issue. However, for all companies the uncertainties in future policies, climate change patterns, and public sentiment mean that this task is not straightforward.

The first step for companies is to understand what their emissions are, both direct and indirect. As we have already noted, a distinction has to be made between a company's direct emissions, and indirect emissions, from, for instance, purchase of electricity from a carbon emitting utility on one side, or from sale of a product that results in emissions, such as coal or automobiles. Corporate emissions inventory guidelines have been developed for most industries (for instance, corporate inventory guidelines prepared by the World Resources Institute – see www.wri.org.). For those companies already facing caps, their historical, direct emissions have a starting point to which an estimate of their indirect emissions needs to be added. It is also important to divide these emissions by type of greenhouse gas (because methane, for example, is weighted at 23 times carbon dioxide), by facility, and by risk, depending on whether emissions are currently capped and are likely to be capped in the future.

Once the emissions are accounted for, it is important to quantify in financial terms the current and future carbon liabilities. A reasonable assumption for companies facing caps on their emissions is to use the current allowance price and the expected shortage (or surplus) of allowances that the company holds. Preparing different scenarios for future prices and expected shortages will also be important.

The company will also need to estimate the financial impact of its indirect exposure to climate change regulations. These may include increases in power prices, and the ability for companies to switch fuels between lower and higher greenhouse emitting fuels. The company's demand for other commodities facing carbon exposure, such as cement and steel, will also be important to calculate.

As with greenhouse gas regulatory exposure, it will also be important to consider the exposure to climate change events. Are corporate assets vulnerable to any of the expected climate change impacts? Are customers likely to face changes in their purchasing habits because of climate change?

Finally, to complete a thorough audit of a company's carbon exposure, it is critical to gauge customer and shareholder sentiment. Do customers view the company as environmentally responsible? How do existing and potential shareholders, especially large institutional investors, rate the company's activities?

Compare your exposure with competitors

Because the carbon issues are ultimately about impacts on a company's competitive advantage, the second key step will be to benchmark a company's exposures with those of its rivals. Although it may not be possible to quantify these as easily as its own, and although it cannot know what steps its competition may be taking to reduce their own exposure, a general idea will be available that can result in a comparison of the various exposures, and thus help guide strategies to differentiate and become more competitive. It is also important to consider substitutes to the product that may be more or less competitive in a carbon-constrained market, which will guide the creation of strategies to either defend market share (if a company is more exposed to carbon constraints), or take market share from other industries.

Assess your options to mitigate carbon exposure

There are a number of options available to most industries to reduce or at least manage their carbon exposure. These include:

- Investing in plant retrofits or new investments to reduce emissions
- Investing in projects to offset emissions
- Purchasing allowances from the emissions market, hedges or other risk management tools
- Divesting business activities with too much current or potential carbon exposure

- Lobbying government to influence decisions on future emissions limits

- Communicating corporate greenhouse-friendly actions with shareholders and the public.

For each of these options, a reasonable assessment of the marginal costs of each action, adjusted for risk, will be useful to decide the most effective strategy.

It is possible that some companies may find that a 'do nothing, but watch' strategy is most appropriate. This is probably only applicable for those companies whose overall exposure is minimal however, and the hidden indirect impacts of the carbon-constrained market need to be identified and evaluated before coming to this decision.

Assess your opportunities to gain competitive advantage in the new, carbon-constrained environment

Companies in all industries will have the potential to differentiate themselves from competitors based on the assessment of future climate change regulations, direct impacts, and public perceptions.

Companies will in most instances also be able to identify actions and investments that will be more profitable in a carbon-constrained business environment. By identifying the company's natural strengths (such as relations with companies that have low-cost emission reduction potential), or a customer base faced with very significant carbon exposure (such as electric utilities), managers will be able to develop strategies that differentiate them from their competitors. For instance, fuel suppliers may be in a position to change their supply to be less carbon intensive than their competitors. This could be direct by producing more greenhouse-friendly fuels, such as shifting from coal to natural gas, or it could be by securing emissions credits at low cost and then bundling these credits with a fuel sales agreement to meet a customer's emissions allowance needs. As we noted above, it is worth considering the potential of turning the supply of carbon credits into a profit centre.

Develop a strategic plan

Once the strategic options are identified, it will be important to create a plan that integrates the various steps and creates clear management of some or all of the following areas:

- Investments

- Divestments

- Purchases

- Hedging strategies

- Sales strategy

- Public relations

Putting the strategic approach into practice

Each industry and each individual company will have a unique set of carbon exposures and different strategies available to maintain or create competitive advantage in carbon-constrained economies. To better understand some of the basic nuances, and the process to create a corporate carbon strategy, we take the examples of three different companies in three continents in very different industries and types of exposure: a small European cement company facing emission caps, a US multinational bank, and an Asian pulp and paper company.

A European Cement Manufacturer

Following the five-step model, the first task was to assess the company's carbon exposure.

Assessing its carbon exposure

Cement making is very carbon intensive. In our example, a Portland cement company with two separate facilities produces a total of 1.8 million tonnes of cement per year. The direct greenhouse gas emissions are calculated for both emissions by identifying accurate emissions factors for its direct fuel consumption of coal, natural gas, propane and diesel, and emissions from the processing of raw materials into cement. The fuel consumption emissions are estimated to be 220,000 tonnes of carbon dioxide, and the process emissions are 350,000 tonnes, for a total of 570,000 tonnes.

Indirect emissions from the consumption of electricity are calculated based on an emissions factor for the power grid in its region. These emissions are estimated to be 25,000 tonnes. The cement maker also considers the emissions from its suppliers (production of limestone, shale, clay, sand and iron) and estimates that the production and transport of these emissions result in an additional 85,000 tonnes of emissions. It then considers the emissions from distributing its cement, and estimates these emissions at 25,000 tonnes.

Finally, it considers the indirect emissions created by its customers. This is a difficult issue to weigh, and it has to consider if substitutes to Portland cement might be higher or lower in their contribution to greenhouse gas emissions. Its preliminary research indicates that less carbon-intensive substitutes, such as use of fly ash in concrete might be favoured in the future, but questions the consistency of resource supply.

It then looks at its overall market value and determines that at an emissions allowance price of €16 per tonne, the 570,000 tonnes of direct emissions each year represent a total potential asset value of €9.12 million. However, the manufacturer has been given 520,000 allowances so it is short 50,000 tonnes at a price of €800,000. On the other hand, it expects demand to increase for its product, so the likely exposure is greater. Without changes in its process, it expects to be short 150,000 tonnes in 2007 at an expected value of €2.4 million and it expects during the second phase of the trading scheme that this shortage will increase. With net revenues of €2.5 million, its exposure is significant.

Looking to the future, the company examined a different set of scenarios for what their allocations were likely to be, starting in 2008. Considering that the allocations were going to be less and allowance prices greater, it assumed for a mid-case scenario that its allocation would drop from 2008

– 2012, resulting in a shortage valued at €2.5 million (which however assumes allowance prices do not increase), or equal to its current net revenues.

The cement manufacturer then looked at the impacts of carbon constraints on the price of its energy. It assumed that power prices would go up, increasing its costs, and that gas prices would also rise as demand for gas, a less emitting fuel, would go up. Coal prices, it assumed, would average the same as before the emissions trading scheme, but the price volatility might increase.

 Since its facilities are not very vulnerable to more severe weather, it assumed that this would not be an important issue, but did assume that demand for concrete may go up as the need for new build for sea level rise might increase.

It also considered if its customers would see the company's position on climate change as an issue, and decided probably, but not to a great extent.

Estimating its competitors' carbon exposure

Ninety-five per cent of the cement company's product is sold onto the national market. As such, it looked at each of the top national cement companies, and also looked at the possible competition from brick making and asphalt production. It also looked at the possibility of foreign companies being less exposed, and thus able to enter the national market. In this case, the cement maker determined that there was little differentiation in the national market, but that cement makers in one neighbouring country may face weaker limits on emissions, whereas in another the limits might be more stringent, making its companies less competitive. However, because of the higher transport costs it became less clear if these differences would amount to anything.

Developing its options to mitigate exposure

Based on the above analysis of its exposure, the cement company then ran through a series of options to mitigate its exposure.

Because it was likely to face a shortage of allowances, it decided to analyse the marginal costs of reducing its direct emissions. It found that it could reduce emissions through a number of investments and changes in purchase decisions, including:

- Increasing its use of gas
  However, for this scenario it also looked at projected gas prices and determined that a likely switch may not be cost effective, even with the lowered emissions. However, from 2008 onwards this scenario becomes economic.

- Alternative energy inputs
  It identified biomass fuel as being economic if its price didn't increase. However, an analysis of biomass demand suggested that the company should wait before deciding on this option.

- Energy efficiency improvements
  It identified six different measures, and found that two were cost effective starting immediately, and an additional two would be economic after 2008. A government grant might help finance four of these measures.

- Supplementary cementing materials
  It found that it could input fly ash into its process and indirectly reduce emissions. However, it found there was no current means by which this would reduce its direct emissions. Nonetheless, because it had a potential supply at a comparable price to its current inputs, it decided to undertake this to show it is doing what it can to indirectly reduce emissions.

The cement company also approached a developer of a project to reduce methane emissions in Vietnam. It found that this project could generate emissions reductions at a lower price than the allowance price. However, it was concerned that this project exceeded its typical investment risk threshold.

The company also discussed the option of purchasing futures contracts with an emissions broker. This option would reduce its exposure risk as the price of acquiring its allowances would be fixed.

The company considered a sales push in a neighbouring country with tighter emissions caps on its cement industry. This option was analysed, and the company calculated that it would be competitive on costs. However, there were additional marketing costs and plans to enter this market were postponed until the (probably more stringent) allocations under Phase II to be announced in 2007.

The company also is a member of its trade association, and could join a working group that would track greenhouse emissions issues. It also considered preparing a public relations campaign. Recognising that the company is not particularly large nor is public visibility particularly related to sales, it calculated that this would be a relatively costly option.

Assembling a strategy for competitive advantage

The cement company then took all the options available to it, and prepared a decision model for how to move forward, and at what stage various emissions allowance, energy, and cement prices would warrant taking different steps.

It has discovered that the options it identified would be likely to result in a significantly reduced exposure to greenhouse gas limits, and suspected that its competitors were not looking at all their options as carefully. As such, it thinks it will be able to increase its market share and, even with emissions constraints, be in a stronger position.

A Multinational Bank

Assessing its carbon exposure

A New York bank, with offices throughout the world, faced no direct caps on its emissions. However, it is a highly visible company with customer perceptions important for its business and it also finances a diverse set of industries, many of which face direct caps on their emissions. Additional investments may be even costlier to cover.

Direct emissions for this company are relatively small; however, these are carefully included in the bank's annual corporate social responsibility reports. CO_2 emissions are divided into energy use (indirect electricity consumption) and travel (car, rail, and air travel).

Fifty per cent of the bank's investments are in the US with 15 per cent of its US investments in industries with planned emission caps. Thirty per cent of its remaining investments are in other countries with emission caps, and a total of 25 per cent of its investments are in the industrial sectors facing emissions caps. The remaining 20 per cent of investments are in countries currently without caps but the majority of these investments are in carbon-intensive activities and could generate emission reduction credits. The bank reviewed the exposure of its clients to emissions caps, and also the likely impact different investments would have on future exposure. It found that it had invested in a disproportionately high percentage of companies with heavy exposure, including a number of manufacturing facilities dependent on coal-fired facilities for production. It also had some investments in tourism and port facilities that had the potential to be impacted by changing temperatures and sea level rise.

Estimating its competitors' carbon exposure

A careful analysis of the competition showed that this bank is moderately exposed. While it has invested a higher percentage into heavily exposed industries than the average, its investments overseas that could generate emissions credits mitigates this somewhat.

Developing its options to mitigate exposure

The bank considered the following options:

- Do nothing. This was rejected because although it had no direct exposure, its indirect investment exposure was significant.

- Augment its sustainable development investment criteria to include a demand for quantification of emissions exposure, and propose means of minimizing these exposures.

- Undertake a progressive divestment strategy from some of the most exposed and at risk industries – in particular coal-fired power in Europe, and some climate-sensitive infrastructure and service investments.

- Serve as an important facilitator and financier of emissions credit creation, and supply these credits (through a separately regulated subsidiary) to many of its European and Japanese clients seeking emissions credits. It is in a position to implement this strategy because of its strong position in overseas emissions generation.

- Strengthen its corporate sustainability message to include a climate change policy. This was viewed as important to maintain good customer relations.

Assembling a strategy for competitive advantage

As a result of adopting a number of these varied measures the bank has significantly lowered the risk of its investment portfolio, and achieved a stronger retail banking image. The emission generation and trading arm has also created a new profit centre for the bank.

An Asian Pulp And Paper Manufacturer

Assessing its carbon exposure

A large paper and pulp manufacturer, with its operations throughout Southeast Asia, faces no caps on its emissions. However, it recognizes that as a major energy consumer and purchaser of wood, that its exposure to carbon is very significant. The company produces one million tonnes of paper and two million tonnes of pulp and exports worldwide. It also consumes four million m^3 of wood. It is facing increased demand for its products in China and plans on expanding production facilities there.

The company recognizes the importance of understanding emissions across its entire supply chain. A competitor faced bad publicity from purchases of timber from companies allegedly clearing rainforest. It also realizes that with the high cost of fuel, steps to improve its energy efficiency may reduce costs significantly.

Direct emissions from this company stem from its consumption of fuel oil, with total CO_2 emissions of 2.4 million tonnes. Its waste water stream results in emissions of methane of approximately the equivalent of 100,000 tonnes of CO_2. It also consumes a significant amount of electricity purchased from the grid, contributing significantly to indirect emissions.

It sources 75 per cent of its timber from its own plantations, but the rest is purchased and the company does not have a well documented understanding of the sources of this wood. Along its supply chain it also has emissions from transport of timber to the mills and shipping to markets, including European and North American. Its shipments to China and other Asian countries are mainly for packaging of manufactured goods, frequently exported to Europe or North American markets.

Estimating its competitors' carbon exposure

This paper and pulp company is growing; some of this is at the expense of competing companies in Europe that face high energy costs and limits on carbon dioxide emissions that it doesn't face. This gives it a window of competitive advantage as it does not yet face emission limits.

Its regional competitors have similar direct emissions to it although many use waste wood products for much of their energy needs. A few competitors are marketing non-wood paper products which they claim reduces deforestation and the resulting net greenhouse gas emissions. If these strategic initiatives taken by competitors gain momentum, they may put the Asian company's product portfolio and entire business model under threat.

Developing its options to mitigate exposure

The paper/pulp company has a number of options to reduce its exposure to carbon. These include:

- Improving its supply chain record. An 'Independent Chain of Custody' (CoC) standard marketed by PriceWaterhouseCoopers would ensure that wood products were grown meeting responsible forest management practices.

- Incorporating carbon costs of transportation into its procurement and sales offers. Thus, wood products and markets closer to its paper mills would be given a slight edge up and net indirect emissions from transportation would decline.

- Improve manufacturing processes to lower net energy consumption. Many of these would come at no cost, would lower energy costs, and reduce carbon emissions.

- Undertake investments in more efficient infrastructure, such as more efficient boilers, insulation of steam valves, flanges, and other pipe fittings, etc.

- Switch to lower carbon fuels, including natural gas or waste wood products such as using sludge as kiln fuel. Waste bio-fuels, if replanted, have zero net carbon emissions; natural gas has about half the carbon emissions of fuel oil.

- Capture and use the methane currently generated from its waste water.

- Consider adding non-wood paper to its product offering. This would have a benefit if it could document that there was no net deforestation from its supply sources.

The company also looked at the potential for generating project-based carbon credits from these measures. If it undertook an aggressive programme to reduce its direct emissions, it calculated it could produce over 600,000 tonnes of credits per year, for investments representing €50 million and energy cost savings of €3 million per year (and the prospect of energy prices increasing further). If it could sell its credits for €8 per tonne, this would represent an additional revenue stream of €6 million per year.

It also reckoned that these measures, if publicized, could provide it with a competitive marketing edge which it did not quantify, however.

Assembling a strategy for competitive advantage

By looking at its competitive 'window of opportunity' against its competitors who face emission caps, at the significant demand for emission credits that it could generate, at anticipated energy market volatility, at the potential for securing finance for these processes, and at the marketing advantages such activities might bring, it decided to undertake an aggressive strategy of emission reductions across its supply chain, incorporating all measures that met a positive investment return threshold.

Conclusion

Managers and boards in most industries are only beginning to come to terms with the new realities of a carbon-constrained economy. Our key message in this chapter is the need to take a strategic approach. First, to ensure that your company looks beyond its direct emissions to properly assess the exposure both to indirect emissions and to the impacts climate change itself will have on your business. Second, to make sure you unearth opportunities to gain competitive advantage over your rivals by developing strategies to creatively minimise the additional costs, differentiate your product by bundling in carbon credits, and turning the capacity to supply carbon credits into a profit centre for your company. The bottom line is that carbon, just like capital, human resources and products, is now a strategic element in the new competitive game.

Notes

1   Schwartz P. and Randall D. 'An abrupt climate change scenario and its implications for United States national security', report for the U.S. Department of Defence, October 2003.

2   See 'Natural catastrophes and man-made disasters in 2003: many fatalities, comparatively moderate insured losses,' in sigma, No. 1/2004. Publication of Swiss Re.

3   Shareholder Resolution on Climate Data at Exxon Mobil Corporation, Annual Shareholders' Meeting, 26 May 2004, Dallas, Texas.

4   Ceres, 'Electric Power, Investors, and Climate Change: A Call to Action', September 2003.

5   Innovest Strategic Value Advisors, 'Value at Risk: Climate Change and the Future of Governance', April 2002.

Investment Opportunities and Corporate Strategies

9

The New Business Model for Investing in the Green Space

Peter C Fusaro, Global Change Associates

Emerging markets for environmental financial investment and trading continue to attract significant global investment interest. Traditionally, private investment has come from the venture capital world, which typically has the requisite patience to invest in many projects for as long as the ten-year life of venture capital funds. More recently, this area of investment has attracted hedge funds. Hedge funds don't have that much patience and usually look for more immediate arbitrage opportunities.

As markets change, so do investment models. The new business model that has emerged for investment in alternative energy and clean technology is a hybrid business model of venture capital and hedge funds. Investment is locked up for shorter periods of time from two to four years rather than with traditional venture capital time periods of up to ten years. Coupled with the project orientation of the investment, there is a dimension of credit trading for emissions, carbon and renewable energy included in this investment strategy. The blurring of the lines between hedge funds and venture capital is also being exacerbated by significant private equity participation in environmental finance. This new hybrid financial green investment model will be discussed and analyzed in this chapter.

The new market drivers

The three global market drivers – sustained high energy prices, accelerated technology shift and increased environmental concerns – form the perfect storm for clean technology investment. Falling renewable energy costs are also increasing investment opportunities in this sector. To put this clean technology market in some perspective, we must look at its origin, what is driving it and where it is headed in the foreseeable future.

Today, clean technology investment is the fifth largest share of early stage venture capital in North America at 10 per cent of market share and rising. US$8.2 billion was invested by venture capitalists in this sector from 1999 through 2005 according to the Cleantech Venture Network. It is now very conservatively estimated that US$8.5 billion more will be invested in this sector from 2007 through 2010.

In addition to early stage venture capital, both private equity and hedge funds will supply additional billions more as new technology is rapidly commercialized and deployed globally. The need is that great. Demand pull of global financial markets is accelerating. We will enter the world of Kyoto Protocol implementation in 2008 and that has already impacted environmental project finance. It is accelerating. Some of that anticipated investment in all stages of development is estimated in the chart below.

Table 1: Clean energy investment today and tomorrow
Source: Clean Edge

	2005	2015
Bio Fuels	US$15.7 bn	US$52.5 bn
Wind	US$11.8 bn	US$48.5 bn
Solar PV	US$11.2 bn	US$51.5 bn
Fuel Cells	US$ 1.2 bn	US$15.1 bn

Global growing pains in this sector are seen in the shortage of wind turbines, polysilica for solar power, and even geothermal parts. The whole world is moving rapidly toward cleaner energy sources at the same time. Rising environmental imperatives will accelerate much of this energy market transformation into a cleaner energy world.

Clean technology investment is accelerating

The opportunities are immense. World demand is accelerating. Renewable energy mandates are proliferating in the United States, the European Union, China and India. The 'Kyoto Factor' arriving in 2008 and the need for carbon credits for the industrialized world are accelerating, as well as the need for less carbon-intensive technology.

Also, this is much more market driven than regulatory driven as before. While there continues to be a focus on the regulatory regime, greater energy demand is pushing out products faster. Biological and materials sciences are also contributing to this effort on a new level in the form of both biofuels and nanotechnology. There is a higher use of information technology than ever before. This tweaks many efficiency gains that make projects fly, particularly in advanced metering and remote sensing. Higher sustained energy prices are setting up the price floor to push it faster than ever before. Technology is also becoming more cost effective.

Energy, agriculture, manufacturing, transportation and water are all under the clean technology tent. This leads to many applications and cross-fertilization between different scientific disciplines. The list includes bio-based fuels, micro-irrigation systems, distributed energy, renewables, energy storage, advanced packaging, natural chemistry, hybrid vehicles, lighter materials, smart logistics software, water recycling desalination, and newer applications of sensing equipment. The opportunities are almost endless and the technology cycles are shrinking as well. This age of technology delivers results.

BOX 1: CLASSIFICATION OF THE CLEAN ENERGY BUSINESS OPPORTUNITY:

Alternative energy

- Solar
- Wind
- Hydro, tidal and wave
- Geothermal

Bioenergy and ethanol

Distributed energy

- Microturbines
- Fuel cells
- Hydrogen generation
- Flywheels

Energy efficiency

- Lighting
- Buildings

Energy recycling

Waste-to-energy

Battery technology & energy storage

Medical & biological crossovers

Environmental technologies

- Waste & wastewater treatment
- Clean coal gasification
- Emissions mitigation

Information technology

- Net metering and real-time pricing
- Demand response (energy efficiency)
- Remote sensing

Source: Energy Hedge Fund Center LLC (www.energyhedgefunds.com)

As one can see, these encompass engineering disciplines, information technology and the physical sciences.

What the new business model looks like

It may be helpful to review recent developments in 'clean technology,' also called 'cleantech.' When mainstream press – Business Week, the Financial Times, Forbes and the Economist – all start covering this sector, they herald the news that the time has arrived for greener and cleaner technology. But the space is very different than many envision. Good venture projects for the clean technology space need three elements to be successful. These are defined as: revenue stream, a seasoned management team to grow the business, and a defined exit strategy (usually by an initial public offering or roll up). Building a business to scale and commercialization is very different than funding research and development efforts that are really science projects. In fact, some of the currently funded technologies are so debt ridden that they will never be commercially viable. Moreover, their cost structure will require an ability to significantly reduce costs in order to become commercialized. They cannot depend on the 'environmental kicker' of emissions reductions (called offsets) making a project economically viable. These are additional benefits for a business, but are not the reason for that business to exist.

What may be more interesting are the second stage investments in clean technology and alternative energy that *do* have revenue and *can* make money for investors. Several venture funds are focused on these later stage investments, and the investment space is beginning to get crowded. There is a great need for viable later stage companies. Angel investing, on the other hand, will fund start-ups in the green space, and consequently take on more risk.

While the outcome is still uncertain, the timing is right. Higher energy prices are now sustainable due to unprecedented global demand coupled with underinvestment in the global energy business for two decades. The real metric is that US$40 oil makes a floor for all these new technologies to take off. Higher global energy demand growth will continue to drive return on investment (ROI) higher in the cleantech space.

But what about the trading markets and the reduction of project costs? The new model that has emerged is a hybrid somewhere between venture capital and hedge funds. They require a capital commitment from investors for two to four years (called a lock up) and a capability to trade the renewable energy credits (Recs) and emissions reductions (sulphur dioxide SO_2, nitrous oxides NO_x and carbon dioxide CO_2). These green streams of revenue or 'green finance' make the cost of capital cheaper, but also bring much needed liquidity to emerging environmental financial markets. They cannot fund projects entirely unless they are a pure speculative play.

There is now increasing interest by investors in how SO_2, NO_x, CO_2 and Recs are related to clean technology projects. It seems obvious to most cleantech investors that we are entering a carbon-constrained world and that their venture capital investments in clean technology will have an environmental kicker at some juncture in the US and from 2008 in the Kyoto world. The question then becomes how this is related to carbon finance and carbon offsets and more importantly investment in the realm of clean energy and cleaner technology.

This hybrid business model of figuring out of the best business structure to participate – not in only in investment in equities and commodities but also in clean technology tied to carbon reductions – is actually becoming quite important for new project development in the area of carbon offsets. The entire concept of 'green trading' is focused on the interrelationship of emissions reductions, renewable energy credits and energy efficiency.

Investment interest is now more focused on how to invest in new technologies and gain investment streams that encompass two or three of these environmental benefits and should benefit from multiple credit streams. Of course, there are those who believe that 'double counting' of credits for renewable energy and carbon reductions is a bad thing, but I think that in the beginning of a market shift these multiple environmental credit streams actually enhance project creditworthiness. They also get us beyond the myopia of subsidizing technologies and push cleaner technologies to more market-centric sustainability. This is a better economic model for the future since it seems inevitable that technology cycles are accelerating and the need to invest in better technologies that are more energy efficient as well as cleaner will deliver better financial results.

Climate change as the new driver

The impending climate change regime in the United States will add an extra dimension to the drive for greater energy efficiency and reduction of emissions footprint for carbon. There is clear movement of capital into 'carbon finance' but this is not very well followed in the United States. This extra dimension of monetization of carbon credits for green project finance will increase ROI for many projects. More energy efficiency and renewable projects will take root as technology continues to shift, and the regulatory scheme for a less carbon-intensive world takes hold.

It also seems reasonable that more rapid deployment of these cleantech investments will be needed to scale to meet the rising environmental and energy needs both in the United States and around the world. It is no accident that there is a shortage of most renewable energy equipment today. A flattened world levels the playing field for new technology and also creates more market opportunities. It should not be forgotten that throughout the world two billion people do not have access to electric power, and three billion people do not have potable water. The scale is mind boggling and has been underestimated by all forecasts. Global demand is evident in the BRIC (Brazil, Russian, India and China) economies with 800 million middle class consumers who have money in their pocket and want consumer goods and products just like the developed world. Most economic projections have underestimated this need, just as no one estimated or anticipated how much electricity the Internet would use.

Everyone has misjudged the scale of the cleantech revolution. The short-term focus on ethanol and solar companies which receive most press and investment attention is only the initial stage of this change over to clean energy. It is a growing global phenomenon that will be rising in developing countries in coming years and cycle in much more innovation than can be imagined today. The market demand is there in both the developing and developed world. One is leapfrogging technology and one is replacing antiquated infrastructure. Green is the new gold, and now is the time to watch it accelerate.

Several funds have invested and made money on the ethanol and solar price moves of the last year within existing funds and are now launching alternative energy specific funds. There are carbon funds in Europe that are oversubscribed and many in the US are growing their asset base. There are alternative energy/cleantech funds in Europe with multi hundred million dollar backing. There are cleantech funds on both sides of the ocean. There seems to be a realization that this market move is sustainable. What is really lacking is in-depth knowledge of the sector. The sector is not as widely followed by Wall Street and City of London investment analysts today.

It would take mainstream investors at least 12–24 months to get up to speed in the cleantech/alternative energy sector. Some investors had allocated into several commodity trading green hedge funds (those that trade RECs and GHG) but felt that the capacity was limited in those existing structures. This time lag of knowledge is significant as it focuses much of today's investment attention on the narrow band of biofuel and solar projects and gives short shrift to the broader dimensions of the opportunity.

The green revenue stream

The ability to trade both emissions and renewable energy credits creates another revenue stream. Green trading is an encompassing term. We define green trading as the triple convergence of emissions reductions, renewable energy and energy efficiency.

Source: Global Change Associates, Inc.

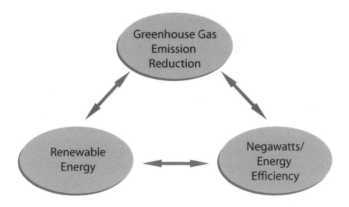

This triple convergence of carbon emissions, renewables and energy efficiency offers multiple risk arbitrage opportunities as well as many revenue streams. They are obviously interrelated in their use of more efficient technology, which reduces the emissions footprint. Similarly, using renewable energy can reduce the carbon footprint of power stations for example.

Green trading is a term coined several years ago to capture the value of the convergence of the capital markets and the environment. It encompasses all forms of environmental financial trading including carbon dioxide and other GHG reductions. Sulphur dioxide (acid rain) and nitrous oxide (ozone), renewable energy credits and negawatt (value of energy efficiency). All of these emerging and established environmental financial markets have one thing in common: making the environment cleaner by either reducing emissions, using clean technology or not using energy through the use of financial markets. Sometimes, both can be accomplished as in reducing emissions and reducing energy usage by moving to cleaner technology. Green trading is one mechanism to accelerate this change.

The trading markets determine the financial value of environmental benefits. The quaint notion that we are 'trading pollution' is an oversimplification of the need for markets to create financial incentives to reduce pollution and accelerate more efficient and environmentally benign technology transfer. This is not an academic exercise but an exercise of rational economic behavior.

BOX 2: SULPHUR DIOXIDE AND NITROUS OXIDE MARKETS IN THE US

For example, in the well established US sulphur dioxide (SO_2) and nitrous oxides (NO_x) markets established in 1995 and 1999 respectively, we have seen a sea change in the past two years in US environmental financial markets. As coal burning increased, due to rising electricity demand and decreasing supply of natural gas, the emissions trading markets responded in kind. The price of emissions allowances rose to a peak of US$1,630 per ton for sulphur dioxide in December 2005 and US$40,000 for nitrous oxide during the past year in the US. Sulphur dioxide credits in the 11-year-old markets had never before risen above US$225 per ton. Prices have leveled off to the US$500 to US$600 range during most of 2006.

The financial penalty for emitting more emissions accelerated the emergence of new technology into the coal burning power generation space that was previously uneconomical. In the past year, at least 20 newly planned coal gasification facilities have either been announced or are on the permitting cycle for siting. Two years ago there were none. The benefits of gasification technology are that they not only reduce the previously mentioned SO_2 and NO_x emissions but also reduce carbon dioxide emissions. They also increase efficiency of coal burning from 30 per cent to the 50–70 per cent range, which means that less coal will need to be burned to produce the same amount of electric power in the future. This additional efficiency benefit is often overlooked by environmentalists, economists and policy makers who tend to view the energy supply picture as static with ever increasing energy demand. Basically, we will be using less energy and it will be cleaner forms of energy in the future due to market-based incentives coupled with financial penalties for noncompliance. These are not voluntary markets but government *mandated* markets. Proved to work and are cost effective, they are essentially the templates for the Kyoto Protocol.

For carbon dioxide and greenhouse gas (GHG) markets, 2005 was a watershed year. In February 2005, the Kyoto Protocol entered into force more than seven years after it was established. With Russia's ratification in November 2004, countries that represent over 60 per cent of the total 1990 carbon dioxide emissions have now ratified the Protocol. They include the European Union, Japan, New Zealand, Canada, Russia and most of the countries known as the economies in transition (the countries that were 'behind the iron curtain' in the decades leading up to 1990). The United States and Australia have not ratified the Protocol, but are nonetheless pursuing programs to reduce GHG emissions on a voluntary basis – hence their prices for carbon credits are less than in the EU.

BOX 3: KYOTO PROTOCOL IN THE GLOBAL ARENA

Under the Kyoto Protocol, countries can use emissions trading to lower the overall cost of reducing GHGs to meet the protocol targets. The protocol provides three flexible mechanisms for trading among countries: (1) An international emissions trading regime. This cap-and-trade program will allow industrialized countries to trade carbon permits in the international market. (2) Joint Implementation (JI) permits trading among industrialized countries and the economies in transition, and (3) the Clean Development Mechanism (CDM) permits developing countries that are not parties to the Protocol to sell emission reductions to Annex 1 countries. By far, the CDM market has been the most developed with over 700 projects globally.

A marked shift in the market began in 2004 as the EU countries prepared to implement the EU Emissions Trading Scheme (ETS), a program adopted to reduce the cost of Kyoto Protocol compliance, permits trading of carbon dioxide. The EU Emissions Trading Scheme officially started on 1 January 2005, and is now trading hundreds of millions of tons per year. It is estimated that €25 to €30 billion will trade in 2006. Trades on the European market have continued to increase on a year to year basis. The European Commission estimated that adopting the EU-wide trading scheme would reduce the costs of attaining its emission target by at least 20 per cent if it covered the energy supply sector.

BOX 4: EMISSIONS TRADING SCHEME IN THE EUROPEAN UNION

12,000 facilities in Europe fall under the purview of the EU Emissions Trading Scheme from 2005 to 2007. In 2008, the Kyoto Protocol takes effect and the program globalizes for the over 160 Kyoto signatory countries.

Carbon prices fluctuate:
In the EU ETS, the price is €12.58 (September 29, 2006)
On the Chicago Climate Exchange, the price is US$3.90 (29 September 2006)

Another venue for green trading has been in the renewable energy area. Wind, solar and biomass markets are accelerating commercially, due to the monetization of 'renewable energy credits' as they are called in the US. Today, 22 states have, or are developing, a Renewable Portfolio Standard (RPS) that is jump-starting markets in Texas, California and the Northeastern states to take advantage of 'green power' programs that are now popular with consumers. In America today there are over 600 green power programs where consumers willingly pay more for green power. The renewable energy projects in these states are able to bank-finance their development and create a revenue stream of green credits that reduce the cost of capital, in effect creating 'green finance.'

Green trading is the mechanism to create market-based incentives. Their application is global. Not only are the US, EU and Japan moving forward, but so are developing economies such as China, India and Russia, on both emissions trading initiatives and clean technology applications.

As fossil fuel prices remain high throughout this decade and as demand continues to increase, clean technology will become a more attractive economic choice for deployment in global markets. Energy and environment issues continue to be more interconnected. Rising demand is accelerating the need to move faster to clean technology solutions. Green trading is the financial mechanism that allows markets to meet that goal of global deployment of new, cleaner technology to meet rising demand for electricity, transportation, heating and cooling applications. What used to be expensive and uncommercial is rapidly changing to economic solutions to global environmental problems.

The new wall of money

This investment sector is getting started. There is pent up demand for renewable and clean technology. There is global demand due to rising Asian economies. The green investment sector is about to really blossom. Wall Street and City of London analysts are gearing up to speed and to start following those companies that can scale. A new asset class has emerged and it is called 'green.'

The implications of this new wall of money are hard to predict at the present time. The hype of markets for ethanol and solar power overshadow many other investment opportunities. However, we are starting to see private equity funds dedicated to infrastructure investment beyond clean technology raise capital in the multi-billion scale.

The rapidly evolving renewable energy and clean technology industry offer attractive investment opportunities. While some funds focus on early stage investment, many funds are focused on mid/later stage development and want to provide developmental capital to fund expansion and scale of operations. There are opportunities across the value energy and environmental chain.

Renewable opportunities include wind, biomass, geothermal, solar, landfill gas, waste-to-energy, hydro, ocean/wave, biodiesel and ethanol. Some funds are offering the traditional private equity project finance component and are extremely well capitalized. For example, Carlyle's Riverstone fund and ARC Light fund is now close to US$3 billion. Others are just ramping up and are In the process of raising US$100 to US$400 million in their first financing. Still others have become standalone investment vehicles as part of larger hedge funds where ethanol and solar projects over the 2005–2006 have paid off handsomely. These fund managers now wish to take the deeper dive by building a wider renewable energy portfolio.

Some funds are seeking to secure a portfolio of projects with different locations so that they can get into the game faster. Others are either looking for co-investment opportunities or partnerships with developers. Law firms have become extremely entrepreneurial and take equity stakes in projects in lieu of fees, as Boston Consulting Group, Bain and McKinsey have all done.

The sector is changing rapidly since the need has become global. It is not surprising to see the emergence of India's Suzlon and the rapid growth of China's Suntech, with global projects in 2006. But what is underestimated is the second wave of new technology companies that will also come from those and other developing countries.

Finding the good green projects globally

The Holy Grail of clean energy investment is finding the outstanding technology projects that can be scaled into a robust enterprise.

Market opportunities for wind, biofuels, photovoltaics, and fuel cells are expected to increase fourfold in the next ten years, growing from US$40 billion in global revenues in 2005 to US$167 billion by 2012 according to Clean Edge, Inc.'s 'Clean Energy Trends 2006.' According to the Cleantech Venture Network, investments increased to US$513 million in the first quarter 2006 – the largest recorded since Q1 2000 representing a 2.3 per cent increase from the US$502 million recorded in the previous quarter.

As in all boom times, there will be a short-term bust, and this most likely will be in the ethanol sector sometime in 2007, but the need for global investment is so great and the technology is shifting so fast that the momentum will carry clean energy as well as clean water initiatives for the next two decades. Climate change risk will be increasingly mitigated by the movement and rapid deployment of clean energy projects on a global scale which has never before been anticipated nor appreciated. The skills shortage of the oil and gas industry will spill over into the clean tech sector. Building out infrastructure will take time. This presents many opportunities for smaller scale technologies in distributed generation and distributed water solutions to take root. Both small and big projects will be built out, licensed and distributed on a global scale following a new manufacturing model of global outsourcing and distribution. It is possible this model may be crimped by supply chain management, too.

BOX 5: TIPS FOR COMPANIES TRYING TO ATTRACT 'GREEN' INVESTMENT CAPITAL

- Create a professional, concise business plan with clear business objectives.

- Have a seasoned management team in place to grow the business and allow experienced external help to assist in global company growth.

- Look for scalable green technologies that have global applications.

- Have strategic investors from the targeted market segment.

- Create attainable financial milestones.

- Don't underestimate the environmental externalities that can be monetized such as carbon credits, renewable energy credits, and other emissions reductions.

- Offer shared saving opportunities so that risk is also shared.

- Be willing to be flexible in management control and providing equity opportunities for investors.

- Look well beyond ethanol and solar for next generation market opportunities.

- Use the knowledge and expertise of the advisory board to leverage global projects.

Source: Energy Hedge Fund Center LLC

This is the end of the beginning

Higher energy prices, national security concerns over oil, global warming, implementation of Kyoto Protocol, modernization of Asian economies, particularly China and India, and a growing movement of multinational corporations to go green and adopt clean technologies have pushed the energy and environmental dynamic faster than anyone imagined five years ago. The need to improve operational efficiency, reduce costs, eliminate waste and pollution have all coalesced to form a new market. It is not hindered by misconceptions that it is a bubble or dotcom boomlet. The energy value chain is now overlaid with an environmental value chain. The clean energy market is large, growing and global with higher rates of market acceptance than anyone anticipated. There are now over 600 green power programs in the US alone where consumer preference is for green energy. This trend is growing.

The competitive landscape has shifted. Government initiatives are helpful but the global capital markets are driving this boom. There will be high-profile market failures during this transition to cleaner technology and cleaner use of energy. The era of coal and oil is plateauing, and not in the production sense. These dirtier, carbon-intensive fuels are being replaced by renewables, cleaner technology, and higher efficiencies. By 2020, oil and coal will plateau in global usage. For example, as clean coal technology takes root with gasification of coal, there is not only an emissions reduction but also a higher efficiency gain from 30 per cent for conventional coal-fired plants to a higher range of 50 – 70 per cent. The same is true of hybridization of the transportation fleet featuring greater fuel economy and reduced tailpipe emissions. If we apply this business model to how cleantech permeates the entire energy value chain, it stands to reason that all applications – to be financially viable – will have to reduce energy consumption and be cleaner. This dual benefit is lost by many observers in the mainstream media. Using renewables to replace fossil fuels brings with it a third layer of benefit by offsetting carbon.

The new green business model is blurring the lines between hedge funds, private equity and venture capital. The arbitrage opportunities combined with the building out of new projects will lead to more incentives to invest in clean energy and clean technology. However, this is a transition that defies a quick fix. It will take decades to remediate the environmental damage done and shift to the more environmentally benign technologies of tomorrow. But the good news is that global investors are now focused on this sector!

References

Fusaro P.C. and James T. *Energy and Emissions: Collision or Convergence*, Wiley, 2006.

Fusaro P.C. *Energy and Environmental Hedge Funds: The New Investment Paradigm*, Wiley, 2006.

Fusaro P.C. and Yuen M. *Green Trading Markets: Developing the Second Wave*, Elsevier, 2005.

Fusaro P.C. (author and editor) *The Professional Risk Managers Guide to Energy & Environmental Markets,* Professional Risk Management International Association, 2006. www.prmia.org

Fusaro P.C. 'Cleantech is More Than a Buzzword', *Utilipoint Issue Alert* April 26, 2006. www.utilipoint.com

Fusaro P.C. 'The New Business Model for the Green Space', *Utilipoint Issue Alert* July 11, 2005. www.utilipoint.com

Fusaro P.C. 'Turbulent Markets Ahead: Why the Energy and Environmental Crisis Will Continue for Many Years' September 20, 2005. www.utilipoint.com

Other useful websites for environmental finance information are www.pointcarbon.com, www.evomarkets.com, www.cleantech.com, www.cleanedge.com, and www.environmental-finance.com

10

Upside of Climate Change – Opportunities in Cleantech A sector study of the auto sector

Andrew White, Innovest

From both a corporate and an investor perspective, there is no doubt that climate change is now regarded as a very real and increasingly relevant value driver, which affects a wide range of industrial sectors. Historically, investors and companies alike have associated climate change with a series of potential risks, which can be summarized under six main headings:

- Physical risks: these occur because of the direct impacts of climate change itself (such as asset damage and project delays caused by extreme weather events)[1]

- Regulatory risks: these result from tightening national and international regulations designed to curtail greenhouse gas (GHG) emissions

- Competitive risks: these are caused by a decline in marginal consumer demand for oil-intensive products

- Reputation risks: these stem from a perceived lack of action to tackle the problems of climate change

- Operational risks: for example, in the form of rising electricity prices in Europe caused in part by the regulation of CO_2 emissions through the European Union Emissions Trading Scheme (EU ETS); and

- Litigation risks: for example, from the threat of climate change-related litigation, as is now being seen in the United States.

When climate change is viewed exclusively as a risk factor, however, investors and companies may be failing to appreciate the other side of the equation, namely that climate change can create new market opportunities. Climate change is also driving a strong degree of technological innovation, helping to stimulate growth in new industries and underpinning the idea that there could be some long-term growth potential for products and services with a low carbon footprint.

This broader take on the impacts of climate change is backed up by the findings of the recently published Stern Review, widely regarded as heralding a new era in climate change thinking, as it is seen as the first major contribution to the global warming debate by an economist, rather than an environmental scientist. It considers not only the risks, physical and economic, but also highlights possible areas of growth. The report, by economist Sir Nicholas Stern, argues that global warming could cause the global economy to shrink by 20 per cent. The Stern Review coincides with the publication of new data by the United Nations pointing to an upward trend in the emission of greenhouse gases – a development for which developed countries undoubtedly share most of the responsibility. While the Stern Review did not recommend specific tax rises, increasing the cost of flying and driving was on the agenda of all three main political parties in the UK.

In the wake of the report, Chancellor Gordon Brown promised the UK would lead the international response to tackle climate change. Chancellor Brown, who commissioned the report, has also recruited former US Vice-President Al Gore as an environment adviser. Chancellor Brown endorsed this new economic paradigm in the 21st century, saying that:

> 'In the 20th century our national economic ambitions were the twin objectives of achieving stable economic growth and full employment. Now in the 21st century our new objectives are clear, they are threefold: growth, full employment and environmental care.' He said the green challenge was also an opportunity 'for new markets, for new jobs, new technologies, new exports where companies, universities and social enterprises in Britain can lead the world'. [2]

Rapid growth of the clean technology sector

A major development in the worldwide carbon landscape over the past two years has been the rapid growth of the clean technology or 'cleantech' sector. According to figures from the Cleantech Venture Network, US investment in cleantech in 2005 totalled more than US$1.6 billion, an increase of US$423 million, or 34.9 per cent from 2004.[3] This makes cleantech the fifth largest venture capital investment category in the United States, behind the other leading sectors – biotechnology, software, medical and telecommunications.[4]

Furthermore, a total of US$513 million in venture capital was invested in the US cleantech sector in the first quarter 2006, representing a 2.3 per cent increase over the final quarter in 2005 and a 52.9 per cent increase over the first quarter of that year.[5] In the UK the government recently published a report stating that the market for cleantech financing could reach US$1.9 trillion by 2020.[6]

Cleantech has been broadly defined as: 'a diverse range of products, services, and processes that are inherently designed to provide superior performance at lower costs, greatly reduce or eliminate environmental impacts and, in doing so, improve the quality of life.'[7]

Examples of cleantech include renewable energy technologies such as solar panels, wind power and wave/tidal power, fuel cells, electric/hybrid vehicles, photovoltaics, water purification processes, bio-based agriculture and nanotechnologies. A variety of market, regulatory and political forces are helping the cleantech sector to expand and prosper, among them:

- rising costs of global energy which, at the margin, make renewable energy solutions more economically attractive

- the increasing volatility of global energy prices

- the pivotal role that clean technologies can play in helping corporations to meet increasingly stringent environmental regulatory requirements in areas such as emissions of pollutants and greenhouse gases (GHGs) waste management, etc, and

- the capacity of cleantech and in particular renewable energy, to provide 'energy security' by offering alternative energy solutions, especially at a time when energy supply and political aspirations are interwoven.

This last point requires further explanation and is an increasingly important one at a time of political tension in some parts of the world. The idea of energy security has attained particular prominence in the United States, due to the fact that the country is highly dependent on imported energy; the US is estimated to consume about 25 per cent of the world's oil while holding only two per cent of its reserves.[8] For this reason alone, the notion of reducing the proportion of imported energy in the country's overall energy mix has achieved broad bi-partisan political support.

As President Bush noted in his State of the Union address, on 31 January, 2006:

> 'Keeping America competitive requires affordable energy. And here we have a serious problem: America is addicted to oil, which is often imported from unstable parts of the world. The best way to break this addiction is through technology. Since 2001, we have spent nearly $10 billion to develop cleaner, cheaper, and more reliable alternative energy sources... and we are on the threshold of incredible advances.'

Growth in clean energy

The growth of the cleantech sector and in particular the renewable or 'clean energy' component, has been impressive to say the least. The global clean energy market reached a value of US$6.7 billion in 2005, up from US$2.8 billion in 2004.[9] According to Clean Edge, global wind and solar markets reached US$11.8 billion and US$11.2 billion in 2005, up 47 per cent and 55 per cent, respectively, from the previous year. A recent report from the International Energy Agency said that global electricity and oil consumption could be reduced by 50 per cent if clean energy technologies that are currently available were applied.[10]

The market for biofuels was valued at US$15.7 billion globally in 2005, up more than 15 per cent from 2004.[11] Clean Edge estimates that the clean energy market (comprising biofuels, wind power, solar power and fuel cells) will grow from its current value of US$39.9 billion to US$167.2 billion by 2015, equating to an average annual growth rate of 32 per cent over the next nine to ten years, as shown in the chart below.[12]

Clean Energy Projected Growth 2005–2015 ($US Billions)

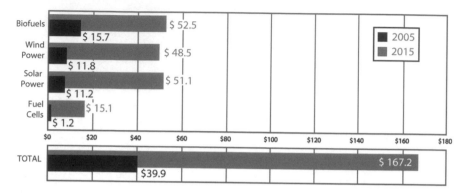

In response to these types of forecasts for cleantech, a growing number of investors are increasing their exposure to the cleantech sector in an effort to tap into the sector's long-term profit potential. Recent high-profile examples of cleantech investments made in the US include:

- The two co-founders of Google, Larry Page and Sergey Brin, invested USD$40 million in Tesla Motors, a Silicon Valley start-up building a mass-market electric sports car; they joined the private equity arm of JP Morgan Chase as an investor in the company

- Bill Gates, through his company Cascade Investment, invested USD$84 million in Pacific Ethanol, which is building a series of ethanol plants in the west coast region of the US

- Goldman Sachs invested CAD$30 million investment in Iogen Corporation, a Canadian company that converts agricultural materials such as straw, corn stalks and switchgrass to ethanol using renewable cellulose ethanol technology (Goldman Sachs joined Royal Dutch Shell as a minority investor in the company)

- Examples of other FT500 companies with known exposure in the cleantech space include: Archer Daniels Midland, BP, Chevron, DuPont, General Electric, J.P. Morgan Chase, Sharp and Toyota.

It can also be observed that the London Stock Exchange's Alternative Investment Market (AIM) with its comparatively lenient listing requirements and focus on emerging industries, has become the premier locus of global climate-driven IPO activity, ranging from environmental technologies and renewable energy to carbon finance. Activity in the AIM has been intensifying over the past year, driven in large part by the fact that, on average, the percentage change in market cap since flotation for AIM-listed securities is 84 per cent.[13] There are currently over 50 companies listed on AIM that can be ascribed to the clean tech/carbon finance space, and this number is set to grow appreciably over the coming years as AIM is increasingly perceived by small firms as a viable alternative to NASDAQ.

Exploiting clean technology opportunities

So far as companies themselves are concerned, the Carbon Disclosure Project (CDP)[14] provides an excellent window on the cleantech activities of the world's leading corporations. In this year's CDP questionnaire, companies were asked if they were developing any technologies, products or services in response to climate change. In reviewing the responses, it was found that companies make such investments for one of two main reasons.

Firstly, companies make these investments in order to improve the energy efficiency and decrease the general environmental intensity of their operations, thereby reducing emissions of various pollutants and GHGs as well as energy costs. These investments are often made in a regulatory environment that is presumed to be tightening.

Secondly, companies are making these investments with the intention of bringing energy-efficient and other cleantech products to market in order to capture some of the growth potential discussed above. On the basis of information provided in this year's CDP questionnaire, Innovest assembled a table (see below) identifying for investors those FT500 companies that report upside exposure to the emerging global cleantech market.

Examples of FT500 Companies with Cleantech Exposure

Sector	Company	2005 Sales (Millions USD)	Cleantech Initiatives
Aerospace and Defense	United Technologies	42,584	United Technologies produces hydrogen fuel cells, and low emissions combined cooling, heating, and power solutions for commercial buildings.
Air Freight & Couriers	United Parcel Services	42,584	UPS utilises an extensive fleet of alternative fuel delivery trucks.
Automobiles	Daimler-Chrysler	177,365	DaimlerChrysler is a leading manufacturer of diesel electric hybrid and fuel cell buses.
Automobiles	Honda	80,872	Honda manufactures hybrid and 'super clean' diesel-powered passenger cars.

Sector	Company	2005 Sales (Millions USD)	Cleantech Initiatives
Automobiles	Nissan Motor	80,182	Nissan Motor manufacturers hybrid and alternative fuel passenger and commercial vehicles
Automobiles	Peugeot	66,371	Peugeot manufactures vehicles that utilize efficient diesel engines, compressed natural gas, and ethanol.
Automobiles	Toyota Motor	173,444	As at March 2006, Toyota had sold roughly 613,000 hybrid cars.
Building Products	Saint-Gobain	41,415	Saint-Gobain produces a variety of building materials that allow for increased energy efficiency and renewable energy production.
Construction Materials	Cemex	15,296	Cemex produces concrete that utilizes waste materials with GHG potential that would otherwise be discarded.
Construction Materials	CRH	17,111	CRH uses alternative materials in cement production, thereby reducing CO_2 emissions associated with traditional production.
Diversified Chemicals	BASF	50,421	BASF has developed a variety of bioplastics and lightweight automobile components. It reports nearly EUR500 million in sales from products that utilise its biotechnological processes.
Diversified Chemicals	Dow Chemical	46,307	Dow Chemical manufacturers a variety of products that address the need for energy efficiency including: insulation and components for hydrogen facilities.
Diversified Chemicals	E I du Pont de Nemours (DuPont)	27,516	DuPont produces lightweight thermoplastics and components for solar panels.
Electric Power – North America	Exelon	15,357	Exelon owns a variety of renewable energy facilities in the United States.
Electric Power – North America	FPL Group	11,846	FPL Group Installs 150KW of solar capacity in Florida for every 10,000 customers that sign up for its Sunshine Energy program.

Sector	Company	2005 Sales (Millions USD)	Cleantech Initiatives
Electric Power – North America	Entergy Corp	10,106	Entergy Corp owns 80MW of wind generating capacity in the United States.
Electric Utilities – International	ENEL	37,747	ENEL has 20,000MW of renewable energy generating capacity worldwide. The company plans to invest EUR1.7 billion over the next several years in additional renewable energy projects.
Electric Utilities – International	Iberdrola	13,846	Iberdrola currently owns 3,800MW of installed wind power generating capacity.
Electric Utilities – International	Scottish & Southern Energy	12,941	Scottish & Southern Energy is the UK's largest provider of renewable energy with 162MW of wind power generating capacity.
Electronic Equipment & Instruments	Hitachi	84,396	Hitachi manufactures systems that allow for the operation of solar and wind power facilities.
Household Durables	Sharp	23,746	Sharp has been the leading manufacturer of solar cells since 2000.
Industrial Conglomerates	General Electric	148,019	General Electric manufactures wind turbines and numerous other energy efficient products under its 'Ecomagination' product line.
Industrial Conglomerates	Minnesota Mining & Manufacturing (3M)	21,167	3M manufactures and develops fuel cell components and products to increase home efficiency.
Industrial Conglomerates	Siemens	90,960	Siemens has developed technology to increase the energy efficiency of buildings and power plants.
Integrated Oil & Gas	BP	249,465	BP plans to invest $8billion over the next 10 years to continue developing solar, natural gas, and wind power through BP Alternative Energy.
Integrated Oil & Gas	Chevron	184,922	Chevron produces advanced battery systems for electric and hybrid-electric vehicles. In addition, the company recently completed a demonstration hydrogen fueling station in California. Chevron reports spending $300 million annually on the development of these and other renewable or alternative energy projects.

Sector	Company	2005 Sales (Millions USD)	Cleantech Initiatives
Integrated Oil & Gas	Petrobras	58,491	Petrobras operates two biodiesel production facilities in Brazil, which required an investment of US$8.3 million.
Integrated Oil & Gas	Repsol YPF	n/a	Repsol YPF currently converts over 140,000 tons of bioethanol into high octane fuels per year.
Integrated Oil & Gas	Royal Dutch / Shell	290,393	Royal Dutch / Shell is involved in the development and installation of renewable energy through: Shell Hydrogen, Shell WindEnergy, and Shell Solar.
Metals & Mining	Alcoa	26,159	In 2005, Alcoa commercialised new high strength to mass ratio automotive components and aerospace alloys to improve vehicle and aircraft efficiency.
Specialty Chemicals	Praxair	7,656	Praxair produces components that increase the efficiency of boiler systems in addition to those that allow the conversion of vehicles to natural gas power.

Source: Innovest

As witnessed in the IT space up until the late 1990s, the cleantech space is currently the province of small-cap pure-plays. However, it is clear from the above table that FT500 companies are now realizing that the cleantech space could be a driver of future profits. This is true not only for industrial or technology concerns, but also for fund managers that view the growth of cleantech as potential investment opportunities.

Certain sectors are making significant strides forward in developing new product lines in response to climate change, and the automotive (auto) sector is one that stands out. It provides a useful case study example of how progressive companies, able to meet the climate change challenge, can develop new markets.

Sector study – the auto sector

The auto sector is faced with a distinct set of sustainability risks and opportunities linked to reducing the environmental impacts of its products (as well as managing the globalisation of the labour force). The ability to develop and commercialise key fuel economy technologies has become the hallmark of leading sustainability and financial performance in the sector. For example, the R&D department at GM has developed, over the past ten years, many of the industry's most advanced technologies to address the need for fuel efficiency and alternative fuels. However, its main rivals, Toyota and Honda, have been much more successful in their ability to take R&D innovations to the next stage and commercialise these technologies for consumers.

While these differences have been highlighted during the recent spike in oil prices, the warnings coming from the scientific community regarding the alacrity needed to deal with climate change implies that these trends will continue to develop and deepen. Rising oil prices and carbon constraints are now the major macro-industry trends. These trends will require significant technological change, pushing new fuels and engine platforms. Therefore, the ability to develop and commercialise engine technology will be the most important strategic strength for automotive OEMs going forward.

The auto industry has experienced a trend towards a more international market with car usage in the rest of the world now outstripping that in the US. The Sport Utility Vehicle (SUV) boom in the late 1990s gave rise to record profits for the auto industry and its suppliers, notably in the US (still the world's largest single car market). However, rising commodity and oil prices, reaching well above US$2.00 a gallon resulted in fluctuations in the SUV category, with this rapid growth followed by a decline in sales. The big three US automakers and their suppliers, especially Ford and GM, highly reliant on the SUV/truck market for their profitability, have experienced overall gains and losses in line with the fortunes of this particular product segment. In addition, the industry has been affected by increasing regulatory standards linked to environmental protection, including increasing tailpipe exhaust regulations, fuel economy concerns, intensifying debate around the issue of global climate change, and growing market demands for safer, higher performance and more environmentally responsible vehicles.

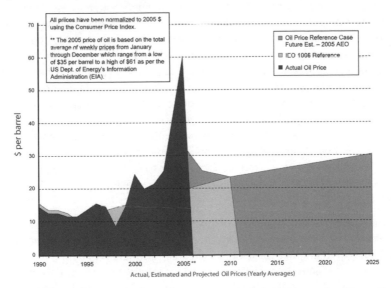

Source: Energy Information Administration – 2005 Annual Energy Outlook, 1995 International Energy Outlook and Monthly Energy Review. (All data normalized to 2005 dollars.)

As the figure above indicates, rising energy prices are highly likely to be something the auto makers will have to address in the future. High oil prices have allowed for leading edge fuel efficiency technology, developed to address Japan's stringent requirements, to be marketed worldwide, in particular in the US. The technology with the highest profile has been the emergence of a new class of vehicles with hybrid-electric engines. Other technology developments include continuously variable transmissions (CVTs), lithium ion batteries and the further enhancement of hydrogen fuel cells and internal combustion hydrogen engines. Car companies face increasing exposure due to shifting market perceptions of climate change risk. Car makers themselves are significant emitters of greenhouse gases (GHG) yet their exposure will vary depending on profile of the fleet of vehicles they produce, the location of their production facilities, their asset base, level of engagement and response to underlying risks.

All companies in this group have significant operations in Kyoto Protocol signatory countries or in locations with increasingly stringent controls on carbon emissions. In countries such as Canada (a Kyoto signatory), the United States, and China, regulations are intensifying. Risks include more stringent fuel economy standards, increased costs of production due to emissions caps, fines, technical mandates, as well as damage to the corporate image and brand if the company fails to address the issue. The emergence of emission trading in the EU and in the United States may serve as a potential opportunity for these companies to mitigate risk and offset impacts. Significant growth in alternative energy technology markets and demand for energy efficiency will be major profit drivers going forward.

Proactive players can also enhance their corporate image through mechanisms such as 'green power purchasing', in addition to the development and marketing of technologies that increase energy efficiency or utilise alternative energy sources. Most important will be the development of technologies that help OEMs meet their obligations to reduce CO_2 emissions from vehicles. The extent to which climate change has the potential to change industry practices can be understood by assessing short, medium and long term responses needed in order to address the problem. Current industry responses can reflect a mitigation and adaptation strategy, that is to say, reducing emissions and decreasing the carbon intensity of both products and operations. Against a backdrop of rising car use worldwide, though, even reduced carbon intensity means growth in the level of absolute emissions. An effective strategy to address climate change can therefore only be delivered via a move away from a fossil fuel-based technology. The chart below summarises the strategic approaches to climate change that can be taken, in terms of mitigation and adaptation, leading to new technologies and in turn, to new markets.

The figures below reveal the growth of the hybrid market and illustrate the expansion of available models planned by various automakers. As the market grows the economies of scale for hybrid engines will allow for cheaper production of hybrid models. Market leader Toyota estimates that it will reach full profitability on its hybrid models by 2008. The expansion of the hybrid engine and other fuel saving technologies has been helped by increasingly stringent emissions standards world-wide, in response to the need to combat high fuel prices and climate change.

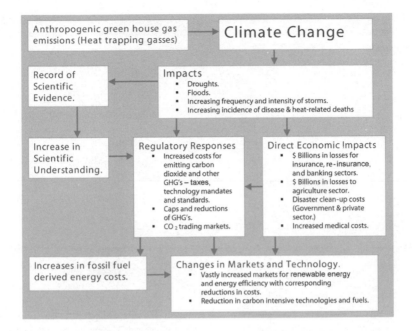

Flow chart – economic impacts of climate change
Source: Innovest Strategic Value Advisors

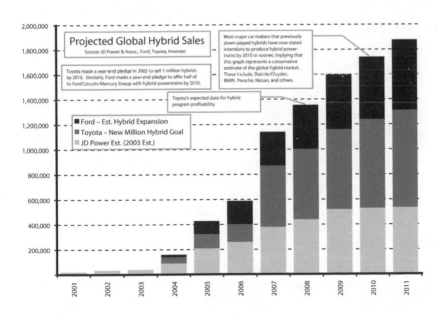

Projected hybrid sales through 2011
Source: JD Power & Assoc., Innovest

Make	Currently Available	Future Models
Cars (Petrol)		
BMW		Un-named models. (Leased from GM)
Ford		Fusion, expected 2008
		Mercury Milan, expected 2008
GM		Chevrolet Malibu Expected 2007
	Accord	
Honda	Civic	
	Insight (Best Performance)	
Nissan		Altima Expected 2006
		Camry Expected 2006
Toyota	Prius (Best Selling)	
		Lexus GS Expected 2006
Cars (Diesel)		
Peugeot/Citroen		Diesel Hybrid Expected 2010 (Likely to be Peugeot 307 and Citroën C4)
SUVs and Minivans		
DaimlerChrysler		Dodge Durango Expected 2008
		Chevrolet Tahoe Expected Late 2007
GM		GMC Yukon Expected Late 2007
		Saturn VUE Expected 2006
		Cadillac Escalade Expected Late 2007
	Escape SUV (Best in Class Performance)	New Version of Hybrid Escape 2007
Ford	Mercury Mariner (Similar to Escape	
		Mazda Tribute Expected 2007
Porsche		Cayenne Expected 2008
	Lexus RX 400h SUV	
Toyota	Highlander SUV	
		Sienna Minivan Expected 2007
Trucks		
DaimlerChrysler		Dodge Ram Expected 2006

Make	Currently Available	Future Models
GM	GM Silverado & Sierra ('Light' hybrids with offer a 10-15% improvement in fuel economy.	

Hybrid models 2005–2008
Source: Innovest

As hybrid vehicle sales have grown from 40,000 in 2003 to a projected million plus by 2008, the batteries that they require to operate have led to a major influx of R&D capital. This development has lead some industry researchers to predict that hybrid petrol/diesel vehicles will transform into full electric vehicles as the battery technology improves and removes the major obstacle to commercialisation – the time needed to recharge a battery.

This contest between the battery-powered and the nascent hydrogen powered vehicle market may determine the ultimate platform for the car industry and may have implications for the entire economy. Ultimately, improved battery technologies and fuel cells will be complimentary technologies for the economy as a whole. Some of the major joint ventures in the industry and the focus of their research indicate that lithium ion battery technology will likely be the technical choice of the future given the promise the technology has shown compared to nickel-cadmium batteries, which are both less efficient as well as significantly more toxic given the presence of cadmium, a heavy metal targeted by the ELV and RoHS Directives.

In the meantime, those car manufacturers that have invested in hybrid vehicles have tended to perform better than their rivals over the past two years, especially in the US where the development of more fuel-efficient vehicles has been timely, with Toyota the main beneficiary. The table below ranks the automotive sector according to performance on environmental factors. Due to the fact that there are high air, water and ground emissions from this sector, together with the importance of environmental technology development, and increasingly stringent global environmental laws, the environmental ratings of the leading companies – in the US market in this case – can be regarded as invaluable indicators of company performance.

Ticker	Company	Country	Environmental Rating
7203-TO	Toyota Motor Corp.	Japan	AAA
7267-TO	Honda Motor Company Limited	Japan	AAA
F	Ford Motor Company	United States	BB
GM	General Motors Corp.	United States	BB

Combined Rating for Auto Companies
Source: Innovest's Rating Model and databases, 2006

Looking at sales of hybrids in the US over the past two years, Toyota and Honda have been at the forefront, with GM and Ford trailing. At a time when fuel prices and environmental regulations are becoming tougher, US consumers were switching to smaller models and to hybrids, and GM and Ford did not have comparable models. Sales of their models did not fare so well over this period despite heavy price cutting.

Conclusion

In conclusion, it can be argued that for many higher impact sectors, such as the automotive market, the main risk factors faced by manufacturers are increasingly environmental in nature. In the auto sector for example, beyond the traditional concerns of smog-forming exhausts and the resulting health impacts, climate change linked to carbon dioxide (CO_2) emissions have become a major concern for auto companies. CO_2 emissions, which are directly correlated to the consumption of fossil fuels, contribute to the greenhouse gas effect and thus have a global impact. Regulatory regimes are arising accordingly.

But as well as having to respond to regulatory and other risks, leading firms are developing products for customers that exploit the potential for new markets. Despite the lack of uniform international emission regulations, most FT500 auto manufacturers would now cite capacity in fuel cell, hydrogen and zero-emission technologies as critical elements of their long-term strategies. In the short run, the strategic imperative remains continued advancement in internal combustion efficiency. It is estimated that the cost of saving one ton of vehicle-life CO_2 emissions through improved emission technologies ranges from US$200 to US$2,000.

In addition, it is likely that energy efficiency design, built without the use of toxic materials and with improved recyclability, will increasingly become the industry standard. Other environmental concerns include fuel efficiency and noxious gases (carbon dioxide, hydrocarbon, nitrogen oxide, particulate matter, sulfur oxide, and other emissions in steel and plastic material manufacturing, as well as vehicle assembly and use phases); noise levels when vehicles are in motion; the disposal recovery rate of materials (in assembly facilities and from end-of-life vehicles); and the reduction of substances of environmental concern such as lead and arsenic.

It has been demonstrated above that, especially in the auto sector, forward-thinking companies can gain competitive advantage by responding to the climate change challenge, while those that are slow to move may lose market share and profitability. For the automotive sector, there are five key value drivers for the 21st century, that can be said to be a direct result of responses to climate change, and that will help to build competitive advantage:

- Awareness of and strategic response to tightening emissions regimes

- Agility and capability to develop new models in the face of fuel price volatility

- Speed of response to the impact of climate change and fuel prices rises on consumer buying habits

- Investment in new engine technologies while being able to market affordable vehicles

- The development of new models that are not only more fuel efficient, e.g. hybrids, but the ability to offer these across all ranges of cars including SUVs.

Notes

1   'Winning the Battle Against Global Climate Change', Communication From The European Commission to the Council, The European Parliament, The European Economic and Social Committee, and the Committee of the Regions, Com (2005) 35 final, September 2, 2005, pp.1–3.

2   See http://news.bbc.co.uk/1/hi/business/6098362.stm

3   See http://cleantech.com/index.cfm?pageSRC=PressReleases

4   Ibid.

5   See http://cleantech.com/index.cfm?pageSRC=PressReleases

6   See Government of the United Kingdom, 'Investing in the Future', Background Paper for European Conference on Corporate Social Responsibility and the Financial Sector, Dec. 2005, p.14.

7   See http://cleantech.com/index.cfm?pageSRC=CleantechDefined

8   Makower J., Pernick R. and Wilder C. 'Clean Energy Trends 2006', Clean Edge, 2006, p.7. See www.cleanedge.com/reports/trends2006.pdf

9   'Cleaning Up: Focus on Private Equity & Venture Capital Investment in Clean Energy Technologies, Companies and & Projects,' New Energy Finance, June 13, 2006, p.5.

10 See www.wbcsd.org/plugins/DocSearch/details.asp?type=DocDet&ObjectId=MTk0ODQ

11 Makower J., Pernick R. and Wilder C. 'Clean Energy Trends 2006', Clean Edge, 2006, p.2. See www.cleanedge.com/reports/trends2006.pdf

12 Ibid., p.2.

13 This data was released at the Cleantech Venture Network's London event. See http://cleantech.com/index.cfm?pageSRC=LondonVentureForum

14 The Carbon Disclosure Project (CDP) provides a co-ordinating secretariat for institutional investor (US$31 trillion of assets under management) collaboration regarding climate change. CDP's aim is twofold: to inform investors regarding the significant risks and opportunities presented by climate change; and to inform company management regarding the serious concerns of their shareholders regarding the impact of these issues on company value. CDP provides a single global request for disclosure of shareholder value relevant information regarding GHG Emissions. With research carried out by Innovest Strategic Value Advisors, CDP expanded and the information request was sent to 2,000 companies globally, of which 900 answered the questions. More than 350 of the world's 500 largest corporations have completed previous information requests regarding their Greenhouse Gas emissions.

11

Business Leadership on Climate Change: Energy Efficiency and Beyond

Mark Kenber and Sophy Bristow, The Climate Group

Imagine the scene. The year is 2026. China is responsible for 15 per cent of the world's energy consumption. California has imposed permanent water rationing. Relief agencies warn that late rains again raise the spectre of widespread hunger in southern Africa. Cases of malaria are being reported among holidaymakers in Greece and Turkey. The Thames Barrier is being urgently extended to protect Canary Wharf after floods caused £100 million of damage.

It's impossible to predict exactly what the future will hold, but given the current knowledge from climate science, this picture is certainly not unrealistic. If it becomes reality, it significantly affects what 'doing good business' is going to entail in twenty years' time, as a diverse set of drivers begin to act more forcefully on the political and economic landscape, radically altering the world in which we live and work.

This chapter looks at the drivers for action and posits energy efficiency as the first step. This will be followed by a more in-depth discussion of the case for moving beyond efficiency – developing new products and services, communicating with customers on climate change and being part of the drive to develop the building blocks of a lower-carbon economy.

Drivers for corporate action

There are a range of factors already pushing companies to act to cut energy use and reduce their greenhouse gas (GHG) emissions. These can broadly be grouped under either risk management – the need to prepare for regulation, a desire to minimise the risks associated with rising energy prices and a fear of litigation, for example – or under new business opportunity. We examine each of these driver areas in more detail and ask what this might mean for the future of corporate action on climate change.

Risk management

Evolving regulatory framework

There is no doubt that the physical effects of climate change will become harder and harder to ignore. Climate projections run by leading scientific institution The Hadley Centre show, for example, that by the 2060s the sweltering summer temperatures we have experienced in Europe in the last few years might be described as 'unusually cool'– particularly worrying when you consider that the 2003 summer heat wave killed 35,000 people across Europe.[1]

It is reasonable to suppose that, in the context of increasingly visible signs of climate change, legislation will become more far reaching and extensive as electorates wake up to the problem and governments react to the consequences of changing weather and the costs of adaptive action.

The seeds of a regulatory framework are, of course, already in place. The best known initiative is the Kyoto Protocol, which covers 164 countries globally and 55 per cent of the world's greenhouse gas (GHG) emissions, and commits ratifying industrialized countries to reduce their GHG emissions in the period up to 2012. In other contexts too, political progress is being made. Several US and Australian states, as well as countless cities around the world, are developing policy frameworks aimed at stabilizing and then cutting GHG emissions. In California, for example, Governor Schwarzenegger has recently signed Bill AB 32 which puts a cap on California's greenhouse gas emissions and lays the foundations for a system based on market and other mechanisms that will bring the state's emissions back down to 1990 levels by 2020.

One of the possible regulatory approaches for meeting the AB 32 target would be to introduce a 'cap-and-trade' system. Indeed, the emergence of emissions trading which, by putting a limit on total emissions and allowing participants to buy and sell rights to emit, creates a price on carbon, is currently the policy of choice for tackling greenhouse gas emissions around the world. Emissions trading systems enable participants to reduce emissions at least cost, giving them the option to buy reductions from elsewhere when their own abatement costs are high. The European Emissions Trading scheme, the highest profile example, traded €7,218 million worth of emissions in 2004.

There are many similar schemes evolving. The Regional Greenhouse Gas Initiative system in the US, for example, brings Northeastern and Mid-Atlantic US states together to reduce emissions from electric power generators via a regional trading scheme. In the UK, the Energy Performance Commitment proposal has been launched for consultation – it plans to extend emissions trading beyond the power generators and energy-intensive industries participating in the EU-ETS and to launch a domestic scheme which energy users with electricity bills of over £15,000 a year would have to join, covering organisations as diverse as Tesco and the BBC.

Litigation

Beyond existing and possible future policy frameworks, the threat of litigation is also increasingly perceived to be a risk, and one which may drive companies to take action on climate change, particularly the large emitters in as yet unregulated markets. There have been a number of landmark cases over the last few years. For example, in 2004, eight US states and New York City filed a groundbreaking public nuisance lawsuit against five of America's largest power companies, demanding that they cut CO_2 emissions because of climate change. The suit did not seek monetary damages, but instead asked the companies to reduce their emissions at 174 plants by 3 per cent per year during the next ten years. More recently, in 2006, the State of California bought a lawsuit against six major car companies demanding 'monetary compensation' for climate change damage.

With the precedents by lawsuits[2] on asbestos and tobacco and the interest shown by other groups in following the example set by New York City, some reinsurers are already requiring that companies have appropriate strategies in place before extending them Directors' and Officers' liability insurance. This in itself should be sufficient motivation for firms to take action.

Energy security risk

The spectre of rising energy prices is another part of the risk management jigsaw, forcing companies to think carefully about their use of energy, with a knock-on positive impact on greenhouse gas emissions when efficiencies, and consequent energy savings, are made. The price of standard crude oil on NYMEX was under US$25/barrel in September 2003, but by August 11, 2005, it had risen to over US$60/barrel, and topped out at a record price of US$78.40 per barrel on July 13, 2006.

The price of oil has since dropped to around US$60/barrel, but there has been extensive discussion looking at the inflationary pressures on oil prices. In particular, world energy demand is expected to increase by 50 per cent by 2030 – to an equivalent of 335 barrels of oil a day – as developing countries, particularly China and India, seek prosperity and as rich nations, above all the US, endeavour to maintain an energy-intensive way of life. More than three-quarters of the increased need for energy is expected to come from developing countries.

Potential business opportunity

The operational need to manage the risks associated with reputation as well as regulation and changing weather patterns will inevitably make climate change increasingly prominent on the corporate radar. But it is short-sighted to think that defensive action will be the main driver of change over the next twenty years. From saving money on the bottom line, through to attracting and retaining high calibre staff, developing new products and building brand value, taking action on climate change is increasingly being seen as a business opportunity. Indeed, as carbon pricing evolves and awareness increases new markets are already opening up.

At the most simple level, energy efficiency can result in significant cost savings and although return on investment decreases as low-hanging fruit is picked off, if the current trends in energy price rises continue, then margins will shift in favour of continued efficiency improvements. It is to this potentially profitable approach that we now turn. This will be followed by a more in depth discussion of the case for moving beyond efficiency – developing new products and services, communicating with customers on climate change and being part of the drive to develop the building blocks of a lower carbon economy.

Energy efficiency – the first step

According to Amory Lovins: 'Increasing energy end-use efficiency—technologically providing more desired service per unit of delivered energy consumed—is generally the largest, least expensive, most benign, most quickly deployable, least visible, least understood, and most neglected way to provide energy services.' So, for those companies wanting to benefit from reducing their use of energy, what are the important steps to take?

Step one – Identify possible cost savings

As Michael Northrop stated in *Carbon Down, Profits Up* 2005, 'energy efficiency is the entry point for action on climate change and a great unrealized frontier of profitability'.[3] In fact, in most commercial, industrial and institutional facilities, there is an opportunity to save on average, 70–90 per cent of the energy and cost for lighting, fan and pump systems, 50 per cent for electric motors and 60 per cent in heating, cooling, office equipment and appliances.[4]

Once energy efficiency projects are identified, they are relatively easy to accomplish and have reasonably quick payback periods (especially with current trends for rising energy costs discussed above). For example, lighting retrofit projects have a typical three-year payback, which is equal to an internal rate of return in excess of 30 per cent. Lighting retrofits may also cut energy use by 50 cents or greater per square foot.[5]

There are numerous examples across all sectors where cost savings have been achieved through energy efficiency. In the area of lighting, Boeing reduced electricity use up to 90 per cent in some of its plants and on the whole achieved a 53 per cent rate of return on its investment in lighting retrofits. Also in lighting, General Electric expects to save US$12.8 million per annum on energy costs from its lighting retrofit program begun in 2005. Alcoa has already saved US$20 million by conducting energy efficiency surveys from 2002 to 2004 and projects a potential total savings of $80 million as a result of further efficiency measures. Allergan saved US$2.3 million from 2001 to 2005 through energy efficiency in its new research and development building and through the use of cogeneration. From 1998 to 2005, BP increased its net present value by US$1 billion by increasing operational efficiency, applying technological innovation and improving energy management.

Identifying cost savings to be made through energy efficiency measures is achieved by carrying out energy audits of employee energy use, buildings and infrastructure and production processes. Once the possibilities for improving efficiency have been identified, steps can then be taken to communicate those possibilities and integrate them into company management systems.

Table 1: Examples of efficiency savings

Company	Measure undertaken	Dates	Savings	Sector
Boeing	Lighting		53 per cent rate of return	Aerospace & Defense
General Electric	Lighting	2005	$12,800,000	Industrial Manufacturing
Alcoa	Energy surveys	2002-2004 Annual savings	$20,000,000	Industrial Manufacturing
BP	Operational efficiency, energy management, technological innovation	1998-2005	$1,000,000,000	Energy & Utilities
Eastman Chemical		1995–2005	$800,000,000	Chemicals
General Motors	Lighting	2005	$2,700,000	Automotive
HBOS		1999–2005	£16,500,000	Financial Services
Johnson Johnson		2005	$30,000,000	Pharmaceuticals
Kimberly-Clark		2000–2005	$70,000,000 annual savings	Consumer Products Manufacturers
Pfizer	900 energy conservation projects	2002–2005	$30,000,000 annual savings	Pharmaceuticals
Verizon		2005	$15,000,000	Telecommunications
Timberland		2004	$275,000	Retail
Investa Property Group		2004–2005 Annual savings	AU$ 600,000	Real Estate
IBM	Real-time monitoring of electrical use	2005	$747,000	Computer Hardware
E I du Pont de Nemours		1990–2005	$3,000,000,000	Chemicals
Deutsche Telekom	Everyday service contracts	2001–2005	$35,300,000	Telecommunications
Caterpillar	Diesel fuel conservation	2004	$2,800,000	Industrial Manufacturing

Company	Measure undertaken	Dates	Savings	Sector
Catalyst	Reduced fuel consumption 2 per cent	2005–2006	$5,000,000	Paper and Pulp
California Portland Cement	Cut electricity consumption		$3,000,000	Construction
Amcor Limited		2000–2005 Annual savings	$5,000,000	Metals & Mining
Allergan	Cogeneration & efficiency in R&D bldg	2001–2005	$2,300,000	Pharmaceuticals
Adobe Systems, Inc.	Lighting	Annual savings	$100,436	Computer Software
Abitibit Consolidated, Inc.	Process Changes; Waste Management; Reduced fuel use	2005	$450,000	Paper and Pulp
ABM Amro	Communication	2004–2008 Projected savings	$3,500,000	Financial Services

Source: Various, see for example Carbon Down, Profits Up, 2005, The Climate Group (op cit)

Chart 1: Significant areas for improved efficiency and energy savings
Source: Author's own

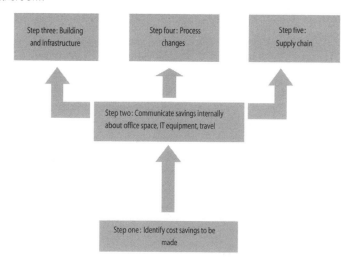

Step two – Internal communications on efficiency and conservation

Once opportunities for cost savings through energy efficiency have been identified, the next step is to develop an internal communications programme surrounding energy efficiency and conservation within the company (see middle tier in Chart 1). Internal communication should result in further cost savings without changing any physical infrastructure. Examples of areas where cost savings can be made are in business travel, efficient use of office space and use of IT equipment.

For example, Verizon has instituted an internal communications programme with employees called Energy Champions, which encourages the creative reduction of energy use with employees receiving recognition for their action. Energy Champions is part of a larger programme entitled Team Energy, which has already saved US$60 million for the company.[6]

Another corporate leader in the internal communication of energy efficiency is British Telecom (BT). BT's corporate and social responsibility team has put in place a number of channels to reach staff with its efficiency message: focus groups; an internal newspaper and intranet; BT Environment Week; and issue-specific campaigns and road shows where the CSR team travels to offices asking for employee pledges to reduce energy. The programme has over 700 volunteers contributing to reducing energy use and cost savings.

Many companies have found that engaging their employees is not only an extremely productive way to reduce energy bills but that it also motivates staff and involves them in an area which, like many members of the general public, is of deep concern to them. Anecdotal evidence suggests that firms that demonstrate a responsible attitude on energy efficiency – and climate change issues in general – are finding it easier to attract high quality employees, especially among recent graduates.

Step three – Buildings and infrastructure

Moving on to the third tier of action in Chart 1, buildings and infrastructure offer another significant potential opportunity for improved efficiency and cost savings. Understanding the changes that can be made here is an important step for all businesses, from banking to metals and mining.

There are opportunities both in existing infrastructure and retrofits and also in new buildings in the form of efficient design. One example of retrofitting existing infrastructure is the lighting programme at General Electric (GE). GE surveyed its facilities' lighting and replaced high-intensity discharge lighting fixtures with fluorescent bulbs at a total cost of US$4 million. The retrofit has cut the lighting load in half, resulting in US$2 million annual savings.

The St Mary Axe building (The Gherkin) in central London and the Conde Nast Building in New York are both examples of buildings where efficiency criteria were integrated into the design at an early stage. The Gherkin, designed by Sir Norman Foster and the UK head quarters of Swiss Re, is one of the most energy-efficient buildings in Europe, using half the energy of a conventional high-rise office, saving Swiss Re and other tenants millions in energy costs annually. The Conde Nast Building in Times Square was one of the first environmentally responsible buildings of its kind, maximising energy conservation through highly efficient gas-fired absorption chillers, excellent insulation and passive solar use.

In the US alone, commercial buildings accounted for 45.4 per cent of national energy use in 2002, so the potential savings to be made are significant.[7] Furthermore, a green building project does not have to cost more up front. And careful 'front-loaded' planning and design can pay for itself – with interest – in avoided downstream costs such as elaborate mechanical systems, expensive redesigns, drawn-out approvals, litigation, and stalled construction.

Step four – Look for process improvement opportunities

Process changes – covering a range of actions from modifications to fuels and chemicals used to changes in procedures during manufacturing – are one of the most significant areas where companies can make efficiency gains.

In 1995 Alumax (subsequently acquired by Alcoa), an aluminum refiner, decided to improve the energy efficiency of its four-pot line dust collection systems at its smelter in Mount Holly, S.C. By installing a three-fan variable inlet valve system energy costs were reduced by US$103,700 per year. The system increased fan efficiency enough to allow for one fan in each of the four systems to be shut down and the project payback time was six days.[8]

Other examples include Philips, which has replaced glass furnaces with oxy-fuel furnaces at factories, contributing to cutting energy use by 25 per cent between 2001 and 2005, and Nestlé where emissions from manufacturing operations were reduced by more than 12 per cent since 1997 – a period during which Nestlé production volumes increased by more than 55 per cent.[9]

Step five – Incorporate efficiency into supply chain

Once in-house opportunities for energy efficiency have been maximised, there is scope to look at possible improvements which can be made throughout the rest of the value chain, from the efficiency of manufacturing facilities (where these are outsourced), through to the product or service which the company in question itself provides.

Some leading retailers, for example, are beginning to introduce clauses on energy efficiency into suppliers' codes, or looking for ways to invest in improving the efficiency of outsourced manufacturing facilities in return for the possibility of owning the emission reductions or sharing in the cost savings that are made as a result.

From the product perspective, Philips is a good example of a business leading innovation in energy efficient lighting – investing €400 million in its development since 2000 alone. Since lighting consumes 19 per cent of global electricity, estimates suggest that a switch to energy efficient lighting could reduce CO_2 emissions by up to 300 million tonnes, resulting in up cost savings of up to €50 billion.

In the field of information technology, Intel helped to develop the US Environmental Protection Agency's (EPA) Energy Star program for computers, and in 1993 demonstrated the first Energy Star compliant personal computer (PC). The Intel innovation that has had the greatest impact on the efficiency of personal computers has been the Instantly Available PC (IAPC) technology which allows PCs to run more efficiently while reducing their energy use by up to 71 per cent. The IAPC technology has a 'sleep state' of lower than five watts which allows the PC to remain connected and perform tasks over a network or the Internet. The US EPA estimates that between 2002 and 2010 the use of the IAPC technology will avoid 159 million tonnes of CO_2 emissions (the equivalent of taking five million cars off the road).[10]

The business opportunities associated with these more efficient, 'climate-friendly' products are discussed further below – growing consumer awareness, in particular, is likely to be a key business driver for new product development. It is also worth noting that although there are a number of voluntary schemes and individual corporate success stories, regulation around product energy efficiency is likely to increase in the future. For example, an action plan to cut Europe's energy consumption by 20 per cent before 2020, recently outlined by the European Commission, included tougher energy standards for electrical goods and more fuel-efficient cars. Officials say the proposals will deliver an annual saving of 100bn euros (£67bn) and help the EU meet its Kyoto Protocol target to cut emissions by eight per cent.

Beyond efficiency

Energy efficiency, particularly the first steps outlined above, is an essential consideration for companies wanting to maximise the opportunities associated with reducing greenhouse gas emissions. However, despite the fact that many companies discover that there are far more opportunities than they originally imagined, there comes a point when most of the easily available reductions in energy use have been made. Many leading companies are therefore starting to take a more holistic approach to minimising their carbon footprints. Furthermore, these progressive companies are no longer looking simply to reduce their own GHG emissions. They are also seeking to maximise opportunities presented by growing interest in climate amongst consumers and shareholders. Step five above, which covers thinking through energy use in the supply chain and also in products and services, is an important part of this more integrated vision. We will now look at a range of the other approaches being taken to reach beyond efficiency: renewable energy and carbon neutrality; responding to consumer demand and building brand value; and playing a part in developing the building blocks of a low carbon economy. It should be noted that none of these are mutually exclusive either with each other or with the energy efficiency steps outlined above.

Renewable energy

In terms of reducing direct emissions, one of the most popular approaches, after improvements in energy efficiency, is to increase the use of renewable and sustainable energy sources such as wind and solar power.

One company that has made a particularly strong commitment to alternative energy is British Telecom. In October 2004, it completed what is reportedly the world's largest green energy deal after agreeing a three-year contract with British Gas and npower for 2.1 TWh (terawatt hours) of electricity from renewables and efficient combined heat and power (CHP) generation.

As well as the purchase of green energy, companies are also looking to develop onsite renewable generation. Sharp, for example, is promoting the use of photovoltaic power systems at all its domestic production sites. Sharp has a 5,150-kW photovoltaic power system on the recently built Mie plant in Japan. This is the world's largest installation on a building and can generate enough electricity for 1,300 average homes.

While the initial costs of green electricity can be higher than for conventional grid-based power, companies are not switching to green sources for PR reasons alone. In many countries, buying green electricity increases the total renewable-based generation capacity and displaces fossil fuels. Even where this is not the case, diversifying energy sources can reduce the risk of disruptions – like the recent blackouts in France and California, for example – and may over time reduce energy bills.

After improving efficiency and purchasing renewable energy, companies like HSBC and BSkyB, are going one step further and going 'carbon neutral' (effectively reducing their net emissions to zero) by 'offsetting' to compensate for their remaining carbon footprints. Offsetting, the process of purchasing emissions reductions made elsewhere (from a renewable energy project that displaces fossil fuel-based generation in the developing world, for example), to count against those of your own emissions which may be more difficult or expensive to tackle directly, is already an option for those companies participating in the European Emissions Trading Scheme (EU ETS) or regulated in other Kyoto signatory countries. But beyond this regulation-driven framework there is now a blossoming voluntary market that demonstrates the increasing number of companies wanting the benefits of flexibility when taking voluntary steps to reduce emissions. While offsetting is only part of a corporate strategy to cut greenhouse gas emissions, it can be an effective way to make early gains, motivate staff and customers and create internal understanding of the opportunities arising from engaging in carbon markets.

Customers

A well thought through 'carbon-neutral' commitment is something which can be easily communicated to customers and other stakeholders as an integrated approach to tackling climate change. For companies outside the regulatory framework, finding ways like this to differentiate themselves in the context of rising consumer awareness around the climate issue is increasingly important – press mentions of climate change increased 20-fold in the ten years to 2003.

As well as thinking about communicating their corporate activities, many companies including Avis (carbon-neutral car hire), BP ('Target Neutral' service to offset emissions associated with driving) and B&Q (domestic wind turbines and solar panels) are also developing lower-carbon products and services and are increasingly thinking about how to effectively market these 'climate-friendly' offers to customers.

A recent study conducted by The Climate Group and Lippincott Mercer, sponsored by BskyB, found that 28 per cent of consumers in the UK and 19 per cent in the US 'feel *very* strongly' about climate change (81 per cent and 58 per cent respectively recognized climate change as an important issue), supporting a potentially much larger market than for organics or FairTrade when those markets first took off.[11] This group shows a latent demand amongst consumers for products, services and brands that would allow people to reflect their climate change concern in their spending.

Unfortunately, consumers are largely unaware of the options currently available. The research showed that once informed they are positive, and surprised by what is affordable. But the barriers that keep demand latent go beyond awareness. Knowledge (lack of understanding about the climate issue), direction (a feeling of powerlessness with regards to the problem), convenience (current offers are seen to be difficult and time-consuming), fairness (a desire for governments, businesses and other consumers to 'do their bit') and wealth (unwillingness to pay more for climate friendly options) are all, according to the research, limiting consumer action on climate change.

There are a range of roles which companies can adopt to enable consumers to overcomes these barriers and capitalize on a very real business opportunity:

- *Educators* can help overcome the knowledge barrier through education, helping consumers understand what they should be worried about, why they can and should act, and what they can usefully do;

- *Leaders* can play different leadership roles depending on their own objectives and legitimacy. They may invite consumers to follow them based on what they do, what they have pioneered or what products they offer;

- *Facilitators* make the desired behaviours easy to do – 'easy' here means accessible, prompted, effortless and assured, something which has been achieved successfully with FairTrade for example;

- *Contributors* act alongside their customers and staff, as with pension provision where companies traditionally make a financial contribution alongside their employees, and;

- *Marketers* are needed to encourage consumers to pay for something which doesn't necessarily have any intrinsic gratification. It sounds tough but has many precedents, from FairTrade to insurance.

Ben & Jerry's has been playing a strong educator role with the launch of its Climate Change College. In 2006, the college will offer the chance for six 18–30 year olds to educate themselves about the causes, politics and potential solutions of climate change with the emphasis on developing their own climate change campaign.

Toyota is a good example of a company which has developed a positive brand association specifically linked to climate change. The company is viewed as a 'leader' largely based on the development and marketing of its Toyota Prius, the world's first mass-produced gas-electric hybrid vehicle. Sales of the Prius passed half a million units worldwide in April this year. The company has integrated environmental criteria into the product at all stages from design and procurement through to manufacture and, ultimately, marketing. The Prius's success is particularly important because motor vehicles are responsible for a disproportionate amount of GHG emissions. Innovative developments in key areas like this form the building blocks of a low-carbon economy and are, in themselves, a particularly significant business opportunity.

Building the low-carbon economy

The move to a low carbon economy – one where development is fuelled by low emissions technologies – is essential to tackle both climate change and energy security. Research has shown that a 60 per cent reduction in UK carbon emissions can be achieved by 2050 using a mixture of energy efficiency, renewable sources of electricity, replacing coal and oil with lower carbon fuels such as gas and the use of hydrogen as fuel.[12] If we get these new technologies right it will be the basis for a new industrial revolution, and many companies are vying to get in on the act early.

As well as Toyota in the motor industry mentioned above, a number of other major companies are ramping up investment in clean technologies. General Electric's ecomagination initiative, for example, is a commitment to invest US$1.5 billion annually by 2010 in this area. By May 2006 it had already increased its revenues from environmental goods from US$6.2 billion to US$10.1 billion. In November 2005 BP launched BP Alternative Energy. Building on the success of BP Solar – which expects to hit revenues of US$1 billion in 2008 – this new venture will manage an investment programme in solar, wind, hydrogen and combined-cycle-gas-turbine (CCGT) power generation, which could amount to US$8 billion over the next ten years.

With the worldwide market for wind, solar, geothermal and fuel cell energy estimated at US$200 billion in 2020, it is no surprise that dynamic companies are looking to establish themselves in this field. And the broader investment sector is also getting in on the act. According to a recent article in the Economist, 'investors are falling over themselves to finance start-ups in clean tech, especially in energy. ... investments in this field by venture capitalists and private-equity firms have quadrupled in the past two years, from some US$500m in 2004 to almost US$2 billion so far this year. New Energy Finance [a research firm], reckons that investments of all sorts in the business will reach US$63 billion this year compared with just US$30 billion in 2004.[13]

TEN LEADERSHIP STEPS FOR CLIMATE CHANGE

1. Understand the situation

2. Accept responsibility

3. Identify risks (regulation, weather, legal, energy security)

4. Identify opportunities (new products and services, brand value, first mover advantage, efficiency savings)

5. Measure footprint

6. Adopt clear strategies and targets

    (i)   Address internal emissions

    (ii)   Look for external opportunities

7. Develop and harness expertise

8. Overcome barriers

9. Communicate with stakeholders

10. Champion further positive action to others

A common denominator?

So what do all these organisations have in common? They have responded to a diverse set of drivers, including shareholder and consumer pressure, rising energy prices and the need for energy security, legislation and the lure of business opportunity. They have used a wide range of approaches – internal energy efficiency, renewable energy purchases, upgrading plant and working with suppliers and customers. What brings them together is that they have all recognised the synergies between cutting GHGs and increased productivity and revenue.

In doing so, they have recognised the need for strong internal and external leadership – a CEO or chairman who is a flag bearer for the cause – and an integrated approach that does not deal with climate change in an internal corporate ghetto but across the board, involving management, production, IT, design and marketing. This is unlikely to be a flash in the pan. There is no doubt that climate change will be with us for the long term and that the shift to a low-carbon economy will only accelerate, be it as a result of ever tougher regulations or the grasping of the opportunities that the shift brings with it. The companies that have taken early action to reduce emissions have realised a series of benefits: reduced costs, better motivated staff and management, new business opportunities and greater customer satisfaction.

There is a clear message here for both policy makers and business leaders: addressing global warming does not have to result in economic cooling. On the contrary, the emerging evidence shows that the first movers in addressing this challenge will be the successful economies of the future. Those who do not take action face an altogether different risk – the risk of being left behind.

In the words of Lord Browne, CEO of BP, 'Addressing climate change will take bold leadership. It's a global problem and will require a global solution. The role of business is not to engage in politics or propaganda. The role of business is to offer solutions.'[14]

Notes

1   Hadley Centre, www.metoffice.com/research/hadleycentre/pubs/brochures/B2004/global.pdf
2   For example, see Myles Allen 'The Spectre of Liability' in K. Tang *The Finance of Climate Change – A Guide for Governments, Corporations & Investors*, Risk Books, 2005.
3   The Climate Group, 'Carbon Down, Profits Up', 2005. www.theclimategroup.org
4   Rocky Mountain Institute, www.rmi.org/sitepages/pid119.php
5   Ibid.
6   Verizon Communications, 'Introspective Energy Conservation Strategies' by Eliza Barclay, www.safeclimate.net/index/stories_verizon.php
7   Environment Protection Agency, Green Building Stats, www.epa.gov/greenbuilding/pubs/gbstats.pdf
8   US Department of Energy, Best Practise Case-studies, www1.eere.energy.gov/industry/bestpractices/case_studies.html
9   The Climate Group, op. cit.
10 Climate Group Intel case-study, www.theclimategroup.org/index.php?pid=521
11 The Climate Group & Lippincott Mercer, *Serving the Climate Change Conscious Consumer*, www.theclimategroup.org/assets/Serving%20CCC%20consumer.pdf
12 The Carbon Trust, *Scoping R&D Priorities for a Low Carbon Future*, www.iccept.ic.ac.uk/pdfs/Carbon%20Trust%20report.pdf
13 *The Economist*, p.83, November 18–24, 2006.
14 Climate and Energy Roundtable Event, Los Angeles, July 2006.

12

Coming Clean: Business Takes on the Climate Challenge*

Jennifer Layke and Samantha Putt del Pino,
World Resources Institute

Introduction

Since the oil embargo of the 1970s, US companies and individuals have been aware of domestic energy security issues. For over twenty years, scientists around the world have warned us that increasing atmospheric concentrations of greenhouse gases could destabilize our climate. In 2006, these issues have taken centre stage as significant concerns for the world's ability to grow and thrive in this new century. While the business community can be a significant force in helping us find technology solutions to these challenges, the stakes are high and there is no time to spare.

Acting alone, single countries or companies will have a negligible effect on reducing the risks of climate change. To achieve long-term emissions reductions on a scale commensurate with the threat, a critical mass of actors – both governmental and private – will need to work together. The question is not so much 'Will we experience the effects of climate change?' but rather 'When will we experience them?' and 'How disastrous will it be?' The economic, human and ecological risks require new management and technological approaches.

So what is motivating corporations to become engaged? While government regulation of the greenhouse gas (GHG) emissions that contribute to climate change is imperative, some national leaders – most notably those in the United States – have been slow to act, and international policy can take years to develop and implement. But smart planning and innovative thinking by corporations will help them profit and thrive in a GHG-constrained world (and in the US, prepare for GHG regulation). Some companies already have shifted their thinking and are taking positive steps to help build a clean energy future. Their experiences are rich with lessons that others can learn from. Companies that fail to act now, however, could face higher costs as they race to keep up, and risk falling behind competitors who are working today to create new technologies, services and products.

This chapter discusses how to build the business case for developing a corporate climate change strategy. It reviews the tangible and intangible benefits companies can accrue by reducing their emissions and outlines the process for identifying emission reductions. The chapter also discusses key avenues for reducing operational emissions and looks at how companies can maximize reduction opportunities by leveraging their supply chain relationships. It then explores how companies can derive new or expanded business by developing new low-carbon products and services. Finally, the chapter looks at the policy environment companies need in order to develop and deploy clean energy technologies and how some forward-looking companies are developing long-term integrated approaches to carbon management.

Developing the business case

There are two reasons businesses are interested in climate change: risk and opportunity. In an increasingly interdependent global economy, companies' value chains may cover activities in multiple geographic locations. Such diversity can make almost any company vulnerable to the impact of climate change, as any effect on an upstream supplier or a downstream consumer may significantly change a company's operations and profit margin.

Climate change may harm businesses' operations and profitability, regardless of sector. For instance, businesses with operations or customers in areas like coastal regions may be at risk from physical damage to property caused by flooding and extreme weather events, the loss of revenue in the aftermath of a violent storm, and the ensuing higher insurance premiums in these regions. Starbucks, for example, cites potential climatic shifts due to climate change as a risk to its ability to source coffee from all over the world. Damage to energy infrastructure resulting from extreme weather events may also create volatility and scarcity for raw materials, basic goods and energy.

Companies will not invest in new technologies, in GHG management systems, or in emissions reduction projects unless they see the value it will provide to their firms. An understanding of an investment's explicit or implicit positive financial outcome is what is often referred to as the 'business case.' While the business case for action may be broadly tied to long-term interests, a company may anticipate specific benefits and returns from a greenhouse gas management program. These outcomes, or value propositions, are indicators of a successful GHG program and strategy.

Value propositions can be divided into tangible returns and intangible benefits (see Box 1). Tangible returns from either reducing costs or increasing revenue can be measured in dollars. Common examples are energy-efficiency projects and the launch of a climate-friendly product that lowers emissions when used by the consumer. Intangible benefits are more difficult to measure yet may be more important as they could have a substantial effect on corporate share value over time. For corporate GHG programs, these benefits are generally tied to three factors: sound risk management, improved reputation or brand image, and early preparation for regulation. Such benefits may be interpreted by an investor as an indication of forward-looking strategy and superior business management, a perception that can be more valuable than any of the underlying factors.

BOX 1: VALUE PROPOSITIONS FOR CORPORATE GHG MANAGEMENT PROGRAMS

Businesses create a GHG strategy by measuring tangible returns and articulating intangible benefits. Anticipated outcomes, or value propositions, are indicators of a successful GHG program.

Tangible returns

- Climate-friendly projects yield a positive return on investment

- Increased income and/or market share from new or enhanced products or services

- Low-GHG technology advances used as new standard by regulators/customers

- Internal emissions-reduction projects allow for the sale of emissions reduction credits.

- Enhanced energy-conservation practices and fuel switching stabilize corporate energy use and protect against energy price volatility.

Intangible benefits

- Competitive positioning

  1. Low-carbon products or services improve the company's position vis-à-vis its competitors.

  2. The public perceives the corporate brand as environmentally friendly, leading to improved public relations.

  3. Strong environmental performance results in higher employee recruitment, retention, and productivity.

- Shareholder-related benefits

  1. Shareholders drop climate resolutions as their conditions are satisfied.

  2. Investors perceive strong environmental performance as an indicator of superior business management, resulting in a premium on the stock price and a lower cost for capital.

  3. The company's stock is included in a specialized stock index, such as the Dow Jones Sustainability Index, and is held by investment funds that track the index.

  4. The company receives higher stock ratings from 'socially responsible investment' (SRI) analysts, resulting in more stock purchases by SRI investors.

- Regulatory preparedness

    1. Company staff are trained to manage GHG emissions, thereby broadening the company's experience and enabling it to adapt more easily to future regulations.

    2. The company's GHG emissions are at or below legal requirements at the time the GHG regulations go into effect, thereby making compliance easier.

    3. A strong GHG management program gives the company greater credibility and thus a greater voice in policy discussions and an opportunity to influence policy outcomes.

- Management benefits

    1. Coordination of GHG management across business units and jurisdictions improves learning, identifies opportunities, leads to innovation, and offers unexpected efficiencies.

    2. The company is protected against potential class-action lawsuits related to corporate governance, specifically claiming breach of fiduciary responsibility for failing to manage GHG emissions and their associated liabilities.

Source: A Climate of Innovation Andrew Aulisi, Jennifer Layke, Samantha Putt Del Pino, World Resources Institute, 2004, p.6)

Getting started

Developing and implementing a corporate climate change strategy is an iterative process and the business case is always being improved and built upon through companies' experiences. Companies that are serious about taking action on climate change will first need to start by developing an annual greenhouse gas inventory – listing their GHG emissions sources and their quantities. A GHG inventory helps companies identify emission reduction opportunities, set reduction targets, and track their GHG performance over time. General Electric (GE), a global, diversified corporation, found that creating a GHG inventory enabled it to better identify its opportunities for emission reductions. This inventory also supported GE's 'Ecomagination' business strategy by generating the data needed to set a company-wide emission reduction target. 'Ecomagination' combines GE's commitment to develop products and services with lower environmental impacts with its corporate-wide emissions reduction target. With 'Ecomagination,' GE is positioning itself as a global leader in a carbon-constrained world. Establishing a GHG inventory was crucial to supporting GE's innovative approach.[1]

Developing a GHG management strategy will require senior-level support within the company as well as operational changes to ensure that data is tracked. Figure 1 illustrates the key steps involved in constructing a corporate GHG inventory. A key challenge for most companies is designing an efficient data collection and management system that is also accurate and auditable. One solution may be to develop an online database accessible by the company's data collection team. Some companies have found success in hiring a third party to manage their data. For example, Staples, the office products company, uses its existing energy management system to gather activity data for its GHG inventory. The web-based energy system is provided through a contract with a third-party provider. Before hiring them, Staples was having trouble keeping track of its energy and water consumption, managing its utility bills and ensuring prompt payment. These problems have been resolved now that the energy management system is in place. And when Staples started constructing its GHG inventory, nearly all the data for its facilities' energy consumption were contained in the energy management system and were easily accessible. Through this third-party-managed system, Staples is able to easily track data for its more than 1,500 retail and non-retail facilities.[2]

Figure 1: Steps to developing a corporate GHG inventory
Source: A Climate of Innovation Andrew Aulisi, Jennifer Layke, Samantha Putt Del Pino, World Resources Institute, 2004, p.11

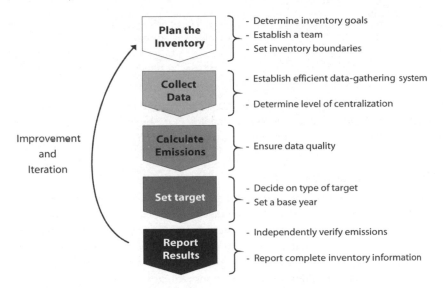

Detailed guidance on corporate inventory development can be found in the *GHG Protocol Corporate Accounting and Reporting Standard* available at www.ghgprotocol. org. This standard, developed to be the 'generally accepted accounting principles' for greenhouse gases, was developed by the World Resources Institute, the World Business Council for Sustainable Development, and dozens of business and other stakeholder contributors.

Once companies have developed a comprehensive GHG inventory, set a credible emissions reduction target, and formulated a strategy to reach their goals, they can share their progress with interested stakeholders. Shareholders, employees, other businesses within the sector and the environmental community all may be interested in learning more about a company's commitment to protecting the climate. Companies can feature their achievements in their annual or sustainability reports, and many companies now seek opportunities to register their emissions publicly (see Box 2 for a sample of reporting programs). This is particularly valuable for global companies, since no national registry may offer the opportunity to communicate about global emissions.

BOX 2: EXAMPLES OF GREENHOUSE GAS REPORTING PROGRAMS

California Climate Action Registry (http://www.climateregistry.org)

Carbon Disclosure Project (http://www.cdproject.net)

Dow Jones Sustainability Index (http://www.sustainability-index.com)

U.S. Environmental Protection Agency Climate Leaders Initiative (http://www.epa.gov/climateleaders)

World Economic Forum Emissions Registry (http://www.weforum.org)

Once a corporate GHG inventory is developed, it can be used to help identify emission reduction opportunities. This is where companies must build internal capacity and processes to identify, select and implement behavioral change in their operations.

Reducing emissions

After measuring their impacts, companies generally seek cost-effective emissions reduction opportunities. As detailed in the business case section above, they do so for a myriad of reasons – for cost reduction, regulatory compliance, marketing and advertising, and/or carbon trading opportunities. Emissions reduction projects can take a variety of forms. These include energy efficiency projects, renewable energy procurement and transportation-related emissions reductions. For example:

- **Supporting renewable energy**: In 2003 Johnson & Johnson offset over 68,000 metric tons of CO_2 emissions with a purchase of renewable energy certificates (RECs) equivalent to roughly 162,000 megawatt-hours of electricity. At the time, the purchase was one of the largest corporate purchases of RECs, and it allowed Johnson & Johnson to efficiently and cost-effectively support the company's climate change commitment.[3] More recently the company has continued to innovate in the area of renewable energy procurement. ALZA Pharmaceuticals, a division of Johnson & Johnson, expects to save 7,256 tons of CO_2 per year – 71 per cent of its business unit target – by replacing the natural gas it uses at three research and development facilities with landfill gas (methane) from a local California landfill that otherwise would be flared.[4]

- **Implementing energy efficiency**: At just one distribution facility, Staples reduced energy consumption by over 80 per cent, cut GHG emissions by 300 metric tons and saved more than $100,000 in annual energy costs by implementing energy efficiency measures. Staples' distribution centres can be upwards of 500,000 square feet. The system of conveyor belts each centre houses can be as long as six or seven miles. Staples was able to accrue the described energy, emissions and monetary savings by installing a sensor-based system that ensures not only that the vast buildings' air and lighting systems turn off in unoccupied areas but that the conveyor belt system is only activated when a package is placed on it.[5]

- **Supply-chain data gathering**: DHL Nordic Express outsources much of its transportation to partners. Under their contract with DHL Nordic Express, these partners are required to provide information on distance traveled, fuel efficiency and other data. This information allows DHL Nordic Express to calculate the associated emissions and screen their partners for environmental performance. DHL Nordic Express is thus able to effectively manage its GHG emissions.[6]

- **Supplier targets**: Time Inc., a publisher, found that greenhouse emissions from one of its paper mills accounted for 61 per cent of the emissions from Time magazine and 77 per cent of the emissions from In Style magazine. To reduce its impact, Time Inc. asked the company's paper suppliers to reduce their greenhouse gas emissions by 20 per cent by 2012, and began actively engaging suppliers.[7]

- **Optimizing shipping activities**: Marks & Spencer, a retailer with 400 stores in the United Kingdom and another 200 operated by franchises in more than 30 countries, has reduced its emissions from transportation by engaging its suppliers. For example, until recently, each of its suppliers shipped goods across the English Channel via separate freight ferries regardless of how full each truck was. The company worked with its suppliers to consolidate shipments from different suppliers in one mainland distribution centre. From there, the products are loaded onto trains that travel via the Channel Tunnel. Marks & Spencer sends two full trains a week across the channel, reducing freight costs, simplifying logistics, and greatly reducing transport emissions.[8]

Corporate emissions reductions offer opportunities for companies to cut costs, support and deploy clean energy technologies and build efficient operations. However, many managers report that when faced with supporting an energy reduction project, a chief financial officer will pass over a solid project that meets minimum internal rates of return in favour of a project that ties in more directly with a technology or product path. Many companies are now beginning to take another look:

- Johnson & Johnson has instituted a US $40 million fund for greenhouse gas reduction projects with acceptable internal rate of returns and significant technology and GHG reduction value.

- DuPont, IBM and the Ford Motor Company joined with over 20 firms in the Chicago Climate Exchange to voluntarily trade emissions reductions and gain experience with carbon markets.

- BP's internal trading program put in a 'shadow price' for carbon that demonstrated how their capital investment and emissions reduction opportunities would fare in a carbon-constrained world.

Some companies find that factoring in the potential carbon value of a project can help managers better understand the full potential of GHG projects. The 'Carbon Value Analysis Tool' developed by the World Resources Institute is a screening tool to help companies integrate the value of carbon dioxide emissions reductions into energy-related investment decisions. It can test the sensitivity of a project's internal rate of return to a carbon value by allowing the user to assign a real or fictitious price for carbon. The tool allows users to build a 'marginal cost abatement curve' across a variety of potential project investments to determine their GHG impact per dollar of investment.[9]

Climate change as a business driver

If the world is to solve the climate challenge, many companies will ultimately need to look beyond the operational aspects of their business to their products and services too. Technology investment, innovation, and deployment are increasingly the realm of the private sector. General Electric's 'Ecomagination' foreshadows a significant shift – companies seeking to 'walk the talk' to align their internal actions with the impact of their products and services. GE's goals did not exclusively focus on emission reductions. Rather, the company took the opportunity to invest in research and development for solutions to climate change, and took on a challenge to grow the company's revenues from 'Ecomagination' products such as wind turbines, compact fluorescent light bulbs, advanced gas turbines, appliances and other core business products. And finally, the company has invested in marketing and educational materials for consumers, and called for public policy on climate change and energy policy standards.

Investors are taking note. Citigroup and other investment houses are beginning to track corporate exposure to climate risk and opportunities for companies with climate-friendly products and services to offer. Citigroup's report 'Investing in Solutions to Climate Change' offers its' analysts views of 'the Clean Dozen' – companies with market opportunities to profit from their climate technologies. Companies such as Archer Daniels Midland, Cypres Semiconductor, Itron, Johnson Controls and others were highlighted.[10] Co-author Suozzo stated that 'for investors looking for exposure to low-carbon technologies, large companies operating in growth areas can offer stable upside potential, while small listed companies with proven technologies can offer more 'pure' exposure to trends toward carbon constraints.'[11]

The technology imperative

It will not be possible to avoid dangerous climate change without the engagement of the business sector to design and transfer low-GHG technologies for use in developing countries – where 80 per cent of the world's population resides and where emissions are growing most rapidly. The private sector, while often citing valid concerns about intellectual property rights and nascent national competitors in key developing countries, must create and be rewarded for new models of technology transfer.

A recent paper by two Princeton researchers offered the world a new paradigm for reflecting on the climate and technology challenge. The 'wedges' analysis quantifies the global emissions reductions required (seven 1-gigatonne carbon wedges per year) to stabilize the climate. The analysis focuses on the investment and policy needs required to scale deployment of technologies such as wind power, biofuels, and carbon capture and storage[12] (see Box 3 for depiction of this concept).

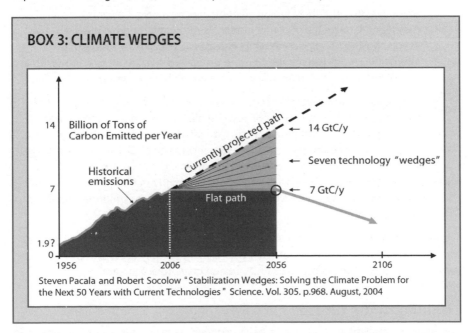

BOX 3: CLIMATE WEDGES

Steven Pacala and Robert Socolow "Stabilization Wedges: Solving the Climate Problem for the Next 50 Years with Current Technologies" Science. Vol. 305. p.968. August, 2004

Sokolow and Pacala choose the technology wedges from technologies that are available today. They conclude in their analysis that 'none of the options is a pipe dream or an unproven idea. Today, one can buy electricity from a wind turbine, PV array, gas turbine, or nuclear power plant…. Every one of these options is already implemented at an industrial scale and could be scaled up further over 50 years to provide at least one wedge.'[13]

To invest in and deploy these clean energy technologies, business needs clear signals, some degree of regulatory certainty and the right incentives to change business-as-usual practice. As Citigroup's Suozzo points out, 'there is sufficient activity at the current session of the US Congress, as well as at the state and local level, to warrant investor attention. A push-me-pull-you dynamic is at work: society and some politicians are 'pushing' for regulation, while business is 'pulling' for certainty and solutions.'[14]

There is extensive literature on the barriers to technology deployment and technology transfer. What is clear is that going to scale with technological solutions will require businesses to invest differently. Some businesses are taking steps now to build out capacity in new clean energy technologies:

- Getting in to the energy business: In 2005, Goldman Sachs began investing more significantly in renewable energy through acquisition of US wind developer Zilkha Renewables and through significant funding for solar photovoltaic company SunEdison. Goldman Sachs' press materials stated that 'wind and other renewable forms of energy will become an increasingly important part of the world's energy mix, and Goldman Sachs aspires to play a leading role in this high-growth industry'[15]

- Beyond fossil fuels: UK-based oil giant BP expanded its renewables commitment beyond BP Solar to a new 'BP Alternative Energy' business. Its solar business is expected to hit revenues of $1 billion in 2008 and BP Alternative Energy will manage a more diversified investment portfolio with a goal of growing to be an $8 billion business over the next ten years.[16]

- Changing the customer interface with environmental products: Retailer Wal-Mart in 2006 charted a new set of partnerships with supplier GE to channel the company's tremendous resources into offering cost-competitive compact fluorescent light bulbs that consume 75 per cent less electricity than traditional lightbulbs. Wal-Mart wants to double US sales for CFLs in a year, and grow it onward from there. If every US household swapped out for one CFL, enough power would be saved to avoid the need for two new conventional coal-fired power plants.[17]

These companies are acting now because technology investments, new business models and updated consumer outreach with climate-friendly choices in products and services can differentiate companies and provide marketplace advantages.

Looking to the future

The analyses of climate change and its consequences and assessments of what can be done to mitigate the most serious risks lead us to a compelling conclusion: action must begin now. The longer we wait, the steeper the curve is to reduce emissions and stabilize the climate. The urgency with which climate change needs to be addressed cannot be overstated. That the world is moving toward a carbon-constrained future is a certainty. Critics who say this will cost too much cannot argue that US economic growth has been constrained over the past 30 years since the oil crisis – a period in which the energy intensity of its economy decreased dramatically. The US now uses 47 per cent less energy per dollar of economic output. This type of efficiency gain must be accelerated even further.[18] Doing so requires price signals, support for innovation, and a long-term energy path that can harness the private sector's unique capability to provide technology innovation.

Forward-looking companies must recognize that climate change is not a quick 'fix-it' problem but rather will require long-term, sustained changes to business practices that are reflected throughout the entire value chain. Innovative companies are building momentum now and some clear hot topics for business engagement are emerging:

- **Energy efficiency** Most companies can be more energy efficient, which benefits the climate and makes financial sense too. Many companies have multiple avenues to slim and trim energy use – from lighting upgrades to installing energy-efficient windows and replacing office equipment with newer, more energy-efficient models. Some companies invest in energy audits to find where they use the most energy and determine where the largest savings opportunities are, and then make systematic changes throughout their facilities. All companies discover that energy efficiency investments save money over time.

- **Clean energy** Much of the world's energy is generated by burning fossil fuels – such as coal and natural gas – which creates carbon dioxide, the most common greenhouse gas. However, there are an increasing number of clean energy options for companies and many leading businesses are tapping into these power sources for a portion of their energy needs, including Kinko's, Johnson & Johnson, General Motors and IBM. In addition to reducing their emissions, these businesses are finding that a wider portfolio of energy sources can lower or stabilize energy costs, especially as oil and natural gas prices rise.

- **Transportation** Emissions from transportation are the fastest growing source of emissions in the world, so addressing fleet efficiency and transport is an important emissions reduction activity for many companies. Opportunities to improve the emissions profile of a corporate fleet include upgrading to the most fuel-efficient models possible, or ones that use alternative fuels. Switching to a less carbon-intensive mode such as train versus truck may be an option for companies that distribute products or raw materials. Ensuring that vehicles are fully loaded and take the shortest possible route can also save money and emissions.

- For some companies, business travel makes up a significant portion of greenhouse gas emissions. This is especially true for companies that have employees traveling by air, which is often the most emissions-intensive mode of transportation. Some companies are finding that by consolidating business trips and taking advantage of communications technology such as video- and web-conferencing, they can reduce emissions and have happier, better-rested employees.

- **Green buildings** Incorporating the right components into the design of a new building or retrofit of an older one can accrue many climate benefits too. From building location to materials use, from the boilers in the basement to the plants on the roof, there are many opportunities for facilities to become climate-friendly. Some companies reach for high environmental standards for their buildings such as through the Leadership in Energy and Environmental Design (LEED) program administered by the US Green Building Council.

Corporate opportunities for operational effectiveness are universal to all companies, regardless of sector, product or consumer interface. Taking on advanced technologies and designing for a carbon-constrained future now can chart a path to reduce environmental and economic risks. But to help solve the problem, business must recognize its central role in engaging society on a shared vision of the future. Luckily, leaders across sectors are looking to each other to build a bridge to a safe climate, sound business future.

* The authors drew material for this chapter from various other published works they have authored or co-authored. The following publications were used significantly:

- *A Climate of Innovation: Northeast Business Action to Reduce Greenhouse Gases*, A. Aulisi, J. Layke and S. Putt del Pino, World Resources Institute, 2004.

- *Hot Climate, Cool Commerce: A Service Sector Guide to Greenhouse Gas Management*, S. Putt del Pino, R. Levinson and J. Larsen, World Resources Institute, 2006.

Notes

1   'Ecomagination Evolution: How GE's Inventory Supported the Foundation of an Innovative Business Strategy', Case study A in Putt del Pino S., Levinson R. and Larsen J. *Hot Climate, Cool Commerce: A Service Sector Guide to Greenhouse Gas Management*, World Resources Institute, 2006.
2   '"Staples" Experience with Third-Party Billing: An Activity Data Management Success', Case study G in ibid.
3   'Executing a Large Corporate Purchase of RECs: Johnson & Johnson's Experience', Case study 5 in Aulisi A., Layke J. and Putt del Pino S. *A Climate of Innovation: Northeast Business Action to Reduce Greenhouse Gases*, World Resources Institute, 2004.
4   http://www.climatenortheast.org/pdfs/2006-WRI-CNE-CS-JandJ1.pdf World Resources Institute, Climate Northeast Case Study, 'Heat and Power from Landfill Gas, Johnson & Johnson's Experience', 2006.
5   http://www.climatenortheast.org/pdfs/2006-WRI-CNE-CS-Staples1.pdf World Resources Institute, Climate Northeast Case Study, 'Lightening the Load: Reducing Costs and Emissions While Maintaining Performance at Staples', 2006.
6   'Including Emissions That Matter: Ikea and DHL Express Nordic Count Their Core Business

Scope 3 Emissions', Case study B in Putt del Pino S., Levinson R. and Larsen J. *Hot Climate, Cool Commerce: A Service Sector Guide to Greenhouse Gas Management*, World Resources Institute, 2006.

7   Story L. 'The Hidden Life of Paper and Its Impact on the Environment', *The New York Times*, 25 October 2006.

8   'Marks & Spencer: Pursuing Innovative Emission Reductions Throughout the Value Chain', Case study K in Putt del Pino S., Levinson R. and Larsen J. *Hot Climate, Cool Commerce: A Service Sector Guide to Greenhouse Gas Management*, World Resources Institute, 2006.

9   The 'Carbon Value Analysis Tool (CVAT)' can be downloaded from http://www. climatenortheast.org/Business_tools.php

10   Citigroup Investment Research and WRI's Capital Markets Research Team, *Investing in Solutions to Climate Change*, 2006.

11   http://www.socialfunds.com/news/article.cgi/2033.html, accessed 26 October 2006.

12   http://www.princeton.edu/~cmi/resources/CMI_Resources_new_files/Wedges%20ppr% 20in%20Science.pdf Pacala S. and Socolow R. 'Stabilization Wedges: Solving the Climate Problem for the Next 50 Years with Current Technologies', *Science*, Vol.305, August 2004, p.968–971.

13   Ibid. p. 971

14   http://www.socialfunds.com/news/article.cgi/2033.html, accessed 26 October 2006.

15   http://www.horizonwind.com/news/articles/2005march21-2.aspx, accessed 30 October 2006.

16   http://www.bp.com/genericarticle.do?categoryId=2012968&contentId=7012352 , accessed 30 October 2006.

17   http://www.fastcompany.com/magazine/108/open_lightbulbs.html, accessed 31 October 2006.

18   Amory L. 'More Profits with Less Carbon', *Scientific American*, September 2005, p. 74. Also: http://www.sciam.com/media/pdf/Lovinsforweb.pdf, accessed on 30 October 2006.

13
Integrating Climate Change into Mission-Based Business Strategy

Tauni Brooker, URS Corporation

Introduction

Climate change is quickly becoming a point of conversation in even the most unconventional arena. Discussions are no longer the domain of the hallowed halls of academia but are instead capturing the attention of world business leaders, filmmakers and the wider public. There is, however, still controversy; what does climate change mean? Is it just an urban myth, or is what we are seeing tangible and irrefutable evidence that proves that the human race is fundamentally changing the face of the planet?

This chapter will not explore the science behind climate change, but will simply assume that climate change is here and that the behaviour of humankind has had a hand in creating a deteriorating situation. Following this assumption the chapter will focus on the role companies can play in reducing greenhouse gas (GHG) emissions and will examine changing corporate behaviour towards the issue of climate change. Indeed, aligning climate change strategy to stated company mission and value statements will ensure credibility and allow a higher possibility of success in attaining valuable climate change impacts.

Ideal behaviour, in corporate terms, is outlined in the mission and value statements of a company. These statements, when setting out the strategy of a company, can be incredibly specific and play a vital role in shaping the company for the future. How then, should a company's climate change strategy fit into these mission and value statements? Should it actually fit into the statements at all? In this chapter two cases will be presented, based on current evolution in the business environment where changing company behaviour is crucial to positively impacting climate change.

Before exploring the link between mission and value statements and climate change strategy, a short explanation of mission-based strategy and how it is to be understood in this context is needed. This will be followed with an exploration of the way in which climate change issues alter the various expectations of companies as they come to terms with their behaviour, and the growth of external pressures as regards climate change. This chapter will also investigate the way in which climate change can impact fixed cost, revenue and business bottlenecks. Finally, two mini-cases will be offered, both based on real companies as they struggle to take climate change into account when doing business. How can changing company behaviour be achieved? Essentially, the focus here is on implementing what is called 'mission-based business strategy'.

What is mission-based business strategy?

Before looking more closely at climate change, we explore what mission-based business strategy is, in this context. Corporations typically set aside time and effort to develop a business strategy that is both forward looking and dynamic. This business strategy dictates how a company will respond to traditional areas of concern – such as marketplace risk or changing market conditions – and clearly indicates how dynamically a company can anticipate external pressures. In addition to the business plan, which is effectively the company's 'route map', clear mission and specific value statements are integral to underpinning the business strategy. It is assumed that the corporation has taken the time and effort needed to complete an internal process, achieving well groomed and discussed value and mission statements. Once the internal refining has been done, it is assumed that the corporation is clear in communicating these statements to a broader audience. Both the mission and value statements should be used in concert to help drive a successful business strategy.

It is generally understood that the mission statement highlights the current goals and targets of a company, and the process required in order to achieve these goals. The vision statement, on the other hand, is more forward-looking and characterizes the type of organization it wishes to become. Of course, the mission should be based on the vision, and should clearly state how current goals can only be achieved through adherence to the company's values.

Figure 1: Mission and value statements underpinning mission-based strategy
Source: Bloomberg, Wikipedia and author's own

Business Strategy
Key strategies a firm intends to pursue
in carrying out its business plan

Mission Based Strategy
Action plan for achieving business goals based on corporate mission and value statements – strategy based on the guiding principles when ethical issues related to realizing the Vision, and undertaking the Mission

Mission Statement
Clear and succinct representation of the company's broader purpose for existence – incorporating goals and targets

Value Statement
Describes in graphic terms where the company want to see themselves in the future

As illustrated, this is a hierarchical process; greater value will be achieved when a company's mission statement is aligned with its business strategy. This solves a couple of distinct problems. One is the issue of perception; if the mission statement is simply seen as 'nice to have' then it is not credible, as it is not related to the strategies it intends to pursue in carrying out its business. This leads to the perception of unreliability. The second issue is that of employee motivation, which, if allied to a well-crafted mission statement, leads to a higher level of productivity.

Real and sustained company value creation and value maintenance will ensure high shareholder value and implies an effective and clear corporate strategy. A comprehensive corporate strategy should, by its very nature, include climate change strategy. The needs and expectations of funders and investors take precedent when company shareholder value is measured – via market capitalization.

Other stakeholders, both internal and external, are important, but a company needs to understand how investors see climate change in order to provide the impetus to integrate climate change strategy into their overall strategy. This alignment secures credibility and illustrates that climate change is not only a cost, but in fact an integrated element of the risk management profile of a company.

Figure 2: Value proposition – addressing climate change and creating true value
Source: Author's own

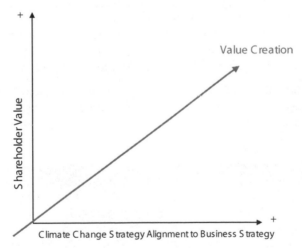

The other side of the equation is that mismanagement of climate change, especially if it is seen as an 'add on' to normal business practices, can be seen as a value destroyer. To ensure that value is maintained, climate change strategy must be fully integrated into a company's business strategy.

Climate change and expectations on companies

The UK Department for Environment Food and Rural Affairs (Defra) has defined climate change as being the greatest environmental challenge facing the world today. Rising global temperatures will bring changes in weather patterns, rising sea levels and increased frequency and intensity of extreme weather events. The effects will be felt globally but most especially by people in geographic regions that are particularly vulnerable to the effects of climate change; these people may experience severe problems. Companies, by their very nature and global extent, have a great opportunity to change behaviour, raise awareness of climate change and positively impact the communities in which they operate.

At this point it is necessary to examine the various levels of discussions that companies need for support and encouragement. Companies participate in the climate change debate at both the local and global level. Locally, discussions will typically be with non-governmental organizations (NGOs), suppliers and the supply stream and will focus upon locally caused and controllable emissions. The physical impact of climate change, through weather events, underwrites the global discourse. These physical impacts, while less controllable by any individual company, may have a significant impact on fixed costs as physical assets are damaged and insurers raise premiums. The direct and indirect impacts on a company will be discussed in the next section.

The expectations of companies come from many areas including: funders and investors, external stakeholders (such as environmental and other NGOs etc.), communities, employees and regulators. The expectations of these groups may not find common ground, and in some cases may work against each other. Nonetheless, the stronger (or louder) the group, the greater influence it is likely to have on a company.

It may be useful at this point to highlight some general 'push and pull' effects that some companies have encountered. Each group has an expectation of a company in terms of climate change strategy and management. The effects are both local and global in scope.

Group	Push	Pull	Expectation
Funders/ Investors	Clear company disclosure on all material risks.	Funding requirements imposed on the company – impacts the cost of capital. Impact of climate change management on reputation.	Effective management of all company risk – maintain growth and ensure revenue streams
External pressure groups	Public naming and shaming	Positive engagement with groups – proactive dialogue	Credibility of the company 'walking the talk'– showing tangible steps to change behaviour

Group	Push	Pull	Expectation
Communities	License to operate – especially in areas of unique natural beauty or heavy industry manufacturing	Proactive dialogue with community members	Align with 'think globally act locally' mantra
Employees	Access to an environmentally savvy workforce	Productivity linking to motivation of workforce	Illustrating credible, public and tangible evidence of the company working toward its missions.
Regulators	Setting down regulation	Participation in lobbying arrangements and active governmental engagement	Compliance is expected

This list sets out in general terms the pressures on a company from various groups. The objective is to give a sample of the broad issues and actions that would facilitate 'pushing and pulling' the company to look more intently at climate change and its effect on overall business.

Expectations on companies are increasing. New company disclosure rules from financial regulators and from external stakeholders are forging a new environment where companies are expected to discuss all risks, both financial and those outside traditional non-financial risks. Current expectations focus on demonstrating tangible, credible and publicly available evidence that its climate change strategy is truly embedded its mission statement. In some companies, stated appropriate climate change targets have become an integral part of the mission and value statements. How then, do these statements help the company achieve its financial targets?

Climate change impacts on business

There is a debate underway in the business world about the *direct* and *indirect* greenhouse gas (GHG) emissions of businesses. The World Business Council for Sustainable Development (WBCSD) and the World Resources Institute (WRI) have defined direct GHG emissions as coming from sources owned, or controlled by a company, while indirect GHG emissions are a consequence of the activities of a company, but occur at sources owned or controlled by another company.[1] The classification of direct and indirect emission is dependent on the consolidation approach (equity share or control) selected for setting the organizational boundary.

In this chapter direct emissions are understood to be those emitted by manufacturing, or those gases emitted in the normal course of doing business; in principle, they should be controllable. For heavy industry, direct emissions are more significant than indirect, whereas for service industries – such as banking or insurance – indirect emission can far exceed direct emissions. Both types of companies are explored in the following case studies.

The strong causality between climate change and catastrophic weather events has been widely explored in the media and in scientific circles. The changes in rain and wind patterns, rising sea and temperature levels, have all been firmly placed on the wide screen of climate change. This section will explore some of direct climate change impacts on business, including weather events and rising sea and temperature levels. The focus will be on the triple concerns of cost reduction; secure revenue stream and the avoidance of bottlenecks. For the purposes of illustration, it is more relevant to use heavy industry as an example.

Production (revenue impact)

Catastrophic weather events can have a material impact on production. Major disruption of production caused by weather events may require significant capital expenditure to return to normal levels of production, if production machinery is damaged. As temperatures rise, heat awareness training will become more widespread; indeed a prolonged increase in temperatures will have an immediate impact on revenue due to business interruption or slowdown in employee productivity for health reasons (not to mention higher energy usage for cooling). In the case of a company whose main manufacturing site is found in a flood plain or avalanche area, if one or both of these events occur, then disruption of production can occur resulting in a serious impact on revenue.

Yet there is an opportunity, based on product design changes, to cater for the demands of a harsher weather environment due to climate change, or to design stronger products that can withstand the effects of climate change. Development of new products can increase revenue through first mover advantage. As the environment changes, so must the design and manufacture of products to reflect the new circumstances that we face.

Funders and investors are very keen to determine how a company ensures continuation of revenue. This is factored into growth models and plays a significant role in the cost of capital. Although the company cannot be held responsible for the general effects of climate change, it will be expected to have planned for such contingencies and to be able to adequately address them, especially if a disruption in production and direct impacts on revenue can be traced back to climate change effects.

Insurance (cost reduction)

Insurance is a necessary fixed cost for a company, but that is not to say that companies cannot manage their material business risks as to have a mitigating impact on premium levels. If climate change is seen as a material business risk to the company, and insurance is needed to insure against high impact events, then a company that clearly indicates to insurers that they are managing climate change risk at an acceptable level, therefore lowering their business risk profile, may see the level of their premiums reflected accordingly.

Insurance is used to cover fixed assets. Increased storm intensity, changing rain and wind patterns and flooding are all becoming more probable, along with higher claims for damage to fixed stock. This will drive insurance premiums up. As temperatures increase due to climate change, in some areas of the world there is also an increase in the risks of diseases, which in turn raises the cost of employee heath care. This cost has to be borne, in some measure, by employers.

There could also be significant costs involved in either re-tooling damaged assets, or designing new production equipment that could better withstand some of the more extreme weather events.

The cost of insurance for companies that manufacture in flood plains is rising to reflect the increasing number of claims made for fixed assets. Insurance matrices are used to calculate insurance premiums. These are based on risk factors that must be made by the insured, to guarantee protection of property under an insurance policy. These well-defined matrices are savvy in taking climate change issues into account, especially in instances of catastrophic weather events, and they are determining (higher) premiums.

Directors and Officers' (D&O) insurance is also rising, as directors and officers are seen as personally liable for any material risks that have not been communicated effectively via normal company disclosure routes. Climate change risks are material for some industries and therefore must be disclosed on all levels.

Changing rain patterns will also shape food production. As droughts occur more often it becomes more difficult to source foodstuffs both for food production and public consumption. Workers themselves may suffer from a lack of nutrition and as a result may end up taking more time off sick. This has a knock-on effect on the company's productivity and may also mean sourcing from supply chains further away, thus increasing the production of GHGs via transport.

Intermediate goods/ procurement (bottleneck)

Procurement bottlenecks are the most challenging company concern because of the inability of companies to truly control the supply of components and intermediate goods (i.e. those which go into the assembling and manufacturing process). This can lead to serious bottlenecks, especially in industries such as automotive and consumer electronic goods, that have typically moved to a 'just in time' schedule of procurement.

Severe weather events impact the procurement of components and intermediate goods, for example a ship blown off course by a hurricane or another extreme weather event could seriously hinder the delivery of products.

Climate change also poses an opportunity on the procurement side, as companies look for local suppliers of components and intermediate goods. There may be a direct positive impact on employment, education and infrastructure in those areas. In addition, when climate change policy is rigorously applied to the supply chain, more environmentally savvy suppliers may emerge who demonstrate lower energy use and higher environmental awareness.

Case examples

The link between the mission statement and climate change can be overt, that is the mission and value statements directly include climate change. Conversely, the link can be covert. Some companies, for instance, have chosen to 'go carbon neutral' – essentially emitting no carbon, offsetting current emissions, or working to achieve GHG reduction – in such a way that GHG reduction is an implied corporate goal without it having to be publicly stated.

The link between a mission based business strategy and a climate change strategy is founded on emissions and managing business strategy with an understanding of how and where climate change may fit. If a company is in an industry where emissions are unavoidable, a clear, concise climate change strategy and implementation plan must fit with the overall business strategy. Ideally, it should fit into the strategy in such a way that it is a driver for the business, not seen as a cost. Transparent implementation is imperative for addressing key concerns with local communities and garnering credibility with NGOs (at the local level). Globally, a comprehensive climate change strategy implies management of the issue at a very senior level, offering a strong signal to investors and insurers alike that risks are being adequately addressed and managed.

Figure 3: Climate change boundaries and the company
Source: Author's own

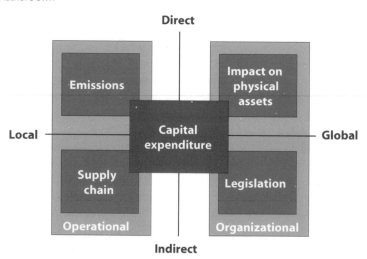

There are examples of companies who have adequately addressed the crucial issue of combining climate change strategy and business strategy – effectively offering an intriguing illustration of how companies are taking environmental risks forward and getting local, divisional and group-level support. The crucial element is doing a 360° in-depth look at the company and its extensive operations, requiring high level buy-in on the climate change strategy and gathering full knowledge on how such a strategy will impact the business at operational, organizational, production and capital levels.

Figure 3 illustrates the boundary issues a company faces when doing a full-scale evaluation of climate change, and the subsequent impact on its business strategy. These impacts could be felt at a local or global level with direct (such as emissions and impact on physical assets) and indirect components (such as the supply chain and legislation).

For example, climate change impacts on the organizational level of the company may manifest themselves, in a direct manner, on the physical assets of the company. Climate change, if fuelling larger and stronger hurricanes, such as the ones that battered the Gulf Coast last year and took out a portion of the oil platforms in the Gulf, will directly impact on the physical assets of companies.

Below are two different companies who have chosen to be publicly accountable on the subject of climate change and what they plan to do about it. These cases are purely illustrative in nature, revealing how two diverse companies are dealing with the issue of climate change. The mission and value statement indicates the path the company will be taking in fulfilling its climate change objectives. The mission statements below are a summary of the corporate statements; this has been done to ensure the anonymity of the specific corporation.

Goods industry

This first case focuses on a multi-national company manufacturing in the extractive sector. The manufacture and procurement of raw materials occurs in areas of high natural beauty and has a significant impact on surrounding communities – both economically and environmentally. The headquarters of the company is located in one of the highly developed countries of the world, but the majority of the extractive sites are found in developing countries.

Location	Areas of high natural beauty
Mission statement	Grow a diversified portfolio of products with transparent and co-operative community partnerships
Climate change issues:	• Rising temperatures • Climate change regulation • Climate variability • Increase in disease • Greenhouse gas emissions & stakeholder concerns around emissions • Energy usage

Location	Areas of high natural beauty
360° look at the company: resulting issues to address	Employee and health care costs Logistics and transportation Pensions Acquisitions Property management Procurement/ Supply chain Recycling Energy procurement and use
Current projects – mitigating some business issues.	This company has focused its attentions on direct greenhouse gas emissions. Some of the projects this company has established to help fight climate change are: • Methane capture • Energy use via clean coal technology • Energy efficiency campaigns • Supporting of R&D into zero emission technologies • Land sequestration, storage of CO_2 in the land, marine or plant organisms. • Clean development mechanisms, via the Kyoto protocols.

Outcome: as a result of the 360° look, the company focused on a number of key projects to directly address as part of their mission based strategy. Climate change is attributed in the direct assessment and measurement of emissions. The climate change strategy loosely links into the mission statement as the company strives toward transparent and co-operative community partnerships.

In this case the tailored climate change strategy has a locality-based approach. The company looks for better and more efficient ways of reducing emissions and their subsequent impact on local communities.

Service industry

This second case concentrates on a financial sector player. Most of the direct climate change impacts are marginal in comparison to the indirect impacts due to services this company supplies. The property portfolio, both owned and managed, is extensive and integral to the management of the carbon footprint of the company.

Location	Urban areas: high number of branches within high density population areas
Mission statement	Integrity, fair, quality and accountability
Climate change issues:	• Greenhouse gas emissions • Climate change regulation • Traditional energy usage • Investment in renewable energy and carbon banking • Adapted risk matrix taking climate change into account.
360° look at the company: resulting issues to address	Transportation Pensions Acquisitions Property management Procurement/ Supply chain Recycling Energy procurement and use
Current projects – alleviating some business issues.	This company has both direct and indirect greenhouse gas emissions. This company has taken steps to lower the carbon footprint by exploring a mix of direct and indirect carbon reduction projects some are: • Recycling and waste management • High performance buildings • Effective transportation of staff, car-pooling and hybrid (dual fuel) vehicles • Energy use via renewable energy and purchase of renewable energy certificates • Energy efficiency campaigns • Supporting of R&D into zero emission technologies • Investment on carbon neutral projects to offset direct emissions

Outcome: as a result of the 360° look, the company focused on a number of key projects which directly addressed a part of their mission statement. This company is vastly different from the previous case in so far as climate change has both direct and indirect impacts; therefore, climate change strategy must cover both boundaries to be effective.

The strategy followed in this case is one of carbon reduction via energy efficiency and investment in carbon offsets. Because of the nature of this service company, an international strategy for climate change is the most appropriate.

The learning from these two cases is that a clear climate change strategy is specific to each company, irrespective of the sector. In both instances the companies have been highly public in their efforts to focus on climate change, and have woven that commitment in to the value statements of each company. By using the value and mission statement as the corporate road map, it became clear which type of climate change strategy was appropriate for each company. Principally, it was the mission and value statements that drove the climate change strategy for each disparate company.

Concluding comments

Based on our research there are some key tips on climate change strategy implementation:

- Value creation and maintenance can be achieved through clear integration of climate change strategy in business strategy.

- Be aware of international guidelines and standards on climate change but define replicable and credible targets tailored for your company.

- Use corporate strengths and skills to benefit impacted local communities.

- Focus on the strategic and tactical opportunities that climate change presents;

    1. Rigorous application of climate change missions and values in design and manufacturing.

    2. Develop new products that anticipate the changing environment.

    3. Accountable supply chain policy; align the policy with the climate change strategy to harvest maximum impact.

Notes

1   WBCSD and WRI, *The Greenhouse Gas Protocol – A corporate accounting and reporting standard* (revised edition), 2004, p.30.

Implementation Strategies

14

The Carbon-Positive Company

Antony Turner, Peter Martin and Fraser Durham,
CarbonSense

Climate change is increasingly being seen as the result of our own actions as human beings. Furthermore, environmental changes that were expected to take decades are turning out to be faster and more abrupt. In the UK and many other countries, discussions no longer centre on whether climate change is actually happening, but focus on what to do about it. Similarly, the emphasis of communications about climate change is moving from interpretation of scientific findings and forecasts to seeking solutions and encouraging action.

Can we do anything about climate change?

At CarbonSense we now normally present only one science-based story, using findings from ice-cores taken at Vostok in the Antarctic (Fig. 1). This shows an undeniable link between the temperature of the planet and levels of carbon dioxide in the atmosphere. By comparing the current concentration of carbon dioxide (CO_2) with historic levels, it becomes clear that we are changing the atmosphere of the only living planet we know to exist, to a potentially irreversible degree.

Climate change is multi-dimensional and necessitates action from many different angles. Importantly, most governments do actually acknowledge that the problem exists, and are starting to suggest that solutions will need to be behavioural as well as technical.

Many eminent figures today are suggesting that we have the technologies available to rapidly decarbonise society. What we have not had sufficiently is the political will to make both structural and behavioural changes; nor have we developed sufficient incentives to encourage everyone to become engaged.

The conventional response of campaigning NGOs to the need for behavioural change is to exhort governments to set tough carbon reduction targets, demand that business cleans up and citizens, everyday people like you and me, 'do their bit' by turning down the thermostat, changing light bulbs, and driving and flying less. Whilst all these actions may help, they do not take account of critical aspects of the problem.

Fig. 1: Carbon dioxide and temperature
Source: Petit et al, Nature, 1999

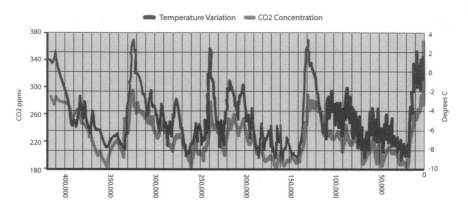

Over twenty years ago, French and Russian scientists in Antarctica drilled into the frozen ice at Vostok in the Antarctic to investigate the gases trapped there. Their analysis revealed an undeniable correlation between the levels of CO_2 and atmospheric temperature (see Fig.1). Their data, which spanned back at least 400,000 years (although new data now takes this relationship back almost further) showed CO_2 in the atmosphere to range between approximately 200 and 300 parts per million (ppm) by volume.

Today, CO_2 levels have risen to over 380ppm, with a growing scientific consensus that this concentration could continue to increase to over 500ppm. An increase in atmospheric levels of CO_2 of this scale and magnitude are unprecedented for at least a million years. The Vostok ice cores show that we are potentially tipping our atmosphere into a position that could initiate severe temperature changes.

Carbon economics

The economic model we have employed for the last two hundred years does not suit the world we now live in. Six and a half billion people and rapid industrialisation have stretched our ecosystems to a level that is unprecedented. We have a choice a little like the captain of the ill-fated Titanic ocean liner – we can continue the party, confident in our invincibility, or we can listen to the warnings and attempt to change course. For twenty years there has been talk of 'sustainable development' but only very limited action. Now we need significant action, for unless development is genuinely sustainable, the human story on this small planet will end. Carbon needs to become an integral part of economic decisions.

Invisibility

Another key aspect of climate change is that it is invisible. When we walk into a room devoid of people and furniture we typically say that it is 'empty'. Yet it is anything but 'empty'. The room is full of air – the amazing mix of gases that allows life to exist. The room is literally full to the brim with the very essence of life.

In many parts of the industrial world we have reduced and cleaned up the effects of local, visible pollution but we continue to produce greenhouse gases (GHGs) without recognising how much we are throwing into the atmosphere.

For an individual, company or government, a realisation of the extent and cause of the problem is necessary. This tends to only come about when we can actually *see* the result of our actions and our effects on the atmosphere, or their consequences. Therefore, in effect we need to make carbon dioxide visible.

In order to help create this visibility, and influence the behavioural decisions of society, we must now work towards developing carbon literacy and numeracy as a necessary basis from which to engage everyone in developing responses to the climate problem.

Carbon literacy

Following ratification of the Kyoto Protocol, carbon-literate solutions have begun to be developed. Market forces are being utilised to deliver reductions in carbon dioxide and other GHG emissions over defined periods. However, these markets are not showing the quick and overarching solutions to the climate problem that some people expected. Globally, major emitting countries are still deliberating as to whether they should be involved in the Kyoto mechanism, while systems such as the Clean Development Mechanism (CDM), and the Joint Implementation scheme (JI) have grown slowly due to limited resources, bureaucracy, over allocation, inadequate scale and other early-stage development issues.

Kyoto led to the definition of initial reduction targets. In Europe, these have then been passed on as specific target reductions for 'large emitter' industries. However, in order to create an accurate economic value for carbon dioxide and other GHGs, the system has to widen quite rapidly to incorporate other sectors. The theory is that if you have only a certain allocation of carbon dioxide 'emission rights' available then the more companies chasing that allocation, the greater the drive to find technologies that allow for carbon alternatives. These 'cap-and-trade' systems have been shown to work well for the regulated reduction of other pollutants such as sulphuric oxide (re acid rain) and nitric oxide (road transport pollutant).

It is important to remember that these market-based initiatives are the result of government-implemented regulation. Without this, it is fair to assume that they would not have existed at all. So, before lambasting the governments with calls for more action, it is worth noting that they have made a start. However, as with most things, governments should not be relied upon to produce the answers to society's problems. They can only be part of the solution. Long-term change can be sustained only through organic shifts in society's actions. As John F Kennedy famously said: 'Ask not what your country can do for you, but what you can do for your country.' We, as individuals and businesses, need to understand our part in driving forward proactive initiatives to combat climate change, rather than the easier short-term option of wait and blame. We must develop our own carbon literacy, pushing the boundaries of our positive influence throughout society.

The 'carbon-illiterate' diagram (Fig. 2) illustrates how society has failed to make progress. However, this vicious circle can be altered by pushing change through at any point.

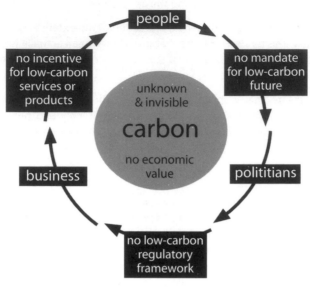

Fig 2: Carbon-illiterate society
Source: CarbonSense

Two problems lie at the core of the problem – carbon dioxide's invisibility, and its lack of economic value. In a carbon-illiterate society each part of the chain is disempowered to provide solutions.

Individuals do not push governments to provide a framework to generate a solution. As a result regulation is not forthcoming, and companies have no incentive to provide the solution. This is starting to change as the Kyoto Protocol, and the markets that have come as a result (EU ETS), start to account for the economic cost of producing carbon dioxide – generating pressure for increased regulation. However, this is still limited in scope and open to the flaws of any system in its infancy.

Somehow this vicious circle must be undone, forcing positive change throughout.

The carbon journey and business

When carbon becomes a visible part of decision making, modes of consumption and production can be transformed. This is what we refer to as the 'carbon journey' (Fig. 3).

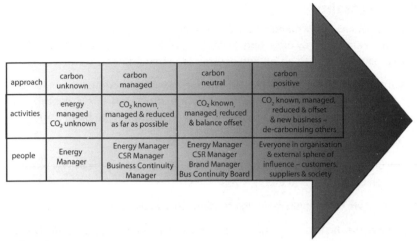

approach	carbon unknown	carbon managed	carbon neutral	carbon positive
activities	energy managed CO₂ unknown	CO₂ known, managed & reduced as far as possible	CO₂ known, managed, reduced & balance offset	CO₂ known, managed, reduced & offset & new business – de-carbonising others
people	Energy Manager	Energy Manager CSR Manager Business Continuity Manager	Energy Manager CSR Manager Brand Manager Bus Continuity Board	Everyone in organisation & external sphere of influence – customers, suppliers & society

Fig. 3: The carbon journey
Source: CarbonSense

It relates to the transition of an individual, business, or society from a point where carbon dioxide (and other GHGs) is unknown and invisible, through to a point where actions are informed through visibility and value.

The Carbon Disclosure Project (CDP) has pushed large companies around the world to wake up to the scale of the problem and embark on their own carbon journeys. This has been encouraged by the co-operation of asset managers, whose capital (US$31trillion of assets under management in 2005) and inherent vote can influence the actions of most companies. Companies are both investigating their carbon profiles, and developing strategies to tackle the problem. Almost one thousand of the world's largest companies have responded, reporting information to the CDP and this momentum will undoubtedly continue.

For companies, understanding is the first stage in the carbon journey. This means they need to move to a point where carbon dioxide emissions are fully understood and accounted for.

Adhering to the basic formulations of the Green House Gas (GHG) Protocol allows companies to meet the minimum level of emissions reporting, yet this is clearly not enough. Climate change is not simply about understanding your GHG emissions exposure, but about trying to provide long-term sustainable solutions and reducing emissions.

Once emissions have been properly accounted for, the next step is to develop abatement or reduction strategies. This should be the starting point for any climate change strategy, and can create quite substantial financial benefits. In the UK, the Carbon Trust estimates that simply 'implementing no- and low-cost [abatement] measures can result in a 20 per cent reduction in energy use and can have the same effect on profitability as a five per cent increase in sales.'

Carbon neutrality

Once all abatement opportunities have been achieved, it is possible to compensate for the remaining emissions by offsetting. Recently several major companies such as HSBC and BSkyB have decided to go 'carbon neutral' or 'climate neutral' by offsetting.

In 2004, John Bond, the chairman of HSBC announced that the company would become carbon neutral within eighteen months, although their own direct contribution to climate change was relatively small. HSBC described its strategy in three stages:

- firstly we manage and reduce our direct emissions, then

- secondly we reduce the carbon intensity of the electricity we use by buying 'green electricity', and then

- thirdly, we offset the remaining emissions to achieve carbon neutrality.

Simply being the first in a sector to move to a carbon-neutral position can bring rewards. In London, Radio Taxis decided to go 'carbon neutral' by investing in offsets, and has reported additional business worth £1.5m as a consequence of using this as a differentiating factor.

The concept of carbon neutrality is fairly straightforward in theory, but in practice the details are complex and in some respects highly controversial. Paying to buy offsets creates uncertainty over the viability of investing in changes to achieve long-term carbon reductions. It could also be construed as 'green wash' in the case of any company announcing its carbon neutrality through the simple purchase of carbon offsets, without any internal carbon abatement policy or in-depth action to reduce its carbon profile through proper business efficiencies, process changes etc.

Offset projects are themselves contentious for many reasons. For example, under the CDM they require 'additionality' – in other words it is necessary to demonstrate that the projects would not have happened but for funding through this regulated route. This reliance on hypothetical futures is open to question. At present, it is also possible, for example, for a project which involves cutting down rainforest and planting oil palms for biofuel to qualify as an offset project under the CDM. Many offset projects involve planting trees. Although in theory the risks of the impact of changing climate, forest fires and so on can be factored in, their overall effectiveness in absorbing and retaining carbon cannot be guaranteed. In addition, many such projects have imposed changes on the livelihoods of indigenous people which have proved to be highly controversial.

Regulated or voluntary offsetting schemes can have a place in a carbon reduction strategy. However, it is clear to us that they are best employed as a means of compensating for emissions only after all possible reductions and efficiencies have been achieved, rather than in the rush to make a claim of neutrality for marketing purposes, as is commonly the case at present. If a carbon strategy ends with such a transaction, then the carbon journey, in our opinion, is certainly only partially complete.

Furthermore, as environmentalists, customers and the general public become more carbon literate, and the media questions those who have used only 'chequebook environmentalism' there are potentially severe risks to brand and reputation. Members of the public will question whether they are being carbon neutral when they watch Sky television or withdraw cash from an HSBC cash point. They will recognise that these activities do cause carbon emissions and continue to contribute to climate change every day. So while these companies may be applauded for taking positive action to compensate for the damaging impact of their activities, they risk being accused of using the term 'carbon neutral' to give the public a misleading impression.

Serious players are questioning the validity of claims of carbon neutrality achieved by offsetting and it is by no means certain that the term will retain any respect in the marketplace over time. The problem is serious, and companies need to be serious about their approach to climate change solutions.

This is where the step to being carbon positive develops importance.

The carbon-positive company

We define a 'carbon-positive' company as one which is fully engaged in driving the growth of the low-carbon economy. It will shape its own business model, and its products and services to reduce CO_2 emissions. It will promote technologies, behaviours, and structural change which support quality of life with low CO_2 emissions. A carbon-positive business will also use its influence to help positively transform society to a low-carbon economy (Fig. 4). We believe that businesses have the potential to play a major role in the climate solution.

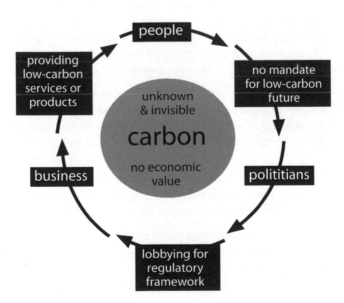

Fig. 4: Carbon-literate society and business leadership
Source: CarbonSense

Businesses have the ability to positively influence society at all levels. Low-carbon products and services are an imperative that *can* be driven through by proactive companies. Businesses can also influence governments to provide the necessary regulatory frameworks to help to make provision of low-carbon products and services viable and sustainable.

For a business to focus purely on its own operations when initiating a climate change strategy is not enough. Businesses touch society in so many ways. Employees, their families, the supply chain, sub-contactors, and, of course, customers and the products and services that they use, can all be influenced by business.

In 2006, BSkyB announced it would make its own operations carbon neutral. The company's own direct carbon emissions are relatively small, so offsetting these will not be costly. CEO James Murdoch announced that they are to introduce set-top boxes that do not offer the 'standby' facility. This will save emissions arising from customers' use of the company's product, as a set-top box on standby typically uses almost a third of the energy it uses when switched on. The company is also encouraging employees to take steps towards lower-carbon living with incentives for leasing hybrid cars and a range of other low-carbon options. Environmental coverage is also being increased on Sky News, raising public awareness and encouraging climate debate. For BSkyB, doing these things makes business sense in a world where the reduction of carbon emissions will become more critical.

Examples of the proactive engagement of stakeholders can also come from those companies whose very existence relies upon carbon-intensive activities. BP has incorporated climate change into its marketing and is offering customers opportunities to participate in positive actions. For example, customers can compensate for the emissions they cause by driving, by offsetting through BP's 'Target Neutral' campaign. This engagement of motorists in the issue can be seen as a positive step.

HSBC have now developed their thinking beyond their initial purchasing of offsets. 'As a bank we are able to deploy capital and help develop projects,' says Francis Sullivan, HSBC's environmental policy adviser. 'If you are looking for serious additionality, that's the way forward – trying to decarbonise our customers as well as ourselves.'

Opportunities

As we move towards a low-carbon economy, any company providing clear information and guidance, and demonstrating a commitment to solutions could stand to gain.

Customers are becoming actively engaged in the climate change issue and are starting to look for those companies that can provide low-carbon solutions that do not entail simply writing a cheque to offset.

As an example, the telecoms industry is one area where opportunities may exist to positively influence society, whilst at the same time bringing in new business. As carbon becomes valued in the economy, rises in the cost of travel will increase the potential value of ICT applications which can replace travel, such as video telephony.

Board engagement

The decision to initiate a carbon-positive strategy has to be made at board level. The vision of a low-carbon business must be translated into the business model – driving change throughout all decision-making processes.

Organisations making this company-wide decision may also achieve greater employee benefits. There is an abundance of research to show higher staff retention, increased productivity, creativity and team working occurs in organisations that care for the community and environment.

Key steps

So how does a company become carbon positive? We suggest that there are five key steps to take in order to move towards this goal:

1. Count carbon

- count and report carbon in a complete, transparent and public way

2. Manage decarbonisation

- engage senior management to ensure decarbonisation is managed as an integral part of running the business
- implement operational strategies to mitigate as much as is practicable
- engage employees to ensure a wide ownership of objectives and consistent actions
- consider compensating for carbon emissions by offsetting

3. Update business models

- integrate low carbon objectives into business strategy

4. Engage stakeholders

- decarbonise the supply chain
- support employee personal actions
- actively engage with government, trade bodies etc

5. Aim for low carbon leadership

Conclusion

Leading companies are becoming more proactive on climate change and starting to demonstrate aspects of a stance we have termed 'carbon positive'. This aims beyond any notions of carbon neutrality and offsetting towards deeper and more fundamental decarbonising strategies.

The costs to companies that are slow to embark on the carbon journey are likely to become greater over time but as the need for deeper action on climate change becomes more urgent, there are likely to be greater opportunities for companies that have taken the proactive step to become carbon positive.

References

BP – see for example, Carbon 100 report by Trucost for Henderson Investors: www.trucost.com

BSkyB press release 18 May 2006: www.younggloballeaders.org

CarbonSense, *What would a genuinely carbon neutral BT look like?* May 2006.

HSBC – see carbon neutrality pilot project:
www.hsbc.com/hsbc/csr/environment/hsbc-and-climate-change/carbon-neutrality

Petit at al., *Nature* (Journal), 1999.

Trucost, *Carbon Management and Carbon Neutrality*, 2006.

15

The Growing Voluntary Market for Carbon: Emerging Strategies[1]

Ricardo Bayon, Amanda Hawn and
Katherine Hamilton, Ecosystem Marketplace

The Ecosystem Marketplace

Ever since US President George W. Bush categorically refused to sign onto the Kyoto Protocol on global warming, there has been a simmering debate on what is the best way to tackle this contentious problem. While this debate has many different facets one of the most interesting is the whole question of whether reductions in emissions of greenhouse gases (GHG) should be voluntary or mandatory.

In this debate there are those who argue that reductions need to be mandatory in order to truly address the problem. On the other side of the fence are those who say that businesses and individuals will voluntarily take the steps necessary to reduce their GHG emissions if given the chance.

As is so often the case in these kinds of dichotomies (false dichotomies as it turns out), both sides are partly right and partly wrong. On the partly right side, critics of voluntary action are correct in saying that emissions reductions can only reach a scale necessary to address the massive problem we face if and when the government decides to implement laws designed to reduce emissions. These critics, however, have underestimated the potential of voluntary action. The advocates of voluntary action, on the other hand, are partly right in saying that there is an important role for voluntary initiatives in our struggle to address climate change. Voluntary action, however, will not be enough to deal with the problem. Solving the climate change problem will in fact require both government regulation and voluntary action.

In Europe, for example, the European Union's Emission Trading Scheme (ETS) is by far the world's largest regulated carbon market. The ETS has already transacted billions of dollars in carbon credits and this is likely to lead to tremendous reductions in GHGs, though this fact has yet to be adequately documented. Similarly, the regulated market for certified emission reductions, approved through the Clean Development Mechanism (CDM) of the Kyoto Protocol, is currently robust. Together these regulated markets traded some US$11.3 billion in 2005, the first year the ETS was operational. For 2006 all indications are that these markets will possibly trade carbon credits worth two or three times this amount.

Creating a US$20 billion market is no mean feat. In fact it is an achievement that has captured the imagination and checkbooks of more private sector investors than any other environmental effort to date. Thus we see it as a real source of hope when it comes to the global challenge of addressing climate change. Perhaps even more promising is the fact that alongside the regulated market, there is also a booming voluntary carbon market in Europe; a market where individuals and companies are choosing, voluntarily, to offset their emissions by investing in carbon sequestration or emission reduction projects.

Europe is not alone; voluntary carbon markets are sprouting up all over the world, from California to Canberra and back again. Even in countries where legislated reductions are not taking place – countries that are currently beyond the reach of the Kyoto Protocol –voluntary markets have begun to gain traction in the public eye.

Is this just a fluke? A blip in time that will usher voluntary markets off the global stage just as quickly as they arose? At the Ecosystem Marketplace we have been looking into this question for some time now and we think that, at the very least, voluntary carbon markets have an important role to play in advancing policy and educating the public on climate change across the next decade. Indeed, many of the experts we have interviewed think voluntary carbon markets have the capacity to grow to levels that will make them interesting to the capital markets for years to come.

To date, no one has put forward a truly comprehensive study concerning the size and value of the voluntary carbon market, but a conservative estimate would probably place the current market value at US$50–$100 million. Even as a notional figure, the idea that this number might quadruple over the next several years is intriguing. If the number of businesses employing the voluntary carbon market as a branding and/or risk management tool continues to increase at its current rate, then the voluntary carbon market may indeed be poised for growth.

Before we explore this hypothesis in depth it is useful to review how carbon markets work and why they are important to climate change:

BOX 1: PG&E ENTERS THE CARBON MARKET

In January 2006, PG&E (Pacific Gas and Electric, the largest investor-owned utility in the US) announced a groundbreaking programme that would help its customers become 'climate neutral'. This programme – the Climate Protection Tariff (CPT) programme – would collect small premiums from enrolled customers and then invest the funds collected in carbon offset projects. The resulting greenhouse gas (GHG) reductions would negate the customers' emissions, thereby rendering them climate neutral. 'It is an interesting programme. We think it's the first of its kind anywhere, in the United States anyway' says Wendy Pulling, Director of Environmental Policy at PG&E. She continues, 'We'll give you your footprint, and we'll offer you the value proposition of being climate neutral.'

The CPT programme is straightforward. Interested customers can voluntarily enrol in the programme. After enrolling, they will be charged a tariff on their monthly electricity and natural gas usage. This tariff – $0.00254 per kilowatt-hour for electricity and $0.0653 per therm of natural gas – would result in an increase of approximately 3% (or US$4.31) for the average residential customer per month. PG&E is making two promises to enrolled customers: 100% of their tariff payments will go towards GHG reduction projects; and the GHG reductions purchased will neutralise their electricity and natural gas consumption.

PG&E is proposing a three-year demonstration period – 2007 through 2009 – for the programme. Structuring it as a demonstration gives PG&E the flexibility to expand or change the programme as necessary, and also recognises the changing nature of the climate change policy environment. 'This is a pilot programme,' says Pulling, 'We're not going into this assuming that we know everything...a lot of folks are learning an awful lot [about combating climate change], and...one of the goals of this programme is to create a forum in which more learning can take place.'

Based on a survey of various US green power programmes and some preliminary market research with PG&E customers, PG&E hopes to enrol 4–5% of its customers in the CPT programme over the course of the demonstration period. 'That number, 4–5%, is our goal. We think it's an ambitious but do-able target to have. We really wanted to set ourselves an ambitious target because putting the effort into this, and trying to maximise the opportunity to learn and make a difference here, we didn't think that 1% enrolling... was really worth doing, and we wanted to make this something really worth doing.' says Pulling.

(Excerpted from the Ecosystem Marketplace story 'The Unusual Suspect' by Charis Anderson, www.ecosystemmarketplace.com)

Market theory

The impetus behind global carbon markets (both voluntary and regulated) is simple: in order to deal with the growing problem of GHG emissions we need a system that provides the right incentives for GHG reductions and increases the uptake of new emissions-reduction technologies. Enter the global carbon market.

The theory is that carbon markets are able to achieve both these outcomes because they punish (monetarily) those who emit more than an established quota, and reward (again, monetarily) those who emit less. In so doing they encourage people to emit less and change the economics of energy technologies, making technologies that emit less carbon more competitive vis-à-vis their carbon-intensive counterparts.

There is other benefit at work as well. By turning units of pollution into units of property the system makes it possible to exchange pollution from Cape Town with pollution from Cape Cod. If business managers find reducing their company's emissions too costly they can buy excess reductions from a facility where reductions are less expensive. The bigger the market, the theory goes, the greater the likelihood that efficiencies will be found.

Finally, by aggregating information about the value of carbon allowances, the market is sending signals to potential polluters. In today's European emissions market, for instance, emitting one ton of CO_2 has in the past cost polluters anywhere from €6 to over €30. In a world where pollution has no price, the default decision will always be to pollute. In a world where pollution costs between €6 and €30, the decision is no longer quite so easy. Polluters must suddenly consider a new suite of options: do they accept the cost of added pollution, change fuel mixes, or simply conserve energy?

The market-based approach also allows other third-party players, such as speculators, to enter the fray. By agreeing to take on market risks in exchange for possible paybacks, speculators assume the risks that others are either unwilling or unable to shoulder. Other interested parties can also get involved. If, for example, an environmental group wants to see emissions decrease below a regulated target, they can raise money to buy and retire emissions allowances. This drives up the cost of emissions and can force utilities to become more efficient.

It is, of course, important to note that some people dispute the net gain of such benefits, and others feel that markets allow companies to 'green wash' previously tarnished environmental reputations without changing their behaviour in important ways.

This debate notwithstanding, experimentation with environmental markets is now widespread. Ever since the US established the first large-scale environmental market (to regulate emissions of gases that lead to acid rain), we have seen environmental markets emerging to trade in everything from wetlands to woodpeckers.

BOX 2: A SKI RESORT GOES CLIMATE NEUTRAL

In addition to being the highest altitude ski resort in the US, Arapahoe Basin in Colorado is also among the first to offers its customers a chance to fight one of the biggest threats to the ski industry as a whole: climate change. In addition to educating skiers about the threats to snowfall and snowpack caused by rising concentrations of greenhouse gases (GHG) in the atmosphere, management offered them the chance to sign up to offset their GHG emissions. In essence, they offered them the chance to take as many tonnes of GHGs out of the air as they had put in by driving to the resort nearly 70 miles west of Denver.

'Most consumers don't know what offsets are so, of course, our partners are tasked with educating consumers about global warming and efforts to offset,' explains Sid Embree, president of Massachusetts-based AtmosClear Climate Club, the offset provider allied with Arapahoe Basin. 'Skiers are a very obvious group. They are concerned about weather and climate, but also most skiers tend to have extra cash.'

Thus far, the club has only about 500 members, according to Embree, but as public awareness grows, so will business. In exchange for this membership, the Arapahoe skiers got assorted 'swag' – bumper stickers, magnets, a membership card and other fringe benefits – and, more importantly, the serial number to one offset, in this case a ton of carbon dioxide equivalent (CO_2e) for methane emissions flared, or burned off, before reaching the atmosphere at a small landfill roughly 30 miles west of Chicago.

'In a way we're structured more like a rewards programme,' Embree says. 'We use partnerships with retailers of different kinds to present to individuals and families a chance to reduce their overall contribution of greenhouse gases.'

AtmosClear is unique in being the only GHG offset provider structured like a rewards programme but it is certainly not unique in being a GHG offset provider. The number of such providers has in fact gone from one to at least five in the US alone in just the past few years (see the Ecosystem Marketplace article *Speaking for the Trees: Voluntary Markets Help Expand the Reach of Climate Efforts*). In the absence of government regulation, such offset providers present one of the few ways for concerned US consumers to make a difference to global warming.

(Excerpted from the Ecosystem Marketplace article 'A Drive to Offset Emissions' by David Biello, www.ecosystemmarketplace.com)

Carbon markets

The term *carbon market* refers to the buying and selling of emissions permits that have been either distributed by a regulatory body or generated by GHG emission reductions projects. Six GHGs are generally included in carbon markets: carbon dioxide (CO_2), methane, nitrous oxide, sulphur hexafluoride, hydro fluorocarbons and perfluorocarbons.

GHG emission reductions are traded in *carbon credits*, which represent the reduction of GHGs equal to one metric ton of CO_2 (tCO_2e), the most common GHG. A group of scientists associated with the Intergovernmental Panel on Climate Change (IPCC) has determined the global warming potential (GWP) of each gas in terms of its equivalent in tonnes of CO_2 (i.e. tCO_2e) over the course of 100 years. For example, methane has a GWP roughly 23 times higher than CO_2, hence one ton of methane equals about 23 tCO_2e. Likewise, other gases have different equivalences in terms of tCO_2e, some of them (perfluorocarbons for example) are worth thousands of tonnes of CO_2e.

GHG emissions reduction credits can be accrued through two different types of transactions. In *project-based transactions*, emissions credits are the result of a specific carbon offset project. *Allowance-based transactions* involve the trading of issued allowances created and allocated by regulators under a cap-and-trade regime. In regulated cap-and-trade markets the regulatory authority caps the quantity of emissions that participants are permitted to emit and issues a number of tradable allowance units equal to the cap. Participants who reduce their emissions internally, beyond required levels, can sell unused allowances to other participants at whatever price the market will bear.

Carbon markets can be separated into two major categories: the compliance (or regulatory) and voluntary markets. Because the voluntary market inherently does not operate under a universal cap all carbon credits purchased in the voluntary market are project-based transactions. (The exception here is the Chicago Climate Exchange (CCX) which is a sort of hybrid system where companies voluntarily agree to set caps on themselves. Once they've agreed, however, they are bound by contracts to meet these reductions. As a result the CCX trades versions of both project-based emissions credits, as well as allowance credits.)

BOX 3: THE CHICAGO CLIMATE EXCHANGE: A HYBRID MARKET

Richard Sandor recounts with glee the fifth-graders from Glens Falls, NY, who decided to combat lung disease by buying and retiring sulphur dioxide allowances on the Chicago Board of Trade (CBoT). 'The kids raised the money to buy the allowances by launching their own 'cap-and-trade' market for chewing gum allowances,' he recalls. 'When twelve-year olds proved their savvy at emissions trading, I knew no CEO or congressman could ever say they didn't get it.'

What's more, those kids executed their trade ten years ago, when more evolved minds were still battling to keep emissions trading out of the Kyoto Protocol, an international agreement that assigns mandatory targets for emissions reductions to industrialised countries.

While emissions trading eventually found its way into the Protocol, the United States did not. And so by 2002 Sandor was tapping into his personal savings and hitting up friends to get the Chicago Climate Exchange (CCX) off the ground as a platform for trading voluntary emission reductions.

Though perceived as a libertarian experiment to test the ability of market forces to drive down emissions without government intervention, CCX was, in fact, first conceived to provide the market-based mechanism for implementing government policy as North America's central platform for trading greenhouse gas (GHG) emissions under a nationwide mandatory cap-and-trade regime.

Instead, its website boasts its existence as 'North America's only voluntary, legally binding rules-based greenhouse gas emission reduction and trading system.' The exchange restricts trading to members who have voluntarily signed up to its mandatory reductions policy. During the pilot phase (2003–2006) members agreed to reduce GHG emissions 1% a year from a baseline determined by their average emissions during 1998 to 2001. The current goal (Phase II) is for members to reduce their total emissions by 6% below the baseline by 2010.

Like the carbon market in general, CCX trades six different types of GHGs converted to tCO_2e. The majority of the credits are allowance-based, created by member companies internally reducing their emissions. Since its launch in late 2003, CCX's membership has grown from 19 institutions to over 131. Ford Motor, International Paper, IBM, American Electric Power, the City of Chicago, the City of Portland, the City of Oakland, the State of New Mexico, the World Resources Institute and the Rocky Mountain Institute are just a few of its wide range of members from the business, governmental and philanthropic sectors.

CCX traded 1.45 million tCO_2e in 2005 for a total value of US$2.7 million, and trading prices spiked in the first quarter of 2006 when – according to sources – a US Senator speculated that the US might someday adopt CCX as its de-facto carbon trading scheme.

In 2005, CCX created the European Carbon Exchange (ECX), a joint venture with the International Petroleum Exchange (IPE, today ICE Futures) and currently the largest exchange trading carbon credits on the EU Emission Trading Scheme (see Creating a 'Wall Street' for Carbon). This year, CCX has announced a flurry of new exchanges and joint ventures around the globe.

(Excerpted from the Ecosystem Marketplace's story 'Richard Sandor: Maker of Markets' by Steve Zwick, www.ecosystemmarketplace.com)

Voluntary carbon market

Voluntary carbon markets are nothing new; in fact, they pre-date all regulated carbon markets. The world's first carbon offset deal was brokered in 1989 (long before the Kyoto Protocol was signed, let alone ratified), when AES Corp., an American electricity company, invested in an agro-forestry project in Guatemala.[2]

Since trees use and store carbon as they grow (an example of carbon sequestration), AES reasoned it could offset the GHGs it emitted during electricity production by paying farmers in Guatemala to plant 50 million pine and eucalyptus trees on their land.[3] AES, like other companies since, hoped to reduce its 'carbon footprint' for philanthropic and marketing reasons, not because it was forced to do so by legislation or global treaty. The deal was thus voluntary, marking the beginning of a voluntary carbon market that remains as controversial and interesting today as it was in 1989.

Unlike the regulated market, the voluntary market does not rely on legally mandated reduction standards or consistent tracking. As a result it suffers from fragmentation and a lack of widely available impartial information. The fragmented and opaque nature of the voluntary market can, in large part, be attributed to the fact that it is partially composed of deals that are negotiated on a case-by-case basis, and that many of these deals neither require the carbon credits to undergo a uniform certification or verification process, nor register them with any central body. As a result, there are as many types of carbon transactions on the voluntary market as there are buyers and sellers and a variety of businesses and non-profits based on different models sell a range of products, certified to a wide array of standards.[4]

The lack of uniformity, transparency and registration in the voluntary market has won it a great deal of criticism from some environmentalists, who claim that it is a game of smoke and mirrors rather than an engine of actual environmental progress. Many buyers also say they are wary of the voluntary carbon market since transactions often carry real risks of non-delivery. Some companies buying carbon credits also fear that they will be criticised by NGOs if the carbon they are buying isn't seen to meet the highest possible standards.

BOX 4: EXAMPLES OF CARBON SEQUESTRATION FORESTRY PROJECTS: FROM MEXICO TO UGANDA

In Mexico, the Scolel Té project has allowed companies, individuals and institutions to offset their greenhouse gas (GHG) emissions through purchasing emissions reductions from agricultural and forestry projects in Chiapas, Mexico's poorest state. The International Federation of Automobiles, for example, purchases credits from a Mexican trust fund called Fondo BioClimático, which provides small-scale farmers with the technical assistance needed to switch from swidden ('slash and burn') agriculture to agroforestry. Projects include tree-based 'living' fences, shade-grown coffee plantations, tree-enriched barren areas and intercropping of forestry and agricultural crops. The carbon benefits generated by these enterprises are expected to range from a minimum of 55,000 tonnes of CO_2 (15,000 t C) up to 1.21 million t CO_2 (330,000 t C). In addition, the plantings contribute to the preservation of the region's rich biodiversity and provide income to farmers to cover the costs of implementing new farming systems, purchasing foods and medicines, and improving households.

In Uganda, farmers in the village Bitereko have entered into a contract with ECOTRUST, a Ugandan NGO, to sell the rights to the carbon sequestration generated by planting native species of trees on their land. Beatrice Ahimisbwe is one of those farmers. She agreed to clear and plant a hectare of her land with native species of trees. In return experts determined she would generate 57 tonnes of carbon sequestered over ten years (assuming the trees survived) and would be paid US$8 per ton, for a possible total of US$416 over 25 years.

Ahimbisibwe's carbon is being sold in Europe, most of it purchased by global packaging company Tetra Pak. Indeed, Tetra Pak UK is the largest single buyer of Ugandan carbon. Every year they buy around 8,000 tonnes from the Ugandan project to offset their emissions.

'In essence,' explains Samantha Edgar, Environment Officer for Tetra Pak UK, 'we like the idea of investing in growing trees because it links back to our everyday business of producing packaging which is largely tree-based...[We] see our offsetting program as a way of pre-empting [compliance with] climate change regulations that will likely affect us more and more in the future. We also see this as a way of strengthening our ability to dialogue with our stakeholders, and to motivate and communicate with our staff... The carbon projects are very important and fit in quite nicely with our company's overall environmental policy.'

Since Tetra Pak began working with Edinburgh Centre for Carbon Management (ECCM) to develop a carbon management programme in 2003, the company has created a computer-based carbon monitoring system that allows them to better gauge their carbon footprint on a yearly basis. By 2004, Tetra Pak UK had managed to reduce their carbon emissions by 13% as compared to their 2001 levels, and their target for 2005 has been to raise the reduction to 15% below 2001 levels. These reductions, however, don't include offsets that, according to Edgar, are used to compensate for unavoidable emissions, thus making the company 'carbon neutral'. In 2004, Tetra Pak UK's carbon footprint was just over 11,780 tonnes, so this is the amount they are buying. To date, 80% of Tetra Pak UK's offsets come from the Uganda projects –including Beatrice's carbon – while the remaining 20% comes from biomass and solar energy projects in India and Sri Lanka.

Tetra Pak UK (the only division of Tetra Pak currently offsetting at these levels), says Edgar, is very happy with their investment in the Uganda project. 'Our carbon management programme [projects], including the offsets in Uganda, have been great stories and recently helped us win the overall Wales environmental award,' she explains. 'So yes, we are quite pleased with this programme.'

(For more information see Ecosystem Marketplace articles.)

Of concern to environmentalists and buyers alike, is the fact that the voluntary carbon market's lack of regulation may mean it cannot reach the scale necessary to impact the problem. Because It lacks a regulatory drIver, demand for credIts can be volatIle and fickle.

The sudden explosion of the Kyoto carbon market in 2005 shows the difference that regulation can make. Clearly, regulation is key to driving large-scale demand. 'The voluntary credit market could grow by an order of magnitude or two orders of magnitude and it's still not going to impact the problem,' explains Mark Trexler, president of Trexler Climate & Energy Services.

Despite the shortcomings of the voluntary market, many feel it is a fast-evolving arena with some distinct and important advantages over the regulated carbon market. For example, while the wide range of products emerging from the voluntary market can be confusing to potential buyers, these products can also be highly innovative and flexible. Numerous suppliers say they benefit from this flexibility and the lower transaction costs associated with it.

For example, Emily Tyler of the Group 'South-South-North' in South Africa, which recently sold carbon offset credits into the regulated carbon market (the CDM), estimates that had her group sold the same credits into the voluntary markets, her revenues may have been lower, but her costs would also have been lower still and her group might have netted some €25,000 as opposed to potential losses of €10,000 or, at the very best, net revenues of €1,000 or less.

Numerous observers have also noted that, for many projects, coming up with the start-up capital to register a project for the compliance carbon market is prohibitively difficult. The voluntary carbon markets, on the other hand, don't have these sorts of transaction costs. They can avoid 'bottlenecks' in the CDM methodology approval process and get carbon financing for methodologies that aren't currently 'approved' by the CDM process. For example, the Nature Conservancy is working towards obtaining carbon financing for forest protection projects (what in Kyoto parlance is referred to as 'avoided deforestation'), a concept not currently approved to produce carbon credits within CDM.

The innovation, flexibility and lower transaction costs of the voluntary market can benefit buyers and suppliers. When an organisation purchases carbon offsets to meet a public relations or branding need, creativity, speed, cost-effectiveness and the ability to support specific types of projects (e.g. those that also benefit local communities or biodiversity) can often be clear and valuable benefits.

Having weighed such pros and cons, many non-profit organisations are supportive of the voluntary carbon market because it provides individuals – not just corporations and large organisations – with a means of participating in the fight against climate change in a way that the compliance markets do not. And since individuals account for most of the GHG emissions, more than 50% by some counts,[5] some environmentalists view the voluntary carbon market as an important tool for educating the public about climate change and their potential role in addressing the problem.

Last but not least, some sellers and buyers of carbon credits prefer the voluntary carbon market precisely because it does not depend on regulation. As the international political community struggles to implement an effective climate-change framework, the voluntary carbon market has the potential to become an active driver of change today.

Some formality, please!

Be they fans or critics, experts agree that the voluntary carbon market is in a critical period right now. Spurred by the success of the regulated carbon markets, the voluntary market is formalising, as investors who cut their teeth on the regulated market look for other places to put their money, and as buyers and sellers consolidate around a few guiding practices and business models from which conclusions can be drawn about market direction and opportunities.

Although nobody has exact numbers on the size of the voluntary carbon market, most think it has grown rapidly in the last two years. Kenber of The Climate Group gives the following estimates of past and projected market size:

Table 1 Voluntary carbon market size[6]

Year	Estimated/Projected Market Volume (million tonnes/yr)
2004	3–5 million tonnes
2005	10–20 million tonnes
2006	20–50 million tonnes
2007	100 million tonnes

To put these numbers in perspective: Kenber's outside estimate that 20 million tonnes of carbon may have traded on the voluntary carbon market in 2005 is probably optimistic, and yet 20 million tonnes of carbon traded on the EU ETS in a single week in April 2006. Despite the comparatively small scale of the voluntary carbon market, it could well be poised for explosive growth and some companies see real business opportunities associated with the creation of carbon-neutral products for retail consumption. If these predictions are to be borne out, most market players think it will be necessary to generate liquidity, and therefore formalise and streamline the market.

At present there are various efforts underway to make the voluntary carbon market more 'investor-friendly' by creating registries, documenting the size of the market, and standardising the credits being sold. These include the standards described above, as well as new registries. In 2006 The Bank of New York, launched a global registrar and custody service to facilitate trading of voluntary carbon credits.[7]

Whatever one's take on the long term prospects of the voluntary carbon market it seems clear that, in the short term, the market is evolving quickly, creating new economic and environmental opportunities for investors, businesses, non-profits and individuals. It is therefore important to understand how this market operates.

A look at the supply chain

Institutions and individuals acquire offsets in a number of ways, but a simplified model of the voluntary carbon market's supply chain includes the following elements: a project or project idea is generated, the resulting emission reductions are verified to some standard to create carbon credits, the credits are sold to an intermediary (including carbon funds) and then the intermediary sells them on to businesses and individuals. Brokers and exchanges may assist in the distribution of offsets by facilitating transactions between buyers and sellers, but they usually do not buy or sell credits.

In some cases project developers may skip stage two and/or three of this sequence, selling either verified or unverified credits directly to consumers. The International Small Group and Tree Planting Alliance (TIST), for instance, has sold verified offsets generated by subsistence farmers in East Africa and India directly to individual consumers via a virtual 'store' on eBay.[8]

Who is 'buying' these credits? In general, carbon credits are consumed in order to offset one of four types of emissions:

Internal emissions: Companies, non-profit organisations or government agencies may purchase carbon credits in order to offset the emissions generated by their facilities and employees in the course of doing business, such as emissions from travel, energy use, manufacturing etc. These emissions are often referred to as direct emissions or internal emissions, and this type of deal probably accounted for most of the carbon credits purchased on the voluntary carbon market last year.

> **Example**: HSBC purchased carbon offsets in order to neutralise its group-wide emissions for the last quarter of 2005. To offset the total emissions amount (approx. 170,000 tonnes of carbon dioxide), HSBC has bought 170,000 tonnes of carbon offset credits from four offset projects around the world: the Te Apiti wind farm in North Island, New Zealand; an organic waste composting project in Victoria, Australia; the Sandbeiendorf agricultural methane capture project in Sandbeiendorf, Germany; and the Vensa Biotek biomass co-generation project in Andhra Pradesh, India. 'A large-scale collective effort is going to be needed to address climate change. Governments must play their part, and help the public to make informed decisions,' says Francis Sullivan, HSBC's advisor on the environment. 'Banks should also do their bit.'[9]

Product life cycle emissions: Companies may also want to offset the emissions generated by the use of their products (known as their indirect or external emissions). In other words, they may be buying credits in order to develop carbon-neutral products for their customers. Such products generally carry a price-premium and are marketed as carbon neutral in much the same way that organically produced food products are marketed as environmentally sound. Theoretically, companies could purchase offsets in order to offset their external emissions as a matter of corporate social responsibility without claiming that their products are 'carbon neutral', but this is less likely.

Example: *BP has launched a carbon-neutral fuel product in Australia. As part of its Global Choice programme, BP offers its commercial customers the opportunity to offset some of their GHG emissions, either by paying more for an Ultimate grade gasoline that comes with a company promise to offset the emissions generated by its use, or by partnering to purchase offsets outright. BP has already neutralised more than 800,000 metric tonnes of GHG emissions from its Ultimate grade gasoline customers. 'We do it because we fundamentally believe that we need to tackle climate change, whether it be from our own operations or customers using our products,' says Kerryn Schrank, business advisor for future fuels at BP. 'Offsets are going to be important for the transport sector for the next 20 years or so, until we can get cleaner transport options.'*[10]

Event emissions: In recent years, steering committees for high-profile events have elected to make events carbon neutral through the purchase of large numbers of carbon credits. As credits become more readily available and certification programmes gain more trust in the coming years, offsetting event emissions may become common practice for many political, athletic and social events.

Example: *FIFA offset the 2006 World Cup through a voluntary 100,000 tonne carbon offset programme called the Green Goal Initiative. Although official figures are a closely guarded secret, the budget for carbon neutrality is estimated at one million euros, which comes to an average price of ten euros per ton of carbon offset.*[11]

Individual emissions: In contrast to the first three types of carbon credit purchases, which involve an institutional buyer purchasing large numbers of credits, the last kind of deal involves individual consumers purchasing carbon credits in order to offset their daily activities and/or travel plans. While this side of the market is small at the moment, many social sector organisations consider it the most important type of transaction, since it allows individuals to take action against climate change, thus increasing public awareness of the market.

Example: *Cyd Gorman calculates the emissions from her commute to and from work using a carbon calculator and then pays Terrapass – a business that buys carbon credits and renewable energy certificates on the voluntary market and then sells them on to individual consumers – to offset them for her. 'Think of it as Kyoto for commuters,' says Dan Neil of the Los Angeles Times.*[12]

Why are companies entering this market?

In general, corporations cite five reasons for participating in the voluntary market:

- Experience and clout as a way to influence future regulatory requirements and policy setting, preparation for potential regulatory requirements

- Competitive differentiation as consumers become increasingly concerned about climate change, including being able to offer products that are 'carbon neutral' (perhaps for price premiums that generate a net profit for the companies retailing the products in question)

- Inclusion in company-wide corporate social responsibility or sustainability strategies

- Better access to capital by helping attract investment and secure project finance

- Ability to recruit, retain and reward staff because of corporate responsibility.

Where is the market heading?

Some investors think that as regulation comes online in the US and more sectors are included in the EU ETS, voluntary carbon credits will see a jump in value not unlike that experienced by CDM credits once the Kyoto Protocol went into effect.

To wit, Climate Wedge Ltd started the world's first voluntary carbon offset fund in July 2005. The Cheyne Climate Wedge Fund invests in high-quality offsets for carbon dioxide emissions for large-scale corporate and institutional buyers. 'Our view of the world is that the use of voluntary carbon offsets is going to grow dramatically,' says Michael Molitor, the Fund's CEO. His reasoning, 'it's the only thing we can do to slow down the growth in emissions over the next two decades'.[13]

For the most part the drivers of the voluntary carbon market look set to grow in the coming years, but it should be remembered that the market is far from mainstream at this point and uncertainty abounds. Fortunately registries, standards and exchanges are evolving to help streamline the voluntary carbon market and consolidate market information as potential buyers push for increased transparency. It should become easier then, for buyers and sellers to grasp both the risks and the opportunities associated with this dynamic market in the coming years.

Voluntary carbon: the future, or a pipe dream?

Fifty years ago, the idea that markets would one day be used to protect the environment was little more than science fiction. Thirty years ago, a prediction that markets would one day help control acid rain would have been seen as fanciful. And five years ago, the thought that a European GHG market would one day be worth US$8.2 billion would have been considered ridiculous. And yet, all of this has come to pass. Yesterday's fiction is today's fact.

And so it may be with voluntary carbon markets. Today the thought that there could, one day, be a large and thriving voluntary market in GHGs – a market where buyers and sellers operate without the threat of regulation – is easily dismissed. And yet, under most people's radar screens, voluntary carbon markets are growing and thriving. As German philosopher Arthur Schopenhauer (1788–1860) once said, 'All truth passes through three stages: first, it is ridiculed; second, it is violently opposed; and third, it is accepted as self-evident.'

Even if the voluntary carbon market does not mature into a truly robust market, it will remain a source of innovation, inspiration, and education. The market will also continue to serve as an interesting barometer of public opinion for businesses weighing options for branding and risk management.

Notes

1   Parts of this chapter are excerpted from *Voluntary Carbon Markets: An International Business Guide to What they are and How they work* by Ricardo Bayon, Amanda Hawn, and Katherine Hamilton (Earthscan, 2006).

2   Hawn A. 'Horses for courses – Voluntary vs. CDM carbon projects in Mexico', The Ecosystem Marketplace, 2005. www.ecosystemmarketplace.com

3   Ibid.

4   The Ecosystem Marketplace has recently begun studying the voluntary carbon market and hopes to publish an annual 'State of the Voluntary Carbon Markets' report beginning in 2007.

5   Biello D. 'A drive to offset emissions', The Ecosystem Marketplace, 2006. www.ecosystemmarketplace.com/

6   Mark Kenber's presentation at 'Green T Forum: Raising the Bar for Voluntary Environmental Credit Markets', New York, 2–3 May 2006.

7   Bank of New York Company, 'The Bank of New York creates global registrar and custody service for voluntary carbon units', Business Wire Inc., 2006.

8   Hawn A. 'eBay Shoppers and Subsistence Farmers Meet on Virtual Ground, The Ecosystem Marketplace', 2005. www.ecosystemmarketplace.com/

9   The Climate Group, *Carbon Down, Profits Up 2nd Edition*, *Environmental Finance*, London, Fulton Publishing, pp.26–27; HSBC, 'HSBC carbon neutral pilot project', downloaded from HSBC website, 2005.

10 Biello D. 'Climate friendly fuels', The Ecosystem Marketplace, 2005. www.ecosystemmarketplace.com/

11 Zwick S. 'Green Goal: Soccer Enters the Carbon Markets', The Ecosystem Marketplace, 2006. www.ecosystemmarketplace.com; www.myclimate.org

12 Neil D. 'TerraPass eases drivers' minds', *Los Angeles Times*, 2 February 2005.

13 Walker C. 'The Voluntary Carbon Markets Difference Maker: Michael Molitor', The Ecosystem Marketplace, 2006. www.ecosystemmarketplace.com

16

Co-operative Strategies for Ecological Sustainability – Environmental Results or Competitive Advantage[1]

Art Kleiner, strategy+business

When companies come together to save the world, what is more compelling – environmental results or competitive advantage?

During the past decade or so, people have increasingly looked to the private sector for solutions to global environmental problems – and the private sector has grown increasingly interested in providing them. BP's CEO Lord John Browne, GE's CEO Jeffrey Immelt, and Nissan CEO Carlos Ghosn, among many other corporate chief executives, have gone on record naming ecological sustainability as a central component of their corporate strategies. For every CEO joining the bandwagon, there are seemingly hundreds, perhaps thousands, of middle-level managers and engineers trying to implement solutions on the ground.

Which naturally raises the question: What kind of effect does the current wave of corporate environmentalism have – both on business culture and on the environment? A particularly passionate consortium known as the Materials Pooling project provides a living answer to that question. Their stumbling but persistent progress demonstrates exactly how difficult the environmental challenge will be for most of the corporate world.

Some members of the consortium are household name companies: Nike, Ford, BP, Unilever, Harley-Davidson, Hewlett-Packard. Others are specialized, innovative manufacturers with an environmental identity: Aveda (a division of Estée Lauder dedicated to ecological cosmetics) and Plug Power (a pioneering fuel cell company). The consortium also includes Sikorsky (a helicopter manufacturer), Pratt & Whitney (the jet engine division of United Technologies Corporation), and about 20 component and commodity suppliers at various times, of which the largest and most consistently present is Visteon, a former division of Ford. They come together under the joint auspices of the Rocky Mountain Institute (or RMI, a well known think tank led by energy-efficiency and 'hypercar' expert Amory Lovins) and the Society for Organizational Learning (or SoL, an international group focused on organizational learning practice, founded by *Fifth Discipline* author Peter Senge).

Materials pooling for environmental ends

Materials pooling is supply chain management across corporate–customer boundaries – in this case, for environmental ends. In its simplest form, manufacturers pool their purchasing power to favour raw materials that are freer of toxins and waste, and easier to recycle or reuse; this gives suppliers more of an incentive to provide such materials. But that collaboration inevitably means sharing information, articulating definitions of such evanescent concepts as 'toxins' and 'waste,' and ultimately opening the door to new inter-company relationships. Hence the attraction of such projects: the managers involved in the RMI/SoL Materials Pooling project are enthusiastic, innovative, and capable, and their story is inspirational – but it is also sobering.

Once, companies thought it would be hard to build partnerships with environmental groups. In fact, that proved to be easy: DuPont and McDonald's have maintained close working relationships with the Environmental Defense Fund (now called Environmental Defense) for almost 20 years. The truly hard part turns out to be forging and maintaining relationships with other companies, especially competitors. In fact, there is a direct clash between the collaboration needed for genuine environmental impact and the control over information that is needed to maintain a competitive advantage. The Materials Pooling project's slow start is a result of these warring imperatives, and thus has something to teach any executive who wonders why his or her company's environmental initiatives – or, indeed, any supply chain initiative – are failing to gain traction.

BOX 1: FROM CRADLE TO CRADLE: REMAKING THE WAY WE MAKE THINGS

The culture of both Rocky Mountain Institute and the Society for Organizational Learning originally helped to attract the man who instigated the Materials Pooling project, Michael Braungart.

A chemist and former Greenpeace activist, Mr Braungart is the co-author, with architect William McDonough, of an unusual and influential book called *Cradle to Cradle: Remaking the Way We Make Things* (North Point Press, 2002). The book points out that nearly every mass-produced product, from chair fabrics to children's toys to printer cartridges, contains trace elements of heavy metals and mutagenic materials. In aggregate, over time, these might well be hidden causes of cancer, infertility, and genetic damage (although it is admittedly difficult to know for certain).

By redesigning such products from scratch, Mr McDonough and Mr Braungart argue, industrial society could transcend mere pollution prevention to eliminate waste altogether and to 'generate nutritious effects on the environment.' Cars would produce not carbon dioxide gas, but carbon pellets, which could be sold to rubber manufacturers as raw materials; clothes could be made of edible fabric, recycled perhaps as animal feed. Nothing would be discarded; instead it would be broken down to its component materials and reused – hence the title, 'cradle to cradle'. To demonstrate how plausible this future could be, Mr McDonough and Mr Braungart produced their book on pages made from a resin-based material that contained no wood, emitted no toxins, and (unlike many materials) was infinitely recyclable; it could be reformed into pages, ground back into resin, and reformed again and again.

And yet, around the time *Cradle to Cradle* was published, Mr Braungart was heard to say at a Society for Organizational Learning event: 'We haven't had any luck in making this happen.' In other words, the industrial world was not leaping to change fast enough. He thought SoL's sustainability subgroup, led by two energetic management/environmental consultants named Sara Schley and Joe Laur, could help jump-start some progress with its corporate members. And indeed the idea proved popular with member companies, who felt their license to operate depended, more than ever before, on meeting and transcending environmental regulations.

Automakers, for example, faced a pending European Union rule called the **'End-of-Life Vehicle Directive,'** with such targets as 85 per cent automobile recyclability by weight by 2006, and 95 per cent by 2015. (Already, if you count scrap metal, 75 per cent of the material in most cars is recycled.) 'The directives had us thinking,' recalls Visteon's Matt Roman. 'If we were to take back and recycle our components whenever a car was scrapped, what would that framework look like?'

Pressure also came from increased liabilities and regulations concerning product toxicity. Consider, for example, hexavalent chromium, which is routinely used in engine parts and fasteners. It is inexpensive, it prevents corrosion, it resists wear, and it shines appealingly even when scratched. But when swallowed or inhaled, it is highly carcinogenic (the crime that triggers the lawsuit in Steven Soderbergh's film *Erin Brockovich* is carelessness with hexavalent chromium). New European regulations have outlawed its use in automobiles beginning in 2006, but other manufacturers recognize the public-affairs benefit and general moral benefit of reducing this material. At Harley-Davidson, Hugh Vallely, the director of motorcycle product planning, raised the point simply: 'If this material is so toxic, why are we using it?'

Cross-organisational relationships in supply chain management

In the last few years, supply chain management in general has moved away from an ethic of squeezing suppliers and pitting them against one another to a more co-operative ethic based on long-term relationships.[2] The materials pooling concept represents a similar move, a shift from fighting regulators separately to collaborating on solutions that regulators never thought of. There are pooling projects for automobile parts (uscars.com), consumer product containers (the Sustainable Packaging Coalition), cotton (the Organic Exchange), and environmentally benign lumber (the Forest Stewardship Council, known for certifying the wood carried in stores like Home Depot). But the RMI/SoL Materials Pooling project is unique: It operates across a variety of industries. Its members have thus learned to talk about highly technical subjects, like materials specifications, with a rare quality of freewheeling transparency.

By mid-2003, there were four active groups of companies in the Materials Pooling project, focusing respectively on replacing hexavalent chromium; sourcing lightweight corrugated cardboard; researching the environmental impact of different types of leather (as used in Nike shoes and Visteon seats); and managing polypropylene, a plastic resin often used in consumer packaging. There was a constant swirl of activity: weekly phone calls for each group and quarterly meetings of unusual enthusiasm. 'We were on the leading edge of a field that was just starting to take off,' says Aveda's vice president of package development, John Delfausse. 'Not only did we really want to be there, but light bulbs started turning on. We could do this.' They talked about rethinking product design in Braungartian fashion. They also found unexpected connections – Mr Delfausse, for example, recalls scoring a potential cache of recycled polypropylene, to be used in lipstick caps, from an electronics supplier who shipped disk drives in plastic racks. 'I've got tons of this stuff, and we would love to harvest it for you,' the supplier said.

Christina Page, the Rocky Mountain Institute project manager for the consortium, recalls the sheer excitement that came from talking informally. 'One of the auto industry suppliers said, "I get to talk to other car people all the time. Where else will I get the chance to work with people from Hewlett-Packard, Harley-Davidson, and Nike?" For a few great months, it seemed as if Michael Braungart's visionary future could become a reality; talk could reshape the world.'

Roadblocks to nirvana

Three years later, the effort is still under way, but momentum has slowed and goals have been scaled back. Nike, for instance, still participates in the broad materials pooling consortium, but its primary participant, project manager Vanessa Margolis, now focuses much of her effort on a separate leather tannery assessment initiative across the footwear industry – an initiative inspired, in part, by her experience in the materials pooling group. 'Braungart's conceptual idea of materials pooling led to a false set of expectations,' says Ms Margolis. 'In reality, when we step back and look at what we accomplished, it's good stuff. But we haven't achieved what the visionaries called nirvana.'

One fundamental roadblock, typical of many cross-organizational collaborations, was the differences among the companies themselves. This showed up most dramatically in the group working on hexavalent chromium. Pratt & Whitney and Sikorsky needed functionality; stainless steel was potentially acceptable. But Harley-Davidson needed beautiful, rust-resistant chrome for the kind of visible engine components that could endure exposure to a beach full of salt spray and emerge gleaming in the sun. If they could not keep hexavalent, they had to find another kind of chrome. And Ford was part of the USCar consortium, which announced a decision to switch to trivalent chromium, a material approved by European regulations. All these differences eroded the group's potential collective purchasing clout.

Sourcing incompatibilities

There were similar incompatibilities in sourcing leather – which must be very soft for automotive seats, hard for motorcycle seats and jackets, and waterproof for shoes. 'We were looking for an environmental attribute or preference that might be shared by the different leathers and production processes that we all sourced,' says Ms Margolis. 'But we never defined what this attribute or preference might be. It's the kind of design problem that probably nobody would choose on their own.'

Getting co-operation from suppliers was also unexpectedly difficult. Having agreed to canvass their suppliers for details about materials, many of the corporate members returned empty-handed. Some suppliers apparently suspected that this was just another tactic to squeeze down prices. Other suppliers had never kept track of their materials' environmental pedigree – the detailed history of its previous uses (if it was recycled), its contact with contaminants, or its exact chemical makeup. And then suppliers had their own constraints; John Delfausse's electronics supplier, for example, discovered that it did not have the contractual right to pass on the polypropylene to Aveda.

Another problem was the lack of formal sponsorship that participants had from their own companies. Materials engineers, in particular, had trouble getting their time and expenses authorized when many urgent needs demanded their attention at home. Harley's Hugh Vallely remembers a technical specialist from a Harley supplier complaining to him about research he'd requested: 'I'm doing this without a charge code.'

Sharing information with competitors – catch-22

Consortium members talked openly about all these issues, but there was another, more hidden factor limiting the growth of the consortium: the discomfort members felt about sharing information with competitors. Ford quietly balked at inviting Toyota; Harley at Honda (even if participation were limited to Honda's automotive, non-motorcycle branch); and Nike at Reebok or Adidas. At Aveda, which has spearheaded some industry-wide recycling projects (such as one for aluminum), Mr Delfausse said he would need to think twice before sharing broader materials information with non–Estée Lauder cosmetics companies. Suppliers were also skittish about competition, which put the whole project in a sort of catch-22, because participating companies feared they could be vulnerable to antitrust charges if no competing suppliers were present, but they were unable to compel competing suppliers to join.

Although members were always conscious of US federal antitrust laws, those laws specifically focus on price-fixing; there has not been an actual federal case related to materials pooling since at least the early 1980s. The real threat is more visceral. It is hard enough to talk openly and honestly with people from other industries about the differences, say, between shoe leather and car-seat leather; to reinvent industrial society and eliminate all potential toxins would require almost unimaginable openness. Manufacturers and suppliers alike would have to entrust competitors with some of their most carefully held secrets.

For this reason, conversations in the Materials Pooling project often took on the precise and laboured formulations that you might expect at high-tech standards-setting meetings (which, in a way, these gatherings were). At one SoL meeting, Ford product development team member Sibel Koyluoglu showed an intricate flowchart she had created to track the multiple conversations required to reconcile the needs and priorities of her own company – design specs from her team, the marketing department's concerns about brand image, and the engineering group's multiple schedules – with the needs and priorities of the other companies in the consortium.

'We weren't just tackling Ford's system,' she recalls, 'but all the system interactions that you see as you take this on as a group. For example, the technical talk about chrome specifications led us to talk about the motives customers have in buying our products. We had to understand the requirements of our products and then work our way back through the material standards and the material chain to reach the point at which we would find commonality.' Though sometimes difficult to maintain, these are also the kinds of conversations that lead to moments of genuine accomplishment: starting out to reduce the solvents used in a welding process, one might end up redesigning the process so no solvents at all are needed.

Key to unlocking environmental problems

Most environmental problems transcend corporate, industrial-sector, and political boundaries, and thus a whole-systems orientation is required to deal with them. As with many other cross-boundary endeavours, the project's momentum depends on the enthusiasm of its participants, which in turn depends on the increased ability it gives them to manage all sorts of cross-industry and cross-platform endeavours in the future.

And the implications go beyond this one project. Corporate environmentalists like Michael Braungart and William McDonough are calling for nothing less than an in-depth revolution in industrial infrastructure. Generating financial results is hard enough, but translating this kind of ideal into day-to-day practice requires a highly sophisticated degree of managerial competence. Many companies have this level of competence, but they do not often exercise it, in part because they do not give themselves permission to take the kinds of risks that corporate environmentalism requires. And there is also a longer time horizon involved. Some observers might argue that the Materials Pooling project is a failure because it has not yet realized its promise. But initiatives that require so much collaborative experimentation and learning, particularly when more than a dozen companies are involved, can reasonably take months or years to show tangible results.

Maybe the Braungartian future, in which all industrial waste output becomes an input somewhere else and all materials are free of hidden toxins, is worth pursuing precisely because it is so comprehensive. In a world where energy and materials technology breakthroughs are seemingly on the horizon, with nanotechnology close behind and global climate change looming as a potential threat, the Materials Pooling project provides a useful way to learn to deal with the next round of challenges. The obstacles are not primarily technological; they stem from the natural reluctance that corporate people have to participate.

BOX 2: SKILLS TO MANAGE CROSS-ORGANISATIONAL PROJECTS

Experience shows that there are five skills and capabilities that can be developed to make this type of cross-boundary, multidisciplinary novel collaboration work. These skills include:

In-depth conversation about difficult subjects: the ability to bring assumptions and attitudes to the surface, get past knee jerk responses and conduct collaborative dialogue.

Mentorship and sponsorship: the ability to bring together coherent teams and develop people's ingrained capabilities.

Risk and resilience management: the ability to see, prepare for, and respond to probabilities and potential harms.

Cross-boundary operations: the ability to manage projects and collaborate across internal 'silos' and organizational boundaries.

Systems thinking capability: the training and ability to explore reinforcing (accelerating) and balancing (oscillating) processes in everyday life, their interactions, and their counter-intuitive effects.

For more information on these skills and capabilities, see 'Further References' below.

Environmental results or competitive advantage?

That is ultimately the question facing CEOs like Lord John Browne, Jeffrey Immelt, and Carlos Ghosn. To what extent will their endorsement of a new environmental ethic include new ways of working with competitors and other companies? What kinds of permission and sponsorship and commitment will leaders of environmentally responsive companies give collaborative initiatives, even when those initiatives threaten their competitive advantage and autonomy? And if they permit their engineers to engage in unprecedented forms of collaboration, will they ultimately make their companies stronger? Or weaker? Although initiatives like the Materials Pooling project show how difficult these questions are to answer, they also show how important it will be to answer them well.

Notes

1   An earlier version of this article entitled 'Materials Witnesses' appeared in *strategy+business*, Fall 2005.

2   See 'Building the Advantaged Supply Network' by Bill Jackson and Conrad Winkler, *strategy+business*, Fall 2004.

Further References

Senge P., Kleiner A., Roberts C., Ross R. and Smith B. *The Fifth Discipline Fieldbook: Strategies and Tools for Building a Learning Organization*, New York: Doubleday/Currency, 1994.

Senge P., Kleiner A., Roberts C., Ross R., Roth G. and Smith B. *The Dance of Change: The Challenges of Sustaining Momentum in Learning Organizations*, New York: Doubleday/Currency, 1999.

17

From Energy Management to Carbon Management – a Strategic Approach

Dana Hanby, Ecofys International

Introduction

It is now a cliché to state that corporate success depends on the distinctive capabilities of the firm. In *The Competitive Advantage of Nations*, Michael Porter (Porter, 1990) stated that positioning involves a firm's total approach to competing, not just its products or target customer group. He then identified two basic types of competitive advantage: lower cost and differentiation. John Kay in turn argued that positioning can be replicated and listed innovation, reputation and architecture as pillars of competitive advantage for companies (Kay, 1993).

This is a strategic area of interest with a number of publications on what competitive advantages are and how to create them. Although we may argue how to best create competitive advantage, it is probably easier to agree with the corollary: that a company cannot afford to ignore positioning or main pillars of competitive advantage without risking falling into disadvantage compared to its competitors.

Corporate response to carbon emissions may affect all of these strategic areas and therefore directly influence the success of a company. Changes in the operational processes will affect cost structure; an improved product or service may influence differentiation; thinking about new ways of doing things should stimulate innovation, and the carbon management process will give a chance to influence a network of relationships ('architecture') both internally within the company and externally with customers and suppliers.

A proactive and effective method in which emissions are managed is therefore very important. In the next section, we discuss major steps which are applied in different carbon management methodologies. These methodologies provide a basic structure for development and implementation of carbon management; however by themselves they do not address individual circumstances and markets of the companies implementing them. Lack of tailored methodology to individual circumstances and markets may result in confusion among your customers – a risk that one definitely does not wish to take. Carbon management is a strategic issue and its implementation reaches far beyond the technical and functional departments of any company. Making the conceptual leap from 'energy management' to 'carbon management' is not a small leap for most companies. The aspects involved in making this leap are also discussed.

A sound methodology for managing emissions is important

There are many different approaches to carbon management, including a number of published approaches undertaken by the public and private sector (examples of which can be found throughout this book). While these approaches may use different phraseology, different formulae and different numbers or sequences of steps, they include the following fundamental foundations:

- Commitment
- Audits and assessments
- Selection of most appropriate options
- Planning
- Prototype testing followed by programme rollout
- Review.

Commitment

Buy-in at all levels is essential and a convincing business case for action needs to be put forward. The business case should focus not only on the contribution to operational efficiency but also on the positive impact on the organisation as a whole, operational requirements and service levels. All of these aspects are important to convince decision makers at different levels in the organisation.

Different decision makers will have different criteria for supporting the project. At higher levels in the organisational hierarchy, usually the financial aspects and operational efficiency improvements are critical. However, in order to obtain wide support within the organisation the carbon management process has to appeal to all stakeholders. Therefore, consideration for all other additional benefits from the project needs to be given, particularly relating to satisfaction of end customers of the organisation and improved service levels. These criteria are sometimes regarded as more important within some parts of the organisation than the actual financial performance.

- Undertaking stakeholder analysis is also important, especially using proven methodologies to highlight strengths and weaknesses of key stakeholders within the organisation and to ascertain whether existing organisational structures can be used for internal communication, buy-in, project development and other processes.

An important aspect of this initial involvement is to gain a detailed understanding of the decision-making processes in relation to energy, existing carbon management issues and investment procedures. These could be different for individual units and an exact understanding of these is essential for the success of the programme.

Audits and assessments

This part of the process aims at identification of the scale of change that may be required and involves taking a close look at technical aspects of the operation and also gaining a good understanding of a company's strategy and the markets in which the company operates. This is usually not a simple task and the complexity increases as the number of sites and countries a company operates in increases. For a company within the EU Emissions Trading Scheme (EU ETS) this may mean different requirements regarding reporting formats in different EU Member States, multiple approaches to issue of tiers in EU ETS installations, the use of different scope for emission factors, multiple verifier accreditation schemes, not to mention different market conditions.

From a technical point of view, this part involves detailed consideration of the processes that are used in a company as well as selection of sites, units and other areas that directly or indirectly influence emissions and need to be included in calculations. The approach may differ for companies affected by the requirements of the EU ETS and those in the voluntary market. The old adage 'what you can't measure, you can't manage' applies here as the process should be supported by sound measurement systems. An example is if a company needs to know their carbon dioxide (CO_2) baseline, which identifies the distribution of emissions across a company's activities. Process studies enable a company to prioritise abatement action.

Another aim of the assessment is to gain knowledge of the company's existing situation and understanding of the options that a company has available to reduce emissions. The options will be affected not only by the technical/operational possibilities, but also by availability of resources, constraints and opportunities that are presented by the competitive environment in which a company operates, the current market conditions and the company's view of future development of the market. As such, a review of strategy and careful alignment of carbon management into the company's processes is essential. A useful tool to flush out ideas may be 'opportunities workshops' (suggestions for a possible structure of such workshops are presented in Box 1).

BOX 1: OPPORTUNITIES WORKSHOP

The purpose of such workshops is to brainstorm the opportunities for carbon abatement within the company, with reference to the draft emissions baseline. The objectives of the opportunities workshop should be identification and prioritisation of suitable carbon abatement options and provision of guidance on related CO_2 savings and payback periods.

Other items that may be discussed during such workshops include:

The top opportunities identified in the opportunities assessments

- Opportunities for on-site renewable energy projects

- Opportunities outside the facilities; for example, transportation and procurement, etc

- Other non-technical opportunities relating to management and organisation.

We would encourage a high level of participation from all involved in these workshops.

To promote cross-fertilisation after the initial workshop, the existing Internet forum may be used or a dedicated forum for the participants in such a project can be developed.

Selection of the most appropriate option should be a natural step after the careful assessment process. By this stage, a company would have their marginal abatement costs curves drawn, gained understanding of market conditions and opportunities and be ready to plan an implementation programme.

Planning

It is hard to overestimate the importance of planning. Shortcuts at this stage very often result in confusion regarding responsibilities and accountabilities or in delays during implementation of the project. A structured approach to work from high-level strategic objectives to concrete actions is essential.

It is also easy to confuse objectives of each individual project (e.g. to reduce energy intensity, increase efficiency, etc) within the programme of work with business objectives and benefits. Planning should ensure clarity of objectives, identify requirements for resources and their availability, specify timescales and methodology. It should also establish who will perform, run and own the programme of works and how it will be ensured that the programme succeeds.

A few key steps that are likely to be included in the plan may involve the following: establishing a plan to integrate carbon into business decision making; proposing short and longer-term measures; developing business cases for selected key opportunities, identifying barriers and actions; preparing marketing and communications plans and presenting findings and recommendations (see Box 2 for more details).

It sounds like a truism, but planning does involve time and is based on a number of assumptions. It is very easy to succumb to a temptation to trim tasks to suit project deadlines or forget that required sign-offs and reviews of each of the project stages may have consequences for the project.

BOX 2: IMPLEMENTATION PLAN

This action plan underpins the recommended actions and is the basis for ongoing carbon management activity within the organisation.

A suitable plan is developed in which an organisation is best able to meet its objectives. This can be done after several workshops, which can be held with each individual unit with the following objectives:

- To focus and confirm a timetabled project/initiative implementation shortlist
- To link the timetable to wider projects, initiatives and milestones in the organisation
- To assign high level responsibilities for those initiatives
- To agree and assign resources (financial or personnel) to specific initiatives
- To understand the key success factors and potential barriers for individual projects.

Such work should result in a plan, which should include:

- Prioritised options
- Detailed best practice guidance
- Resource allocation plan; including assigned responsibilities and internal and external input requirements
- Implementation time schedule
- Ongoing carbon management activities – for example monitoring and reporting carbon considerations during procurement maintenance and other decision-making processes. Selected ongoing activities will have to be anchored in policy documents
- Each plan should also include a template for periodic updating.

Prototype testing and programme rollout

This stage requires a combination of a few disciplines – change management, project/programme management, etc – and as such calls for proven methodologies from each of these areas. It is beyond the scope of this chapter to discuss methodologies of each of these disciplines but perhaps it is worth looking at a few common issues.

Change management has its own pitfalls. Very often, even if a change process follows well established methodologies, there is still a danger that significant actual changes in organisational behaviour will not occur. We have all heard about change programmes, where a CEO publishes new mission statements and in a quick succession of moves establishes a company-wide programme to push change down through the organisation – a new organisational structure, a performance appraisal system, training programmes to turn managers into 'change agents' and periodic surveys to chart the progress of the change effort – only to find a result far from that desired.

Some suggested solutions (see Beer and Eisentat, 1990) to this potential pitfall are prototype testing or implementing a project of a smaller scale which would not only contribute to the learning process, but also demonstrate a successful effort, which is easier to follow by others. Depending on the scale of the change programme the 'prototype' may be limited to a particular geography or indeed particular units in the organisation. This suggestion, however, should not be followed blindly, as each organisation has its own specifics and different processes may be more appropriate (an example of a mix of change management and technical services is presented in Box 3).

Indeed 'programme rollout' suggests that it is a programme – i.e. a group of projects, which very often would have common objectives, same reporting lines, same time horizons, shared resources and cross-dependencies. It is possible to isolate an individual project (say in a given geography) which is run as a prototype, but it is also possible to manage the entire programme.

The programme does not exist in a vacuum. It impacts a number of business units that have their own business objectives and may ultimately ask 'why do we need this project?' Also the risks assessment now would need to include business and project risks. Therefore, already at the initial stages, it needs to be clear how the programme will impact individual businesses and what the business objectives of the programme are.

The business view of project priorities needs to be interwoven in the implementation programme and may include the following:

- 'Must have' objective (for example legal or regulatory requirement)

- Significant goals (e.g. delivering to meet strategic vision)

- Business improvement (customer/market driven; improving cost/quality/ efficiency)

- Nice to have (which may include everything else).

BOX 3: MIX OF CHANGE MANAGEMENT AND TECHNICAL SERVICES

Due to the various experiences and requirements of individual organisations, the exact mix of change management and technical services needs to be tailored to each project. A portfolio of tools and available services can be used to tailor the programme to the specific requirements of each individual organisation. Separately it needs to be assessed which tools and services are most appropriate for individual units. Some of the services may include:

Technical services

- Energy audit/survey
- Review and update of existing audit
- Renewable energy audit/implementation support
- Transport planning
- General support for calculating savings, whole life costing, performance indicators, etc
- Guidelines for prioritising opportunities
- Energy performance benchmarking
- Emissions trading

Change management services

- Attitude survey
- Energy management assessments
- Mapping of stakeholders and decision making processes
- Trainings & workshops: for example awareness, presentation of business cases etc.

Review

As in any other change programme, carbon management is implemented with clear objectives. Depending on the scale of the programme, the implementation process can last a reasonably long time. During this time and also after the programme has been implemented, involved parties need to be able to monitor progress and clearly see how the deliverables from the programme meet the objectives. A tool that may be used for such periodic reviews during the implementation phase can be a 'benefits map', where deliverables are clearly listed in a matrix against objectives.

Earlier stages of implementation of the carbon management process would have already identified factors that need to be monitored on an ongoing basis as well as after the programme has been successfully implemented.

Embedding carbon management into a company's policies is an important part of ensuring that the implementation phase of carbon management projects outlives the involvement of a carbon management consultancy team, even for the small number of companies who rely on the ongoing input of external carbon management experts. As policies are fundamental in many decision making processes within any organisation, a key focus is to ensure that the carbon considerations have been sufficiently incorporated into a wide range of policies as appropriate, including procurement, investments and budgeting, maintenance, health and safety, environmental and energy policies and policies relating to external contractors and/or the company's supply chain. Relevant policies should be identified during the earlier phases of the project.

A good methodology on its own may not result in corporate success

The previous section covers the general structure of the carbon management process. It is important however to remember the pressures that companies are facing, as markets and expectations of customers vary widely. Each company will have its own specific circumstances. A carbon management project therefore needs to reflect the position of each organisation engaged and to tailor the response to climate change accordingly.

Individual circumstances of companies and the level of awareness and engagement of customers in the carbon management process are just two basic reasons why 'off the shelf' solutions may not work as expected.

Tailor-made support

The carbon management methodology used is inextricably linked to corporate strategy and business objectives of individual units. A successful carbon management change process will need to be tailored to the specific circumstances of each company, and will generally require a number of elements, including making direct contact with individual business units in the company, working both top-down and bottom-up within the company, close attention to end customers and perceptions of the target market for the company and promoting innovative carbon solutions from inside the company

In order to be able to provide tailor-made support and to gain commitment, it is important to establish direct contact with business units that will be affected. Here, direct engagement through a combination of on-site time, and clustered events may be a way forward. Selected approaches will differ and depend on the specific circumstances of the organisation. The format of the contacts and interventions should be also adapted to the requirements of the participants.

Some of the most innovative carbon solutions and ideas often come from within the company itself. Hence, a key element of a successful carbon management approach is to nurture, harness and capitalise upon this existing internal capacity. For example, some of the business units within an organisation might be more advanced in energy efficiency and carbon emission reduction. Usually these units would be very supportive for an implementation of carbon management. Units that are already very proactive are potentially also interested in the implementation of more innovative solutions, for example relating to on-site renewable energy or innovative transportation technologies. Identification and implementation of such innovative solutions can be supported by external consultants with expert knowledge in a given field. These innovative projects can make a real contribution to internal case studies to promote the company's carbon management scheme during a potential rollout phase.

BOX 4: EXAMPLES

Many companies are already actively engaging an effective carbon management approach requiring a programme tailored to the individual organisation, with the right mix of change management, strategic and technical tools.

For example, a large multinational communications company is seeking to uniquely and strategically integrate carbon management into their brand identity. Initial studies carried out in the company indicated that energy use exceeded a few million pounds. The potential impacts of energy and carbon costs on profitability and competitiveness, as well as on the environmental image of the company and its reputation with key stakeholders, are significant. Also, in the highly competitive communication retail sector, brand value and perception is one of the most important differentiators between products. Improving the energy efficiency of their large network of retail shops is one of the initiatives and includes installing high-quality low-carbon lighting to tangibly reduce emissions, as well as provide visible evidence to customers of their efforts.

Another example is the UK subsidiary of a large multinational food and beverage company, which was under risk of UK production being transferred to the company's manufacturing operations in India and China. This was due to several factors, including cost-effectiveness and the fact that the UK factory comprises older plants compared to the Indian and Chinese factories, with an internal company perception that being posted to the UK factory was a low-status position. The UK subsidiary wanted to develop a carbon management approach that, given these challenges, would improve and protect competitiveness. A carbon management programme, including energy efficiency, energy monitoring and management resulted in significant cost savings and carbon reductions, which received external recognition and profiling from the Carbon Trust. The detailed analysis of the factory's processes and performance, also resulted in a number of opportunities to improve quality being identified and implemented at the same time. With factory performance being boosted in a number of areas, and the factory being featured by the Carbon Trust as a carbon front-runner, the position of the UK subsidiary within its parent holding company was assured and UK production was safeguarded.

Perception of benefits

Some companies make a tacit assumption that implementation of carbon abatement processes in itself will result in a number of benefits. While such efforts may result in cost and carbon savings, improved company culture and/or favourable customer perceptions do not automatically follow.

A good carbon management methodology would provide a platform for all these things. However, for sustained (and not just 'one-off') benefits to be delivered, an organisation needs to also navigate a change and learning process in order for carbon management to take root within an organisation and for the strategic aims sought from undertaking carbon management to be achieved.

The test of the success and perception of a company's new product by customers will depend on the detailed understanding of their markets and competitive positioning. This should take into account (but not be limited to) the awareness of climate change issues in target markets, availability of other competitive products, economics and impact on lifestyle among other factors.

Although a number of customers will welcome change in products that incorporate environmental benefits, this may not always be the case. Indeed, reactions of customers to changed products can vary and may be negative. Even if the new product or service will benefit customers, this may not necessarily be immediately apparent. It is good if a tailored marketing approach is a part of a carbon management programme. Requirements, of course, are different depending on the type of customers that we are serving – for example institutional or individual.

Sometimes, ingrained perceptions that 'green' products are more expensive or inferior prevails and some educational activity and marketing approach is required to ensure that the change benefits all parties.

A very good example here is a small printing company that is very enthusiastic to implement a carbon management programme. The company looked in detail at their processes, identified opportunities for carbon abatement, reduced cost and brought new, environmentally friendly products to their wholesale outlets. Unprepared wholesalers started to reduce orders as they were not sure how to position this new product in their portfolio contributing to confusion among their (retail) customers. A quick educational campaign was swiftly put in place to avoid further serious impact on the bottom line. On the other hand, there are many examples of companies (also in the SME sector), which successfully launched their new environmental approach or service, differentiating themselves from competitors.

Making the conceptual leap from 'energy management' to 'carbon management' is not a small leap for most companies. Not only do each of these areas have a different focus within an organisation but the process of getting there is not easy.

Energy management

Energy management is traditionally concerned with the effective measurement, monitoring and projection of energy consumption levels and energy procurement, with the aim of reducing and accurately measuring energy consumption and obtaining a good deal on energy contracts.

An in-house procedure of emission reduction usually involves use of either demand-side measures (to prevent or reduce excessive energy consumption within the company) or supply-side measures (to switch via a supplier to a lower-carbon energy supply or a different process method or equipment). While these procedures are an essential part of the carbon management process and will have an impact on the cost structure of the company, they should not be understood as the sole element of the carbon management change process.

The key driver of energy management is making sure that the company isn't paying more on their energy bills than they should be and obtaining good prices and value for money on energy contracts.

Functionally, within organisations, responsibility for emission and energy management issues do not traditionally sit in a place from which carbon management is best enabled. Energy management often sits within the facilities/maintenance or operational part of an organisation, or even the procurement/contract management part of an organisation. These departments are seldom able to provide the strategic approach required for carbon management.

Carbon management

Carbon management is a major strategic change with a long-term impact. It requires a company to extend 'energy management' conceptualisation to include a much broader range of company-wide issues involving the financial opportunities and risks of the carbon market, embedded carbon with the company's products and services, brand management, and the carbon implications of different policy decisions.

With such broad impacts of carbon management on an organisation, ensuring congruence of the interrelated elements and the effectiveness of the process itself (during and after the transition period) is a major challenge for any organisation.

The complexity of the carbon management process will differ depending on the scale of operation and obligations that the company is facing. For sectors impacted by the EU ETS (and indeed for companies in the voluntary markets who are addressing climate change issues in a proactive manner), managing CO_2 emissions becomes important at a number of levels: as a legal compliance concern and development in various regulations that may impact their sector in the future; as a new market that presents a number of opportunities and threats; as a new investment consideration and as a shift in minds about the dangers that climate change poses to all of us.

Carbon management is designed to identify the risks and opportunities linked to CO_2 emissions within a company and to include analyses of both the traditional remit of energy efficiency within a company as well as its strategies, structures and attitude towards climate change. Strategic opportunities will vary depending on the industry, scale of operations, appetite for risk, geographical or operational focus of any given company.

Consideration could be given to:

- Financial opportunities of the carbon market- JI/CDM, EU ETS trading

- Brand management – corporate social responsibilities

- Products with added carbon value (i.e. carbon-neutral products)

- Investment trends

- Awareness of the issues (internal and among customers and suppliers).

Some challenges are posed by the difficulty in making investment decisions and calculating financial benefits of carbon management projects due to longer-term regulatory uncertainty and carbon prices, which so far defy to strictly follow fundamentals. While the emergence of the global carbon market has had an overall supportive impact, the newness and uncertainty of this market make a number of participants delay investments.

The key driver of the carbon management process is to appropriately position the company in the new low-carbon economy. As such, it is a strategic consideration for the board and the change can be properly assessed and implemented only with support of the senior levels of management.

Some key aspects that need to be carefully considered are:

- **Vision and strategy formulation**
  This stage of the project is concerned with creating the necessary vision and strategy for the organisation. Both vision and strategy have to be engaging and have buy-in from all sections of the hierarchy. Separate methodology should be prepared to achieve this.

- **Establishing and agreeing on feasible but challenging carbon reduction targets**
  The target level should be based on the list of prioritised abatement opportunities identified earlier in the project.

- **Preparation of clear internal and external communication plans**
  To ensure that the vision and strategy are known throughout the organisation, both internal and external communication plans are required. These communication plans have to ensure that all stakeholders are aware of the organisation's ambitions, which will further contribute to wider support for the programme.

BOX 5: EXAMPLE OF CARBON MANAGEMENT ANALYSIS

An initial study carried out in a large multinational non EU ETS company indicated that energy use exceeded £5m. The potential impacts of energy and carbon costs on profitability and competitiveness, as well as on the environmental image of the company and its reputation with key stakeholders, were significant.

In addition, the emerging carbon-constrained economy gives proactive companies new business opportunities. An integrated carbon management approach was suggested to address both these issues – *direct energy issues* on one hand, and *carbon-related products and services* on the other. It was important to realise that these were related. Additionally, a carbon management policy needed to be developed using a process that includes stakeholders involved in both types of activities.

Direct energy issues

The company looked at their direct energy issues, which included their hosting centres, travel and supply chain. The company operates internationally. More detailed plans were required on a country level to consider and assess levels of energy use and opportunities.

A range of opportunities were identified, which included but were not limited to:

- Investment decision options
- Use of renewable energy
- Energy efficiency at all sites
- Reduction of staff transport emissions
- Work with suppliers of equipment and systems to reduce demands for energy and cooling, and to relax constraints.

Carbon-related products and services

The group was already working closely with business partners along the supply chain to consider the whole-life resource and energy impact of equipment and systems. Numerous opportunities for carbon-related products and services existed, and needed to be further developed during the carbon management project.

A rigorous carbon management programme was developed, which encompassed direct and indirect emissions, including upstream and downstream activity, from suppliers to customers. This built on the existing environmental policy, as well as benefiting from and contributing to the group-level programmes, including the sustainability guidance developed in the group EHS policy.

Also, a scoping study was required to build on the current understanding of energy and carbon management. This defined the boundaries and priorities for a full carbon management project for one country of operation. It also indicated the likely financial implications of executing it, and outlined the steps to be followed, the timescales, milestones and outputs to be delivered, and the resources required.

A number of brainstorming sessions were carried out in order to identify issues, drivers and potential opportunities. This included a session discussing activities of other companies in carbon management. This session was to ensure not only that all ideas and knowledge were taken into account, but also to raise awareness of and interest in energy and carbon issues. It also highlighted areas where particular attention was required:

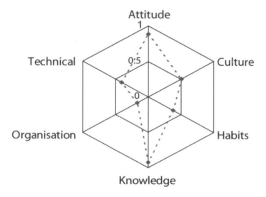

It was vital to understand the general business drivers and competitive context, as well as regulatory or other pressures on energy and carbon in the company's operation in any given country, and to gain an understanding of the organisation and the key operations. The value at risk was assessed using a risk assessment approach, and ideas generated for carbon abatement options.

Issues considered included:

- Emissions from energy, electricity and fuels, electricity used for equipment, back-up systems and other engineering sites. Impact of change in operations, growth in the operations, new site design, use of different systems and energy efficiency actions. Examples of the last category include enhancing energy management information systems (including forecasting and smart metering)

- Staff transport, offices and engineering/ maintenance

- R & D into new network equipment

- Carbon opportunities arising with business partners, suppliers and other stakeholders including customers

- New products and services

- Market drivers including energy prices, cost structures, growth in customer numbers and operational traffic, competitors' investments and responses to all the above.

Conclusions

The greatest threats to the competitive advantage of most firms are changes in the 'rules of the game' to which managers have been accustomed and the creation of new competitive advantages by competitors. It is very tempting to presume that based on historics, durable competitive advantages and their rewards will continue into the future. The dangers of such a presumption accounts for the surprises of both managers and equity markets for they overestimate the prowess of once secure firms. In general, markets differ widely in how long competitive advantage can be sustained before competitors imitate, neutralise or leapfrog. The biggest threats, even for firms that have highly durable advantages, are from changes in the environment such as, for example, new carbon regulation or a new technology that delivers superior benefits.

Changes in the environment, and related changes to company operations, can be perceived as a threat, but proactive response to the changes brings a number of opportunities which can strengthen a company's position in the market and its competitive advantages.

In reality, real change is hard to achieve. But in a carbon-constrained economy and a marketplace that is very aware of climate concerns, companies will need to be more, and not less, attentive to carbon management to remain competitive. However, unless corporations can demonstrate real commitment to carbon management and show tangible sustained progress, corporations risk being accused of 'window-dressing' by an increasingly sceptical and savvy marketplace.

References

Beer M. and Eisenstat R.A. 'Why Change Programs don't produce Change', *Harvard Business Review*, Nov–Dec 1990.

Kay J. *Foundations of Corporate Success*, Oxford University Press, 1993.

Porter M.E. *The Competitive Advantage of Nations*, The MacMillan Press Ltd., 1990.

Schaffet R.H. and Thomson H.A. 'Successful Change Programs Begin with Results', *Harvard Business Review*, Jan–Feb 1992.

Financial Strategies – Valuing Carbon and Climate Change

18

Climate Change and Business Valuation Techniques

Daniel Wells, Ernst & Young

Introduction

The magnitude of the threat that climate change presents demands the development of valuation techniques to understand and quantify the likely consequential value shifts between businesses. There are a range of valuation techniques that can be used to support critical decisions for both companies and investors, but the challenge of building in climate change considerations is significant. Valuation techniques attempt to translate risks and opportunities into quantifiable terms and climate change poses possibly the greatest threat to the ability of businesses to meet expectations in the coming decades. The complexity, however, of the relationship between climate change and value creation makes it very difficult to quantify. In this chapter we first set out the current range of techniques used to value businesses, then go on to consider their potential for adaptation for this purpose, supported by the use of a case study.

The use of valuations

Financial valuation techniques can be used for different purposes by a variety of users. These uses can be broadly separated into two categories, commercial valuations and regulatory valuations:

Commercial valuations: Investors can use valuations to benchmark companies to assist in the portfolio selection process. During mergers and acquisitions both the vendor and the purchaser will need to make an assessment of value to assist in their price negotiations. Similarly, private equity houses and venture capitalists require an understanding of valuation techniques when setting ownership structures of companies in which they invest (consequently it is critical that the owner managers or entrepreneurs of the companies invested in understand such techniques themselves). Investment banks, accounting firms, management consultancies and boutique valuation practices can all provide such valuation services. Aside from valuing companies in their entirety, valuation techniques can also be used in investment appraisal decisions to attribute an implied return to investments, which can be compared to a company's cost of capital or other investment options that are available. Specific assets may be valued, whether they be tangible assets (such as plant and machinery) or intangibles (such as brands, customer relationships or 'know how'). Brand valuations may be used as a support to the marketing function; brand assets can be managed more effectively by tracking the value of a brand over time, or by valuing a portfolio of brands. Accounting firms, boutique practices, management consultancies and branding consultancies all carry out brand valuations, though their methods may vary considerably.

Regulatory valuations: Companies may require valuations for tax, litigation or financial reporting reasons. On the whole, such valuations are required to be performed using particular accepted techniques and are usually carried out by accounting firms.

Valuation methodologies

There are many ways to come to a view on the 'value' of a business and practitioners require flexibility to be able to choose the technique that is most applicable for a given situation. There is inevitably a degree of subjectivity involved, given the inherent uncertainty over the future, which is why valuation is often described as an art rather than a science. Corporate valuation techniques can be grouped into several categories:

Cost-driven valuations: The cost incurred to create an asset may be used as a proxy for value. This method should, however, only be used as a last resort as the original cost of an asset may have little correlation with its actual current value.

Relative valuations: The value of a company can be inferred by using price to earnings ratios (often referred to in terms of multiples) of comparable quoted companies. Relative valuations are, however, a blunt tool in many ways, as variations in earnings over time or the different patterns of income streams are not modelled in full; instead they can only be reflected via relatively crude adjustments. Relative valuations, however, are certainly useful as a cross check when other techniques are used.

Income-based valuations: Companies can be valued by estimating the sum of the total future cash flows that will derive from the business (which will be discounted by a cost of capital to reflect both the time value of money and the risk associated with achieving them). Though they are dependent on the availability of robust, reliable forecasts (indeed establishing the validity of the forecasts is often the most difficult – and sometimes overlooked – area of the exercise), Discounted Cash Flow (DCF) models are the most common tools employed by valuation practitioners. They have the flexibility to map earnings patterns over time and can be adapted to incorporate new costs and incomes to illustrate the impact of different variables on overall corporate value.

Asset-based valuations: When income projections are not available or a company is loss making, it may be more applicable to consider the value of the underlying assets of the business using a 'mark to market' valuation.

Real options valuations: The development of techniques for valuing financial options has given rise to an interesting and potentially powerful concept, that of 'real options'. By adapting the financial option valuation techniques and applying them to businesses, it is possible to capture the value of 'options' (i.e. the value of having specific flexibilities open in the future), a key consideration that may be missed by DCF-based valuations.

Brand valuations: Brand valuations are particularly challenging due to their inherent subjectivity. There is not time here to describe the range of different techniques available, but as brands now represent such a large proportion of some companies' assets their impact on overall value may be significant.

Incorporating climate change into valuation techniques

The impact of climate change on the way businesses create value is far reaching and it is important to realise that climate change isn't simply an extra line that can be inserted into a company's profit and loss account. Climate change has the potential to affect the ability to generate sales, to price sales, the extent and nature of a business's costs, its reputation capital, its risk profile, its tax exposure and its financing structure. Panel 1 illustrates this complexity in a graphical form.

PANEL 1: Incorporating climate change into the process of value creation

The creation and measurement of value can be broken down and linked to the constituent elements of the financial statements by means of a 'Du Pont' analysis. The diagram that follows illustrates this, showing how the overall value of a company is built up, starting with the individual financial accounts, and working through various measures of profit (such as EBIT – Earnings Before Interest and Tax) and value creation. At the overall level, value creation is measured by Return on Invested Capital (ROIC) measured against the companies Weighted Average Cost of Capital (WACC).

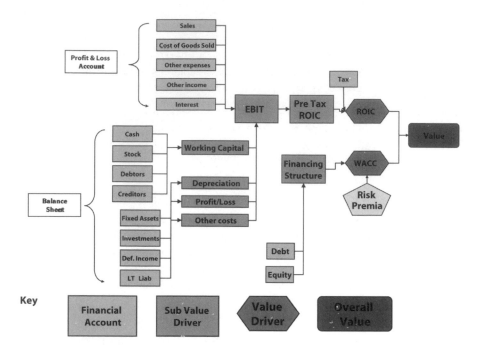

Introducing climate change into this process can be illustrated by linking environmental considerations to the original financial accounts:[1]

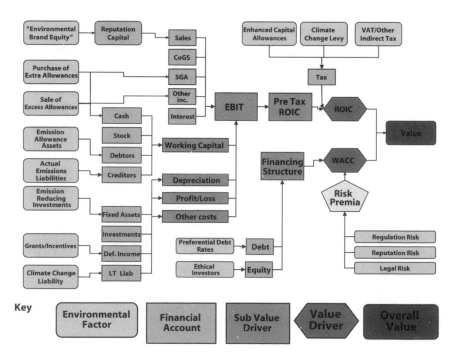

A company, for example, with a robust, integrated climate change strategy, is likely to have a high 'environmental brand equity' which will increase sales. Energy and carbon costs are likely to decrease due to energy efficiency projects and carbon management strategies, while tax savings will accrue from 'green tax' incentives. Consequently overall ROIC will increase. Concurrently, the reputation, legal and regulation risk will be minimised and consequently the WACC will be reduced. Overall value would therefore increase.

The diagram highlights how the entire process of valuation creation is dependent on the relationship with the environment. It is highly difficult, therefore, to quantify the overall impact of climate change on the value of a business. Merely adding a consideration of 'carbon costs' into a valuation will not capture all of the impacts on value, though even the introduction of simple 'climate change variables' into valuations produces unexpected complexity, as we will see later.

We will now consider, in turn, each of the techniques listed above in terms of their ability to model the effects of climate change:

(a) Cost-based techniques

Crude instruments on their own, cost-based valuation techniques are not much more use in the context of quantifying the impact of climate change on value due to the generally low correlation between the amount spent on investment and the actual return. That said, in companies' financial reporting, cost is often used as a measure of carbon management initiatives undertaken ('this year we spent €x million on emission reductions' being a common phrase in annual reports). Though useful, if there is no other way of quantifying costs or benefits to a business, cost-based methods should only ever be used by valuation practitioners as a starting point in the process of understanding the impact of climate change on a business's value.

(b) Relative techniques

Relative, or 'multiple', based valuation techniques are not particularly useful in respect of climate change analysis as they lack the sensitivity to be able to measure individual variables independently. It is possible to adjust multiples to reflect some assessment of climate change risk. For example, a particular percentage premium added to an earnings multiple used to value a steel manufacturer, could be applied to reflect a strong carbon management strategy. Reducing the overall consideration of climate change to a single, lumpy, adjustment, however, inevitably leads to over simplification and unacceptable levels of subjectivity. In this context relative techniques are simply too blunt a tool to give meaningful insights.

(c) Income-based methods

DCF-based models offer plenty of scope to begin building climate change considerations into the measurement of value. Their flexibility allows new items to be added to forecasts, and variations over time can be modelled. Changes in risk can be accounted for in a general way by adjustments to the discount rate, while more specific adjustments can be made to cash flows and other variables based upon knowledge or assumptions about the future market. It is important to remember that, due to the opacity of the future carbon market, it is very difficult to quantify with any great precision how a company's value will be affected. By formulating a series of likely scenarios, however, and analysing their impact on value, DCFs can be an extremely powerful tool. With this foreknowledge businesses can plan their carbon management strategies more effectively. Companies can assess both the impact of variables that are out of their control (the price of carbon, for instance) and those within their control (such as changing the rate of emissions over time). Relevant considerations can be added to a DCF one at a time, starting with the most obviously quantifiable – direct carbon costs. The introduction of the European Emissions Trading Scheme (ETS) has given the financial markets the first major opportunity to quantify an environmental cost in financial terms. Carbon costs – previously an 'externality' (i.e. borne by the environment) – must now be 'internalised' (i.e. recognised as a normal business cost), with a consequent and direct impact on earnings and hence corporate valuation. The ETS, therefore, is the first step towards cost internalisation, the ultimate objective of which is to make business costs more accurate representations of the resources they utilise. We will examine a DCF case study later, to illustrate the issues involved in modelling carbon costs.

Aside from modelling specific estimated scenarios, further – more general – adjustments can also be made via the discount rate used in the valuation. A company's discount rate is built up from an aggregation of the 'risk-free rate' (defined as the yield on a government bond for the territory in question), a market risk premium (to reflect the overall systematic risk in a given market) and finally a company specific risk premium (defined by its beta and any further specific adjustments for known risks). In the example that follows the 12 per cent discount rate used represents a risk-free rate of approximately 5 per cent, a market risk also of 5 per cent and a further 2 per cent of company specific risk. These risk premia base some of their estimates of future risks and 'uncertainties' (put in simple terms, risks that we are not yet aware of) on historical analysis of risk and return however, therefore there is a good chance that they will underestimate future risk, as we enter a period of unprecedented anthropogenic environmental degradation. Due to the extent of strains currently placed upon the planet it is possible that environmental risk represents a large question mark over the future returns of the market. Clearly more research is required in this area, but there is a cogent case for building in an extra premium to account for this environmental risk, which will have a significant impact on the value of companies across many sectors. Building a 'climate change beta' or 'climate change discount rate' is one of the most interesting challenges of the near future, though the concept requires more work to establish its viability.

(d) Asset-based valuations

In cases where a company is loss making, or is not a 'going concern' (i.e. will not be trading beyond the immediate future), earnings-based models are not particularly useful. In these situations it is more appropriate to consider the underlying assets and liabilities that the company possesses. The introduction of the ETS means that – in theory – companies possess new classes of intangible assets (in the form of emission allowances) and new liabilities (actual emissions). This gives rise to the concept of 'carbon accounting', which will affect the balance sheet value of a company, particularly given the high proportion of overall value in stock markets that is now represented by intangible assets. This is not the time or place to embark upon a detailed analysis of current practice, primarily because consensus has not yet been reached on accounting treatment and therefore an evaluation of current practice will have a very short sell-by date. The main issue that a valuation practitioner must be aware of however, involves the measurement of carbon assets and liabilities and whether they should be revalued to market rates (ie 'fair value') on a regular basis, whilst being wary of a potential mismatch if – for instance – a liability is revalued whist the related asset is left recorded at an historical amount. Currently accounting standards have not been agreed upon; the International Financial Reporting Council (IFRIC) attempted to do so with *IFRIC 3: Emissions Rights*, but this was subsequently sent back to the drawing board by the International Accounting Standards Board (IASB) as it was feared that the proposed treatment would lead to excess volatility in companies' accounts (mirroring wider issues with the development of international accounting standards). Still, this is an interesting and evolving area and one that will have a considerable impact on balance sheet based valuations. Once consensus on accounting treatment has been achieved it will be very interesting to compare the impact on intangible asset values of markets that operate emissions trading schemes, with those markets that don't.

(e) Real options

The power of real options techniques to capture the inherent value of possessing a future option can be readily employed by businesses and investors alike. It is important to understand that the advantage of real options is to measure the value of *future* options, as opposed to *current* options. Consider a power plant, which currently produces a certain, relatively high level of emissions. Imagine in this case that the power plant had been built relatively recently and in such a way that emissions could be significantly lowered at some point in the future for a relatively affordable investment cost. The actual internal rate of return (IRR) on this investment will be linked to future carbon prices; the higher prices are, the higher the return (through cost savings from not having to buy permits and income from selling excess allowances). It may be that, at the current time, the price of carbon and future uncertainty about how short the ETS market will be, will mean that such an investment cannot be presently justified. However, if at a future date the price of carbon reaches a trigger point, then the option can be taken up. Compare this position to an older power plant which may not have the flexibility to be able to affordably reduce emissions. Clearly there is a value advantage to the former over the latter. Real options can measure this value. Of course in this case this is little use to the power plants themselves – they either have the flexibility or they don't – but to potential investors this can be a critical consideration.

Furthermore, real options techniques can be employed by companies when considering future investment and hedging strategies and are particularly useful when considering a subject as complex and uncertain as climate change. The crucial advantage of this technique over DCF is that the latter can only tell you whether to invest or not to invest, whereas real options can value the ability to defer a decision. Consider again our hypothetical power plant with its option to invest and the issue of *when* to invest. In reality, over time, the investment may have either a positive or negative effect on value depending on future carbon price. In this case imagine that the return on investment will have a negative, zero or positive IRR, depending on whether long-term prices are €20, €30 or €40 per tonne respectively. A DCF valuation of this investment will value the sum of probablised resulting cash flows; uncertainty over future carbon prices will diminish the value (effectively meaning that €30 per tonne will be used as a normalised carbon price). However, real options techniques, make it possible to measure the value of being able to defer the investment decision until, for example, the next ETS phase starts. At this point the decision can be made based on better information on carbon prices; if prices are €20 then the investment shouldn't be made, but if they are €40 it should. The valuation, based on this deferral option, will be higher than the DCF valuation; therefore the plant should take the decision to defer making the investment.

Read[2] has demonstrated how real options can be used to value a strategy to enhance a company's 'social license to operate' (which will become ever more an issue as climate change concerns become more acute); they can equally be applied to climate change specific considerations. However, a note of caution must be sounded when considering real options, due to the fact that as a technique, they remain in the realm of 'potential for the future', as opposed to 'currently in practice'.

(f) Brand valuations

A company's brand is in many cases its strongest and most durable asset. Coca-Cola's brand is over 100 years old and is still going strong. Paradoxically, however, the brand can also be the most ethereal of assets. It is subject to risks that other assets aren't. A brand's value can dissolve almost literally overnight as recent high profile cases have shown. In many cases a brand's failure can be traced to an inability to manage a form of risk that could have been avoided through effective corporate governance. Climate change risk is an obvious example. The consumer reaction against Shell during the Brent Spar controversy displays the fragility of a company's reputation capital, even in circumstances where a company may follow an arguably reasonable course of action from an environmental perspective. This raises the intriguing question of how to quantify the aspect of a business's brand 'equity' that relates to climate change. On the one hand negative connotations (the extreme manifestations of which are consumer boycotts) associated with perceived 'sin companies' will hinder a company compared to its more virtuous peers. The corollary of this, of course, is that paragon brands may try and capitalise on their green credentials, or indeed build a brand strategy entirely around them. Quantifying 'climate change brand equity' is not a purely academic exercise; with increasingly vast amounts being spent on cause-related marketing campaigns, CEOs will wish to see and measure a commensurate increase in the value of their brand asset. Such techniques from a financial point of view are not yet on the drawing board. Non-financial brand analysis techniques ('brand *evaluations*') are beginning to measure the social and environmental dimension of brands' but only in a peer-to-peer benchmarking capacity. Adapting traditional brand *valuation* techniques however, remains an engaging concept.

Case study: valuation of a European cement manufacturer

We will now consider a case study based on a fictitious cement manufacturer. Some of the assumptions and simplifications we will make here for the purposes of illustration will greatly underestimate the true characteristics of such a company and the nature of its interaction with the environment. However, it is also worth noting that even in this abridged universe life gets complex very quickly.

To begin with we built a basic DCF model to value the business on an 'as is' basis (i.e. as if the ETS was never introduced). We projected eight years of discrete cash flows (to cover the known Kyoto phases as they stand) discounted at an assumed cost of capital (12 per cent in this case) and a 'terminal year' cash flow, which is assumed to extend into perpetuity and capitalised (i.e. valued) using the Gordon's Growth Model.[3] All cash flows were assumed to take place midway through the year for discounting purposes. For simplicity's sake we assumed both revenues and all costs will stay flat for the valuation period and that there would be no capital expenditure or depreciation. The results of the valuation are summarised in the following table:

	31 Dec 2005 €'m	31 Dec 2006 €'m	31 Dec 2007 €'m	31 Dec 2008 €'m	31 Dec 2009 €'m	31 Dec 2010 €'m	31 Dec 2011 €'m	31 Dec 2012 €'m	Terminal year €'m
ETS phase	N/A	N/A	N/A	N/A	N/A	N/A	N/A	N/A	N/A
Revenue	100	100	100	100	100	100	100	100	100
Energy costs	(12)	(12)	(12)	(12)	(12)	(12)	(12)	(12)	(12)
Direct carbon costs	0	0	0	0	0	0	0	0	0
Other costs	(60)	(60)	(60)	(60)	(60)	(60)	(60)	(60)	(60)
Profit after tax	28	28	28	28	28	28	28	28	28
Depreciation	0	0	0	0	0	0	0	0	0
Capital expenditure	0	0	0	0	0	0	0	0	0
Cash flow	28	28	28	28	28	28	28	28	28
Discounted cash flow	26	24	21	19	17	15	13	12	
Terminal value									89
Total values of cash flows 2005–2011	147								
Total values of terminal cash flow	89								
Total value	236								

We then began building in estimates of the impacts of the ETS into the model. Factors that we considered included:

- The phasing structure of the ETS: we split the scheme into three: Phase 1 (assumed to be 2005–2007), Phase 2 (assumed to be 2008–2012) and Phase 3 (post-2012). The average price of carbon permits in each phase then needs to be estimated. Furthermore the proportion of permits that are allocated 'free' (in other words the proportion of a company's current emissions that are covered by allowances issued) in each phase must be considered.

- The underlying emissions data for the business (we made an estimate of tonnes of carbon dioxide per tonne of production).

- The ability to sell excess permits: we set up our model to allow this function to be turned on or off, to explore the impact of scenarios where excess permits cannot be sold (which may occur if the market were not sufficiently liquid, for instance).

- Penalty costs each year – this required particular attention as the model must contain an automatic calculation to decide whether the company should pay the fine or buy allowances each year. Remember that if a company does not purchase sufficient allowances to cover its shortfall then it must both pay a fine and roll over the emissions that aren't covered by allowances into next year's requirement; the model must reflect this.

- The effect that carbon prices will have on energy costs (which therefore have to be split into energy source; coal, electricity, gas, oil etc.) through cost passed through from the electricity sector. We based our assumptions on general estimates for the level of cost pass through that would maximise energy sector profits, but again this was for illustrative purposes only.

Initially we ran the model with the following assumptions:

		2005–7	2008–12	>2012
		Phase 1	Phase 2	Phase 3
Price of carbon	€ per tonne	25.0	35.0	50.0
'Free' allocation	%	95%	90%	60%
Penalty for shortfall	€ per tonne	40.0	100.0	100.0
Increase in energy prices	%	8%	16%	39%

This gave a revised valuation approximately 19 per cent lower than the original case, due to the introduction of basic carbon costs and increases in energy prices:

	31 Dec 2005	31 Dec 2006	31 Dec 2007	31 Dec 2008	31 Dec 2009	31 Dec 2010	31 Dec 2011	31 Dec 2012	Terminal year
	€'m	€'m	€'m	€'m	€'m	€'m	€'m	€'m	€'m
ETS phase	N/A	N/A	N/A	N/A	N/A	N/A	N/A	N/A	N/A
Revenue	100	100	100	100	100	100	100	100	100
Energy costs	(12)	(13)	(13)	(14)	(14)	(14)	(14)	(14)	(17)
Direct carbon costs	(1)	(1)	(1)	(2)	(2)	(2)	(2)	(2)	(11)
Other costs	(60)	(59)	(59)	(59)	(59)	(59)	(59)	(59)	(55)
Profit after tax	27	27	27	25	25	25	25	25	17
Depreciation	0	0	0	0	0	0	0	0	0
Capital expenditure	0	0	0	0	0	0	0	0	0
Cash flow	27	27	27	25	25	25	25	25	17
Discounted cash flow	26	23	20	17	15	14	12	11	
Terminal value									55
Total values of cash flows 2005-2011	137								
Total values of terminal cash flow	55								
Total value	192								

The mechanics and structure of building carbon costs into models are therefore relatively straightforward, but scenario building is required to address uncertainties over future conditions. Carbon prices are extremely hard to forecast given the wide range of factors that influence them and the lack of clarity over the shape – or even existence – of a future market. Scenario planning makes it possible to map the most likely general future paths for the market to take. To begin with, we built two new scenarios around the case outlined above. In one (referred to as 'low') we assumed that emissions trading receives little buy in as a means to mitigate climate change and that carbon prices remain low throughout the forecast period. In the second (referred to as 'high') carbon prices continue to rise as the restrictions are tightened and the market becomes increasingly short. Re-running the model in the three scenarios gave the following results:

Price scenario	2005–7	2008–12	>2012	Value	% Change vs Pre-ETS value
	Phase 1	Phase 2	Phase 3		
	€	€	€	€	%
Low	15.0	15.0	15.0	211.4m	-11%
Original	25.0	35.0	50.0	192.2m	-19%
High	30.0	50.0	70.0	180.9m	-23%

Of course in reality these scenarios would be updated on a rolling basis as new information becomes available, but they provide both management and investors alike with a view as to how future carbon prices could impact a business's value.

A further critical consideration that the model must take into account is that of cost pass through. The ability of our cement manufacturer to pass on costs has the potential to nullify much of the impact of carbon costs. In fact, there is theoretical evidence to suggest that the introduction of the ETS may increase profitability in some businesses. This is based on the assertion that sales price is determined on marginal cost (i.e. the cost required to produce the next 'marginal' unit). For carbon the marginal cost is determined by the price required to buy the extra permits needed to increase production (and therefore a genuine 'high' cost). However, the average cost of carbon is relatively low since the majority of costs are actually 'free' (i.e. the majority of permits are issued free by the government). Therefore although marginal costs are high (and hence so are sales prices), average costs stay low meaning margins are increased.[4] Of course theory doesn't always translate into reality and in this case it bumps up against the issue of demand elasticity. Some sectors may be better placed than others to pass on costs; cement is not easily transported, for instance, and therefore substitutes from outside the EU will be hard to source; in theory therefore the industry can pass on costs more readily than for example the steel sector (steel is more easily transported). Furthermore, there is an opportunity for the firm that achieves the highest efficiency to set the price for the rest of the market.

More scenarios can be built therefore to examine the impact of what proportion of the marginal cost can be passed on. Re-setting the model to the original scenario for carbon price we ran the following scenarios through the model:

Price scenario	2005–7	2008–12	>2012	% Marginal cost pass through	Value	% Change vs Pre-ETS value
	Phase 1	Phase 2	Phase 3			
	€	€	€	%	€	%
Original	25.0	35.0	50.0	0%	192.2m	-19%
Original	25.0	35.0	50.0	10%	207.1m	-12%
Original	25.0	35.0	50.0	20%	222.0m	-6%
Original	25.0	35.0	50.0	30%	236.9m	0%

Given these assumptions, therefore, it would appear that if the business can pass on an average of around 30 per cent of its marginal cost increases over the course of the ETS, it will approximately break even. Our model has been structured so that the proportion of marginal cost that is passed through adds directly to the selling price; because the average cost of carbon is lower than the marginal cost (as explained above) break even can be achieved without 100 per cent of marginal cost increases being passed on.

The scenarios considered so far have considered the impact of factors largely outside the control of business. However, valuation techniques can equally be applied to assessing various paths of action open to businesses. It is important to remember that when reviewing its carbon management strategy a firm has a range of options:

(1) To minimise its emissions through investments in improved efficiencies

(2) To purchase credits on the spot market (possibly supported through a hedging strategy)

(3) To invest in other recognised schemes such as Clean Development Mechanism (CDM) credits

(4) To ignore the issue and take the fine.

The cost and benefits of taking path 1 can be modelled robustly using DCFs and then compared to the other options (indeed the model will also pick up the value in taking option 4). Capital expenditure costs to achieve a certain level of emissions reductions can be fairly accurately projected and then fed into the model. We ran three scenarios through the model, using the mid cases for both carbon price and cost pass through cases listed above. The investments were assumed to take place in year 1 and the resulting emissions reductions were applied over three years. The correlation presented here between investment and emission reduction is purely hypothetical, but it does represent the diminishing returns that will be experienced when making investments of this nature (it will cost successively more to reduce each further tonne of emissions). It is useful to include a switch in the model to quantify the effects of whether or not the capital expenditure incurred qualifies for Enhanced Capital Allowances (ECAs). Capital allowances (the tax deduction equivalent of depreciation) are usually given at

25 per cent per year on a reducing balance of the outstanding net book value basis; if the expenditure qualifies for ECAs then a business can claim 100 per cent of the value in the first year. This does not have a significant effect on overall business value but the cash flow timing considerations are clearly important from a business planning perspective.

We re-ran the model on the assumption that 20 per cent cost pass through could be achieved, the results of which were as follows:

	Price scenario	Marginal cost pass through	Capital expenditure	Emissions reduction (over 3yrs)	Business value	Change vs Pre- ETS value
No investment	Mid	20%	€0m	0%	222.0m	-6%
Low investment	Mid	20%	€5m	-15%	236.4.m	+0%
Medium investment	Mid	20%	€15m	-24%	249.9m	+6%
High investment	Mid	20%	€25m	-26%	246.9m	+4%

Based on this data the company should make a €15m investment in emissions reductions, which would make the summary of the valuation appear like this:

	31 Dec	31 Dec	31 Dec	31 Dec	31 Dec	31 Dec	31 Dec	31 Dec	Term-inal
	2005	2006	2007	2008	2009	2010	2011	2012	Year
	€'m	€'m	€'m	€'m	€'m	€'m	€'m	€'m	€'m
ETS phase	N/A	N/A	N/A	N/A	N/A	N/A	N/A	N/A	N/A
Revenue	100	103	106	110	110	110	110	110	107
Energy costs	(12)	(13)	(13)	(14)	(14)	(14)	(14)	(14)	(17)
Direct carbon costs	(1)	0	0	0	0	0	0	0	0
Other costs	(60)	(61)	(62)	(63)	(64)	(64)	(64)	(64)	(62)
Profit after tax	27	29	30	33	33	32	32	32	28
Depreciation	2	2	2	2	2	2	2	2	2
Capital expenditure	(15)	0	0	0	0	0	0	0	0
Cash flow	13	30	32	34	34	34	34	34	30
Discounted cash flow	13	26	24	23	20	18	16	14	

Terminal value								95
Total values of cash flows 2005–2011	155							
Total values of terminal cash flow	95							
Total value	250							

In summary, the DCF methodology possesses sufficient adaptability to be a powerful tool for both management of and investors in companies who will be affected by the ETS. In the future if more market-based responses to environmental challenges are implemented then DCF-based models can be developed further. However, it should be noted that this methodology is just one of several options available.

Conclusion

Valuation techniques can be potent tools in aiding the understanding of the impact that climate change and its market-based responses will have on corporate performance. Investment decisions made by management and investors alike can be supported by these techniques. None of the methodologies examined here are new, they are merely enhanced applications of existing techniques. Valuation practitioners will not have to learn new processes therefore, though there is a steep learning curve in terms of understanding the risks and opportunities climate change presents. Of the methodologies examined above, DCF appears to have particular applicability, with real options presenting an interesting, if as yet unproven, potential for the future. We have used the ETS as an illustration of the way climate change can impact value. However, the ETS may prove to be merely the first step towards cost internalisation and therefore a better understanding of the true value of natural resources. As pressure on these resources increases, the ability to manage them effectively and the issue of sustainability will translate ever more directly into the value of the businesses that consume them. In this case the ability to model valuation effects will become increasingly crucial. Incorporating climate change into valuation techniques for businesses is not really a quantum leap at all; it is merely another step in the path towards better understanding of how much value something really is to us.

Notes

1   The concept of a 'sustainable Du Pont analysis' was conceived in conjunction with P3 Capital (http://www.p3capital.com).
2   Read D.J. (CFA) *Stalking the Elusive Business Case for Corporate Sustainability*, 2001.
3   The GGM is most regularly used within the DCF methodology when it is applied to calculate the terminal value. In such instances the final year of the cash flows are normalised and capitalised using a factor generated by the model. The GGM is described formulaically as follows: (1+g)/(WACC – g), where g represents nominal growth of free cash flows into perpetuity and WACC represents the Weighted Average Cost of Capital for the business.
4   Refer to the Carbon Trust Report *The European Emissions Trading Scheme: Implications for Industrial Competitiveness*.

19

Valuation Applications in a Carbon-Constrained World: Qualitative and Quantitative Tools for Investment Managers

Daniel Wells, Ernst & Young

Introduction

Climate change means that corporate decision makers must become smarter, wiser and more far-sighted. The long-term direct and indirect effects on business may be difficult to predict but those businesses that proactively adapt and see beyond the obvious will survive and indeed flourish. Climate change means businesses have to operate within tighter boundaries and be more aware of the resources they consume. No longer can all environmental costs be externalised in the name of financial expediency; market-based responses, however, are creating new asset classes that could generate high returns for those sufficiently fleet of foot to react. The benefits of taking sector leadership in addressing climate change are potentially huge. The threats posed by ignoring climate change are twofold; ignoring climate change risk jeopardises a company's future and ignoring climate change-induced opportunities will cause competitive advantages to be missed. This chapter will explore the use of tools for businesses to support their decision-making process by examining the perspective of an Investment Manager (IM). First will be an introduction to the concept of 'climate change due diligence' (CCDD). As with traditional due diligence (DD), CCDD should identify risks and opportunities, quantify them and explain how they can be managed. Following this will be a section describing the qualitative tools available to assist in the risk identification process. Finally the chapter will build on the work of my preceding chapter to explain how financial models can be used to quantify risk and support risk management through a case study of an IM investing in clean development mechanism (CDM) assets.

The impact of climate change on investment decisions

Corporations are now facing questions from both mainstream and socially responsible investors (SRI) regarding their direct climate change exposure. Answering these questions is challenging, particularly in sectors not normally considered to have a high climate change risk. An operator in the media sector with assets in areas exposed to extreme weather events, for instance, is now required to have a coherent climate risk management strategy. Though these may be new areas of interest for mainstream investors, the asset management community has a long history of incorporating environmental analysis into stock selection, dating back to the emergence of ethical investing and SRI. More sophisticated approaches are now built on the concept that sustainability-related research should be built into normal stock selection and not bolted on as an extra, nor used as a negative screen. A company's approach to climate change is reflective of its approach to risk and its overall business strategy. A company's climate change strategy can therefore be taken as a proxy for overall governance and management ability and an indicator of future performance. Quantifying the relationship between sustainability and performance is a major obsession for the SRI sector[1] and though proving direct, linear correlations may be elusive (especially since the stock market itself displays very few predictable trends) the essence and spirit of this hypothesis is already diffusing into the mainstream asset management community.

As climate change is a material threat to both the short-term (in the case of carbon risk) and long-term viability of a potential investment, CCDD should be introduced to the normal DD process. As in the case of traditional DD, CCDD should identify risks and opportunities, quantify them and explain how they can be managed. It is important to distinguish CCDD from traditional Environmental DD (EDD), as CCDD involves looking beyond relatively straightforward issues such as contaminated land. Comprehensive CCDD involves understanding the sector in which a target works, its relationship with climate change, the attitudes of management and its overall climate change strategy. It certainly goes deeper than solely examining direct carbon risk. A Du Pont analysis was used in my previous chapter to illustrate how the entire process of value creation exists within the context of environmental drivers. CCDD must map the process by which a company creates value and form an understanding of how this process affects, and depends on, the natural environment.

CCDD of, for instance, an international oil major would certainly involve quantification of its carbon intensity and its investment in renewable technology. It should also, however, appraise the entity's attitude to 'secondary' climate change consequences. Questions to ask should include: has the entity considered how climatic refugees will affect its business? Has it considered how the spread of disease through the increase in habitat ranges of vectors (organisms such as mosquitoes that are capable of transporting infectious agents) will affect its future? Such questions can be framed from a business or ethical standpoint, but either way a proactive approach to address these questions, indicative of a well-directed business, is more likely to produce high long-term returns. Similarly, issues that are currently deemed 'ethical' will soon become business critical; an entity, for example, that ignores the effects of increased pandemics will have the issue forced upon them when it begins to affect their workforce.

An asset manager's stock selection is in many ways analogous to the DD process carried out by an acquisitive company. In both cases the 'acquirer' has a fiduciary duty and commercial imperative to consider the long-term potential of the prospective target or investment. Climate change, however, does not currently feature in standard DD approaches. When appraising a potential target, ignoring climate change would jeopardise shareholder value. A consequence of this is that is can only be a matter of time before Mergers and Acquisitions (M&A) transactions are delayed or cancelled due to climate change risks. More troubling is the prospect that many historical transactions have been processed without considering climate change, the results of which will become apparent in the medium- to long-term future.

INVESTMENT QUESTIONS: ASSESSING CLIMATE CHANGE

Whether in an asset management or M&A context, the following are examples of questions that could be explored to facilitate an assessment of a target's climate change exposure:

(1) Does the potential investment have a significant direct carbon exposure (for example a fossil fuel based power generator)?

(2) Does the entity have a coherent carbon management strategy?

(3) Does the entity have a litigation exposure with regards to climate change – i.e. could it be sued for emissions?

(4) Does the entity have assets or infrastructure in areas exposed to direct climate change effects, such as extreme weather events, rising sea levels or permafrost melting?

(5) Is the entity exposed to any secondary climate change effects, such as climate change refugees or pandemics?

(6) Has the entity proactively explored the potential opportunities presented by climate change, for example by investment in renewable energy or carbon reduction projects?

(7) What is the extent of the entity's reputation risk?

(8) Is the entity linked in some way to other companies or assets that have a significant climate change exposure? For example it may have investments in or alliances with such a company, or it may be the company's auditor.

(9) Is the entity aware of its entire climate change exposure, both direct and indirect?

(10) Finally, does the firm have an 'integrated' (see below) climate change strategy?

Investment decisions, whether in traditional investment management or M&A capacity, require the same rigour when analysing climate change. Investors and acquirers have an obligation to carry out appropriate DD on targets, while management of companies must anticipate the questions that will be asked of them by means of a coherent climate change strategy. We now turn our attention to some tools that can support this process.

Qualitative tools to support decision making

Not all of the issues associated with climate change can be modelled in the same straightforward manner that carbon risk can. Indeed, as we will see, even the most sophisticated mathematical models depend on inputs that are inherently subjective. This was, however, also the case for traditional 'pre climate change' modelling. Qualitative considerations have always been critical in business strategy and climate change issues are no exception. As for any other business critical issue, when making an investment decision it is crucial to build a detailed, textured picture of the target and its relationship with climate change. Context mapping is an important part of this process. Wilber has developed the following model for mapping the context within which an individual, or in our case, a company, operates,[2] by means of a quadrant analysis. The model divides the context into *subjective* and *objective* issues; the former concerns outlooks, prejudices, cultures and so forth, while the latter examines the basic definable circumstances involved – i.e. the objective nature of the business and its environment. Issues are further divided into *individual* (pertaining to the entity itself) and *collective* (the sector in which it operates, i.e. 'it' and the competition). The resulting quadrants appear as:

(1) *Individual subjective factors* (such as entity values, the way in which the world is perceived by the entity, prejudices etc.)	(3) *Individual objective factors* (the skills, capabilities and limits of the entity)
(2) *Collective subjective factors* (shared cultural values or biases within the industry in which it operates)	(4) *Collective objective factors* (for instance, the economic and legal environment)

For instance, an operator in the oil and gas sector may have the following characteristics:

(1) *Individual subjective factors*: The company has the view that long-term commercial advantage takes precedent over profit maximisation in the short term and believes that long-term success stems from innovation and the ability to pre-empt future trends.

(2) *Collective subjective factors*: The sector as a whole perceives the ability to extricate maximum short-term results as the prime indicator of success.

(3) *Individual objective factors*: The company has a strong engineering and technical energy expertise that it can utilise to produce new technologies and products.

(4) *Collective objective factors*: Costs previously externalised to the environment are

increasingly being forcibly internalised (e.g. carbon costs) and litigation for poor environmental performance is becoming a possibility.

The mapping exercise here reveals that the target is potentially an attractive long-term investment proposition. It has the cultural values and technical capabilities to respond to climate change, yet it operates in a sector where these attributes are not generally considered in the valuation process. There is a good chance, therefore, that the market, led by sector analysts, is undervaluing the target. In technical valuer's terms a discount could be applied to the target's beta (risk profile in comparison to the market as a whole), relative to its peers, thus increasing its value.

By separating the issues associated with a company into objective and subjective considerations, often new and interesting insights are revealed; often the latter category (cultural attitudes and prejudices) in particular are ignored in traditional analysis. Companies have not been blind to the positive impacts that realigning their culture and strategy can have on their valuation, hence the realignment undertaken by firms such as General Electric.

When appraising potential investments, decision makers are often advised that the three key criteria are 'management, management, management'. Management attitudes are crucial in forming a corporate culture and behavioural models can be used to better understand them. It has been proposed, for instance, that human (and hence corporate) thinking consists of loops of action and reflection.[3] There are different levels of loops – in level one, strategy and thinking run along traditional lines; solutions to problems are constructed based on solutions to prior problems. Difficulties occur when new problems dictate the need for new methods of thought; if the overall frame of reference is wrong then attempts to solve a problem by modifying behaviour will fail. Climate change is such a problem. Unlike many threats to businesses it is not immediately visible, nor is it entirely external (the problem stems from human actions). The consequences of climate change are both direct and indirect and predicting the consequences of especially the latter group is highly difficult. A level one response to climate change by a project finance (PF) provider may focus on paper usage by the head office, but the entity may find it makes little progress with this strategy; 'level two' thinking is required. Climate change necessitates an *integrated* approach and awareness that a company's relationship with climate change is not just its direct carbon exposure. An entity responding in a creative and far-sighted way may be exhibiting level two thinking, which may indicate a 'strong buy' proposition. In the PF example this would entail not only an analysis of the lending portfolio and wider stakeholder relationships, but an understanding that the internal business practices (down to the level of office paper usage) are also crucial as having one's 'own house in order' is essential to being seen to be a responsible business. The paradigm shift required would be to view climate change as a strategic issue.

Investment managers and potential acquirers should build up CCDD procedures that are sensitive enough to pick up the indicators of a company's climate change risk, some of which may not be immediately apparent. Models developed for this purpose can be expanded in the future to appraise other sustainability-related issues. These issues will become business constraints, in the same way that carbon has, as we move closer to the planet's capacity to support our economy and way of life. Along with more objective measures of a company's systems and procedures (for example an assessment of the Environmental Management System being used), these models can help form a deeper understanding of potential investments. As their use and sophistication increases, companies will need to establish robust climate change strategies to attract capital and potential acquirers.

Quantitative tools to support decision making

Internalising some of the cost of carbon has made it possible to begin to develop quantitative models to support strategy. My previous chapter described general approaches that can be adopted to quantify the impact of emissions trading on a business. Here we will build on this by examining how these tools can be applied to more specific investment decisions.

Kyoto's flexible mechanisms have created a new asset class, based on carbon reductions, which can be acquired, created, sold or generally managed, just like conventional assets. This affects the decision making needs of a variety of entities with a vested interest, including Annex 1 governments, NGO buyers (such as the World Bank), institutional and investment funds, offset purchasers and industrial sectors covered by emissions trading schemes.

Whether carbon assets are acquired for compliance or speculative reasons, the nature of this new asset class should be carefully considered as they make an interesting, if enigmatic, investment proposition. Stomach-churning volatility has characterised the early trading period, presenting both high risk and high-potential returns. As an alternative asset, hedge funds may find carbon particularly to their taste, with the possibility of relatively high returns for a given risk for those with sufficient understanding of the market. Scheme participants, however, have faced a steep learning curve by being forced into the trading market for compliance reasons; they have been forced to become traders.

To illustrate the complexities involved in 'Carbon Finance', we will focus here on the investment opportunities presented by the CDM. To enable us to cover the full range of relevant investment issues we shall consider them from the standpoint of a fully flexible trading entity, participating in the market for speculative purposes, though the questions raised could equally apply to a scheme participant using CDM-generated 'Certified Emissions Reductions' certificates (CERs) for compliance purposes.

To quantify risk we must first examine some of the risks associated with CDM ventures:

- *Delivery risk:* the risk that the project will not deliver the credits projected, on a timely basis, either due to failure to achieve approval with the CDM board or technical failure

- *Market risk*: the risk that the credit stream will not achieve the forward market prices projected

- *Liquidity risk*: the liquidity risk in the investment

- *Compliance risk:* the compliance spread between project-generated CERs and the market price for European Union Allowances (EUAs). For instance, limits on CERs being sold into various emissions trading schemes may affect their transferability

- *Political/Sovereign risk*: the inherent risk in the host country.

Based on these risks and the investment strategy proposed, the trading entity will need to decide on the most appropriate vehicle for investing in these assets. Investing in CERs can take several forms:

- Equity investments in CDM projects

- The purchase of CERs on the spot market for future sale

- Forward purchases of CERs by means of an Emissions Rights Purchase Agreement (ERPA), the details of which may vary and include the purchase of:

    - an option for a future purchase

    - a right of first refusal

    - an outright purchase of future CERs subject to delivery risk

    - an outright purchase of future CERs with guaranteed delivery.

An asset manager may wish to include a variety of the categories listed above in their portfolio, to take advantage of opportunities and to hedge against risk. For different categories of asset held there will clearly be different considerations:

	Market risk	Delivery risk	Liquidity/ compliance risk
Equity investments in CDM projects	✓	✓	✓
Fully delivered CERs	✓	✗	✓
ERPAs with guaranteed delivery terms	✓	✗	✓
ERPAs without guaranteed delivery	✓	✓	✓

The choice of category held can also influence the business model adopted. Illiquid assets such as equity investments would favour a Private Equity (PE) model, while portfolios of CERs and ERPAs would be better suited to a Hedge Fund (HF) format. An asset manager may set up separate funds for different business models.

Deconstructing overall risk into its constituent parts enables us to begin to build quantitative models. Valuation models can help project developers price projects, for both internal investment appraisal reasons and to attract third-party investment. Such models will, in many cases, be a mandatory audit requirement. Though there is not yet a consensus on best practice for carbon accounting, nor specific guidance from accounting standards, a common current approach is to treat carbon assets as 'Financial Assets' (as opposed to Inventory) and as such, under International Financial Reporting Standards (IFRS), they are valued at 'Fair Value'. In the first instance Fair Value will mean marking assets to market. For portfolios of owned credits such as EUAs that have readily ascertainable spot market values, this will be a straightforward process. Less vanilla assets require increasingly complex valuation approaches, however. Owned CERs can be valued using the forward EUA/CER 'exchange rate' (referred to here as the compliance spread) and by considering a potential liquidity discount. For options on CERs, forward agreements without guaranteed delivery clauses or equity stakes in CDM projects, however, the complexity is sufficient to require a supporting model. The case study below illustrates how such a model could be constructed.

Case study: CDM asset structuring for an investment manager

We will examine the valuation tools available to support the Investment Manager (IM) in the structuring of their portfolio. Let's suppose the IM has spotted the opportunity to create returns in the carbon market and to this end has hired an experienced trading team. It markets itself to high net worth individuals or institutional investors and is not bound by the strict regulations that would affect a conventional retail fund. The IM, therefore, can invest in any of the categories of carbon assets listed above, or any derivatives associated with them. It can also short sell, which will aid its hedging strategy. After some consideration, the IM decides to launch two funds, one illiquid and based on a PE model and one investing in more liquid assets along an HF strategy. The investment options open to these respective funds are:

(1) *Private equity fund:* an equity stake in a CDM generating project

(2) *Hedge fund:* acquisition of portfolio of forward agreements to purchase CERs via ERPAs.

In each case careful analysis will be required to understand the risks and properly price the investments.

(1) Private equity fund

The PE fund will be based on relatively long-term, illiquid investments, which may be levered by securing debt based on the investments, to increase returns to shareholders. An appropriate mechanism, therefore, may be to make equity investments in CDM projects to generate CERs that can be sold into the ETS. Projects such as this can be modelled fairly simply once the risks discussed above have been separated into their component parts. In this case imagine that a target Internal Rate of Return (IRR) of 26 per cent has been set by the IM for the project. As explained above, the discounts here (especially for delivery risk) are only robust when used across a portfolio of projects, but for illustrative reasons we will focus here on the valuation of a single project.

Decision required:

How should the IM structure its PE investment to maximise returns?

Relevant questions:

i. What level of debt and capital expenditure should the project undertake?

ii. How sensitive will the project be to changes in risk assumptions?

iii. How high do future prices of EUAs have to be to support the desired IRR?

To answer these questions we must build a model. As in my previous chapter the most appropriate model would be a Discounted Cash Flow (DCF) model, due to its flexibility. For illustrative purposes assume that the IM has the opportunity to invest in a Methane Capture project in a hypothetical developing country. The project is partly through the CDM approval process and reasonable, quantitative methods have been employed to estimate the delivery risk, compliance risk, overall country risk, market risk and, of course, the actual volume of CERs expected. The key inputs to the DCF will be:

	Units	Input
Market risk	€	Varies
CER stream	tCO_2k	Varies
Delivery risk adjustment[4]	%	60
Compliance/Liquidity spread	%	10
Discount rate	%	12[5]

Using these inputs it is possible to calculate both the project's Net Present Value (NPV, i.e. the sum of all its risk adjusted cash flows) and IRR – the effective annual return of the project expressed in percentage terms – using a DCF model. For simplicity's sake we will assume that the project is wholly owned by the IM (in reality it will more likely take the form of joint ownership with a local party). The valuation appears as follows:[6]

CDM equity investment – no debt								
	Units	2006	2007	2008	2009	2010	2011	2012
Risk adjusted CER stream @ 60%	tCO_2k	0	120	143	155	157	160	158
Revenue from CERs	€'000	0	1,800	2,210	2,531	2,632	2,793	2,871

CDM equity investment – no debt								
	Units	2006	2007	2008	2009	2010	2011	2012
Administration, depreciation and interest costs	€'000	(1,014)	(814)	(814)	(814)	(814)	(814)	(814)
Profit before taxation	€'000	(1,014)	985	1,396	1,716	1,818	1,979	2,057
Profit after tax	€'000	(1,014)	985	986	1,201	1,273	1,385	1,440
Remove non cash items/add other cash items[7]	€'000	(4,286)	714	714	714	714	714	714
Free cash flow:	€'000	(5,300)	1,700	1,700	1,916	1,987	2,099	2,154
Discounted cash flow @ 12%	€'000	(5,008)	1,434	1,280	1,288	1,193	1,126	1,031
Total values of cash flows 2006–2012	€'000	2,344						
	IRR:	26.5%						

The forecast NPV of the project is therefore €2,344k. The key inputs to the model have been highlighted and can be flexed easily to determine the impact on the overall return. This is useful as it allows the IM to gauge the magnitude of the impact of, say, an increase in delivery risk. Sensitivity tables can be used to establish the sensitivity of the project's value to the various inputs. In this case, for example, taking a 50 per cent delivery adjustment as opposed to 60 per cent reduces the IRR by around 7 per cent.

Decisions regarding the funding structure of the project can then be made. Project returns can potentially be increased by either replacing equity investment with debt or assuming debt to enable extensions of scope. This can be modelled in a straightforward manner by adding cash flows for debt drawdown and repayments. If structured appropriately, assuming a level of debt should increase the IM's return. The risk of the project will, of course, be increased, as it will need to generate enough cash flow to make the debt repayments. Debt could be used to replace equity funding to increase returns. Imagine in this case, however, that the IM has the option of extending the project to generate more CERs. Once the total cost of the extension and the number of forecast extra CERs are known, the marginal cost of producing the CERs can be calculated. For our case assume:

- Debt required to fund project extension: €2,000k

- Extra CERs produced: 400 tCO$_2$k extra

- Marginal cost of producing extra CERs: €5.00/tCO$_2$

The IM's cost of borrowing will also be a factor on overall returns. If the interest rate on the debt is 5.5 per cent, the valuation would appear as follows:

CDM equity investment – €2,000k debt								
	Units	2006	2007	2008	2009	2010	2011	2012
Risk adjusted CER stream @ 60%	tCO$_2$k	0	160	183	195	197	200	198
Revenue from CERs	€'000	0	2,399	2,826	3,182	3,302	3,490	3,596
Administration, depreciation and interest costs	€'000	(1,410)	(1,197)	(1,183)	(1,168)	(1,152)	(1,136)	(1,118)
Profit before taxation	€'000	(1,410)	1,203	1,644	2,014	2,150	2,355	2,477
Profit after tax	€'000	(1,410)	1,203	1,213	1,410	1,505	1,648	1,734
Remove non cash items/add other cash items	€'000	(4,242)	745	731	716	700	684	666
Free cash flow:	€'000	(5,652)	1,947	1,943	2,126	2,205	2,332	2,401
Discounted cash flow @ 12%	€'000	(5,341)	1,643	1,464	1,430	1,324	1,250	1,149
Total values of cash flows 2006–2012	€'000	2,920						
	IRR:	28.9%						

The model shows that the NPV has increased from €2,334k to €2,920k. In this case, therefore, assuming the debt and taking on the project extension has increased both the project IRR and NPV. A model like this could also be used to back solve the marginal cost of CER required to achieve a certain return. Such models will, therefore, be vital tools to IM's considering such investments.

Conclusion:

(1)   In this case it would be sensible to take the option of the €2,000k debt to maximise returns. Capital expenditure of €7,000k is required in year one to support the extended project.

(2)   Increasing delivery risk by decreasing the delivery risk adjustment from 60 per cent to 50 per cent, decreases the project IRR by around seven per cent.

(3)   Future EUA prices have to be between €16.00/tCO$_2$ and €20.00/tCO$_2$ to support the IRR of 29 per cent. Note that this, relatively high, IRR is required to compensate investors for the illiquid nature of the asset.

(2) Hedge fund

A more likely investment for the HF would be assets with a higher liquidity, such as credits bought on forward contracts. The investment assumption underpinning this would be that forward CERs could be purchased via ERPAs and sold at a profit to other market participants. In this case, assume that the investment vehicle will be ERPAs with guaranteed delivery terms and that there is, therefore, no requirement for an adjustment for delivery risk. This investment vehicle can be modelled and valued in a similar method to the equity investment. Imagine that a lower target IRR – say 17 per cent – has been set. As the assets can be liquefied more easily than the PE fund, a lower return will be acceptable.

Decision required:

What fund structure and price should the HF set for forward ERPA purchases to maximise returns?

Relevant questions:

(1)   What price for CERs must be set in the ERPA to achieve a 17 per cent IRR – i.e. what should the 'exercise price' of an ERPA be?

(2)   What price should the IM pay for the option to buy the ERPA at the given exercise price?

The following example models the income from the investment as CER sales into the ETS using the forward curves (again adjusted for the compliance spread), which is offset against the cost of obtaining the credits via an ERPA. We have assumed that the ERPA sets a single cost per CER across all years in the forecast; also that the number of CERs purchased via the ERPA will equal the risk adjusted CER stream calculated above. The ERPA payment will consist of two parts: an initial down payment to secure the contract (the 'option cost') and a stream of balancing payments as the CERs become available at the exercise price stipulated by the ERPAs. In this example assume that the IM has been offered the right to buy ERPAs at an option cost of €1.75 per CER.

CDM – ERPA portfolio								
		2006	**2007**	**2008**	**2009**	**2010**	**2011**	**2012**
		€'000	€'000	€'000	€'000	€'000	€'000	€'000
CERs sold into ETS:	tCO2k	0	160	183	195	197	200	198
Revenue from CERs	€'000	**0**	**2,399**	**2,826**	**3,182**	**3,302**	**3,490**	**3,596**
Option cost @ €12.80	€'000	(1,986)	0	0	0	0	0	0
Exercise of ERPA payments @ €1.75	€'000	0	(2,048)	(2,347)	(2,501)	(2,524)	(2,562)	(2,539)
Total cost		**(1,986)**	**(2,048)**	**(2,347)**	**(2,501)**	**(2,524)**	**(2,562)**	**(2,539)**
Admin costs	€'000	(50)	0	0	0	0	0	0
Taxation @ 30%	€'000	0	0	0	0	(77)	(279)	(317)
Net income from CERs	€'000	(2,036)	352	479	681	702	650	740
Discounted cash flow @ 12%	€'000	**(1,923)**	**297**	**361**	**458**	**421**	**348**	**354**
Total values of cash flows 2006–2012	€'000	**317**						
	IRR:	**17.0%**						

The model shows that the necessary ERPA price per CER is €12.80, if the cost to buy the option of the ERPA itself is €1.75 per CER, to support an IRR of 17 per cent.

Note though that the NPV of the ERPA option is considerably lower than the equity investment. Investment managers often like to work with IRRs as the percentage output facilitates comparison of the return of €1 invested in one project versus another. However, the natural limitations of IRR should not be forgotten – for example, it assumes that all intermediary cash flows can be re-invested at the IRR rate for the project and it gives no impression of the absolute return from each option. The IM should carefully consider which indicator to use, therefore, when choosing the funds to allocate to investment vehicles, given the options open.

The IM can now employ a different range of techniques to establish whether the option cost of €1.75 is good value. Assuming the contract stipulates the *right* and not the *obligation* to buy CERs at a certain price at a specified future date then the ERPA is effectively a call option. The value of this option can, therefore, be calculated using options valuations techniques. In my previous chapter, the application of options valuations techniques to value real options open to a business was discussed. In the case of an ERPA secured by an advance payment we are able to work through an illustrated example of the application of options valuations in their original form. The Black-Scholes-Merton formula is the most well known and widely used such formula. The key inputs for a general call option are:

- the present price of the 'stock' (in this case the price of carbon)

- the exercise price of the option (i.e. the price stipulated in the ERPA)

- the interest rate (which is used as a proxy to reflect the overall, general upward drift expected in a market and to reflect the discount rate used to calculate the present value of the option)

- the length of time until the option expires

- the volatility of the underlying asset (i.e. the price of carbon).

These inputs are reasonably intuitive. The value of the option increases as the difference between the exercise price and possible future price increases; the possible future price increases with greater volatility, a higher interest rate and greater period to maturity. In the case of the ERPA, however, the inputs need to be modified somewhat. Due to the fact that a readily available forward price exists, the present spot price for carbon can be replaced and there is no need to adjust for the projected 'upward drift' of the market. The value of the option is discounted back at the risk-free rate (given by the interest rate, as above). This modified formula is known as Black's model.

Taking the exercise price from the above ERPA portfolio valuation, we can set the inputs for the model as follows and value the option on a 2009 vintage CER, by way of an example.

	Units	Input
Exercise price	€	12.80
Forward EUA price	€	17.70
Compliance discount	%	10
Forward CER price	€	16.28
Risk free rate	%	4.5
Market volatility	%	35

Of all these inputs the volatility is the hardest to quantify, due to the immaturity of the carbon market.[8] Volatilities of spot prices have been extremely high since the inception of the European ETS; anecdotal evidence from traders has suggested that at times volatilities have reached 100 per cent and average volatilities over the period have been around 80 per cent. However, we will assume that the movement in forward prices is less erratic and therefore will assume volatility to be 35 per cent – higher than the volatility one would expect for a normal stock (normally of the order of 20 per cent to 30 per cent) but significantly lower than spot price volatilities. Again, however, the measure of volatility will become increasingly robust as the market matures.

Running with these inputs we can now value the option using Black's model:

ERPA option valuation		
Current year:		2006
CER vintage:		2009
ERPA purchase price	€	12.80
Term	Years	3
2009 Current EUA price	€	17.70
CDM to EUA conversion premium	%	8.0 %
2009 Current CER price	€	16.28
Risk free rate	%	5.5 %
Volatility	% p.a.	35.0 %
Value of option		
d1		0.70
d2		0.09
Call option	€	4.66
Put option	€	1.69

In this case, therefore, each option to buy a 2009 vintage ERPA is worth €4.66 (note the model also calculates the value of a 'put' option; that is the right to sell a CER at the stated price at a stated date in the future). Applying the model to the entire portfolio the overall value per ERPA can be calculated:

ERPA option valuation – multi vintage							
Current year:	2006						
CER vintage:		2007	2008	2009	2010	2011	2012
ERPA purchase price	€	12.80	12.80	12.80	12.80	12.80	12.80
Term	Years	1	2	3	4	5	6
Value per call option	€	**4.00**	**4.41**	**4.66**	**4.80**	**4.87**	**4.89**
Number of ERPAs per year:		160	183	195	197	200	198

ERPA option valuation – multi vintage							
Value of options	€'000	640	809	910	946	975	971
Total value of options	€'000	5,250					
Number of ERPAs:		1,135					
Total value per ERPA:	€	4.63					

Black's model therefore values the overall ERPA portfolio at €4.63 per option (the average option value per ERPA). As the cost to the IM was €1.75 per ERPA (see above), it follows that in this (hypothetical) case, it would appear that something of a bargain has been achieved.

Conclusion on HF fund:

(1)   The price stipulated in the ERPAs should be €12.80 to achieve an IRR of €17.00.

(2)   With this exercise price in the ERPA, the option cost of €1.75 should be taken.

In summary, therefore, the IM will be able to make important decisions about the pricing of the various investment approaches and will be able to allocate capital according to the investment priorities. Capital can be spread across liquid and illiquid assets in the two funds operated. A hedging strategy can also be employed to minimise risk to investors.

We've seen with this case study that quantitative tools can be used to support the carbon finance strategies of market participants. In this complex and volatile new asset class this can be of particular use, especially in price setting and risk disaggregation. This section will, however, end with an important caveat; the models proposed here are only as good as the inputs used. DCF-based valuations will be of little use at best (and misleading at worst) if inputs (e.g. delivery risk) are not based on rigorous, empirical calculations. Equally, the options valuation techniques will be flawed if the volatility estimates are erroneous. Like the drunk who misuses the lamppost as a means of support, these techniques should be used as a tool to help illuminate a particular strategy's merits and not as the sole basis of propping up an investment approach.

Conclusion

Despite the obvious uncertainty that climate change introduces into corporate decision making, there are a range of techniques available that can support the process. Conventional corporate finance techniques can be adapted for use in carbon management strategies. The case study here examined the options of an IM investing in CDM assets. Other implications of climate change cannot be directly modelled, but the use of qualitative tools can greatly enhance an investor's or an acquirer's ability to construct an impression of an entity's relationship with climate change. These tools enable the patterns of thoughts necessary for investors to go beyond the immediately obvious climate change effects and form a meaningful, multi-dimensional map of a company's profile. Ultimately this will enable better decision making and a more effective allocation of capital to those businesses best equipped to withstand or indeed flourish in the twenty-first century. Though carbon costs are only one of many relevant issues, they make it possible to build robust quantitative models to support some investment decisions. This is a strong precedent and gives grounds for optimism for the future as we endeavour to integrate economic optimisation with environmental sustainability.

Appendix 1: CDM risks

Project delivery risk

This refers to the risk that a given project won't produce the expected credits, either due to technical failures or a failure to achieve CDM approval. As a rule the further down the approval process a project is, the more likely the project is to generate CERs. The risk of non-delivery is reflected by means of a direct adjustment to the estimated CER volumes. The proportion of CER volumes included in the valuation, therefore, will depend largely on what stage the project is at. Equally, different types of projects (methane capture versus hydro electricity generation, for instance) will have differing risk profiles. The following are fictional examples of the proportion of estimated CERs actually included in the valuation ('delivery adjustments'), based on several different project types at each stage of the approval process (note that the example figures given here are purely illustrative and not based on any real data):

	Project design	Validation	Registration	Monitoring	Verification	Issuance
HFC capture	30%	50%	80%	80%	90%	100%
Methane capture	15%	25%	60%	60%	75%	100%
Renewal energy (e.g. wind)	15%	20%	45%	45%	70%	100%

On an individual project level it is unrealistic to apply a certain factor to reflect the possibility of non-delivery. The credits will almost certainly either be delivered or not and there is little chance that only, say 30 per cent, will be supplied. However, by applying the discount across a portfolio of projects a statistically realistic projection can be obtained.

It is critical that the most robust methodology available is used to estimate the delivery risk. The discounts taken should be based on historical data from, where possible, third-party sources indicating the likelihood of success given the approval status and the project's nature. As the CDM board processes more projects this data will become more robust and an industry consensus will emerge. As the calculation will be closely examined by the funds' auditors, employing empirical rigour from an early stage will ensure the audit process passes more agreeably.

Delivery risk can be mitigated through sensible preventative courses of action. Where delivery is dependent on a third party (in the case of a forward agreement with no delivery guarantee) the contract can be structured to maximise the incentive for the counterparty to produce the agreed CERs on a timely basis. In the case of owner- managed projects, use of third party consultants with CDM project management expertise can expedite the approval process.

Market risk

The second primary risk faced by CDM developers and credit purchasers, is that the future market price of CERs will be lower than forecast. The most likely cause of this would be an overall long position in the market leading to decreasing prices, but due to the complexity of carbon price drivers, a price decrease could be caused by many externalities. This risk should be reflected in valuations through the use of a forward price curve, representing the market's view of future carbon prices.

The impact of market risk on financial performance can be mitigated through hedging strategies such as short selling one carbon-based asset to protect a long position in another asset.

Compliance risk

Due to the ongoing implementation of relevant EU legislation governing the transferability of CERs (by means of the 'Linking Directive') a degree of uncertainty remains over the future system by which CERs can be sold into emission trading schemes such as the European ETS. Possible caps on the use of CERs imposed by member states presents a further complication. This risk is reflected through the CER/EUA 'exchange rate' – the ratio of CERs to one EUA – or the compliance spread. Calculation of the spread will entail both qualitative and quantitative analysis and should reflect the most up-to-date information available. Clearly this too will become more accurate as more data becomes available.

Liquidity risk

For practical purposes the market for EUAs is liquid. Liquidity risk for CERs however, is closely tied to the compliance risk and calculation of the appropriate discount may be combined with the compliance risk calculation. The liquidity of CERs depends on their transferability into EUAs (or other emission assets in the future). The liquidity of an asset can often be estimated using the bid/ask spread; from this an appropriate discount rate can be calculated. Consequently, in the case study, we consider liquidity risk to be incorporated in compliance risk and accounted for in the valuation by means of the 'compliance spread'.

Currency risk

Revenue derived from CERs is likely (for the near future at least) to be denominated in Euros, but clearly if CDM projects generate revenues from other sources (electricity generation for the host country market, for instance) or where costs are borne in foreign currencies, currency risk is a consideration and appropriate hedging strategies should be employed.

Political and sovereign risk

Due to the nature of CDM projects and the variety of host countries in which they may be undertaken, political risk should be considered in the valuation if necessary. Due to the general nature of this risk on projects it would be normal to reflect it by means of the overall discount rate used.

Other risks

Depending on the nature of the assets (forward agreements, options or project investments, for instance) a variety of other risks, including counterparty, taxation or terrorism may also be a consideration that will have to be reflected in the valuation.

Notes

1   Refer, for instance, to Société Générale, *Socially Responsible Investing: SRI and Valuation: The Missing Link?* 2006.
2   Wilber K.*Integral Psychology*, Boston: Shambhala, 2000.
3   Ballard D. *Learning Approaches to Change*, 2000.
4   In this case, therefore, only 60 per cent of the projected CER volumes are converted into revenue in the valuation to reflect risk that the project will not actually deliver.
5   Note that to avoid double counting the discount rate should not include a tax shield in the cost of debt calculation, as tax in the model below is calculated on a post-interest cash flow basis, and therefore already includes an interest tax shield.
6   The model makes various assumptions regarding costs, tax calculations and other issues; these should be taken as purely illustrative and not reflective of real practice, which may vary by country.
7   This adjustment removes non-cash items in the profit and loss account, such as depreciation and accrued interest, and adds cash items such as capital expenditure and cash in from debt drawdown. The large negative adjustment in 2006 is due to the high capital expenditure required on commencing the project.
8   Volatility is given by the standard deviation in prices away from the mean. Around 68 per cent of values over the period measured will be within one standard deviation of the mean and around 95 per cent will lie within two standard deviations. If a price of say €15/tCO_2 has a volatility of 30 per cent over a year, then 68 per cent of the time the price will lie from €10.50/tCO_2 and €19.50/tCO_2, while 95 per cent of the time the price will be between €6.00/tCO_2 and €24.00/tCO_2.

Communications Strategies – Engaging Consumers and Employees

20

Companies, Customers and Climate Change: the Impact of Public Opinion

Arlo Brady, Freud Communications and Judge Business School

Introduction

Over the past few years, climate change has obstinately emerged as a top government priority in many countries around the world. In the UK, for one, Prime Minister Tony Blair is prominent for having stated that *'climate change is probably, long-term the single most important issue we face as a global community'*. He and his advisors have suggested that it represents a more serious threat to UK security than terrorism or other more traditional threats.[1] This belief led to it being given significant priority in the discussions between the leaders of the world's richest nations at the 2005 G8 summit, which took place in Scotland. Eileen Clausen, president of the US-based Pew Center, sums up the problem: *'Every generation faces a challenge. In the 1930s, it was the creation of Social Security. In the 1960s, it was putting a man on the moon. In the 1980s, it was ending the Cold War. Our generation's challenge will be addressing global climate change while sustaining a growing global economy'.*[2]

In a democracy where this high-level governmental and NGO support exists, we could assume that climate change is also an issue high on the public agenda. This chapter seeks to establish the extent to which this is true, and then goes on to explore the implications of this awareness on the business community.

The evolution of climate change

Climate change as a concept has only really been a significant issue in the public psyche for the last ten years. Prior to this it was largely scientific hypothesis and conjecture, written about and discussed in elitist journals such as *Nature* or *Science*, but not featured in the mainstream press or on televised media. There are a number of conspiracy theories suggesting that industry lobbies, namely the now defunct Global Climate Coalition (GCC) and other vested interests, collaborated and conspired to keep the real story from the public eye. It is certainly true that a number of quasi-scientific organisations were (and still are) founded and funded with a view to muddying the waters. The biggest problem facing climate change activists, however, is gathering incontrovertible evidence. The earth's climate is inherently complex and, as my geological training is often a reminder, has always been changing. It has been very difficult to prove that the recently identified changes are out of the ordinary, and that they are directly caused by human activity, as opposed to being the result of natural variation. Having said all this, over the past five years the evidence has mounted, and now it looks beyond doubt. This is largely due to the efforts of the Intergovernmental Panel on Climate Change (IPCC), an influential group established in 1988 by the UN, whose remit was to assess the 'risk of human-induced climate change'. Their 2001 report[3] stated authoritatively that 'most of the warming observed over the last 50 years is likely to be attributable to human activities'.

According to NASA, the six hottest years on record have now all occurred in the last eight years, with 2005 being the hottest ever. Data gathered from tree rings, ice cores, ancient coral and the fossil record, show that the Earth has probably never warmed this quickly.[4]

In a 'shrinking world' marked by globalisation, the results of this warming are unfolding in front of our very eyes. The everyday man and woman on the street would have to be relatively unaware of their surroundings to avoid the, by now regular, newspaper and TV news broadcasts profiling disappearing glaciers, forest fires and fatal heat waves, Arctic ice melting, drought in the Amazon rainforest, and lethal floods in Latin America and Southern Asia. In the face of this omnipresent coverage, even the sceptical President of the United States, George Bush, has recently expressed his concern: *'We must address the issue of global climate change. We must also act in a serious and responsible way, given the scientific uncertainties. While these uncertainties remain, we can begin now to address the human factors that contribute to climate change. Wise action now is an insurance policy against future risks.'[5]*

President Bush's concern did not extend to signing the United States up to the Kyoto Protocol, nor did it suggest that the uncertainties were diminishing with each day, but it is a step in the right direction. It is interesting to note that despite President Bush's scepticism, nine north-eastern states, California's Governor Arnold Schwarzenegger and 194 mayors from US towns and cities, have pledged to adopt Kyoto-style legal limits on greenhouse gas (GHG) emissions.

As might be expected, recent years have seen a number of business leaders boarding the climate change bandwagon – some with more sincerity than others. Lord Browne, the CEO of oil giant BP, made a famous speech at Stanford University in 2002 stating that he believed that *'the American people expect a company like BP […] to offer answers and not excuses.'* He also said:

'Climate change is an issue which raises fundamental questions about the relationship between companies and society as a whole, and between one generation and the next. […] Companies composed of highly skilled and trained people can't live in denial of mounting evidence gathered by hundreds of the most reputable scientists in the world.'[6] Lord Browne has since repositioned BP as an energy company – not an oil company. He instigated a

high profile re-branding exercise and has made climate change a central feature of the overall business strategy.

More recently a group of heavyweight companies, including Ford, Motorola and Dow and Baxter Healthcare, collaborated to set up the Chicago Climate Exchange (CCX). The exchange represents North America's only, and the world's first, GHG emissions registry, reduction and trading system. By the end of December 2006, all members will have voluntarily reduced direct emissions four per cent below a baseline period of 1998-2001. A number of prestigious businesses like HSBC (see Box 1) and Sky have pledged to go 'carbon neutral', calculating and offsetting their own individual carbon dioxide (CO_2) emissions. Businesses like ABN AMRO, Alcan, Johnson & Johnson, Starbucks and Timberland have joined forces to create 'The Climate Group'– an independent, non-profit organisation dedicated to advancing business and government leadership on climate change.

BOX 1: HSBC GOES CARBON NEUTRAL

In 2004 HSBC, the world's third largest bank, became the first major bank in the world to commit to going carbon neutral. The bank made the announcement on the opening day of the 10th Conference of the Parties of the UN Framework Convention on Climate Change. Then chairman of the bank, Sir John Bond, said that *'It is our judgement that climate change represents the largest single environmental challenge this century'*. The following year HSBC pledged to plant trees, reduce energy use, buy 'green' electricity and trade carbon credits to cut CO_2 emissions – estimated at more than 550,000 tonnes in 2003. In addition to the carbon-neutral plan, the bank is investing £650,000 in environment research at two UK universities and is developing a range of socially responsible investment funds.

It would seem that opinion formers all over the world are choosing to acknowledge the precautionary principle.[7] The problem with climate change is that we have already 'done the deed'. Moreover it is getting worse, as countries like India and China follow a traditional (Anglo-Saxon) economic development path. However, even if we stopped emitting CO_2 now, it would not be enough to prevent climate chaos. Pandora's Box is wide open. We certainly need to reduce our emissions but we also need to think about adapting to the climatic changes that will occur, regardless of our behaviour.

Understanding the sceptics

Despite the mounting evidence to the contrary, there are still a number of vocal climate change sceptics at large. The majority of these sceptics are now focusing their efforts on the nature of the societal response, rather than disputing the science. There are, however, a number of groups who still dispute the science: notable groups include CO_2 Science (www.co2science.org) and the Greening Earth Society (www.greeningearthsociety.org). Both of these organisations are based in the United States, and are allegedly funded by large corporates with vested interests in fossil fuel extraction and/or use. All of these groups have produced academic-style dossiers explaining why they believe that their viewpoint is correct, but the majority of these documents have since been publicly discredited in peer review journals.

To my mind, the climate change sceptics have made a significant error in their strategy – not only have they backed the wrong horse, but they have lobbied the wrong group of people. Groups like the Competitive Enterprise Institute in the US and the UK-based Scientific Alliance have focused all their efforts on influencing government policy. A sensible short term strategy, but flawed in the long term. Governments within democracies eventually respond to public opinion – it is their Achilles heel. Not only this, but we live in a world defined by trust; and opaque, unaccountable organisations with disputable funding streams like the Greening Earth Society are outplayed by respected Nobel laureates, nimble NGOs such as Greenpeace, and increasingly, by 'enlightened' businesses who are willing and able to voice their opinions.

In a significant attempt to influence public opinion, the Competitive Enterprise Institute recently resorted to producing TV advertisements with the tag line: *'Carbon dioxide. They call it pollution. We call it life.'*[8] Clearly, unlike most businesses, they are unaware of the huge distinction in credibility between public relations and direct advertising. Incidentally another distinction between the two approaches is cost – advertising is much more expensive. It would seem that the funding stream for these types of organisations is yet to dry up.

This lack of success of the sceptical lobby is borne out by research. In the United States, for example, while President Bush responds positively, a majority[9] of the American public favour their country's participation in the Kyoto Protocol. George Bush had better hope that climate change does not become an electoral issue.

Public perception of climate change

Climate change has only recently become a 'real issue' in the eyes of the general public, and even now it is only an issue in certain countries. To get to the bottom of the reasons for this perception it is important to understand the role of government, sceptics, NGOs, celebrities and the media. Armed with this understanding it is easier to consider an appropriate corporate response.

In order for the public to begin to develop an opinion about a specific subject they must first have a degree of understanding, perceived or otherwise. Climate change in its broadest sense is a difficult concept to grasp, particularly if the individual concerned has no formal scientific training. It is therefore important, not only to focus on explaining the concept in clear, logical language, but also to highlight its local-level observable effects. *What does it mean for me, my life, and the lives of my children? How can I make a difference without impacting my quality of life?* These are questions that the media are very good at tackling, but they are also questions that the government of the day should be focused on answering. They may not want to, but if the media has decided to run with the issue, then the government may be forced into responding.

The UK and the US are good examples of different evolutionary approaches. In the UK, climate change has become very much a political issue and has been for some time (see Box 2), whereas in the US it is largely a media, NGO and business issue.

According to a Harris Interactive 2002 study[10] 85 per cent of Americans are aware of the concept of global warming, and 74 per cent of Americans believe the theory. Rather worryingly, a more recent 2005 MIT (Massachusetts Institute of Technology) study[11] found that 17 per cent of Americans had not heard or read about climate change, global warming or a whole list of other associated terms during the past year. In contrast, a 2006 Ipsos-MORI survey[12] in the UK showed that 62 per cent of respondents polled indicated that, not only did they know what climate change was, but that they thought every possible action should be taken to limit it and a further 32 per cent felt that some action should be taken. Divided public attitudes toward global warming, and modest expressions of concern over the issue, distinguish the United States from other industrialised countries. A 2006 Pew Global Attitudes Project survey showed that only 19 per cent of Americans expressed a great deal of personal concern about global warming. Among 15 countries surveyed, only the Chinese expressed a comparably low level of concern – 20 per cent.[13]

While there is a clear difference in public attitudes in Britain and the US, it is a difference that is changing quickly. The American media is increasingly drawing tenuous links between extreme weather events – like the 2005 Hurricane Katrina in New Orleans – and climate change. While these conclusions are difficult, if not impossible to prove, they do have the effect of increasing awareness of the concept of climate change. Following the path-breaking example of Al Gore who has recently produced a documentary film called 'An Inconvenient Truth', we are likely to see a correspondingly fast response from American politicians in the coming months and years.

BOX 2: CLIMATE CHANGE AND UK POLITICS

In the UK there is arguably little difference between the main political parties, therefore any controversial issues that are seen to strike a chord with the public (i.e. voters), will also strike a chord with politicians. Approach and understanding of sensitive issues is seen as a potential competitive differentiator. British Prime Minister, Tony Blair and David Cameron (the Conservative leader of the opposition) are currently engaged in a battle to see who can appear to be 'greener' – climate change being the defining issue.

The Conservative party has traditionally held a very sceptical position on major environmental issues. This is primarily due to their reputation, forged under the leadership of Margaret Thatcher, of being a 'friend' to British industry. Having been in opposition for almost the past ten years, and having changed leaders frequently, they have recently had a long overdue rethink of their approach and stance.

The majority of their historical support comes from Britain's middle class – the same people who have largely converted to Tony Blair's 'New Labour' over the past ten years. In the main, these people live very comfortable lives and their economic security means that they are capable of concerning themselves with environmental and social issues perhaps outside the scope of interest of Labour's working-class, economically less secure, core supporters. David Cameron's Conservative party have realised that they can afford to go further on environmental issues than Labour, and in an effort to win back support in middle England, they are rapidly developing a sympathetic approach to issues such as climate change that BBC Radio 4 is discussing on its afternoon talk shows. David Cameron has already installed a wind turbine on the roof of his Notting Hill house as a symbol of his intent, and he has replaced the traditional Conservative 'torch' logo with a tree.

The Liberal Democrats, Britain's third largest political party, have always traditionally been perceived as the most environmentally friendly mainstream party. This image is now under threat from the Conservatives, and their leader Sir Menzies Campbell has responded with a hard-hitting pledge to cut income tax and switch to green taxes on pollution instead. Under a Liberal Democrat government, British citizens would be financially incentivised to cut their CO_2 emissions.

Unwittingly UK political parties have reached an 'all-party' consensus on the importance of climate change. Based on this, it looks likely that climate change policy will evolve into a key battleground in the next British general election, perhaps influencing its outcome.

Influencing public opinion

While businesses are assessing how they can leverage their approach to climate change for competitive advantage, the same is true of governments and political parties; and financiers and insurers are therefore considering the risk implications. This frenzy of 'grasstops' interest has certainly been stimulated by the urgency of the issue and emerging scientific consensus, but it is primarily the result of 'grassroots' level NGO activity, media promotion and the activities of Hollywood and celebrities.

In Britain it is now quite unusual to scan the front pages of the ten or so national newspapers without seeing at least one reference to climate change. Some of the more liberal papers like *The Independent* and *The Guardian* have regular front-page features on the science, and the implications for society. Meanwhile more popular newspapers like *The Daily Telegraph*, or *The Daily Mail* run smaller, less detailed, and often more sceptical pieces. While many of these articles are undoubtedly published with good intentions, the papers have recently come under criticism from the think-tank IPPR (Institute for Public Policy Research)[14]. They suggest that the British media is over sensationalising the issue – reports are allegedly either too alarmist, or too sceptical. The IPPR describes most UK media coverage of climate change as being little more than 'Climate Porn'. Their primary concern is that the British public are being frightened off by the macro story, and are not given much in the way of insight into what, if anything, they can do as individuals to make a contribution.

While there is some sympathy for the IPPR's perspective one would, however, dispute that it is the role, or responsibility, of the media to help individuals to make choices. Clearly the media has an impact, but the government, and to an extent businesses also have a responsibility. If the media has any responsibility, it is to report what they consider to be newsworthy, and political perspectives aside, climate change certainly fits squarely into this camp.

IPPR's criticism of the current attitude of the media towards the issue of climate change is surprising as it mirrors the famous Kübler-Ross[15] process by which people deal with grief and tragey.

Figure 1: The five stage Kübler-Ross model

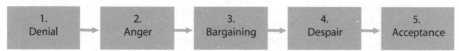

publications are espousing despair (stage four). In my view it is now only a matter of time before we fully accept the situation, and therefore turn our minds to solutions. The fact that newspapers of all persuasions are increasingly publishing stories about the actual impact of climate change is very positive – stories are one of the few ways that we can avoid denial and undergo catharsis. It is like going to the theatre – people suspend their belief long enough to appreciate an alternative input.

Climate change, along with a number of other sustainability issues, has recently benefited from a renaissance of social and environmental consciousness in Hollywood. Tired of accusations of 'dumbing down', endorsing smoking, encouraging violence etc., filmmakers, funders and celebrities alike have focused on raising awareness about a number of social and environmental issues. Climate change has been, and is, at the forefront of their efforts. Blockbuster movies like *The day after tomorrow*, and more recently Al Gore's documentary film *An Inconvenient Truth* have introduced the issue to an influential audience of a younger, traditionally less politically active group of viewers. Al Gore's film even attempts to engage children – it features several cartoons, one featuring a Mr Sunbeam trapped by the bullies known as Greenhouse Gases. To the surprise of many commentators, the movie's average per-screen box office earnings beat the romantic comedy *The Break-up,* starring Jennifer Aniston, which was released in the same week.[16]

Hollywood's knack of (over-)dramatisation has gone a long way to dispelling the common public perception in the Northern hemisphere that climate change is harmless and will just mean nicer weather – a perspective that was famously underlined by Vladimir Putin, the Russian President, when in October 2003 he said that '*An increase of two or three degrees wouldn't be so bad for a northern country like Russia. We could spend less on fur coats, and the grain harvest would go up*'.[17]

BOX 3: CLIMATE CHANGE AND CELEBRITY IMPACT

Movies have, broadly speaking, raised the public's awareness of the macro issues, while celebrity endorsement and high-profile behavioural change has helped to show people that what they do at home can play a role in meeting the challenge. For example, BAFTA-winning actress Thandie Newton very publicly wrote to all of her celebrity friends asking them to trade in their 4x4's and replace them with hybrid cars. Interestingly this was her response to having had Greenpeace put one of their 'Climate Criminal' stickers on the windscreen of her car. She is quoted as saying *'My concerns for the environment had been growing for a long time but I had not connected them with the car I drove. When I saw the sticker it just connected all the dots up'.*[18]

Earlier in the year, on the other side of the Atlantic, Hollywood friends George Clooney and Julia Roberts starred alongside environmentalists Al Gore and Robert F. Kennedy in a photoshoot for the first ever environmentally focused issue of *Vanity Fair*. Not to be outdone, *Elle*, the fashion magazine, also launched a 'green' issue in the US titled *Green is the New Black*.[19] Their research, conducted prior to the magazine launch, had shown that 63 per cent of Elle readers were willing to pay more for a product that is environmentally safe. *Time* magazine seems to concur that sustainability is *de rigeur;* their 2006 *Style and Design* supplement was entitled *Green Living: Is Sustainability the New Luxury?*[20]

Clooney, like Thandie Newton, has also traded in his BMW 4x4 for a less polluting alternative – in his case a Commuter Cars 'Tango' battery electric car – which featured prominently in the photo spread inside the special issue of *Vanity Fair*. Not only is Clooney walking the talk in his day-to-day life, he also produced and starred in the thought-provoking 2006 movie *Syriana* about oil consumption and corruption – a movie that was incidentally billed as the world's first 'climate-neutral' major motion picture. While undoubtedly high-profile, these actions are eclipsed by the biggest climate change-related celebrity PR stunt of the last few years: former Soviet Premier Mikhail Gorbachev's Green Cross organisation succeeded in persuading the organisers of the Oscars (an event watched by an estimated one billion viewers worldwide) to ditch their gas-guzzling stretch limousines in favour of a fleet of hybrid vehicles.

It is not only the movies that are getting star treatment – climate change is now also a regular feature on TV. Matt Damon, the star of the *Bourne Identity* and Harvard dropout, has recently hosted a popular series of documentaries on PBS examining the defining environmental problems of the 21st century. Capitalising on the current appetite for reality TV, and targeting a different audience to Matt Damon, Cameron Diaz stars in an MTV series profiling her celebrity friends and their interest in environmental issues. The music world is also seemingly plugged in; rock group Pearl Jam donated US$100,000 this year to several groups that focus on climate change, renewable energy and other environmental causes, as part of an effort to offset the carbon emissions the band churns out on tour, and the British band Coldplay has released a carbon-neutral album – X&Y[21] – that went on to debut at number one in the charts of 28 different countries around the world.

Bob Dylan, the legendary American singer-songwriter once said that *'Television shows what people perceive, music shows what they are feeling'*. Following this argument it is interesting also to note that Thom Yorke, the lead singer from British band Radiohead, managed to reach number two in the charts this year with his album *The Eraser* containing a series of songs inspired by the British environmental activist Sir Jonathon Porritt and focused on global warming.

While celebrity endorsement is a step in the right direction, the cynical 'hard-core' climate change campaigner may suggest that they are doing little other than massaging their own reputations. The question is *does all of this promotion really make a difference to the way that we spend our money?* The answer, according to the results of a 2006 'Celebrity Influence Study'[22] by market research firm NPD Group, is an emphatic *yes*. A celebrity alone won't sell a product, but the 'right' celebrity may help grab the attention of some consumers who wouldn't have otherwise noticed the product. Fortunately for climate change protagonists, many of the celebrities who are active in this area are also considered to be the 'right' people and consumers (and most importantly children and young people) notice their every move.

The business implications of public attitude/perception

What is the role of business? It is a question that has engaged business school professors and businessmen struggling with their conscience for many years. At a simplistic level and in a nutshell, business is about the generation of a financial return in exchange for work – usually the delivery of a product or service.

Any business, regardless of the nature of its work, has customers, and keeping those customers happy – both with the product or service that they purchase, and with the behaviour of the business – is clearly of paramount importance. Businesses that display an awareness and responsiveness to issues that are capturing the public imagination at any one point in time (like climate change) will benefit from a significant competitive advantage over their peers. They can develop new products and services that help customers to meet emerging challenges, or they can just leverage on the fact that the business and its customers are 'of the same mind', interested and concerned by the same issues. Behaviour of this nature also has a legislative advantage: where public opinion goes, legislation usually follows. Businesses that have taken early note of public opinion and pre-empted changes in the legislative framework, can reduce the cumulative cost of compliance whilst benefiting from the early mover advantages.

Some businesses, perhaps because they have a monopoly, or because they have a unique product, have not fully exploited these intangible advantages. However, for the majority of forward-looking businesses in the 21st century, intangible advantages are critical to success. Whilst competitive pricing can represent an advantage, it is one that can usually be replicated easily and quickly. In a globalised world, the intangible advantages of image and reputation rule – they are difficult if not impossible to replicate.

To exemplify this point you may think about how a consumer chooses between a range of MP3 players – they all have many of the same features and are roughly the same price, but some are just 'cooler' than others. That coolness or desirability is hard to define; scarcity and price clearly play a role, but there is more to it. The same is true of a whole host of consumer products and services: cars, TVs, holidays, mobile phones, and even certain premium food items.

The wallet is mightier than the sword

The modern consumer is interested not only in the functionality of the product – they expect this to reach a certain standard – but also in how buying the product makes them feel. For example, Fairtrade coffee tastes the same, if not better, than other premium brands; it costs the same, but 'feels much better' to buy – and of course, it looks great in the shopping trolley or cupboard. It says something positive about you as a person and as a consequence, sales of these kinds of products are rocketing. There are now a number of magazines and internet sites designed specifically to advise consumers on how to make choices that are environmentally and socially acceptable (see Appendix). Some of these sites screen products and services for their sustainability impacts. In 2002 ICM conducted a poll[23] designed to examine the shopping habits of the British consumer – they found that one in four of us always, or usually, considers ethical issues when shopping, a quarter of us have boycotted products on ethical grounds, and a further one in three would consider doing so in the future.

Of course, buying products that are more environmentally or socially friendly is not a new idea. *The Green Consumer Guide*[24] was published in 1988 and sold well over a million copies globally. It profiled a series of everyday products with a reduced environmental impact. While this book was undoubtedly a pathfinder, it did not herald the beginning of a paradigm change in the way that we shop. This is because business – in particular retailers – were behind the game. Unless you were willing to shop in small, local health food shops you could not conveniently find the products.

Following almost 20 years of malaise, this situation is changing. Proactive businesses now know that a substantial number of consumers are willing to pay extra for these kinds of products. What does this mean for the business setting out to try to address climate change? Firstly, it suggests that a corporate approach towards climate change can contribute significantly towards desirability – desirability for customers, but also for other stakeholders like investors and regulators who, whether they admit it or not, are influenced by imagery. Secondly, as climate change is so intricately linked to energy consumption, it is possible that by redesigning products and services with this in mind you may actually be able to reduce costs for consumers, perhaps not at point of sale, but certainly in use. For example, Whirlpool is focusing on producing more energy-efficient washing machines.

It is not rocket science to suggest that consumer-facing businesses should always be on the lookout for issues that catch the imagination of the public. Climate change is not yet a selling point for all consumers, but it is certainly of interest at the higher, premium end of the spectrum. This observation is relevant for all consumer-facing businesses, primarily because issues that influence the definition of luxury at the premium end of the spectrum eventually find their way onto the high street.

As Juliet Schor notes in her book *The Overspent American*,[25] '*What [people] acquire and own is closely bound to their personal identity. Driving a certain type of car, wearing particular designer labels, living in a certain kind of home, and ordering the right bottle of wine create and support a particular image of themselves to present to the world.*' If climate change is currently pigeonholed as an optional extra, a 'luxury', it is one that very soon everyone will demand – no one, regardless of income, wants to be thought of as a polluter, and everyone wants to improve their social status.

It should not come as a surprise that spring 2007 will see the launch of *The New Green Consumer Guide*. Nor should it surprise you that 2006 is the year in which the world's biggest retailer, and long time environmental sceptic, has pledged to go green. Wal-Mart was recently profiled in *Fortune* magazine under the title 'The Green Machine'.[26] They have set up 14 different taskforces to look at how they can adapt every aspect of their business – including one to look specifically at climate change.

Climate change represents a huge opportunity for the proactive business. Following relentless media coverage and peer pressure, stakeholders will reach the fifth stage of the Kübler-Ross model – acceptance. When they do they will be actively looking for leadership, partners and, above all, solutions.

When London 'black cab' company Radio Taxis went carbon neutral in 2005 they were not expecting an immediate payback. However, their head of marketing Michelle Nunan subsequently admitted that '*going carbon neutral was a significant factor in winning five accounts with a total value of over £1.2million. And this was all achieved within the first months*'.[27]

This example, coupled with the consumer statistics mentioned above, points to the fact that there is a market out there for products and services that have been designed with climate change in mind. Individuals, and customers at all levels, all over the world are starting to realise that, as Gandhi said some 80 years ago, they can '*be the change that they want to see in the world*'. The wallet is mightier than the sword.

Taking action – a ten-stage framework for consumer-facing businesses

Climate change will affect all businesses directly to a greater or lesser extent, but it also has the potential to affect them indirectly – via consumers, employees, supply chain and other influential stakeholders. If a business is reactive by nature, the primary impact will take the form of a risk. If a business is proactive, it will still be a risk but it can also be an opportunity, delivering desirability and valuable product distinction. Either way, businesses should look to take action to meet current (premium/luxury market), mid-term (mainstream/high street) and future (potential legislation driven) demand for products and services designed to mitigate or reduce the impact of climate change.

A ten-stage process for consumer-facing businesses to consider when approaching the issue of climate change is set out below:

1. **Benchmark**: In the first instance it is important for a business to establish the actual climate change implications/footprint of its operations, products and services. At this stage it is advisable to seek expert advice to help management to understand the carbon footprint of the business and its products and services across their full life-cycle.

2. **Consumers**: Armed with this knowledge the business should then talk to its current consumers to discuss their hopes, fears and desires within an environmental context. This can be easily achieved through the use of surveys and/or focus groups – perhaps making use of existing channels. Assuming that current consumers are regularly engaged for their views, then climate change-related questions should be integrated into the long-term analysis so that changes of opinion can be tracked.

3. **Trendsetters**: Following this, the company should conduct exactly the same process with other groups of consumers – consumers who perhaps would not choose to purchase the businesses products and services, instead opting for niche, premium or cheaper alternatives. Particular attention should be paid to those groups who are considered to be setting trends within the sector.

4. **Horizon scanning**: The information obtained in stages 1 and 2 should then be used to provide input to a horizon scanning process to understand threats and opportunities relating to climate change. This process, perhaps modelled on the 'Delphi Technique',[28] will identify potential substitute products and services, and highlight emerging competitors.

5. **Scenarios**: The information obtained in stages 1, 2 and 3 should now be used to develop a series of scenarios or written descriptions of possible futures. These scenarios can then be used to evaluate the potential success of current products and services. The process will identify shortcomings in current product/service strategy, and will highlight the changes that will need to be made to maintain and increase market share. It will also highlight opportunities for the development of new, climate change-related, products and services within your sector.

6. **Strategy**: An evaluation of the scenarios will inform the development of a corporate climate change strategy and official corporate position. The strategy should not only examine products and services, but also the impact of the business itself. The strategy should include targets not only for the reduction of the carbon footprint, but also market-facing sales targets.

7. **Responsibility**: A board-level director should be made responsible for the implementation of the climate change strategy; he/she should ensure exposure and profile for the business and receive a portion of pay linked to performance.

8. **Partnership**: With the strategy, position and responsibility in place, the business should seek to partner with other like-minded organisations that can help to achieve mutual climate change aims and objectives. This organisation may be an environmental NGO, but it could equally be another business. It is important to ensure that the two organisations share more than climate change concerns in common – other activities of the partner should be examined to ensure there is no conflict of interest.

9. **Action**: The business should now be armed with the appropriate knowledge to be in a position to take direct action to reduce the carbon footprint (perhaps the phased introduction of new, or altered, product and services), and to reduce exposure to risk.

10. **Communication**: Throughout the duration of the climate change response process the business should ensure that it is communicating regularly with stakeholders, letting them know what the corporate position is and what changes have been made, otherwise they will not be aware of the environmental benefits of doing business with the company over and above a competitor. While an aspect of communication should undoubtedly be formal (e.g. an audited sustainability report), businesses need to use other more informal, practical and inspiring ways to engage with consumers. Advertising can clearly play a role in the communications mix, however, the large trust gap between consumers and businesses means that communications should be primarily two-way, transparent and, where possible, involve a third party.

By following a process similar to the above, a business will find that it invariably reduces its carbon footprint and at the same time enhances creativity and ingenuity. In this way the business will be more likely to stay ahead of the competition for longer. By taking note of the bigger picture, the business will have helped consumers to do the right thing, making them feel like they are part of something big, something that can make a real difference. By showing that the organisation cares about the same kinds of things that the general public cares about, the business will likely enhance employee and customer loyalty. By showing that the business takes climate change risks seriously, the business will be more likely to attract investment from more stable long-term investors (i.e. pension funds) with significant interests in the long-term impact of climate change. Of course all of this costs money, but I would argue that for any business interested in exploiting the public perception of climate change and producing products and services attuned to this, it is an investment worth making, and one that will be returned many times over.

Appendix – Ethical consumer websites[29]

New American Dream: http://www.newdream.org/

Ethical Consumer Magazine: http://www.ethicalconsumer.org/

Be, Live, Buy Different – Make a Difference: http://www.ibuydifferent.org/

GOOSHING – the free ethical shopping tool: http://www.gooshing.co.uk/

Green Choices: http://www.greenchoices.org/

Ethical Junction: http://www.ethicaljunction.co.uk/

The Green Consumer Guide: http://www.greenconsumerguide.com/

Get Ethical: http://www.getethical.com/

Ethics Score: http://www.ethiscore.org/

Eco Mall: http://ecomall.com/

US Environmental Protection Agency guide to green shopping: http://www.epa.gov/
epaoswer/education/pdfs/shopping.pdf

Notes

1   Sir David King, UK government chief scientific adviser, January 2004.

2   Testimony of Eileen Claussen before the US Senate Committee on the Environment and
Public Works, 24 March 1999. See: http://epw.senate.gov/107th/cla_3-24.htm

3   IPCC Third Assessment Report: Climate Change 2001: http://www.ipcc.ch/pub/un/syreng/
spm.pdf

4   Hansen J., Sato M., Ruedy R., Lo K., Lea D., Medina-Elizade M. 'Global Temperature Change',
Proceedings of the National Academy of Sciences, 2006, 103(39): 14288–14293.

5   http://www.whitehouse.gov/news/releases/2002/02/20020214-5.html#

6   http://daily.stanford.edu/article/2002/3/13/
ceoOfBpDiscussesEffortsToMakeOilMoreEnvironmentallyFriendly

7   The Precautionary Principle refers to the idea that if the consequences of an action
are unknown, but are judged to have some potential for major or irreversible negative
consequences, then it is better to avoid that action.

8   To view the video clips visit: http://www.cei.org/pages/co2.cfm

9   Brechin S. 'Comparative Public Opinion and Knowledge on Global Climatic Change and
the Kyoto Protocol: The U.S. versus the World?' *Int. J. Sociology and Social Policy*, 2003, 23:
106–134.

10   http://www.harrisinteractive.com/harris_poll/index.asp?PID=335

11   http://www.eurekalert.org/pub_releases/2005-03/miot-ccp032305.php

12   http://www.mori.com/polls/2005/uea.shtml

13   http://pewresearch.org/reports/?ReportID=34

14   See BBC news report: http://news.bbc.co.uk/2/hi/science/nature/5236482.stm

15   See Kubler-Ross E. *On Grief and Grieving: Finding the Meaning of Grief Through the Five
Stages of Loss*, Simon & Schuster Ltd., 2005.

16   See Fox News report: http://www.foxnews.com/story/0,2933,198124,00.html?sPage=fnc.
foxlife/celebcouples

17   See *New Scientist* article: http://www.newscientist.com/channel/earth/climate-change/
dn9911-quotes-climate-change.html;jsessionid=BLPEOFFLOLGF

18 http://www.greenpeace.org.uk/climate/climate.cfm?ucidparam=20060403100749&CFID= 1044260&CFTOKEN=

19 http://www.elle.com/article.asp?section_id=51&article_id=7996&page_number=2

20 *Time* Magazine: Style & Design, Summer 2006, *Green Living: Is Sustainability the New Luxury?*

21 Coldplay's involvement in a tree-planting project organized by the Carbon Neutral Company has attracted considerable controversy. Of the 10,000 mango trees that were planted in the band's name in Karnataka, India, a later report by a British newspaper, the Sunday Telegraph, claimed that only a few hundred still alive. The Carbon Neutral Company has made up for the shortfall by alternative investments.

22 http://www.npdinsights.com/corp/enewsletter/html/archives/may2006/cover.story.html

23 ICM Ethical Shopping, 2002, http://www.icmresearch.co.uk/reviews/2002/retail-week-ethical-shopping.htm

24 Elkington J. and Hailes J. *The Green Consumer Guide: From Shampoo to Champagne – High-street shopping for a better environment*, London: Victor Gollancz, 1988.

25 See: Schor J. *The Overspent American*, New York: HarperPerennial, 1999.

26 http://money.cnn.com/magazines/fortune/fortune_archive/2006/08/07/8382593/index.htm

27 See: http://www.carbonneutral.com/casestudies/client.asp?id=1

28 The 'Delphi Technique' is a forecasting aid based on a consensus reached by a panel of experts.

29 The author is not responsible for the content of any of these websites.

21

Engaging Consumers through Corporate Marketing and PR Programs

Cecilia (Sid) Embree, AtmosClear Climate Club

Introduction and purpose

This chapter explores some of the many alternatives that have been attempted for retail sales of emission reductions, and questions the size of the retail market for emission reductions needed to grow a profitable business in this sector.

Engaging individuals to reduce emissions

Individuals contribute GHG emissions directly and indirectly through daily and lifestyle activities. The heating and lighting of homes uses energy, often through the burning of fossil fuels in homes or in power plants that supply electricity to homes. Driving vehicles also contributes emissions, ranging from about three tons of carbon dioxide per year for a hybrid vehicle that is driven 12,000 miles to six to seven tons for a large sports utility vehicle that is driven 12,000 or more miles. In addition, individuals contribute indirectly to emissions through demand for products that are produced using electricity generated from burning fossil fuels or from direct fuel combustion. Using carbon dioxide (CO_2) as an example, the average family in the United States causes air pollution, directly and indirectly, in the following ways:

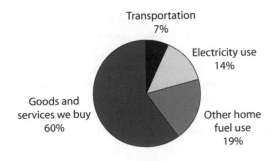

Transportation
7%

Electricity use
14%

Goods and services we buy
60%

Other home fuel use
19%

Research by the Natural Resources Defense Council in the 1990s found that global warming and climate change are complicated issues for individuals to understand. Further, while information on the issue is available, there is often too much information or it is conflicting and difficult to digest.[1] Consequently, most individuals are not aware of their personal contribution to emissions like CO_2, let alone how they can reduce their emissions and/or offset them by buying verified emission reductions.

Nevertheless, over recent years, awareness of global warming has increased in the USA. Clean Commodities LLC (CCLLC), for example, polled individuals in 2004 through a national research firm and found that out of 1,000 US adults, 73 per cent were 'somewhat' or 'very' concerned about global warming. In 2006, the National Wildlife Federation found that 85 per cent of US sportsmen (the majority of whom are conservatives) believe individuals have a moral responsibility to do something about global warming. In Canada, research in September 2006 found that two-thirds of Canadians feel desperately concerned about the issue.[2]

Through its poll, CCLLC also asked individuals, 'How interested are you in learning about ways you can personally reduce the threat of global warming and climate change?' Seventeen per cent of adults were very interested, and 51 per cent were somewhat interested. Unfortunately, few programs actively engage consumers in the fight against global warming. The most common programs offer consumers choice to purchase renewable-based electricity products (generated from wind, biomass, solar and other renewables such as geothermal energy). The objective is to promote markets for renewables by giving customers an opportunity to choose a clean electricity supplier. Despite some progress in getting consumers to purchase 'green power', however, an evaluation of several programs found that a market for renewable energy stimulated by customer choice has been slow to develop.[3]

Governments, schools and non-profits are also making efforts to educate consumers. Any web search will reveal government programs at national and local levels. Schools, too, are making efforts to educate children about energy conservation and pollution. But are there ways for corporations to educate and engage the public and customers to take action on the issue of climate change?

Corporate action to engage consumers to reduce emissions

At GreenTForum, a May 2006 conference on voluntary climate change and trading initiatives in New York City, many businesses outlined programs to reduce emissions and combat global warming. Kathy Loftus, National Energy Manager at Whole Foods, described the purchase by her company of enough renewable energy credits from wind farms to offset 100 per cent of the electricity used in all of their stores, facilities, bake houses, distribution centers, regional offices and national headquarters in the United States and Canada. This was the largest wind energy credit purchase by that time. This purchase generated interest on the part of consumers, who contacted Whole Foods to learn how they could do the same.

Many other companies have launched efforts to engage consumers or to help them reduce their climate impact, including Stoneyfield Farm, Clif Bar, Interface Carpet, WalMart, NativeEnergy and CoolClimate LLC's AtmosClear. Some companies offer opportunities for individuals to take action to reduce emissions, or offer offsets, or they provide products or services that reduce emissions or that are emissions neutral (compared to other offers in the market). Some of these programs are complemented by initiatives promoted by non-profit organizations.

Encouraging consumers to reduce emissions

	Climate-neutral products or services	Encourage consumers to take actions
Climate-neutral products/services	Stonyfield Farm, Land Rover UK, Whole Foods, Clif Bar	Wal-Mart, Stonyfield Farm, Whole Foods
Offers offsets/VERs	AtmosClear, NativeEnergy, Land Rover UK	Clif Bar
	Non-profit	**Non-profit**
Call to action	fightglobalwarming.org (Environmental Defense and The Ad Council)	stopglobalwarming.org (stopglobalwarming)

Source: Author's own

Stonyfield Farm's six-ounce yogurt cup lid program educates consumers on health and environmental issues and motivates them to take action. Messages on the aluminum lids expose millions of Stonyfield customers to activities of non-profit environmental groups, and issues that threaten human health and the health of our planet. Stonyfield was the first US manufacturer to offset 100 per cent of their CO_2 emissions from the energy used at their facility. According to its website, since 1997, the company has offset over 40,000 metric tonnes of global warming gases. Stonyfield has also prepared and distributed free of charge a 'how to' guide for businesses that want to offset emissions.[4]

Wal-Mart is also addressing global warming. It will eliminate 30 per cent of the energy used by stores, with the corporate goal to be fuelled 100 per cent by renewable energy. Wal-Mart also encourages customers to buy at least one compact fluorescent (CFL) light bulb, which reduces emissions by half a ton of CO_2 over its life. With over 100 million customers, use of one CFL by each would keep 22 billion pounds of coal from burning at power plants and 45 billion pounds of GHGs from being emitted.

Clif Bar encourages consumers to reduce their ecological footprint, including by supporting renewable wind energy. Clif Bar sells 'cool tags' to avoid emissions of an estimated 300 pounds of CO_2 out of the air. This is equivalent to neutralizing the global warming emissions generated by traveling 300 miles in the average car (approximately 3 per cent to 5 per cent of a car's annual emissions). Stickers can be purchased via their website, which links to Native Energy's website, a retailer of the cool tags.

In 2006, Land Rover UK introduced a program to reduce its overall impact on global warming. The company will offset emissions generated by Land Rover vehicle assembly at two production facilities in Britain, and provides a mechanism for customers to offset emissions from driving their vehicles. Land Rover has outsourced the program to Climate Care, an independent offset provider.

Interface Carpet Inc. has committed to take GHG emissions out of their business by becoming climate neutral. They have reduced energy consumption in the manufacturing process and offset their remaining emissions. Interface therefore offers consumers a climate-friendly rug product.

Each of these companies has developed a unique strategy to educate individuals about global warming or to encourage consumers to reduce emissions through purchasing climate-friendly products or offsetting their emissions.

The consumer market for emission reductions

In November 2006, Tony Blair, Prime Minister of Britain, published a Climate Change bill with the UK government's long-term goal of a 60 per cent reduction in carbon dioxide emissions by 2050 a legally binding target[5]. Britain has also considered the possibility of imposing individual limits on carbon emissions. For example, people who accumulate unused carbon quotas, say, by driving less or switching to less polluting vehicles, could sell them to people who exceed their quotas by driving more than their quota allows.[6] Is this a viable option for engaging individuals to reduce emissions?

BOX 1: UK PERSONAL CARBON PROJECT

In November 2006, the UK-based Royal Society of Arts (RSA) launched a three-year project to investigate how domestic emissions can be reduced within the UK using market mechanisms. It includes launching a pilot trading scheme, which will enable individual households to trade emissions quotas with other households, similar to the way in which businesses in the European Union trade quotas with each other.

The RSA project will study administrative costs and the practicality of individual trading quotas in areas such as heating, air travel and ground transportation. Individuals are encouraged to register their emissions on the RSA website, and compare their 'carbon footprints' to others', including those of British parliamentarians, who may have also submitted their footprints.

Already, several businesses and non-profits offer emission reductions, or offsets, to consumers. Some offer independently verified emission reductions that have recently occurred, some offer emission reductions that will occur in the future, and yet others offer emission reductions that are assumed to have occurred due to the generation of electricity from renewable sources. Reductions may or may not be independently verified, a factor which could affect the acceptability and therefore the viability of the offset market. In reality, there is no uniform standard for measuring and verifying emission reductions for sale to the public.

While there is no single standard, there are models for creating and verifying emission reductions based on experience in other successful emissions markets. Emission reductions are decreases in pollutant emissions (or 'avoided' emissions) that result from actions like switching to cleaner fuels, improving energy efficiency, and increasing renewable energy use. Renewable energy avoids CO_2 emissions by displacing, or delaying the need for, power plants that use fossil fuels to generate electricity.

Emission reduction occurs when an entity (e.g. a power plant) that is an actual source of air pollution reduces its emissions (by avoiding or eliminating all or a portion of emissions that would have been emitted) and then transfers ownership (legal title) of the independently verified emission reductions (avoided emissions) to another party. A verified emission reduction (VER) is a financial instrument that can be used to transfer GHG emissions reduction rights in the national and international marketplace to businesses and other entities that need them to 'offset' (or create a 'net' reduction of) their own emissions.

BOX 2: HOW THE PROCESS OF TRADING VERS WORKS

Purchases of VERs are typically made according to a contract between the seller (creator) of emission reductions and a buyer. Ideally, the contract requires that all VERs meet the criteria of an independent registry or verifier, preferably according to a widely accepted standard or criteria. The buyer will hire an independent auditor to verify or confirm that emission reductions meet such a standard or criteria. Once verified, the legal title to VERs is purchased and VERs are deposited into the buyer's account at the independent registry, where each ton of reduced (avoided) CO_2 equivalent is assigned a serial number. The buyer will purchase enough VERs to cover its needs, whether to meet a corporate commitment to offset emissions or to supply customers in the retail market, or even to trade on to another buyer. In the retail market, when a customer purchases one or more tons from the retailer, they are provided with a certificate confirming the retailer's purchase of a specified volume of VERs in their name, including the serial number or numbers associated with the VERs the customer has paid for.

The retailer typically maintains two accounts with the registry. The first includes all VERs (and serial numbers) purchased by retailer. VERs sit in this account until they are assigned to individual customers. The second account is a retirement account. Once serialized VERs are assigned to customers, the retailer notifies the registry of the sale(s) and the associated serial numbers, and these specific VERs are then moved to the retailer's retirement account. At that time, these VERs are removed from the market and cannot be used by other parties for either compliance or voluntary purposes.

Currently, there is no global standard for VERs, although an effort is underway by The Climate Group, the International Emissions Trading Association and others to establish such a standard. Generally, VERs should meet strict creation-and-use criteria to ensure the process yields continuous environmental improvement and the VERs are, therefore, a credible, valuable commodity. Verification of emission reductions should be conducted by independent auditors who then provide written assurance of the integrity of the VER, similar to the role of a financial auditor.

Using the retail market for VERs as a tool to engage individuals

Is there a way to engage consumers to reduce emissions and generate profits simultaneously? Market research commissioned by CCLLC in 2004 in the USA suggested that consumer interest and willingness to pay could in fact open the door to a profitable business opportunity. This market research found, and experience shows, that if emission reductions are readily available and can be made 'appealing' – for example by rewarding consumers for their purchase – people will buy them. Fifty-seven per cent of all respondents in a commissioned nationwide USA survey indicated they would buy emission reduction credits to offset or neutralize their GHG emissions from driving (approximately six tons per year). The percentage increased when they were asked if they would be more likely to buy at a specific gasoline retail company, or another store they shop at regularly, such as their favorite supermarket, if that gas company or store offered them a product or service to reduce their emissions. It increased yet further, above 70 per cent, when asked if they would be more likely to buy products or services from a business that offered them rewards in return for their decision to reduce emissions. What this all means is that people say they will buy if sufficiently motivated and if they are presented with the opportunity.

The research results generated an additional, unanswered question. Is there a way to use rewards programs to get consumers to reduce emissions, or to at least get them to offset their emissions? As is evident with the popularity of rewards programs, consumers are always looking for some benefit. And, at the same time, companies are always looking for ways to build customer loyalty. So, is there a profitable business model under which consumers can be motivated to purchase VERs? AtmosClear has tried one model.

AtmosClear experiences

The goal of AtmosClear Climate Club is to enable individuals and families to participate in emission reduction and further advance environmental awareness and reward individuals for doing so in an enjoyable and interesting way. AtmosClear is the first ever environment-focused rewards program and was structured as a multi-faceted marketing and promotional tool. AtmosClear's two main customers are consumers (members), who obtain VERs and other economic benefits/rewards when they join, and retail partners, who serve as distributors of memberships and member benefits and rewards. As it turns out, toward the end of 2006, only 30–40 per cent of AtmosClear's sales are for memberships, while the balance are for VERs (offsets only, without any member benefits).

AtmosClear's club rewards program can be used by retailers and businesses as a promotional marketing tool. Firstly, individuals (members) obtain two bundled services: a) membership in an environmentally focused, socially conscious rewards program; and b) verified emission reductions (VERs). Secondly, partners get a marketing, promotions and public relations tool that enhances their environmental/social image(s). From the perspective of the consumer, the membership is priced so that collectively the discounts, offers and VERs are considered 'a good deal' and they understand 'it's good for the environment'.

A rewards program: Arapahoe Basin ski area

Under this program, AtmosClear relies on partners to market memberships. Arapahoe Basin (A-Basin), a ski area in Colorado, is one such partner. AtmosClear has worked for a number of years with A-Basin to offer to its guests a rewards program that includes emission reductions. Members join by purchasing memberships at the ski area[7], and obtain discounts and other offers from the ski area. Offering the memberships provides A-Basin with a unique rewards program, only offered by a few other ski areas in the USA. A-Basin decides which offers to provide to motivate guests to join.

Available at points of purchase at the ski area (or as an option with season's pass sales), guests buy non-transferable AtmosClear Climate Club memberships that give them discounts on ski area merchandise or products selected by A-Basin (e.g. food, beverages, equipment, passes, day care, lodging). When purchasing the Climate Club membership, guests provide the ski area with their contact information. A-Basin can use this information as a permission marketing tool, for example to inform Climate Club members of special events and where they get discounts on merchandise and products/services. While A-Basin sells Climate Club memberships, AtmosClear administers the Climate Club's VER purchase and transfer program. After receiving purchasers' contact information from A-Basin, AtmosClear sends to members their member materials including certificates with VER serial numbers, member cards, and UndoYourCO$_2$ stickers.

Overall, the program serves to increase awareness of global warming, and provides A-Basin with positive public relations, especially on designated days when members get substantial discounts on ski area offerings. The challenges of offering this type of reward program are that it must be integrated with a business's own marketing and PR efforts. Even though AtmosClear is a turnkey program, a partner, such as A-Basin, must consciously decide how to balance the Climate Club program with its other public relations, marketing and promotional initiatives. This is a challenge, as all partners have multiple priorities and audiences that they need to cater to. The reality is that AtmosClear is one of many promotional programs offered by the ski area. In addition, of course, the ski industry is seasonal and weather-dependent; achieving high sales volumes depends on good weather!

Taking this program to a large retailer with thousands or millions of customers can present challenges. So far, very few large companies in the USA have been willing to make global warming a centerpiece of, or even a major pillar of, their marketing or promotional efforts. This reluctance appears to be declining somewhat as evidenced at least by Wal-Mart's campaign to promote CFLs.

Direct sales of VERs to consumers: fightglobalwarming.com campaign

AtmosClear Climate Club was selected as one of five retailers to sell VERs through a link at the fightglobalwarming.com website established through a partnership between Environmental Defense, a non-profit, and The Ad Council (an association of advertising agencies).[8]

The retailers that were selected to be linked to the campaign website were required to prove that the emission reductions offered to the public through the campaign meet the following criteria:

- Emission reductions are achieved with sound methodologies and practices

- All emission reduction claims are verifiable by a third party

- All emission reductions are permanent

- If there is the potential for a reversal, in which emission reductions are returned to the atmosphere in the future, insurance must be kept to protect against those scenarios

- The carbon offset was generated in a way that produced net positive environmental and community impacts

- Offsets are serialized and tracked so that they cannot be sold twice.

The campaign website was launched on 22 March 2006, when the campaign launched a series of motivating ads suggesting that climate change will happen sooner rather than later. (While the jury is still out, six months after the launch of the campaign, 4,300 tons in total had been purchased by consumers from all five retailers).

AtmosClear Climate Club makes available both memberships and straight (non-membership) offsets to campaign website visitors. Of those that made purchases, membership sales were 38 per cent of all sales attributable to the campaign, while the balance of purchases was for VERs (no membership). Having been selected as one of the retailers for the campaign is good for AtmosClear's credibility, and of course the campaign drives some traffic to the AtmosClear website and motivates some sales. However, the success of this approach to achieving sales at a level that makes a business profitable has yet to be demonstrated. Certainly, the volume of sales would be inadequate to achieve break-even for a retail business.

Why limited success? Visitors must go to the campaign website, and they usually click through several pages of information. They may watch a brief video-clip intended to motivate them to become concerned about global warming, and to learn about their own emissions footprint. It is only toward the end of the process of estimating their emissions contribution that they are invited to offset their emissions. If they decide to purchase offsets (VERs), they must choose from five retailers. If more sales are to be achieved through this campaign, television, print and other ads will need to reach a larger audience, the audience must be informed that they can and should offset their emissions, and they need to be told where to go to get offsets. Or is even more needed?

Herein lies one of the dilemmas of selling VERs. It is difficult to promote offsetting without informing individuals of their contributions of emissions, and encouraging them to reduce their emissions through personal action. People need a lot of information before they decide to purchase VERs. Wading through the websites of many of the non-profit organizations is an overwhelming process, with plentiful information, multiple requests for donations, and numerous calls for action. Sales of VERs have plenty to compete with!

Lessons learned for engaging individuals and consumers

Several challenges arise in the business of selling VERs to individuals. First and foremost is the limited public understanding of climate change and concern about the issue. Focus group research by Yale University in 2006, revealed that a lack of knowledge about the science behind climate change is a barrier to understanding the concept of offsets. Fortunately, in the USA, both understanding and concern are increasing, thanks in part to weather events such as Hurricane Katrina, as well as efforts of celebrities like Al Gore, and focused information campaigns. All of these and other factors have contributed to increasing the information that has become available in the press.

Selling offsets directly to consumers via a retail website and shopping cart requires both education about global warming and offsets, as well as direction to get customers to visit the site. Getting to the shopping cart requires a commitment that only the most concerned and committed consumers seem willing to make. In addition, there are any number of steps in the purchase process where an individual could drop out, particularly if the learning curve is steep.

A review of the stopglobalwarming.org campaign website in late 2006 indicates that over 500,000 people signed up to join their 'virtual march' to show politicians that the public is concerned about global warming. Sign-ups occurred either directly or were encouraged through partner organizations (e.g. myspace.com). Interestingly, no partner organization has managed to sign up more than 100,000 individuals. In fact, the most support any partner has garnered has been about 50,000 sign-ups, with no cost to the individual signing up. Properly priced, 50,000 purchases of VERs, (not merely just sign-ups to join a campaign), could sustain a retail business for one year, perhaps for two, depending on the cost structure of the business. However, it is highly unlikely that 50,000 sign-ups would be converted into 50,000 purchases. Beyond that, based on experience with more conventional member programs, a portion of consumers that do purchase (join) can be expected to drop out in subsequent years, so repeat sales cannot be relied on exclusively to make sure the business achieves sufficient sales for continued profitability. Therefore, it is important to examine more closely the need for education and incentives to get consumers to buy VERs.

Another challenge with selling offsets directly to consumers is that the customer must self-select. AtmosClear has found that many customers who purchase via its website are environmentally aware, members of existing environmental groups, and often 'donate' to several environmental causes. The Yale focus group research revealed that while people are interested and want to know more about buying offsets, including how to get them, they still debated who should have the responsibility to pay for offsets. Ultimately, only a couple of participants in both groups stated that they would consider purchasing carbon offsets for their vehicle.

Some retailers have experimented with selling VERs through partnerships with large corporations or non-profits, which have large customer bases or memberships. Developing these partnerships requires an extensive marketing effort to educate corporations, and work with their environmental experts and marketing and public relations staff. In some cases, internal lawyers get involved to ensure that the company is not exposing itself to potential liability issues. Retailers do not typically have large budgets for direct-to-consumer marketing. So far, few large corporations have demonstrated an interest to go out on a limb and promote offsets. However, Ford has dipped its toe in the water, and now offers customers a link to TerraPass through its own US website.

Even large non-profits emphasize education and taking action to reduce personal emissions. Purchasing offsets is often the last option on a long list of things people can or should do. What about requiring people to offset their emissions? Is there a role for regulation? While unappealing politically, regulation would force people to take responsibility for their emissions. Due to the strong relationship between energy use and emissions, individuals who use more energy could be expected to buy more offsets. Administering a mandatory offset program could prove complicated, but – at least in the transport sector – it could be relatively easy if vehicle owners were required to offset emission as part of their vehicle license purchase or renewal.

Another way to get individuals to take responsibility for their emissions would be through taxing high-carbon products and services. Taxes send a signal to consumers, and should encourage them to make more climate-friendly choices. The Swiss Climate Penny program is a voluntary commitment by oil importers in Switzerland to contribute between one and two Swiss cents per liter to a fund, which invests to reduce emissions or acquire offsets. Experience in the US in late 2005 and early 2006 demonstrated that significant rises in gasoline prices are needed to affect consumer driving behaviour.

While worthwhile and well-targeted, a one cent charge is unlikely to affect US consumer behaviour, as one cent is too small to be felt by the consumer. The Climate Penny is probably most valuable as an educational tool bringing attention to the role of fossil fuels in contributing to climate change. A significant rise in gasoline prices will increase demand for more efficient vehicles, as seen by the increase in demand for hybrid vehicles in the US in 2006. Taxing is less palatable politically than a voluntary program but, if priced properly, could force some change in behaviour.

Going forward

Based on experience and the reality of competing options for consumers, VER retailers need a strategy that will bring them to large pools of consumers and that makes it easy for consumers to make a purchase. Education is key, as people need to understand their contribution to emissions before they are motivated to offset and actually make a purchase of VERs. Offsets must be presented as an essential element on a menu of actions that individuals can take to reduce their overall contribution to emissions. Corporations can play a role in the educational process, as many of the examples in this chapter demonstrate. In the end, however, consumers will decide, so how they are motivated to act is key. Profits can be a significant motivator for a business, and this suggests that what is needed is an appropriate incentive structure to get businesses and consumers to join together to reduce overall emissions.

Notes

1   Jon Coifman and Joanna Krinn, NRDC, personal communication, 2003.
2   See http://www.ipsos.ca
3   Welch K.A., Aeschliman L. and Baxter L.W. 'Environmental Progress in the Electric Sector: Lessons Learned', *Trust* magazine, February 2004, Pew Charitable Trusts. See http://www. pewtrusts.com/ideas/ideas_item.cfm?content_item_id=2205&content_type_id=11&page =11&issue=19&issue_name=Global%20warming&name=
4   See http://www.stonyfieldfarm.com
5   BBC News website, 'Climate bill sets carbon target', www.bbc.co.uk, 15 November 2006.
6   Fox News, 'Tony Blair joins forces with Gov. Schwarzenegger to Fight Global Warming', 31 July 2006.
7   Note: a few A-Basin guests buy directly from AtmosClear, but f than 2 per cent.
8   The link to AtmosClear's and other retailers' shopping carts can be found at: http://www. fightglobalwarming.com/page.cfm?tagID=270

22
Engaging Employees in Climate Change

Trewin Restorick, Global Action Plan

The challenge of engaging employees

International business leaders have identified the potential impact climate change could have on the world's economy. Many have realised the urgency of the problem and are using their contacts and influence to encourage politicians to act more quickly. For example, UK Prime Minister Tony Blair has recently had a steady stream of business leaders urging him and his government to create a framework that will enable businesses to act more effectively to reduce carbon dioxide emissions.

Such proactive leadership is to be applauded and encouraged, yet in the experience of the environmental charity Global Action Plan, many of these leaders are finding it hard to communicate the same sense of necessity and urgency within their own companies. All too often we discover that these companies have a small committed team armed with strong corporate statements about the need to cut carbon and to act sustainably, but when they try to implement them they face a brick wall of inertia amongst their colleagues.

From our experience, we hear the same three underlying messages from these committed teams no matter what the culture, sector or underlying principles of the business. Firstly, the teams feel small and overwhelmed with the scale of the challenge facing them. How can so few influence the values, lifestyles and beliefs of so many? Secondly, there is a common sense of frustration that they cannot get through to their colleagues to understand the enormity of the threat of climate change. Thirdly, there is also a sense of real isolation – a knowledge that when push comes to shove, financial performance and the demands of shareholders will overwhelm any corporate commitment on sustainability.

Aware of the similarity of the challenges facing such corporate teams, we decided to create a range of communication tools that would help address some of the problems they were facing. Based on a mixture of practical experience and academic research, we created three programmes each containing the four key components that are essential to encourage people to change their behaviour to reduce carbon emissions. These four components are:

- High quality communication
- The involvement of facilitated groups
- Measurement and feedback
- A clearly structured process.

High quality communication

From our experience, communication has to be relevant to people's needs, and be creative and dynamic. Initially, communication about the impact of climate change has consisted of dry, doom-laden text littered with obscure references to biodiversity, sustainability and carbon footprinting. For many people the scale of the problem, the complexity of the issue and the lack of any connection with their everyday activities is an immediate turn-off particularly compared to more pressing issues such as money, health and reality TV programmes such as Big Brother.

The abstract nature of climate change and the uncertainty that many people have about the science that lies behind it, demands that communication tools are used that bring climate change to life for people making it real and tangible. Words on paper – however well crafted – often fail to achieve this difficult task; they need to be backed up by other forms of communication. This chapter describes how Global Action Plan used a mobile gym to get the key message across. In addition to this gym, we have also used actors dressed in huge boots to demonstrate the impact of our carbon footprint and comedians acting out sketches for employees during their lunchtime or when they arrive at work.

The involvement of facilitated groups

Many people are increasingly questioning the moral authority that others have in telling them how to live their lives. They instantly recognise hypocrisy when government ministers urge them to use their cars less but then use their ministerial car to drive them the 200 yards from their hotel room to a conference centre. They question it when management encourages them to use energy more frugally, seeing it as a thinly veiled cost-cutting exercise. They question the validity of scientific statements partly because the media always treats such statements as an opportunity to hold a verbal boxing match with anybody holding an opposing view, regardless of the validity of their position.

Given this increasing scepticism, we believe that it is important to avoid the 'talking head' and 'thou shalt' approach to communicating climate change. Instead, we believe that change occurs more effectively where you bring groups of people together in a facilitated discussion. Such discussions not only enable people to test out their views and positions with others, they allow them to share understanding and, crucially, they enable people to decide upon the actions that they can take both individually and as a group that are viable within their own personal circumstances.

Measurement and feedback

The third key component is the importance of measurement and feedback in the process of change and individual action. In many companies the responsibility for measuring energy use and waste sits within the fiefdom of one key person. This is the 'Graphs King' who can tell, down to the smallest and most tedious detail, how energy is used within the company. Containing all this knowledge within one person can be disempowering to others.

From our experience, we discovered that if you ask people to find out for themselves how much energy their company uses, how much paper it throws out, how little the recycling bins are actually used – they are shocked and amazed by the results. To maximise impact, we use their findings to translate the environmental impact into tangible items like how high the tower of waste paper thrown out by the company would reach or the number of road tankers the amount of carbon dioxide produced would fill.

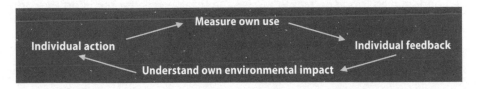

Source: author's own

Once people have a tangible grasp of the environmental impact caused by their activities it motivates them to take the small actions that will make a difference. Being given feedback about the impact of these changes generates a positive response and encourages people to make further ongoing changes. When dealing with huge intangible issues such as climate change it is important to illustrate to people that they can make a difference. Positive feedback is also motivational, in stark contrast to many typical environmental campaigns which tend to be full of doom and gloom.

A clearly structured process

The final component is to provide employees with a clear structure and process of change within which they can take action. In most companies, promoting environmental change is seen as an additional and voluntary activity. Many employees are willing to make this extra effort, but only for a defined and clear period of time. Within that time they want to know what is expected of them, how their activities will link with others, what support they will get and what difference they are likely to make.

Our programmes require the company to identify 'environmental champions' who are willing and able to promote environmental change within the organisation. These champions are brought together in teams. We ensure that these teams also include key people from within the organisation who are able to translate change into action, such as facilities managers. These teams are crucial, they provide mutual support for the champions and they enable them to interact directly with key people who are in a position to change through modifying or enhancing systems or procedures within the company.

Running teams – with such a disparate group of employees dealing with environmental issues requiring knowledge that is often outside their skill set – requires skilled facilitation. We perform this role as facilitator to enable the group to run the initiative more effectively. Crucially, the facilitators leave the group to decide what actions they wish to undertake. They support this decision-making process by providing information and guidance when it is sought.

Typically, the teams work together for a period of between four and twelve months. From our experience, periods under four months do not provide sufficient time to enable change to take place, whilst going beyond twelve months causes a loss of motivation amongst the team.

Keeping the environmental champions motivated and enthused is essential. Global Action Plan feels it is important to reward and thank people for the effort they are making and we provide employees who complete the programme with a UNEP endorsed certificate. It also encourages companies to reward through their standard appraisal and incentive systems.

These are the four key components that we feel are essential to effectively communicate climate change to employees. How, then, is this theory translated into practical activities? Here are three examples of Global Action Plan's work in practice.

The carbon gym

The award winning carbon gym brings climate change to life. The aim of the gym is to help employees understand how their everyday use of energy links to climate change, the volume of gas caused by their activities and the weight of gas created by different travel choices.

The energy bike is an exercise bike – just like any you would come across in any gymnasium – but with a subtle difference. The bike is connected to an alternator which translates the energy created by the cyclists into electricity. The electricity is then used to power a range of different appliances including a mobile phone charger, an energy efficient light bulb, an inefficient light bulb, a computer screen and a radio. A laptop connected to the bike shows the cyclists how much electricity they are generating, how much carbon dioxide this energy would create and the cost of the electricity.

The energy bike invariably attracts a large number of employees eager to take up the challenge. The bike manages to get across a number of clear messages. Cyclists are always deeply shocked about the amount of extra pedal power it takes to power inefficient light-bulbs compared with efficient bulbs. As the switch between the two bulbs is made, the speed of pedalling noticeably slows and a look of surprise flickers across even the fittest cyclist's face!

Cyclists are also amazed about the amount of energy used by a computer monitor left switched on. This message is particularly pertinent as the bike is often used by employees in their lunchtime when they have frequently left their screen left on over the lunch period. Finally, cyclists are also surprised at the fact that phone chargers use electricity when they are left plugged in even when they are not charging the phone.

The energy bike was built just over a year ago. Already over 50 organisations in the UK have used the bike as part of their climate change communications strategy and it has been used or seen by over 5,000 people. It appears to be highly effective in encouraging people to change their behaviour. Based on an online survey with users of the bike:

- Over 80 per cent have installed low energy light bulbs

- 96 per cent now turn off standby functions on electrical equipment

- 92 per cent now turn their mobile phone chargers off at the wall

- 50 per cent now switch off their computer monitors when away from their desks at lunch AND in the evening

- 68 per cent of people fill the kettle only with the amount of water needed.

The second equipment of the carbon gym is the carbon rower. The rowing machine is attached to a pump which can be connected to a range of different balloons. Each balloon represents the volume of carbon created by different travel choices. Rowers are challenged to fill different balloons, enabling them to visualise the amount of carbon produced by their travel choice. The faster someone rows, the more air is pumped into the balloon.

Each of the three balloons shows the volume of carbon dioxide produced by travelling two kilometres on different forms of transport. The plane balloon demonstrates that travelling two kilometers by air produces one kilogramme of carbon dioxide, the car balloon shows that travelling the same distance by road produces 0.4kg of carbon dioxide whilst the train column illustrates that the same journey produced 0.22g of carbon dioxide[1].

The final equipment is a set of carbon weights. Like the carbon rower, the weights illustrate the different levels of carbon created through our travel choices, although this time demonstrating the weight of carbon produced rather than the volume. People can see how much extra weight of carbon is created by making the same journey by plane, an in-efficient car, an efficient car or by train. They are challenged to lift the weight of carbon their travel choice produces.

The carbon gym is an effective communication tool because it gets the message across in a physical, inter-active and engaging manner. Crucially, the Gym also enables people to visualize the impact that their lifestyle choices have by demonstrating to them the volume and weight of carbon dioxide produced through their activities.

Environment champions

The second programme is environment champions which enables companies to reduce their impact on climate change through the active involvement of employees within the workplace.

Companies participating in the project establish a team of volunteer 'environment champions' consisting of up to about 20 employees who ideally represent all parts of the organisation and with varying degrees of seniority. The team is facilitated through an initial training session in which they meet, learn the aims of the programme and carry out an initial audit of the organisation's environmental impacts.

The facilitator then compiles an audit report detailing the organisation's environmental impacts. The team is reconvened for a second meeting where it designs a strategy to reduce these impacts. The strategies generally have two elements. The first establishes the structural changes required such as installing low-energy light bulbs, etc.

The second involves planning a communications campaign to the rest of the employees. Campaigns have historically involved face-to-face communication, displays and events, email and intranet messages and poster displays. Creative variations on this theme have included a glass-painting workshop to encourage employees to use their own individually designed glass rather than disposable plastic cups, or an employee dressed up as a 'green man' who welcomed employees to work and encouraged them to reduce energy use.

The implementation of the strategies generally lasts for between three and five months during which time the facilitator meets with the team on a monthly basis for progress meetings designed to iron out problems and maintain momentum.

At the end of the campaign a second audit is performed using the same methods as in the first and the facilitator compiles a report detailing the changes made and the environmental savings achieved. The team then meets again to celebrate their success and plan the next steps.

A total of 62 organisations have participated, or are participating, in environment champions. These organisations come from across the UK, represent businesses and local authority/civil service organisations and range in size from 22 to 6,442 employees. In total, 924 people have been through the environment champions process and this has impacted upon more than 54,000 people.

Environment champions has achieved an average saving of 12.1 per cent of energy used per annum. Chart 1 shows the distribution of savings across the organisations and indicates substantial savings in all but one of the programmes analysed.

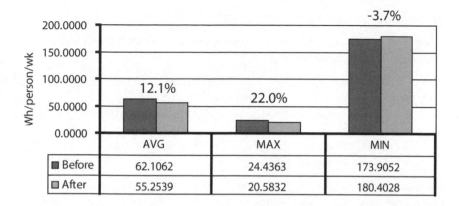

Chart 1
Source: author's own

EcoTeams

The third programme run by Global Action Plan that contains all the elements we believe to be essential within a successful behaviour change initiative is called EcoTeams. Unlike, environment champions, this project encourages people to reduce the impact that their own homes have on climate change.

EcoTeams are groups of six to eight people who meet once a month for approximately four months. At each meeting, EcoTeam participants decide together on the environmental actions that they are able and willing to do at home, and share experiences of the actions they have already taken.

EcoTeams originated in the Netherlands in the late 1990s and since then over 150,000 people have taken part worldwide. In the UK, participating households have on average achieved the following results:

- Before the EcoTeam programme, the average waste to landfill per year per household was just over 400kg. After EcoTeams, this had fallen by 28 per cent to just under 300kg.

- Electricity consumption was reduced by 25 per cent, saving 2.8 tonnes of carbon dioxide per year.

- Gas consumption was reduced by 26 per cent (adjusted for seasonal change), saving 2.2 tonnes of carbon dioxide per year.

BOX 1: BRITISH GAS AND ECOTEAMS

In late 2004, British Gas decided to run EcoTeams with a group of their employees. The reasons for their involvement included:

- A desire to increase employees' environmental awareness
- A wish to help employees to live more sustainably at home
- A belief that positive changes at home would be translated into better practices in the workplace
- A desire to illustrate innovation and leadership to the wider community
- A belief that EcoTeams would strengthen communication within the organisation.

British Gas recruited 18 volunteers from across the country to act as EcoTeam co-ordinators. They were surprised at the level of response received from parts of the company that they sometimes had found difficult to involve in corporate projects – such as the call centres. The reasons people volunteered varied enormously and included:

'I thought it would be a good thing to get my seven year old daughter involved in.' – Cheryl Marshall, Leeds

'I have been recycling for some time but felt I could learn more and have a better structure to it.' – Rachel Pouso, Edinburgh

Global Action Plan ran a training day for the volunteer co-ordinators. The training outlined the project, the role of the co-ordinators and sought to enthuse and motivate the volunteers. Feedback from the training included:

'I really enjoyed the learning aspect of the training – it was fun and interactive – you only get out what you put in!'

'Lots of things to think about – it's not all recycling.'

'Really enjoyed it – emphasis is on anything can be done, if only in a small way – it's up to you and what suits you... lots of support on creating teams.'

After the training event, each volunteer co-ordinator was asked to recruit six colleagues to join them in an EcoTeam. The volunteers succeeded in recruiting 130 households who participated in the four-month EcoTeam programme.

Each EcoTeam was shown a video that explained the project and provided ideas and inspiration as to what could be achieved. Each participant was given an EcoTeam workbook setting out the programme, giving ideas as to what actions could be taken and including measurement sheets so that participants could measure their achievements.

At each EcoTeam meeting the participants discussed an environmental issue including waste and shopping, energy and transport, water use and actions they could take in the wider community. Participants researched the issue to inform their discussions, and measured their waste, energy and water use to set improvement targets. The meetings were facilitated by the EcoTeam co-ordinators and usually took place in a lunch break or immediately after work.

Based upon the measurements taken by the households involved, the British Gas employees succeeded in:

- Reducing the level of waste being thrown into their dustbins by 31 per cent
- Increasing their recycling rate by 25 per cent
- Cutting their electricity use by 16.5 per cent
- Reducing their gas consumption by 10 per cent
- Cutting the carbon dioxide emissions from their direct energy use by 16 per cent.

In addition to these environmental savings, the impact of EcoTeams was felt within British Gas. Participants translated their environmental concerns back into the workplace. For example, many of them sought to further improve their recycling facilities in the office and encouraged their colleagues to put the right paper in the right bins. The Head of Environment commented that she now had a new group of environmental zealots through whom she could communicate new initiatives.

Five of the EcoTeam volunteers presented their achievements at an event at the House of Commons sponsored by Peter Ainsworth MP. They shared the platform with Professor Sir David King – the Government's Chief Scientist, and Elliot Morley – the then Environment Minister. The presentation illustrated to the 100 delegates how the need to take action on climate change can be translated into practical action.

The EcoTeam programme illustrates that communication to employees need not be solely directed at changes in the workplace to be effective. Once people understand what changes they are being asked to consider, and receive support and guidance helping them to make these changes, they are willing to introduce them across all aspects of their life.

Top ten tips

Based upon the experience gathered to date, here are ten dos and don'ts in running climate change initiatives with employees:

1. Do communicate imaginatively using a wide range of communication tools that are interactive, visual and unusual.

2. Do use the energy and inventiveness of your employees.

3. Do measure actual environmental savings and use this as a form of motivation for employee engagement.

4. Do bring employees together in teams. Ensure that these teams are effectively facilitated.

5. Do give employees the time to enable them to participate in climate change initiatives.

6. Don't set employees up to fail by encouraging them to start initiatives with no ongoing support.

7. Don't run awareness campaigns that have no tangible impact on behaviour.

8. Don't give employees an open-ended challenge. Provide them with a clear structure and end date.

9. Don't set employees arbitrary environmental targets, with no mechanism for reaching these targets.

10. Don't forget to thank people for their involvement.

Conclusion

The success of the three programmes outlined illustrates that tools are available to enable business leaders to effectively engage their employees in the fight against climate change. The business benefits are many and varied:

- The environment champions project has achieved an average 12 per cent reduction in energy use across 62 different organisations. These savings were achieved largely through behaviour change rather than large capital outlays meaning that the financial savings were almost totally transferred to the bottom line.

- Fifty per cent of the users of the energy bike have changed their work habits by turning off their computer monitors during lunchtime and in the evenings.

- EcoTeams has enabled British Gas employees to reduce their domestic carbon dioxide emissions by 16 per cent and has also created a group of environmental enthusiasts better able to create change within the company.

- EcoTeams has also enabled the environment team within British Gas to connect and engage with staff in parts of the business that had previously shown no interest in environmental issues.

- All the organisations with whom Global Action Plan has worked have reported that the initiatives enhance staff morale, build new connections within the business and increase employee loyalty to the company.

Another common feature of all the initiatives is that they appear to have been successful in shifting the culture within the companies. Anecdotal evidence suggests that once people make small changes in their daily routines they not only maintain these improved habits, they also explore what else they can to reduce their environmental impact. This anecdotal experience is supported by research from the University of Leiden who tracked the behaviour patterns of people who participated in EcoTeams in the Netherlands over a five-year period. This research concluded that EcoTeams stimulated many people to enter a 'virtuous circle' of continual environmental improvement in all aspects of their lives.

Despite these many tangible benefits, there is a marked reluctance within businesses, with a small number of notable exceptions, to devote the time and resource to implement these types of initiatives. For most businesses, short-term operational and financial need takes precedence over slightly longer-term investment to address climate change – even when this investment cuts costs, improves environmental performance, motivates employees and enhances corporate social responsibility.

In order for this situation to change, business leaders need not only to use their influence to shift government policy, they also need to lead a cultural change within their own companies.

Notes

1   The figures used are from the book *How we can save the planet* by Mayer Hillman (Penguin Puttnam 2006).

Further References

www.globalactionplan.org.uk

How green is your lifestyle? www.greenscore.org.uk

Measure your CO_2 emissions: www.carboncalculator.org.uk

Sector Perspectives and Strategies: In Their Own Words

23

Climate Change and the Insurance Industry

Trevor Maynard, Lloyd's of London

Introduction

The climate is changing and human activity is playing a major role. This is now recognised as fact by a growing body of expert opinion. Most worryingly, the latest science suggests that future climate change may take place more quickly than previously anticipated. One reason for this is the discovery of tipping points, which can result in rapid and unpredictable change. Interaction between climate and society is complex and forms one of the main sources of uncertainty in our future. It is clear that this uncertainty is of intense interest to the insurance industry (and business more generally) as rapid change would call into question the viability of the world's economic systems.

The past few years bluntly highlight the cost of weather-related catastrophes for the global economy and the insurance industry in particular. The insurance sector's response has proven that it is financially strong and well equipped to respond to these financial shocks. It is, however, clear that until recently the industry had not taken changing catastrophe trends seriously enough.

This chapter considers some of the changes in climate that are possible and suggests the impacts these might have on the insurance industry. We do not solely restrict ourselves to the consensus view; whilst it is important not to scaremonger, it is also crucial to monitor developments relating to more extreme possibilities. Over the past decade many risks that were thought extreme are now becoming the consensus view. Key actions are also proposed which highlight the fact that adaptation to climate change is fast becoming part of business-as-usual.

The insurance industry is global. Many insurance companies based in the UK will be affected by climate changes all around the world and this chapter therefore takes a global view of the issues raised.

Climate change and weather risk

Hurricanes

There has been much debate over whether global warming has influenced the extreme hurricane seasons of 2004–5. A recent scientific paper undertakes a careful analysis and concludes that man-made climate change has caused the global air temperature to increase, which in turn has caused the sea temperature to increase, leading to greater hurricane destructiveness. Following this train of logic, it argues that man-made climate change has increased the destructiveness of hurricanes, and hence has *already* impacted insurance losses. Note however, that we don't have to restrict our attention to the largest events; arguably every hurricane is a little stronger than it 'would have been' had man-made climate change not been present, because the sea (the hurricane's power source) is a little warmer. There is strong evidence that we will also see a higher frequency of hurricanes with more of them making landfall. Also, the sea is higher now than previously, therefore they will do more damage. This trend is expected to continue.

Natural rhythms in sea temperatures certainly play a significant role, as analysis in the North Atlantic shows. Under natural cycles alone we can expect very severe hurricane activity to continue for the short to medium term.

Figure 1: Atlantic multidecadal oscillation

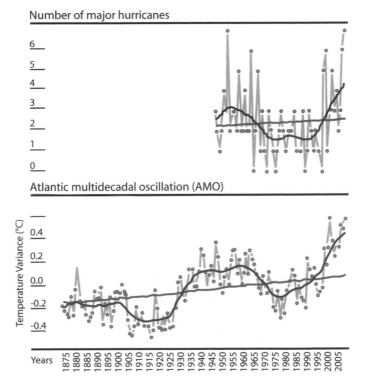

The lower graph illustrates the combined impact on sea surface temperature of natural cycles (darker line) around a suggested climate change trend (lighter line); the cycle is referred to as the Atlantic Multidecadal Oscillation (AMO), as it takes place over several decades. The graph above this tracks the actual number of major hurricanes (category three and above) per year, with the darker line illustrating a cycle over the period and the lighter line showing an increasing trend. There is clearly a strong correlation between 'warm' phases of the sea, surface temperature cycle, and more intense hurricane activity. On this basis, the intense hurricane seasons in 2004 and 2005 should have come as no surprise as they were predicted in 2001 by academics. Another important feature of the graph is that hurricane statistics are highly volatile, in some years there are no major hurricanes, in others, there are up to seven. Even in a period of heightened risk, therefore, it is plausible to have no major land falling hurricanes in a given year. It is vital that, should the insurance industry experience such 'quiet' seasons, it does not relax its pricing discipline and allow premiums to fall below sustainable (risk-based) levels.

With higher temperatures creating the right conditions for storm formation, we can also expect windstorm seasons to lengthen, thus causing the insurance industry to be 'on risk' for longer each year. For example, the recent tropical cyclone *Monica* that hit Australia was the most intense cyclone in southern hemisphere history, yet it occurred at a time when the season is usually all but over. Events over recent years could also cause the industry to become on risk over a wider geographical area than previously. A hurricane hit the coast of Brazil in 2004 for the first time, and in 2005 *Vince* was the first tropical storm to make landfall on the Iberian Peninsula. In 2006 Hurricane *John* had a small probability of threatening Los Angeles; possibly a more significant risk in the coming years? While these three events do not alone prove the impact of climate change, they do illustrate that areas previously 'hurricane free' or at lower risk may become more susceptible.

It is believed that a major reason that Hurricane *Katrina* intensified so suddenly was that it passed over a particularly warm deep current. We could hypothesise that such currents may become more regular, and more extensive; this will be a key question for scientists to answer in the short term.

Ice sheets and rapid sea level rise

One of the major concerns about the effects of global warming is the stability of two land-based large ice sheets, Greenland and the West Antarctic Ice Sheet (WAIS). Rapid melting from these has the potential to increase sea levels significantly and create the conditions for the reorganisation of the oceans, with subsequent severe climatic impacts. Projections regarding the stability of the ice sheets suggest that large portions of them will melt during the coming centuries. There is, however, a probability of significant ice sheet collapse over shorter time scales. Evidence from palaeoglaciology (where proxy data is used to infer information about the long-past climate) shows us that land-based ice sheets were largely stable and melted slowly. Conversely, the more ocean based ice sheets broke up rapidly, resulting in rapid discharge of icebergs and significant sea level rise from displacement. Most of the Greenland Ice Sheet is not marine based and therefore, the scientists argue, not likely to be in imminent danger of collapse. In contrast, much of the WAIS lies at, or below, sea level and hence is potentially able to collapse rapidly. Its stability is regarded as a key issue in the debate concerning the nature and occurrence of 'dangerous climate change'.

The East Antarctic Ice Sheet (EAIS) might also contribute rapidly to sea levels. Lake Vostok is a sub-glacial lake under the EAIS at almost 3500m above sea level in East Antarctica. The lake is 260km long and has a volume of 5400km^3. Erlingsson (2006) suggests that 'Lake Vostok is now almost full, and a [rapid and catastrophic outpouring] of several thousand cubic kilometres appears possible at any time'.

An additional factor is the presence of ocean currents, which raise the sea surface level along their lengths and along the coasts they reach: thus, the Gulf Stream causes the sea surface to lie at a higher altitude (a few centimetres) on the western coasts of the UK than on the eastern coasts. It is believed that, with global warming, a change may take place in the global ocean current system. Whilst current consensus is that this will not occur during the 21st century, one effect of this might be an increase in the sea surface of up to one metre around northwest European coasts during a very short period, perhaps as little as a few decades.

Even a 30cm rise at the eastern English port of Immingham has been shown to convert a one in 120 year flood event to a one in seven year event. So a one metre rise could be very significant indeed. This is often the case with climate change statistics; they often appear to show quite small changes (a one metre sea level rise doesn't sound much, a four degree temperature rise also seems quite bearable) but global averages can conceal great local variations, which is a major concern. Indeed one of the challenges for academic and insurance communities is to convert their statistics into more meaningful measures of impact for public, business and government attention.

It is important that the insurance industry monitors scientific developments in this area and considers how it would react to these rapid and significant events; their probability of occurrence is very low but may be approaching the levels of risk that capital within insurers is expected to withstand; particularly for those with better credit ratings.

Flooding

Flooding is an international problem set to increase under climate change over the next 50 years and beyond. Globally, it accounts currently for 40 per cent of all natural hazards and half of all deaths caused by natural disasters. Both observations and computer models suggest increasing river discharge and flood risk.

There are several types of flooding that are likely to be affected strongly by climate change. Principally these are:

- *Lowland river flooding in larger river channels*: primarily caused by long-duration rainfall from one or more frontal systems, or by springtime snowmelt. For example the flooding in Lewes in October 2000.

- *Flash flooding of small river channels or along drainage pathways*: primarily caused by short-duration, intensive rainfall from convective thunderstorm events. For example, Boscastle, UK, August 2004.

- *Coastal flooding*: primarily caused by localised sea level rise induced by storm surges, including those from tropical cyclones. The major 1953 UK flood event is a good example of this, as is Hurricane Katrina in 2005.

It is likely that events with an intensity of today's one hundred year floods may recur every ten to fifty years by the 2070s. Thus, despite a general trend to drier summer conditions in Europe, episodes of severe flooding may become more frequent due to short (one to five days) episodes of heavy precipitation. To a climate model, thunderstorm events are very small and therefore they are extremely difficult to model and predict. Hence, studies that use climate change predictions to quantify the likely change in flood risk and its economic impact, may well underestimate the risk of flooding from 'small' and short duration events (such as those from flash flooding) and subsequently may underestimate the likely future economic damage. Insurers would do well to be aware of, and adjust for, these parameter uncertainties within models when allowing for impacts on their business.

Climate and climate change is only part of the flooding problem: how the flooding is managed is as important. White and Howe (2004) show that poor surface water management can exacerbate the severity of flooding and its impact. For example, urban drainage systems tend to move water rapidly to the watercourse, leading to a reduced lag time between a precipitation event and the stream discharge peak. In turn, this causes higher *streamflow*, leading to a greater risk of flooding. Further urbanisation, combined with an increase in the frequency and intensity of storm rainfall events, will increase the risk of flooding. This highlights the need for insurers to work with, be aware of and influence the decisions of planners and engineering firms. These decisions may materially affect claims experience in the future. Sustainable Drainage Systems will be a crucial feature to reduce flooding risk and insurers could consider offering lower premiums to households that have invested in them. However, this may not be possible if the success of the system relies on the majority of householders in an area to have taken the necessary steps, and underlies the need for partnership with central and local government.

Insurers can have a role in adaptation after a claim has occurred. Some insurers have promoted and paid for refitting of more damage resistant materials (for example plastic kitchens). This additional upfront cost should significantly reduce claim costs and also help the policyholder recover more quickly in future.

Drought

Global warming is already imposing a change on the 'average' climate and this is expected to accelerate during the 21st century. In the case of heat waves, for example, temperature extremes resulting from climate variability will be more likely as a result of the increased average temperature alone. Under global warming the climate is expected to become more erratic as well, leading to yet higher possible temperatures. Periods of extremes are not usually maintained for longer than a few months, nevertheless, it is these anomalies (arising from variability) that tend to pose the key problems for power generation, agricultural output, human health and insurance.

Unlike floods, which can result from small-scale features such as individual thunderstorm systems (e.g. the Boscastle floods), droughts result from persistent, large scale and organised features of weather and climate, which act to suppress normal rain producing systems.

In many cases droughts can be traced to recognised patterns of climate variability, such as El Nino-Southern Oscillation (ENSO) and the North Atlantic Oscillation (NAO). The last three decades have witnessed the most unusually strong and persistent positive phase of the NAO. Droughts across the Mediterranean countries and North Africa associated with this pattern have led to alarming water resource conditions in some countries. Sustained periods of drought may well lead to increased frequency and severity of subsidence events; a major cause of UK losses for insurers.

Actions for the insurance industry

Assets – choose carefully and use your influence

Insurers hold reserves against claims that have yet to occur, or have occurred but have yet to be reported or paid. These reserves are significant, running into many hundreds of billions of dollars worldwide. Reserves are largely based on expected claims. Insurers also hold 'capital' in addition to reserves; regulators require this as a cushion against the unexpected.

The insurance industry (but more generally the financial services industry as a whole), therefore, holds a significant proportion of the world's financial assets. Assets of insurers in the UK amount to £1488bn of which 45 per cent is invested in equities, 40 per cent in corporate and government bonds, six per cent in cash and six per cent in property; the remainder is held in other assets (such as derivatives held for hedging purposes).

These assets (stocks, bonds, cash, property, options etc) are themselves at risk of climate change; the economy in general may be affected adversely by more regular and larger natural catastrophes and this may affect prices and returns from these investment sectors. As the impact of climate change becomes clearer, investment markets may adjust rapidly to anticipate future impacts. Thus the apparent long-term nature of some climate change impacts may have a far earlier and potentially more sudden impact on asset values than some might think.

The balance sheet of an insurer is thus vulnerable from two directions: the assets may perform worse than expected and the liabilities may increase above expectations. This is particularly true if the insurers hold significant amounts of equity investments, which not all do. However, many companies have pension funds with very significant amounts of assets under management, typically invested heavily in equities and corporate bonds and deficits in a company pension fund require financing. This adversely impacts company revenue accounts and balance sheets. This interaction of the liabilities and assets of the insurer adds to the volatility of their financial position and needs careful management.

Insurers should consider carefully the assets they hold. In particular they should perhaps avoid those that are at risk of adverse impact from climate change, as they need to be able to mobilise cash quickly for claims. They might also be well-advised to hold a little more of those assets that might perform well under climate change scenarios (such as alternative energy stocks).

As large investors, the insurance industry can also use its influence to encourage 'climate wise' behaviour from the boards of large corporations either by the investment choices they make, or directly engaging with these boards and exercising their voting rights at AGMs. We expect that the investment community will have an opportunity to flex its muscles more in this way in the future. Groups already exist like the Carbon Disclosure project and the Institutional Investors Group on Climate Change, which seek to facilitate this process.

Monitor legal judgements

Insurers offer cover to companies against third party liability. They also offer cover to business leaders and to their advisors. Leaders take decisions, often based on the opinions of their advisors. Sometimes these decisions turn out to be the wrong ones. In this case, if shareholders or other third parties believe they have suffered financial loss as a consequence they may take legal action – either against the company, the leaders or in turn against the advisors. Legally speaking, companies and their leaders and advisors are at risk of legal challenge for not having considered an issue if the courts deem it to have been 'reasonably foreseeable'.

Many believe that the implications of climate change, whilst uncertain, are sufficiently well understood that companies should now be taking its impacts into account when deciding strategy. It is far from clear whether the courts will agree with this; indeed this is a highly complex area and the outcome will depend on social attitudes as well as science. Social attitudes have a tendency to change, however, often rapidly; and compensation can be retrospective. We foresee an increasing possibility of attributing weather-related losses to man-made climate change factors; in 2005 scientists succeeded in ascribing a probability to the man-made component of the 2003 heat wave in France. This opens the possibility of courts assigning liability and compensation for claims of damage. Legal liability is now being actively pursued by several groups of lawyers and scientists who wish to use the same lines of argument as used against tobacco companies, though there are many obstacles to successfully winning damages. If the courts conclude that damage was reasonably foreseeable then liability could follow, as would the search for 'deep pockets' to meet the costs, with insurers a likely port of call.

Stick to risk-based pricing

Like most industries there are periods when profits are made and periods where the insurance industry is less profitable. These are often due to cycles in the supply of capital into the industry. During profitable times investors seek to share in the rewards and the well-understood economic theory of supply and demand drives prices down. Eventually (as profits reduce) some investors leave the market in search of better rewards elsewhere. Profits are then allowed to increase again, as there is less competition, and so on. For the insurance industry this cycle is particularly affected by two major factors:

- Catastrophes (both natural and man made) tend to cause a sudden large loss followed by higher premiums and an end to unprofitable times as insurers raise premiums to rebuild their capital base; the 'insurance cycle' can be more like a tooth of a saw, a fairly steady reduction in profits followed by a rapid move into profitability. Indeed some in the industry suggest that such catastrophes are often the only reason for the unprofitable times to end;

- The size and amount of claims often take some time to emerge. Take, for example, employer's liability cover (known as 'workers' compensation' in the US). This appeared to be a profitable business until the disease 'asbestosis' and its variants became known; suddenly there were a significant number of material claims that turned past profitable years into loss making ones. Most businesses largely know the cost of their raw materials in advance of making a product; hence the price they charge can be set to cover expenses. For insurers, the key 'expenses' are the claims arising under the policy, and these are necessarily estimated, not known at the time of selling their product. Insurers make assumptions about the level of claims they will experience over the period of insurance, on the basis that the past is a good proxy for the future. They do attempt to adjust for future trends but inevitably this process is full of uncertainty.

The periods when companies are making less profit, or even losses, are known as the 'soft' part of the cycle. Profitable times, conversely, are termed 'hard'. During the soft phase insurers are much more at risk as, in the event of a large catastrophe, there isn't a layer of profits to absorb part of the cost. The 2005 hurricane season came during a hard part of the insurance cycle and this is one of the reasons why the insurance industry emerged from the largest losses in its history relatively unscathed.

The (valid) argument insurers use for writing less profitable, even loss-making, business is that they wish to stay as major players in a market. If they walk away from business because they can't get the premium they would like, they lose market share and relationships can be very hard to rebuild. They hope to stay in the market so that when premium rates go up they will be available to take their share of the considerable profits. Over time, this 'moving average' approach has worked well; particularly for business (such as catastrophe covers and liability-related business) that it is very hard to price in the first place.

Global warming may change things. The moving average approach only works if irregular large losses are followed by a few years of good profits in a fairly regular pattern. Climate change raises the spectre of multiple catastrophe years (2004/5 for example), and larger losses than experienced before – often over several territories simultaneously.

Against this changing risk, it is vital that insurers maintain an ongoing level of financial strength. A large catastrophe like Katrina during a soft period of the insurance cycle is an unpleasant prospect.

For this reason, insurers must maintain 'risk-based' pricing. Insurers should use their best endeavours to calculate a premium, based on scientific probabilities, with allowance for future trends and the cost of capital. They should think carefully before accepting a premium that is lower. Insurers can be innovative with product design and climate change does indeed present opportunities as well as risks to insurers. We argue, however, that research should be shared; this would be much more efficient and will lead to a healthier industry.

Capital bases must be allowed to build up to prepare for the unknown. When catastrophes occur only every few years the so-called 'profits' in one year can be thought of as savings to be put towards large losses in later years.

Given the very large risks that shareholders are taking (they stand to lose their entire investment), it is reasonable that they get rewarded for those risks. High returns should be expected and are not a sign of a greedy industry; if they do not materialise the shareholders will take their capital elsewhere.

Regulators can help here. In many regions they are responsible for ensuring that premiums are appropriate. Their encouragement to maintain risk-based premiums will be crucial. Governments can also help in encouraging a balanced debate amongst those tasked with ensuring fair trade and competition.

Don't reward 'bad' behaviour

Individuals and companies don't like risks that can overwhelm them. This is understandable and is the reason why insurance has evolved. Insurers can pool the risks of many people on the basis that unfortunate events happen randomly: an accidental fire from a lightning strike, a theft or a car accident being just some examples. The premiums they charge are a tiny fraction of the individual cost of each event because they can share the losses of the unlucky amongst all the policyholders that were lucky.

This is why catastrophes are a problem for the insurance industry. They tend to happen to lots of policyholders at the same time. A hurricane can decimate a very large area of property. Direct insurers (those that sell to the public and businesses) often have aggregations of policyholders within one geographical region. They seek to mitigate their risk by buying their own insurance; this time from reinsurers. Reinsurers pool risks from around the world on the basis that catastrophes in one region might occur but other parts of the world will be lucky.

This is why climate change could be such a potential problem for the global insurance industry. Suddenly catastrophes have increasing probabilities of occurring simultaneously around the world; and when they do, being larger and more devastating.

When extreme risks become more and more frequent, the concept of insurance can break down. You don't buy insurance against replacing your car tyres because it is certain that you will have to replace them eventually.

General insurance contracts are typically annual. Cover is provided for the risks over the coming year. Some have called on insurers to take their 'share of responsibility'. Insurers are keen to work with policyholders to keep premiums down by changing behaviour (for example keeping trees and shrubs trimmed to avoid debris in windstorms). These actions will naturally lead to lower premiums through lower loss experience overall. Insurers in general must not, however, charge premiums that are lower than the risk requires. There has, for example, been a rapid and material migration to coastal locations recently; this has been coupled with considerable increases in contents values. Also, during major catastrophes supply of building materials and skilled trade workers is stretched very thin and prices for both typically increase, leading to larger insured loss than might be expected. Mathematically this has to result in higher premiums.

In some regions prices are agreed or capped by regulators; they then become a political issue. It is vital that markets are free to charge risk-based prices. Economically this tends to encourage appropriate behaviours from policyholders seeking reduced premiums.

Clearly there are considerable risks to the brands of insurers over this issue; insurers must be innovative and willing to work with government, regulators, business and individuals, but they must also stick firmly to good economics.

Think the 'unthinkable'; keep your models updated

It will be important for the insurance industry to consider the financial impact of various scenarios even if they are currently thought to be unlikely.

For example, Lloyd's recently responded to this issue by introducing a Realistic Disaster Scenario to test the financial impact of a hurricane making landfall in New York State, with a second hurricane hitting the Carolinas in the same season. We have also upgraded our existing hurricane scenarios to test US$100bn losses, to take account of the expected increase in storm severity. With more and more accurate scientific information now available, insurers are increasingly able to respond to the scientific predictions of each season ahead. This means a shift in emphasis when pricing catastrophe risk, away from basing price on a long-term baseline trend, which only very gradually allows for the impact of climate change.

Some of the catastrophe modelling companies have issued, so called, 'near-term' projections of hurricane activity which take account of the heightened risk at present (whether due to climate change or natural cycles). We would expect companies to use these near-term views as their 'base' scenarios, and to consider whether the models have gone far enough in assessing the risk.

Companies should continue to pressure their catastrophe modelling advisors to keep their models updated and in line with the latest scientific views on the subject. However, companies should also ensure that they improve on data quality and granularity; it is becoming more and more important to capture exposure data (insured values, type of property, use of building, precise location of building) as quickly and accurately as possible. Brokers should help with this process where they can.

Companies must ensure they keep pace with the latest research both within the academic community and business. Clearly, the insurance industry should do as much as it can to sponsor and share new research going forward.

Don't ignore operational issues

Insurance companies should not forget that they have their own operational issues to manage and climate change may affect these. Transport systems are vulnerable; telecommunications infrastructure can be impacted by wind, flood and heat (fluctuations between summer and winter may lead to more pipe damage and thus affect the water supply of major cities). Most companies have disaster recovery plans; climate change is a key reason they may be called upon. Companies can adapt to many of these problems; for example the possibility of home working is a partial solution to many of them, though companies should not assume that the telecom infrastructure is capable of working on that large a scale (i.e. with 'everyone' logging in at once).

Some academics warn that certain diseases will move away from the tropics and head towards the poles as temperatures rise, which may affect sickness rates of insurance staff as well as potentially leading to Employer Liability issues. This is still highly debatable but is a risk that needs to be monitored carefully. Clearly businesses in one region can learn from others already dealing with such risks. This is yet another example of the teamwork that will be required globally.

Conclusions

We don't know exactly what impact climate change will have but we do know that it presents society, and the economy, with an increasing level of uncertainty. We believe that it is time for the insurance industry to take a more leading role in understanding and managing the impact of climate change. Understanding and responding to it must become 'business as usual' for insurers and those they work with. Failure to take climate change into account will put companies at risk from future legal actions from their own shareholders, their investors and clients.

Climate change must inform underwriting strategy, from the pricing of risk, to the wording of policies. It must guide and counsel business strategy, including business development and planning. It is far from certain whether insurers will be able to continue to offer cover in all areas within current policy terms; to do so may require increases in capital over the coming decades in order to ensure solvency and thereby protect policyholders against ever larger, and more frequent, climate related catastrophes. Additional capital may also be required to cover the increased levels of uncertainty. This is one of the key features of climate change, which is expected to lead to increased *variability* in climate, as well as a change in average levels. The variability is, if anything, more worrying to the insurance industry than the trend in average values. Additional capital must be built up gradually and will lead inevitably to increases in premiums. It is vital that the insurance industry continues to base its premiums on a full assessment of the risks and cost of capital; in an increasingly uncertain world the industry must be strong and the insurance cycle managed actively. Ill-prepared, undercapitalised insurers are no good to anyone, especially policyholders.

Much excellent work on climate change and its likely impacts is already available in academic circles and other industries. The insurance industry must work with these groups to understand their work and take it into account in pricing and planning. The industry must, however, remember that computer models of loss are at best approximations and may omit crucial factors. Whilst highly complex and triumphs of scientific thought, models are still not able to capture all aspects of the climate including key tipping points. Though understanding shifting level of extreme losses is certainly the priority, there are many lessons to be learnt from reconstructions of past climate and it is crucial to monitor this area of science as well, as it is now suggested that rapid climate change is a risk we cannot ignore.

Based on long experience, we believe that insurance markets operate most efficiently when left to free market forces, and the vast majority of natural perils are insurable – as long as the market is free to price risk adequately. However, if this freedom is removed, or if the pace of climate change grows faster than expected, this could change our view. In this event, industry strategists will want to consider the long-term insurability of weather-related risk. Insurers will continue the development of alternative risk transfer tools such as catastrophe bonds and weather derivatives.

Policyholders will quite rightly want to control premium levels and retain insurability of their property. To help with this process the insurance industry must engage with the wider world through meaningful, tangible partnerships to mitigate risk. In turn it is to be hoped that the public, media and consumer groups will understand that at its simplest, the insurance industry shares losses of the few amongst the many. If losses go up because the risk changes or, crucially, behaviour is not modified, then so will premiums. This is not the act of an uncaring industry, it is just mathematics.

Much of this chapter has focussed on adaptation to climate change, as this is clearly within the power of insurance companies to influence. We recognise that mitigation of the risk itself (i.e. the reduction of CO_2 emissions) is also crucial. Not least, the financial services industry as a whole is a vast investor in stock and bond markets and can use its influence as investors to encourage climate proof behaviour from boards of large corporations.

Working together and more widely with business and government, the insurance industry must now seize the opportunity to make a difference, not just to the future of our own industry but also to the future of society.

References

Many of the scientific points raised in this paper are based on advice from Climate Change Risk Management (http://www.ccrm.co.uk/), a specialist scientific consultancy.

Elsner J 'Evidence in support of the climate change–Atlantic hurricane hypothesis', *Geophysical Research Letters*, Vol.33, L16705, doi:10.1029/2006GL026869, 2006.

Erlingsson U. 'Lake Vostok Behaves Like a "Captured Lake" and May be Near to Creating an Antarctic Jökulhlaup', Vol.88, doi:10.1111/j.0435-3676.2006.00278.x, March 2006, p.1.

Levermann A., Griesel A., Hoffmann M., Montoya M. and Rahmstorf S. 'Dynamic sea level changes following changes in the thermohaline circulation', *Climate Dynamics* 24, 2005, p.347.

Silver N. and Dlugolecki A. 'The day before tomorrow', *Environmental Finance*, February 2006, pp.28–9.

Westerling et al. 'Warming and Earlier Spring Increase Western U.S Forest Wildfire Activity', *Science*, 2006, Vol.313.

White I. and Howe J. 'The mismanagement of surface water', *Applied Geography*, 24, 2004, pp.261–280.

24

Valuing Carbon Requires a Fundamental Change in Thinking: How climate mitigation can become affordable and widely accepted

Georg Rosenbauer, Siemens Power Generation

'Global warming is a reality. A disturbing reality of staggering and potentially disastrous consequences. A reality that demands action. Today.'- Dr. Uriel Sharef, member of the Corporate Executive Committee, Siemens AG[1]

Siemens shares the belief that climate change poses a significant challenge for the 21st century, in addition to other issues like the need to ensure economic growth, alleviate poverty and provide access to adequate supplies of energy and water. The issue demands the attention of governments and consumers as well as that of the business economy.

Addressing environmental challenges in all our markets is a cornerstone of our understanding of corporate responsibility. In this context, we are dedicated to responsibly address the global challenges that climate change poses. Part of this involves improving the environmental and operating performance of our customers' assets, as well as our own environmental protection measures and management systems.

To address this, we offer our customers a broad range of energy-efficient products, solutions and services for both fuel and power production with low emissions, power transmission, the power demand side, and for energy conservation. To further push a soft transition into a low-carbon economy, a joint effort of governments, businesses and consumers is required to create both market pull and technology push.

We are committed to co-operate with customers and governments alike to find an optimum balance between greenhouse gas mitigation and sound economic development. Working in partnerships we can identify effective solutions, while ensuring long-term value for customers, shareholders and the environment.

Climate change – a challenge with a completely new dimension

Climate change has new dimensions in almost every aspect:

- *Complexity*: the climatic system is very complex and it is difficult to prove the need for action without any doubts

- *Time lag*: major impacts will hit future generations, even if we act now, the mitigation effect will be felt with a delay of decades

- *Regional mismatch of cause and impact*: the biggest emitters will not necessarily bear the hardest impacts

- *Global nature*: due to its large scale the problem can only be solved through global actions

- *Required structural change*: mitigation costs are at least one order of magnitude higher than all other air pollutant reduction costs (SO_2, NO_x, particulates etc.) put together

- *Potential dimension of threat*: although hardly understood in detail yet, it becomes obvious that the dimension of threat might by far exceed the dimensions of other environmental issues known until now.

These dimensions act as huge roadblocks for further actions and commitment. In international climate negotiations, nations find themselves in a classical 'prisoners' dilemma'; there is hardly a strategic advantage from taking action when others don't.

Although this dilemma may be hard to solve in the field of politics, from a technical and economic perspective there is some reason for optimism. There is a clear rationale that the economic threats and costs of 'not taking action' by far exceed the efforts of 'taking mitigation action'[2]. Climate mitigation is technically feasible and economically bearable, although it requires immediate action towards a fundamental change of energy infrastructure. This is the outcome of many recent studies, for example 'Pathways to 2050' published by the World Business Council for Sustainable Development[3].

Business impact analysis

Even though the lives and environment of millions, if not billions, of people must be the primary concern, an analysis should focus on business impacts. Industry is not only part of the problem, but becoming more and more a key contributor to the solution. The better the impacts on businesses are understood, the more likely it is that industry will support actions to mitigate global warming.

- **Direct regulatory impacts:** The impact is obvious. A company's operations covered by an emissions trading scheme will probably face some shortage of allowances that has to be evaluated.

- **Indirect regulatory impacts:** Examples are higher power prices or a change in investment behaviour. These are much more difficult to anticipate and analyze, but for an equipment supplier like Siemens, they have a much higher impact than the direct regulatory impacts.

- **Commercial opportunities:** For an equipment supplier, commercial opportunities will primarily be the result of changed investment behaviour (see Box 2).

- **Shift in competitive position:** One particular aspect here is pace of business adaptation. Those who anticipate changes earlier and are ready to support customers' needs under the new market conditions will have a competitive advantage. When facing regulatory impacts, many players tend to underestimate the resulting opportunities.

- **Distributional effects:** The distributional effects of environmental regulation can be enormous and are to some extent inevitable. Market-based environmental regulation instruments without any distributional effect cannot be environmentally effective. Of course there are also unnecessary distributional effects beyond the purely environmental regulatory rationale. For Siemens, one major distributional effect is that CO_2 is priced into fuels. At least on the basis of CO_2 opportunity costs, the life-cycle cost optimum of power plants is slightly shifted towards a layout with higher efficiencies. In the long run, more money will ultimately be spent on highly efficient equipment and less on fuel. The same applies to all power-consuming equipment, as CO_2 is indirectly priced into power as well.

- **Regulatory risks:** Assessing the impact of today's regulatory schemes is too short-sighted, particularly when large long-term infrastructure investments are involved. Thus the direct and indirect regulatory impacts will have to be extrapolated, typically on a scenario basis. Generally the entire carbon footprint of a company's activities, including direct emissions, indirect emissions (e.g. from power consumption or raw materials) and mitigation options and costs will have to be considered. For Siemens, as a high-tech equipment and service provider, the value creation per ton of emitted CO_2 is fairly high (see Box 1). Thus for us the primary focus will be on product-related changes, rather than production-related risks. Many of these scenarios conclude that it is not so much a question of if, but when, climate mitigation will be on the agenda globally and CO_2 will have a stable, reasonable global value. Testing strategies and decisions under the different timelines of regulatory regimes remains difficult. Investing too early could be as painful as investing too late. Early movers do not always have an advantage.

- **Physical risks:** All the items above deal with climate mitigation, possible regulations and the resulting business impacts, but no matter how we succeed in mitigation, global warming is already happening. The cumulative nature of climate change effects leads to long time constants. To a certain degree, adaptation to climate change is inevitable, even if mankind were to take strong mitigation actions today. Impacts may be assessed on at least two levels. First, extreme weather events will put exposed facilities at risk and shortage of water or power or property damage caused by hurricanes may arise. The hurricane Katrina, for instance, caused €5 million damage to a Siemens operation in New Orleans. As a consequence, insurance costs will rise and thus generally costs for exposed operations. Second, on a national or global economic basis, overall economic growth is at risk.

The Carbon Disclosure Project (CDP)[4] analyzes this business impact in a stringent manner from an investment perspective and contributes a lot to drawing management attention to climate change. Representing investor funds with US$31.5 trillion capital, CDP assess the companies' exposure to climate related risks and opportunities in a structured way.

Summary

- Companies should use general impact analysis as a basis. Good examples of this can be found in the Carbon Disclosure Project.

- Focus on the opportunities – these are often much harder to identify than threats.

BOX 1: SIEMENS CO_2 FOOTPRINT

The majority of our production and the production of parts from suppliers are not energy intensive. The costs of energy consumption were €170 million for electricity and €43 million for fossil fuel in the fiscal year 2003/04. Thus the energy costs accounted for 0.3 per cent of the turnover or 6.3 per cent of the profit. In terms of value creation per ton (t) of CO_2 the carbon productivity of Siemens reaches more than 10,000 €/t. This is one order of magnitude higher than, for instance, the paper or glass industry reach (1,000 – 2,000 €/t range) and even two orders of magnitude above the steel industry (approx. 100 €/t).

Nevertheless, Siemens is currently building up a comprehensive global corporate greenhouse gas reporting process and is aiming at increased energy efficiency. The following data was compiled by Siemens' companies and subsidiaries worldwide (where Siemens owns more than 50 per cent of shares). It covers most of the productions sites and activities of Siemens. The current reporting system accounts for and reports direct CO_2 emissions and indirect CO_2 emissions from electricity consumed. Around 65 per cent of all Siemens employees worldwide are covered by this approach within the reporting system

Company Inventory of GHG Emissions Fiscal Year 2004/05

	Electricity CO_2 [t]	Fossil Fuel CO_2 [t]
Worldwide	2,152,000	547,000
EU	1,362,050	253,497

This data does not include district heating, the emission of other gases with global warming potential and CO_2 emissions resulting from transport (people, supplies, goods).

The 2005 reporting includes 25 new locations, amongst which are 18, energy-intensive, Osram Sylvania sites that emitted 422.000 t of CO_2 in 2005.

In order to increase its environmental performance – for example, the reduction of emissions, Siemens is implementing a worldwide environmental program. One part of this program is dedicated to Siemens production facilities. It includes a mandatory energy efficiency check for each major production site, i.e. sites with energy consumptions over a certain threshold.

Communication

As climate change is a reality and mitigation a necessity, CO_2 regulations have become a reality and will be extended with regard to scope and region. Simply lobbying against these regulations would not only contradict corporate responsibility targets, it would also be a waste of effort and resources.

A far more promising approach is to focus lobbying activities on the practicability of regulations, minimization of competitive distortions and reduction of planning uncertainties. The primary target must be to set a level playing field for the carbon-constrained economy to achieve climate mitigation at lowest overall cost.

Summary

- Lobbying – focus on making the new rules practicable and to get them working in a level playing field.

Uncertainties

Particularly in the infrastructure sector, investment decisions have to be made with two or more decades in mind. For R&D decisions the situation is even more critical: strategic marketing has to anticipate investment decisions at the time of market entry, often five to ten years in the future.

This planning uncertainty is not new and has always been a key success factor for involved players. Fuel price risks are well known and have been dealt with for a long time. Neither are regulatory changes new. These risks are integrated in financial models and will lead to a risk premium in the required margin. Thus every planning uncertainty will raise the threshold above which an investment will be considered feasible. In the power industry for instance, fuel price risks will lead to postponed investments until the achievable price for power is high enough to offset the required profit premium. Risk is not new and will always be part of the business, however, it will lead to delayed investments, high-risk premium in financial models, and a market development with strong boom-and-bust cycles.

With regard to climate policies it is not an option to 'wait and see' until the framework is predictable in the long run. Delayed action and unnecessary high abatement costs are the undesirable consequences. As an example, the European Union Emissions Trading Scheme (EU ETS), in its present form, bears huge volume and price risks. Allocation schemes can be modified every five years and price developments can only be predicted in a very wide price range. Currently, suitable structural incentives are available only in some aspects (see Box 3). If, under these conditions, the break-even for a power plant with carbon capture and storage (CCS) would be at an European Union Allowance (EUA) price level of 20 €/t, investors would still have to wait for far higher EUA price signals before an investment would pay off.

A good indicator for the quality of regulatory incentives is the response of the financial market. If, one day, banks are willing and able to integrate EUAs into financial models and, for example, lend against future emissions savings, the trading scheme will have achieved the desired impact on investment decisions. Today we are not at that stage.

Summary

- Uncertainty is here to stay – making decisions despite uncertainties is a key success factor.

- Every uncertainty will delay investments, add a risk premium to margins and thus increase overall costs for society. Weaker, but steady commitments will give rise to much better pay off than stop-and-go policies.

- The ability of the financial sector to integrate CO_2 market products in financial models is a valid indicator for the effectiveness of regulatory incentives.

Valuing carbon requires a fundamental change in thinking

Particularly during the first year of the EU ETS, players strongly mistrusted the scheme. Given all the uncertainties mentioned above, planners intuitively assumed that planning with a close to zero carbon price would be 'conservative'. However, if business cases are tested under different carbon scenarios, it will turn out that decisions designed for a 0 €/t world are definitely not the most robust ones.

The economic implications of a cap & trade scheme are still not fully taken in by many players. One tends, for instance, to judge abatement opportunities differently depending on the availability of EUAs (i.e. if one is short or long). If for instance a certain plant modernization could deliver CO_2 reductions at 5 €/t, it should be an attractive opportunity to save EU allowances. These could then be sold on the market at a higher market price. Furthermore, thanks to the modernization, the plant owner does not have to purchase these allowances at the same market price The modernization will, however, hardly be tackled as long as the plant is not short of allowances under its current operating scheme.

Summary

- 'Conservative assumptions' must be oriented to future carbon market scenarios, not to the past.

- Valuing carbon requires a fundamental change in thinking.

Carbon pricing is not all – only long-term incentives induce structural change

Currently, the global CO_2 policy landscape is split into cap & trade-focused countries – at the moment primarily Europe – and technology-focused countries, most prominently the US. The latter argue that new technologies are key to the solution and once they are available, the market will deliver the carbon cuts without further incentives.

Both positions have some logic. From an equipment supplier's perspective, however, these are not alternatives. Both technology push and market pull are required at the same time to make drastic carbon reduction affordable and widely accepted.

Economic theory might suggest that a plain CO_2 price signal should be sufficient to bring new technologies into the market. In reality, any market introduction of new technologies will bear considerable risks. A price signal from the EU ETS may serve well to drive the market diffusion of proven technologies with abatement costs well below market prices. However, it will hardly be sufficient to push large technological shifts.

On the other hand, technology funding without the perspective of a promising long-term market will not motivate CEOs to allocate billions of Euros to R&D and the market introduction of new technologies.

The technology development path of wind turbines shows impressively how highly predictable incentives and a sound competitive environment helped to develop the technology. Countries like Denmark and Germany, which provided planning certainty for investors and funded a reasonable number of units in the first technology generations, are now the operating base of a sound and quickly growing new industry.

Today, there is a broad consensus amongst stakeholders from industry and NGOs that CCS will be a necessary bridging technology towards a carbon-constrained economy, combining secure energy supply, bearable costs and climate mitigation[5] (see Box 4). These will only be successful in the market, however, when CO_2 avoidance costs can be reduced from approximately 40 €/t to 20 €/t.

How can this be done? Three forces need to pull together to make CCS a sustainable, affordable and globally accepted technology.

The first is largely in the hands of power plant and equipment providers – companies like Siemens. To refine CCS, the energy industry needs a concerted and strong technology push. We need to intensify research and development in key technologies and components. We need pilot projects and demonstration plants to optimize cost reductions and increase reliability, and we need to share the risks among stakeholders in these technologies – including equipment suppliers, investors, operators and the public.

The second force needed is market pull. Ultimately, the willingness to invest in plants and technological developments depends on a reliable regulatory environment. Investors must be reassured that a given market has stable and dependable conditions. European equipment suppliers also need to have global perspectives. Equipment suppliers have to be able to refinance the enormous R&D spending on a global market.

Finally, public acceptance of the technology and the corresponding solutions is necessary, not so much for the actual process of carbon capture but for transport and storage of CO_2. An open dialogue is needed to address all public concerns and to convince people of the advantages of the process. Equipment providers are not in the forefront in this mainly political task, but are naturally interested in contributing to this dialogue.

If CCS is really made attractive for investors, it will become a reality. This depends, however, on all three forces working jointly toward a common goal.

Summary

- Three forces need to pull together: technology push, market pull and public acceptance.

- Equipment suppliers have to refinance their R&D spending in a global market. A coherent global regulatory scheme will dramatically increase the incentives.

Conclusions for investors and companies

- Conduct a general business impact analysis

- Focus on the opportunities – they are often much harder to identify than threats

- Concentrate lobbying on making the new rules practicable and getting them work in a level playing field

- Uncertainty is here to stay – decision making under uncertainties is a key success factor

- 'Conservative assumptions' must be oriented to future carbon market scenarios – the past can only serve as reference

- Valuing carbon requires a fundamental change in thinking.

Conclusions for policy makers

- Every uncertainty will delay investments, add a risk premium to profit margins and thus increase overall costs for the society. Weaker, but steady commitments will much better pay off than 'stop-and-go' policies.

- The ability of the financial sector to integrate CO_2 market products in financial models is a valid indicator of the effectiveness of regulatory incentives.

- Three forces need to pull together: technology push, market pull and public acceptance.

- Equipment suppliers have to refinance their R&D spending in a global market. A coherent global regulatory scheme will dramatically increase the incentives.

BOX 2: OPPORTUNITIES – A SELECTION OF CLIMATE-FRIENDLY SIEMENS INNOVATIONS

Among the approximately 400,000 Siemens products and components there are many that have improved environmental performance. Some highlights are:

Piezo injection technology for diesel and gasoline engines:
In 2005, Siemens and Robert Bosch, GmbH, received the German Future Prize 2005 for the joint development of the Piezo injection technology for diesel and gasoline engines. Piezo technology allows extremely precise metering of the amount of fuel injected into the combustion chamber. This allows a substantial reduction of fuel consumption and pollutant emissions. Direct Injection was introduced for large-scale production of diesel engines in 2000, and for gasoline engines in 2006.

The world's most powerful gas turbine:
The world's most powerful gas turbine, built by Siemens for E.ON Energy's Irsching site, will set new benchmarks in terms of performance and operating economy. In a first step, Siemens will build a newly developed gas turbine plant. With a capacity of 340 megawatts, it will be the world's largest and most powerful gas turbine. After the test phase, the gas turbine plant will be extended to form a high-efficiency combined cycle power plant with a capacity of approximately 530 MW and an efficiency of over 60 per cent. Commercial operation is scheduled for 2011.

Wind turbines:
Siemens has become a major player in the wind power business with the acquisition of the Denmark-based company Bonus Energy in 2004. At the time of the takeover, the company was the industry's fifth largest player with an installed capacity of 3,321 megawatts in 20 countries. In November 2005, Siemens acquired the German wind power company AN Windenergie, which installed 1,300 MW of wind power capacity in Germany. The portfolio of Siemens Wind Power focuses on highly reliable wind turbines with lowest overall life-cycle costs. For Siemens Wind Power, it is not a question of building the largest turbines, but of offering the highest lifetime value for its customers. In July 2005, Siemens CEO, Dr. Klaus Kleinfeld, stated in the magazine *Business Week* that he sees wind power as a 'mega trend,' driven by rising electricity demands, soaring oil prices, improved economics of wind power and efforts to reduce CO_2 emissions as stipulated under the Kyoto Protocol.

Biomass power plants:
The Siemens Power Generation Group supplies components for biomass power plants. One such plant is located in Lockerby, Scotland, where 44 MW of electricity will be supplied to the grid as green energy. The plant will use fresh and old wood as fuel, as well as different grades of plant matter, such as willow, which is specially grown for the use in power generation.

Superconductive electric motors:
Siemens is among the world leaders in the development of equipment based on superconductivity. At temperatures well below minus 100 degrees Celsius, superconductors made from ceramics and cooled with liquid nitrogen are capable of carrying electricity without resistance. This reduces power losses to virtually zero. In 2001, Siemens became the first company in Europe to construct a motor with rotor windings made of superconducting wires and with an output of 400 kilowatts. Today, Siemens developers are working on a motor expected to deliver 4 MW of power, which could be used as an electric drive in ships.

Performance contracting for energy management in buildings:
Siemens Building Technology supports customers in enhancing building performance and energy efficiency for the lifetime of buildings. Especially for public owners, budgetary constraints are often a barrier to investing in even highly profitable energy saving measures. In such cases, Siemens Building Technology steps in with a performance-based contract and by financing the measures. The benefits from energy savings are shared with the customer.

Zero-emission casings:
Siemens Corporate Technology and BASF are jointly developing plastics based on glycol. The goal is to produce standard casings from renewable resources. If these synthetics are incinerated at their end of life, carbon dioxide emissions will be neutral.

BOX 3: EU ETS – IT IS THE STRUCTURE OF INCENTIVES THAT MATTERS.

It seems that in the heat of the first allocation battle sometimes the primary goal of the EU ETS (i.e. achieving carbon reductions and, subsequently, the required structural change at lowest overall costs) has been lost. From a very generic economic point of view, this can be achieved with any kind of cap and trade scheme as long as policy makers stick to the appropriate overall cap. However, a closer look reveals that structural aspects of the allocation rules do matter[6]. There are, primarily, two ways for the industry to reduce CO_2 and thus comply with the overall cap:

Short-term production shift:
The largest short-term mitigation is provided by the switch from coal-fired to gas, or biomass-fired power generation in the existing fleet. In industries other than power generation, other opportunities in the value chain can lead to CO_2 savings. These measures can be quickly realized and have a low risk as they are reversible and do not imply investment risks. The downside is that the overall reduction potential is limited and the CO_2 reduction costs are very high – depending on fuel prices in the 20 to 70 €/t range.

Longer-term structural changes in the capital stock:
Options are modernization of old plants, early replacement of mature plants by state-of-the-art technology and, especially in case of replacements, shifting to low-carbon technologies. As all these measures require investments and deployment of equipment, they require a few years lead time, a planning horizon of two decades, and they are not easily reversible. Our estimates show, however, that CO_2 reduction costs, with these investment-based measures, can be in the five to 30 €/t range and are thus way below the short-term production shifts. Precondition for this cost range is that advanced low-carbon technologies are developed and available.

Both these pathways of CO_2 reduction are incentivized by different structural properties of the trading scheme. The production shift is driven by the integration of full CO_2 costs, including opportunity costs, in the variable costs of production. This is the case for almost any allocation scheme (grandfathering as well as benchmarking), as long as it does not use individual ex-post adjustments. However, integrating CO_2 costs into variable costs is not enough to incentivize the longer-term structural changes in the capital stock:

Remove investment barriers:
Above all it is essential to create trust in the long-term value of CO_2 and the predictability of the regulatory environment.

Incentive to invest:
The new investment has to create an absolute benefit in terms of reduced shortage of allowances or increased surplus of allowances. What counts is the difference between the situation before and after the investment. In the case of a close to 100 per cent free grandfathered allocation for existing plants and a best-available-technology benchmarking for new plants, there is absolutely no incentive to invest in new equipment. Keeping new plants short in allowances relative to existing ones – namely on the basis of best available technology benchmarks – is the wrong way to go.

Incentive to choose low-carbon technologies:
In case of new investments, low-carbon technologies will be costlier and need a financial compensation corresponding to the CO_2 savings achieved. It is well known that this can easily be incentivized by strictly output-related benchmarks. Fuel-specific benchmarks only incentivize the selection of lower carbon options inside a given fuel option. Considering supply security, protection of coal-based production is definitely justified. A really sustainable option for coal-based production must then be low-carbon coal power

plants based on Carbon Capture and Storage (CCS). To bridge the development lead-time towards CCS, developing capture-ready coal plants may be a wise step.

It may be questioned whether it is necessary to provide incentives to replace old equipment. This would speed up mitigation at the cost of stranded investments. However, the incentive to choose low-carbon technologies is indispensable.

To be successful in terms of cost efficiency, the EU ETS must lead to a long-term structural shift towards a low-carbon infrastructure. If this does not happen, the entire mitigation will have to be implemented through extremely costly short-term mitigation options or it is impracticable with the existing infrastructure. In that situation even the environmental effectiveness would be missed. It is not only the overall cap that matters, but also the structure of the incentives.

BOX 4: CARBON CAPTURE AND STORAGE

If climate mitigation is taken seriously, CCS is a necessity rather than an option. The main technological options, pre-combustion, post-combustion and *Oxyfuel*, are well known and frequently discussed. Based on a benchmarking of CO_2 avoidance costs, various studies[7] come to the conclusion that carbon capture is most economic for coal-fired power plants. In gas-fired power plants, the efficiency loss from carbon capture has to be offset through the use of a much costlier fuel. Furthermore, CO_2 savings would be much smaller than with coal as fuel. Thus, gas-fired power plants should be used without CCS to reduce the CO_2 emissions in the fleets according to gas availability. These plant types will primarily serve for highly economic and environmentally sound intermediate load operation. CCS primarily makes sense in coal-fired power plants operating in base load.

Today, only pre-combustion capture using Integrated Gasification Combined Cycle (IGCC) power plants can be commercially built in large scale. This, however, is connected with high avoidance costs. Improvement of components and system integration is required to achieve CO_2 avoidance costs below 30 €/t for coal or even below 20 €/t for lignite. Efficiency improvement is key in all processes to compensate for the efficiency losses incurred through the carbon capture processes. This holds true for gas turbines in an IGCC process as well as for steam cycles, relevant for all plant types.

Given the high uncertainties in cost estimates, we concluded that in terms of avoidance costs there is no clear winner yet. Other aspects such as technology risk, fuel capability, or suitability for retrofit, will have a major bearing on decisions.

We have decided to prioritize the IGCC based pre-combustion capture process for green field plants and post-combustion for retrofit of existing plants given our many years of operating experience with IGCC power plants.

The Siemens Power Generation Group has enhanced its power plant business with products and solutions for the conversion of coal to electricity by acquiring the technology and engineering activities of the Sustec Group. Through this acquisition, Siemens is securing a key technology for environment-friendly power generation.

In addition to a wide range of coal grades, the gasification technology of the Sustec Group can also utilize biomass as well as petroleum coke and refinery residues as feedstocks. To accelerate development and testing of the next gasifier generation, we also plan to build a large-scale coal gasification plant with an overall thermal capacity of more than 1000 MW at the location Spreetal, in Saxony.

Finally, the IGCC option opens the door to polygeneration processes. The syngas produced though a coal gasification process can be the basis for various chemical synthesis processes. Producing synthetic fuel via the 'Fischer Tropsch' process is only one example. This is currently pursued in China to mitigate the dependence on oil imports. With CO_2 removal, even hydrogen can be provided. Thus the Zero Emission IGCC opens the door to an economically viable hydrogen economy, which is one of the promising ways of decarbonization of road traffic. With this type of polygeneration plants the deployment of clean coal enters a new era.

Notes

1   Sharef U. (Member of the Corporate Executive Committee, Siemens AG) 'Three forces to bring CCS into the market: Perspective of an equipment supplier', Speech at General Assembly of the European Technology Platform Brussels, 12 September 2006.
2   Stern N. *Stern Review on the Economics of Climate Change*, Cambridge University Press 2006. Also: www.hm-treasury.gov.uk/independent_reviews
3   WBCSD (World Business Council for Sustainable Development) 'Pathways to 2050 – Energy & Climate', 2006.
4   Carbon Disclosure Project, www.cdproject.net
5   EU ZEP (EU The European Technology Platform for Zero Emission Fossil Fuel Power Plants), 'Strategic Research Agenda', 2006.
6   Matthes, F. et al. 'The environmental effectiveness and economic efficiency of the European Union Emissions Trading Scheme: Structural aspects of allocation', a report to WWF, November 2005.
7   EU ZEP (EU The European Technology Platform for Zero Emission Fossil Fuel Power Plants), 'Strategic Research Agenda', 2006.

25

Sustainability and Sustainable Vehicle Strategy at Ford Motor Company

Benjamin Diggins, Ford Motor Company

Introduction

For a long time the term 'sustainability' inhabited the vocabulary of the fringe of industrial thinking globally. With a few notable exceptions very few commercial operations talked in terms of sustainable business models. However, in recent years, sustainability has come to occupy the centre ground of geo-political and industrial thinking to a point where it has started to influence the forward strategies of countries and companies alike.

Despite the increased use of 'sustainability' in business lexicon, questions remain: what is it, what falls under Its ever increasing canopy of influence and how does it affect individual companies? In basic terms companies are like organisms, they need feeding and nurturing to survive and thrive. However when the organism's Inputs and outputs have a disproportionate effect on their local environment the organism is said to be unsustainable and its ability to survive, let alone thrive, is brought into question.

What does this all mean for Ford Motor Company and how can we measure it? One index that Ford Motor Company is looking at more and more to define operations, products and services is the volume of CO_2 they generate. As a base line, CO_2 generation encompasses the energy to transform a range of raw materials into an automotive product, how much energy that product will consume in its operational life and finally how much energy is consumed in converting that product back into raw materials at the end of its operational life.

Here is what sustainability means to some of the leaders of Ford Motor Company.

BOX 1: SETTING THE VISION

Bill Ford, Chairman and CEO

Our view is that sustainability is the effective use of environmental and social, as well as economic, capital and is essential to corporate growth and prosperity. Over time, business can only succeed financially if it offers products and services that enhance society or the environment.

We are more convinced than ever that our long-term success depends on how our company addresses issues such as climate change, energy security, working conditions in our supply chain, safety, congestion, noise and the innovative use of renewable resources and materials. Our business connects fundamentally with society and its growing need for sustainable mobility and it is, therefore, in our material interest to anticipate and respond to that need. I refer to this as the sustainability imperative.

Integrated strategy

At the end of 2005, we issued an industry-first report on the business implications of climate change. The report sets out our long-term climate strategy, which calls for our company to contribute to climate stabilization by reducing the greenhouse gas emissions of our plants and products, and working co-operatively across sectors to develop comprehensive solutions. One sign that the strategy is being mainstreamed into our business processes is that climate stabilization is now a consideration in our product planning process – and nothing is more core to our business than product planning.

Technological innovation

In the UK, we will be doubling our previous rate of environmental spending in the region, investing at least US$1.8 billion to develop a range of global environmental technologies for our Ford, Jaguar, Land Rover and Volvo brands. This initiative will deliver more than 100 models and derivatives that offer improved emissions or fuel economy performance through the use of lightweight, hybrid electric and bio-fuel vehicles, among other technologies.

On the manufacturing side, over a five-year period, our North American facilities improved energy efficiency by over 18 per cent, greenhouse gas emissions by 15 per cent and water use by more than 5 billion gallons, saving millions of dollars in the process.

We've started several projects to help our customers reduce their climate impact. In 2005 we announced the Greener Miles™ partnership with TerraPass to help customers offset remaining emissions. In the UK, our Land Rover brand began a programme that provides a mechanism for customers to offset emissions from the use of their vehicle and also offsets emissions generated by its two production facilities.

At home and abroad, our customers are changing. I'm confident that the day is coming when customers will no more accept a car that emits greenhouse gases or contains non-recyclable material or has parts made under substandard working conditions than they will accept a car without seat belts today. We must – and will – take these trends into consideration as we plot the course toward our future. Sustainability is a business imperative.

BOX 2: FORD AND CHINA'S GROWTH

Tim O'Brien, Deputy Chief of Staff

When Ford came to China, the company brought with it a strong social conscience and the desire to be a good corporate citizen. We take these responsibilities extremely seriously, particularly in terms of human rights and environmental policies. This is part of how we do business. It's also a response to our customers. Chinese citizens themselves are becoming more aware of environmental and social issues. They want to see some of the world's worst air quality cleaned up. The government is responding in several ways, including adopting the world's tightest standards for pollution from vehicles.

In terms of the environment, we have built our plants with state-of-the-art equipment to minimize their impact on the country's resources. For example, our new assembly plant in Nanjing, Jiangsu Province, was designed to collect rainwater for use in our plant. Storm water retention ponds will prevent any impacted water exiting the site. The paint shop is designed to reduce CO_2 emissions by more than 25 per cent and to use less energy than a conventional process. In Jiangxi, we are installing the latest in air emission control systems to reduce the emission of volatile organic compounds from our paint processes.

One major issue we are wrestling with is explosive growth in vehicle sales in China, which are surging by as much as 50 or 100 per cent a quarter. As a developing economy, China wants to enjoy the same things as developed nations – including vehicle ownership. Given this context, it is even more important for the government and manufacturers to set limits on emissions and to look at alternative fuels.

You must have economic development and environmental friendliness. It's not a question of either/or. The sustainability challenges for the auto industry vary around the world, but there are common threads.

BOX 3: SUSTAINABILITY – SHORT-TERM VERSUS LONG-TERM

Lewis Booth, Executive Vice President, Ford Motor Company, Premier Automotive Group and Ford of Europe

Sustainability at Ford is a balancing act. If a business is not giving shareholders a good return on their investment then there is enormous pressure to turn that company's financial performance around. With that kind of pressure, you must find the right balance: first to survive, and then to thrive. But you can't do that by turning the dial fully one way or the other. If you spend all your time focusing on surviving the next one to two years, you can't possibly expect to thrive five, 10 or even 50 years down the line and vice versa.

Most people do not see sustainability as part of the short-term survival mode. But if we don't spend time envisioning how these concepts fit in with our plans to move forward, we will be unable to position ourselves for the future.

In order for Ford to do this successfully, we must re-engineer how we work. The enemy in a large organization like this is not brainpower, but time. In the 1950s, Ford was an efficiency-based manufacturing company with a finance system that focused only on numbers. We successfully used that business model for many years. The problem, however, was that it did not coincide with the changes going on in the world – changes that we now recognize as essential to sustainability, from environmental impacts to shifting demographics.

Ford Motor Company outline globally

Though Ford Motor Company is a truly global company with over 320,000 employees, this chapter discussed the strides it is making in the UK to address energy sustainability in key facets of its operation.

Ford Motor Company in the UK

Employing over 14,200 at 10 locations, Ford has been the UK market leader for 28 consecutive years in an increasingly competitive new car market. The Premier Automotive Group including Jaguar, Land Rover and Aston Martin employ over 20,000 more in the UK at sites across the Midlands and North West.

Ford Motor Company's sustainable vehicle strategy

Ford and the automotive industry looked for a long time at the energy balance of their products and developed this basic ratio within the total energy consumption. Manufacture takes up 10 per cent of the total energy used for a product; 85 per cent of the total is used in the life of the vehicle on the road; and 5 per cent of the total energy balance is used in the disposal and subsequent recycling of the vehicle. Clearly this is a complex calculation and there is some variance in it from vehicle to vehicle. However, the underlying ratio has gone a long way to determining the sustainable strategy Ford is now adopting. Based upon what we have control over, what we can design into the product and what we are legally required to do, we looked at these three areas in some detail.

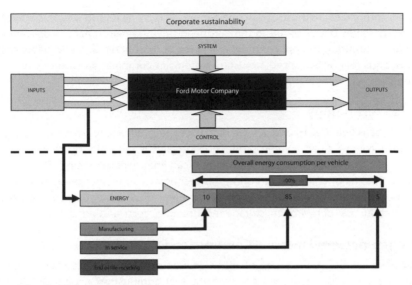

Figure 1: Sustainability at Ford
Source: Ford

Product-based approaches to sustainability

Flexi-fuel

The technologies range from environmentally friendly products already available in selected markets, through to mid-term and long-term potential alternatives. The Ford portfolio embraces two bio-ethanol-powered Focus Flexi Fuel vehicles (FFVs), a Ford Escape Full Hybrid from the United States, a Fiesta Micro Hybrid prototype and a hydrogen-powered Ford Focus Fuel Cell Hybrid (FCEV).

This extensive portfolio demonstrates Ford's commitment, expertise and leading role in working to make future mobility more sustainable.

Market-leading Ford FFVs

Ford FFVs are capable of running on a blend of E85 (85 per cent bio-ethanol and 15 per cent petrol), petrol only, or any mix of both. The use of bio-ethanol, in combination with FFV technology, can lead to a 70 per cent reduction in overall CO_2 emissions compared to a traditional petrol engine.

Hybrids

Different levels of hybridisation will help to optimize the efficiency of both gasoline and diesel engines. However, vehicle fuel efficiency is also dependent on vehicle usage and local driving conditions.

In contrast to the US, the diesel market is already well established in Europe, and state-of-the-art diesel technology offers cost and fuel consumption benefits for the customer comparable to those of gasoline hybrids. This is one reason why 'micro hybrid' technology seems better suited to the European driving environment in delivering a valuable contribution to improved fuel efficiency at reasonable and affordable costs. Micro Hybrids rely on advanced stop/start systems in combination with regenerative braking.

Fuel cell technology

The Ford Focus Fuel Cell Hybrid vehicle has successfully advanced from the prototype stage to become a small volume production car and is currently operating in fleet programmes around the world, including the Clean Energy Partnership (CEP) in Berlin, Germany. The major challenges to bring this technology to market predominantly lie in the development of a suitable infrastructure and environmentally friendly, high-volume production of hydrogen, storage technologies, costs and durability.

Hydrogen-powered Internal Combustion Engine (ICE)

We are also working on a range of other environmentally advanced technologies, including a prototype hydrogen-powered internal combustion engine (H2 ICE) to analyze its technical and environmental potential. In pursuing the goal of sustainable mobility, Ford regards this technology as an important step towards a 'hydrogen' future where even more energy-efficient fuel cell technology might be the ultimate solution.

Vehicle disposal and recycling

Ford was the first of the large auto manufacturers in the UK to declare a fully operational take-back network for their vehicles. Within this contracted network, both partners work together to establish technology partnerships that increase the recycling rates of end-of-life vehicles entering the network. To meet European recycling targets, the network providers are working closely to recycle single material streams back into automotive grade products. Where that is not possible, the use of technologies as diverse as aggregate manufacture and the production of energy from waste projects are being investigated to divert this material from landfill.

The de-pollution process

When a vehicle is presented to a Ford-approved treatment centre it will be professionally de-polluted. This involves:

- The draining of all fluids

- The removal of the battery and tyres

- The neutralisation of the airbag systems.

Any saleable parts will be removed and sold. Further treatment of the vehicle will take place at a shredding facility where the vehicle is crushed and separation techniques used to recover metallics for recycling into new steel and non-ferrous metals.

The remaining material known as 'shredder residue' can be treated at heavy media plants to retrieve any lost metallics and non-metallics. The remaining residue can be further sorted and used in a number of applications. For example glass and stone recovered can be used as an aggregate for road building and road surfaces. Once these processes have been completed only then will the remaining residue be sent to landfill (typically less than 20 per cent of the original weight of the vehicle).

Once the vehicle has been dismantled and shredded, the materials gained from that process can be segregated and reintroduced into the automotive supply chain.

In many cases the technology is in its infancy but great strides are being made to bring not only automotive recyclate but post-consumer recyclate into their products.

Future recycling

To take the process of vehicle recycling to the next level, Ford has invested heavily in the design of their products to reduce the diversity of materials. This primarily improves the polymeric yield rates for future ELVs. In the past, vehicles were engineered for ease of assembly; now they are also engineered for ease of disassembly, increasing the throughput yield at our contracted ELV recycling network providers in the future.

These actions also have the effect of increasing the residual value of the materials, thus promoting a stronger recycling market. This in turn brings a level of stability to the supply chain for such recyclates. As a large consumer of materials, stability is a key factor in any supply chain decisions regarding sustainable and recycled materials.

BOX 4: VEHICLES OF THE FUTURE

Environmental responsibility is a major part of Ford's business philosophy. We worked steadily over the past several years to integrate environmental considerations into how we do business. Through the core business processes, improvement goals and targets are set and progress monitored with the aim of producing as economical and clean a car as possible. The policy considers the wider environment and producing recyclable vehicles in a pollution-free production process. The end of the life of the car is also considered, the treatment of old vehicles and the recycling of the materials from them. Re-use and re-utilisation of materials have priority before disposal and, where economically possible, are re-integrated into the product.

In the Ford Focus, 39 parts are made of plastic from recycled materials with a total weight of over 21 kilograms. For example, screw-type caps from plastic bottles are used in the housing of the heating and air conditioning system. In current European Ford models, approximately 440 different parts are made from recycled content. More importantly, the material used can be fed back into the material cycle again and be re-used for further manufacture of new automotive components or for non-automotive purposes.

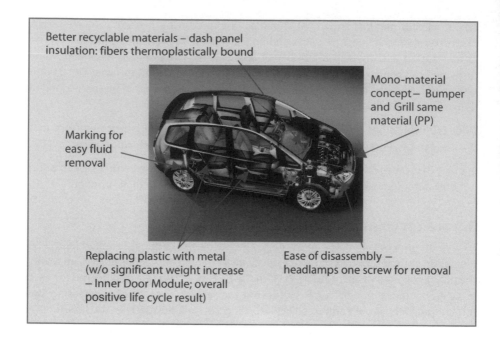

Better recyclable materials – dash panel insulation: fibers thermoplastically bound

Mono-material concept– Bumper and Grill same material (PP)

Marking for easy fluid removal

Replacing plastic with metal (w/o significant weight increase – Inner Door Module; overall positive life cycle result)

Ease of disassembly – headlamps one screw for removal

Plant-based approaches to sustainability

When Henry Ford first conceived large mass-manufacturing facilities, he decided that plants should be self sufficient in almost every aspect of their operation. To this end, many of the major facilities such as the Rouge plant in the US and the Dagenham plant in the UK had their own power sources. However, as the cost of operation and external market influences increased and evolved, many of these 'home grown' power sources were either mothballed or dismantled. Since then, the cost of energy has increased as a percentage of the overall cost of vehicle manufacture and, in some cases, the stability of those energy sources has declined. This led to a re-evaluation of the concept of internal power sources.

In the UK, this is done by taking a full suite of sustainable generation and reduction technologies and applying them in a desk-top exercise to each location. By making this first sweep, clearly inappropriate technologies are discounted immediately. Each technology is then assessed on a business case basis, addressing such issues as sustainability, profitability, planning and stability.

Clearly there is a hierarchy, both globally and in the UK, with regards to the sustainability of the facilities associated with energy. Where at all possible, the company looks first at reducing the levels of power consumption used to manufacture its products, from the machinery used to make discrete components to the level of insulation afforded to each building. However, these actions can only go so far: any manufacturing process will require energy to operate and in many older facilities there are legacy issues that can preclude the retro-fitting of certain energy reduction measures.

Energy reduction examples in the UK

Vegetable-based cutting fluids

As an example of reduction in manufacturing power requirements, vegetable cutting fluids have an impressive track record – both in reducing the power required to machine a component with their greater lubricity and the reduction in power associated with their disposal, all from a sustainable vegetable source.

These coolants give a range of performance, safety, cost and environmental advantages. Latest products include high performance, renewable vegetable-based oil phases with a range of performance, safety and environmental advantages. All these congruent products are designed to positively enhance emulsion performance instead of acting as contaminants when they find their way into the coolant system. The benefits of this secondary use are enormous in terms of usage, cost, performance and waste reduction.

Conclusions

Ford Motor Company has identified sustainability as a key component of future company prosperity and this is being driven from the top of the company. The current climate of the automotive industry presents many challenges, but the fact that sustainability has been identified and is being engineered into future plants and products means the CO_2 footprint will be dramatically lower than it has been in the past.

These are exciting times in which new technologies are tackling two of the major issues of our age: sustainable waste disposal and sustainable energy generation. Waste is no longer seen as a burden to dispose of, but an asset that needs to be harnessed. With the potential of converting that asset into fuels and polymers there is the potential to close the material loop at many levels, driving the carbon footprint down still further.

In this century, recycling and sustainability have ceased to be the rhetoric of the fringe and have become the vocabulary of corporate life:

- Waste is a resource
- Power is a luxury
- Competition is a way of life.

In a business sense, it is incumbent upon all of us to look at what we use and how we can reduce consumption, to look again at what assets and resources we have around us and to reduce and recycle where we can. The task is to marry these aspirations with our efforts to meet the new market challenges.

The following are examples of sustainable manufacturing:

- Natural fibres replacing glass reinforcement in polymeric components
- Old tyres recycled into components for new tyres

- Plastics from our old vehicles recycled into roads for our new vehicles

- Glass bottles recycled into water filters for our industrial water

- Closed-loop paper recycling

- Closed-loop metal recycling

- Further waste to energy projects.

With all these actions, Ford Motor Company will drastically cut not only its landfill input, but also that of the local communities where it operates.

In our aspiration to be a leader in sustainable development, it should be the role of corporates and large organisations in the future to be the propagators of environmental and sustainable best practice. As big consumers, they have the ability to divert increasing tonnages of material away from landfill in the form of raw materials. In effect, an organisation that has a high percentage of recyclate in its raw material inputs becomes the alternative to landfill.

26

Tackling Climate Change is Vital for Business Success: BT as an Example

Adrian Hosford, BT Group plc

This chapter looks at the importance of climate change for business by highlighting some of the approaches that BT is currently taking to tackle the issue in its daily operations and the ways that it will need to change to 'future proof' its business.

Six priorities for action have been identified that will hopefully prove useful to all organisations in thinking about how to make a real difference to climate change and gain some business benefit at the same time.

> 'The pressures on the world have never been greater, with population growth, economic development climate change and social exclusion all combining to create a potentially unsustainable future unless things change'
>
> **Sir Christopher Bland, BT Chairman, July 2006**

Accepting the 'problem'

The evidence of climate change is overwhelming. There is now universal recognition that man-made emissions, primarily from the burning of fossil fuels, are causing the climate to change at an unprecedented rate. Media coverage has meant the public is well aware of the issue, although people remain confused as to what can be done to help.

At the same time, and with a few exceptions such as the UK where manufacturing has been in long-term decline, energy demand continues to be strongly coupled with economic growth. For example, between 1980 and 2002 South Korea's energy use per head rose by 300 per cent, while its GDP rose 270 per cent. If China and India follow a similar path then by 2030 these two countries combined would consume at least three times as much energy as the USA does today.

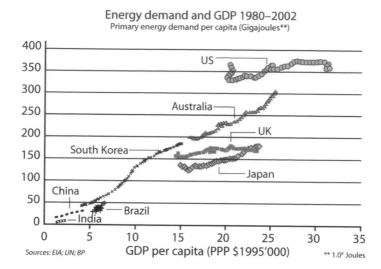

Energy demand and GDP 1980–2002
Primary energy demand per capita (Gigajoules**)

Sources: EIA; UN; BP   GDP per capita (PPP $1995'000)   ** 1.0⁹ Joules

Over the longer term (five years +) these two fundamentally intertwined issues will have profound impacts on global economies and the climate. Urgent and committed action is required to tackle climate change at all levels. Countries need to ensure continuity of energy supply and CO_2 emissions need to be reduced by 60 per cent against 1990 levels for climate. This means every business needs to act.

What this means for companies, using BT as an example

BT needs to ensure it protects its energy supply and, over the long term, keeps its costs to a minimum. There will also be increasing pressure to be seen to be taking more action on climate change, from customers, investors, government and employees.

In order to do this we have identified six priorities for action:

1. Need to reduce exposure to inflated energy costs and uncertainty in supply
Recent increases in the price of energy reflect the fact that world demand for oil and gas is already outstripping supply. As a result, BT's gas and electricity costs have doubled in the last two years. Our total energy costs including vehicle fuel for the 2006 financial year were approximately £175m and under business as usual conditions our electricity costs are projected to rise by 30 per cent over the next 12 months.

The UK is walking a tightrope as the North Sea runs out of gas and the Magnox nuclear power stations are reaching the end of their life with no replacements (either renewable or nuclear) yet in the pipeline.

Energy costs are not only reflecting shortage of supply but are also being affected by economic instruments introduced by governments to address climate change – for example the UK climate change levy and the EU Emissions Trading Scheme. Increasingly there will be a cost to emitting carbon on top of the cost of energy.

In order to meet this need, BT is experimenting with wind and solar power, natural cooling and new technology all of which can reduce our energy costs and provide new sources of sustainable energy.

2. Need to reduce exposure to extreme weather

More extreme weather conditions affect our network, our ability to deliver service and ultimately customer satisfaction. To rectify faults takes resource away from other planned network enhancement work causing further customer dissatisfaction. The wettest summer on record in Scotland in 2004 followed by the worst gale in 40 years in 2005 are examples of where major service disruption took place and fault levels doubled. We can't afford to fall over when our customers need us most.

As our corporate customers such as banks and the transport industry evaluate their own vulnerability to climate change they will want to assure themselves that we have resilient systems in place. In order to reduce our exposure, BT is experimenting with a new network which requires fewer nodes and avoids at-risk areas such as flood plains. We are also building in greater resilience and greater tolerance of extreme temperature fluctuations. We are ensuring that new equipment uses less energy and requires less cooling.

3. Need to reduce CO_2 footprint

In order to reduce our CO_2 footprint we have to examine the full array of activities that drive our CO_2 emissions and to prioritise our efficiency programmes in line with the biggest opportunities. Our main product is delivery of communications services via the telecommunications network. We measure the energy used in transmission and switching of these services with one of the largest computer-based energy management systems in the UK. This allows site by site monitoring and separation of energy consumption by the network and that used to run our buildings. Our estimated emissions for the period April 2005–March 2006 arising from network energy consumption are 300,525,480 kg.

New initiatives can make efficiency savings, reduce output and also lead to more cost-effective operations. A range of prioritised investments, together with measurement tools and targets are being put in place and monitored.

The annual CO_2 savings arising from our energy and fleet efficiency initiatives alone, which began in 1991, equate to almost 1.4 million tonnes of CO_2. We have been measuring our total equivalent CO_2 emissions from energy use (electricity, gas and oil), our commercial fleet, company cars, cars on BT business, refrigerant gas, rail travel, air travel and hire cars since 1996–7 since when BT has reduced its CO_2 emissions by 60 per cent.

4. Need to help others to reduce their CO_2 footprint through ICT solutions

There is a real opportunity for BT to be a significant part of the solution as opposed to part of the problem. Telecommunications services can be used to substitute for travel and in this way reduce society's overall emission of greenhouse gases. Flexible working solutions such as home working (Teleworking) and the use of audio and video conferencing reduce the need for commuting to the office and travelling for meetings. We have monitored BT users of this technology and found that :

- 71 per cent thought their last conference call had definitely or probably replaced a meeting

- 46 per cent of trips avoided would have been by car

- 78 per cent of trips avoided would have been at peak travel times (showing that conferencing helps to relieve congestion on roads and free space on public transport)

- 35 per cent of meetings replaced would have been in London.

We estimate that every conference call saves a minimum of 32kg of travel-related carbon dioxide emissions which is 47,400 tonnes per annum and virtual working across distances also saves buildings and extra heating/cooling costs.

BT already has over 11,000 permanent home workers and another 50,000 part-time or agile workers. Our research also shows that home workers are at least 20 per cent more productive, a great deal happier and more motivated and save significant quantities of CO_2 when compared with office workers, even allowing for any 'bounce back' effect with local traffic.

In the knowledge-based economy where project working can be done by audio conferencing and co-working on the Internet, there is the potential for people to manage most of the workload from home. People will always need to get together but this can be planned off peak at convenient locations where the socialisation 'catalyst' can also best be accommodated.

There is an opportunity for more and more products to become 'dematerialised' to software i.e. downloads as opposed to CDs, entertainment at home, or competitive games played over the Internet. These can be delivered over energy-friendly high-speed networks. Even in manufacturing, advanced digital communication networks can enable 'just in time' stock control, sharing of best practices and download of design changes directly into the production process.

5. Need to involve customers, employees and suppliers

Tackling climate change involves an enormous effort which involves all stakeholders who are often willing to help, but don't know how. A recent survey of BT people showed that 100 per cent felt that tackling climate change was the right thing for BT to do, but only 18 per cent thought that we were doing enough yet. We need to show them exactly how they have the opportunity to contribute at work, at home and on the move. BT is also looking at a range of tools and incentives to help employees participate directly in the initiative to reduce CO_2. Likewise, with our supply chain partners, we are endeavouring to involve them through a range of voluntary initiatives and commitments.

6. Need to win hearts and minds

Customers, employees and everybody involved will be more willing to make the necessary changes to their lifestyle if they see this as something that is desirable. It's important that they want to do it, rather than feel forced to do it. It is therefore critical to make sustainable living a desirable and inspirational thing to do, rather than something which they are told is good for them. In other words, it is about motivation rather than threats. This means going with the grain of consumer needs and shaping it with desirable examples to maximise the positive impact.

Fundamental to this approach is the need to market a more sustainable lifestyle as a more desirable lifestyle. We need to paint a picture (based on proven facts and real possibilities) of a sustainable lifestyle which, when contrasted with an unsustainable lifestyle, has much more appeal and motivation.

UNSUSTAINABLE		MORE SUSTAINABLE
Office heating, cooling, waste costs		Home working – marginal cost
Commuting – stress, congestion, CO_2		Less travel, more flexibility
Routine stress, rushing about		Thinking time – internet, conferencing
No time at home, commitments squeezed, relationships strained	Vs.	Increased leisure time; relationships thrive
Social life limited; rushed between commitments		More social time planned in, at convenient locations
Outputs – productivity average		Outputs – productivity increased by 20 per cent
Job satisfaction – motivation average		Job satisfaction – motivation high

Enhancing the BT brand and BT's marketing proposition

By associating BT with a desirable, more sustainable lifestyle in large part achievable by advanced communications capability, we will be establishing BT as a key enabler of a better life. BT is well placed with a leadership position in this space. Last year we were awarded a Climate Leaders Award by the Climate Group; we remain the top telco in the Dow Jones Sustainability Index and now climate change is a key strand of our CSR strategy.

In summary, the BT brand will represent a better choice for the customer because they know that as well as it representing a good solution and good value, they can also rely on BT to be responsible and sustainable; making sure that BT customers can contribute to a more sustainable future.

Conclusion

We hope that by examining the implications and opportunities for BT in helping to tackle change, we have helped others to think about what their business or their organisation can do. It is only by every organisation and every individual doing their bit that we can tackle such a large problem. It is those who lead the way that will make the greatest difference but also gain the most from the opportunities.

For more information see www.bt.com/betterworld and www.cdproject.net

Strategies on Climate Change – Cities and Businesses

27
Local Governments for Climate Protection – a Sustainable Business Approach

Margarita María Parra and Maryke van Staden, ICLEI

This chapter describes the opportunities presented to local governments, in the current global challenge of climate change, to regard their own actions from a sustainable business perspective, and to work with the business sector to achieve effective greenhouse gas (GHG) emissions reductions. ICLEI's Cities for Climate Protection (CCP) Campaign is a movement of more than 800 cities worldwide that are leaders in the implementation of local climate change policies and actions. The CCP experience includes innovative mechanisms involving successful public–private partnerships and cost effective actions to reduce emissions that promote clean and productive business. ICLEI is an international association of local governments dedicated to sustainability.

The business of local governments

As of 2005, more than half of the global population now lives in urban areas. The shift in energy requirements that has resulted from this population concentration also means that cities are the areas where the highest percentage of human-produced greenhouse gas (GHG) emissions is generated. More than 75 per cent of all energy on the planet is consumed in cities. Local authorities, as the closest level of government to the community, hold tremendous power to influence both the causes of global warming and the solutions to advance climate protection. The onus consequently falls on them to take responsibility and provide direction to the citizens they represent – towards a sustainable future, addressing climate change amelioration, mitigation and adaptation.

Many local governments have recognised this role and have been active leaders in the implementation of climate change policies and actions worldwide. Mutual exchange of experience has benefited many cities and towns in the development and implementation of strategies and actions. In this context, the organisation ICLEI – Local Governments for Sustainability leads capacity building between local governments and offers advanced tools and technical expertise to cities to reduce their environmental impacts. ICLEI is a worldwide membership organisation of local authorities and their associations active in different campaigns, programmes and projects in support of its overall aim – tangible improvements in global sustainability with a special focus on improving environmental conditions through cumulative local action.

Local governments as businesses

In their day-to-day operation local governments are businesses be it as service providers, building and facility owners or community leaders guiding strategic direction. Municipal operations need to run efficiently, with the aim of offering quality services to their constituents without adversely affecting the bottom line. Local governments own and run buildings and vehicle fleets and provide a variety of social and public services such as managing schools, hospitals, water supply, sewage treatment, depending on the different local or national systems and customs. City government services, whether directly managed by the municipality or offered through public–private partnerships, normally utilise a business management approach.

A local government, as any other business, has a procurement team or department which looks after all purchases the authority needs across departments. Sustainable procurement can provide the opportunity for the integration of good governance practice, while addressing sustainable development. Sustainable procurement is a mechanism through which the full range of ecosystem impacts can be addressed in relation to specific products and services whilst ensuring that social and economic factors are also taken into consideration. This practice not only allows the city to lead by example, but can also result in substantial GHG emission reductions in various sectors.

The most common sustainable procurement practices cities implement include: acquiring more energy efficient products such as printers, monitors and heating and cooling equipment; 'greening' their municipal fleets by incorporating biofuel vehicles, hybrid cars, car sharing and bicycle pools; and by improving energy efficiency levels of infrastructure such as street lighting, traffic signals and the built environment such as buildings.

There are various examples of cities around the world implementing sustainable procurement practices that have led to GHG emission savings. See the box that follows for ICLEI related activities.

BOX 1: ICLEI'S LEADING PROGRAMMES IN PROCUREMENT THAT SAVE ENERGY, GHG EMISSIONS AND MONEY FOR CITIES

Mexico City along with 27 other cities in Mexico participate in the Promoting an Energy-Efficient Public Sector (PEPS) program, a joint initiative between ICLEI and the Lawrence Berkeley National Laboratory (LBNL) focussing specifically on the benefits of energy savings for local governments. The goal of the program is to introduce cost-effective, energy-saving purchasing practices in several municipalities, with the hope that other municipalities as well as state and federal agencies will follow these examples. The program has important national partners such as the Mexican National Commission for Energy Efficiency CONAE.

For more information visit:
http://www.pepsonline.org/countries/mexico.html and
http://www.conae.gob.mx/wb/CONAE/Programa_PEPS_ICLEI (in Spanish)

ICLEI Procura+ campaign in Europe, launched in 2004, aims to support the demand side of the market, to foster the economic supply of environmentally friendly and socially accountable products and services, from green electricity to organic food. Thirty local authorities have joined Procura+.

For more information visit:
http://www.iclei-europe.org/procurement

In many countries local authorities own, control or greatly influence the community water, sanitation and waste collection, and disposal systems. These energy-intensive services, when adequately managed, can save natural resources. By reusing or recycling waste (bio-compost or plastic/paper/glass), energy is saved on the production of new items, actively contributing to reducing harmful emissions. In addition, these practices can also boost local economies through job creation and service provision in the areas of recycling, composting, and local energy options from sewage and landfill gas recovery projects. This can be very effective, in particular to support the development of the Small- and Medium-sized Enterprise (SME) sector.

Greener fleets are another effective way to reduce GHG emissions and save money over the medium term. More efficient fuels include bio-fuels, such as ethanol and biodiesel; less carbon-intensive fuels, such as natural gas; and the combination of these options in hybrid or flex-fuel vehicles. In most countries, the use of greener fleets represents a high up-front investment. However, considering a full-cycle analysis, these investments result in significantly lower greenhouse gas emissions and money savings.

In this context the City of Stockholm, a world leader with the target of becoming a fossil-fuel-free city by 2050, has implemented an effective range of actions in the area of sustainable transportation. In addition, the City of Chicago has an environmental agenda that both encourages and works with the private sector. The City has implemented a series of energy saving practices in their municipal buildings. The cases of Stockholm and Chicago are detailed below.

A local authority that acts for climate protection also acts in its own interest – from an economic and environmental perspective, and to improve its resilience, infrastructure and ultimately livability. Like the private sector, cities view their operations with the same fundamentals of fiscal health, quality of services and consistency as the baseline principle from which to work.

On the other side of the coin, local governments regulate business as well as interact, contract and partner with them. There is a relationship that is driven by innovation and leadership from both sides.

Local governments work with business

City governments draft and enforce environmental regulations to ensure inhabitants and businesses comply with standards, mostly with municipal laws and ordinances set by city councils, but also including federal/national and state/provincial level regulations. Some examples are the Clean Air Act in the USA and the Resource Management Act in New Zealand. The application of these regulations should result in lower emissions, also for the industrial and business sectors.

Green building and innovative construction codes are another mechanism that can be used to minimise emissions using a preventative approach. Here the focus is on reducing the energy use of buildings without compromising the indoor environment and services. The European Union Energy Performance of Buildings Directive (EPBD) is one example of a step being taken to promote the improvement of energy efficiency in buildings.

Cities such as Barcelona and Madrid have also initiated their own regulations, solar thermal ordinances, to encourage the use of solar water systems in new buildings or retrofit designs. This type of code has two effects. Firstly, it improves demand for sustainable products (in this case solar thermal systems) which leads to increased business investment in such technologies, with increased demand leading to more affordable prices. Secondly, by enforcing these codes and stating specific targets for the city, the local authority can lead by example with municipal building compliance, encouraging others to follow through awareness-raising and educational programmes.

Another area impacting a local authority's link with business is land-use planning, where regulations can be used as a key resource. With a combination of tax exemptions and incentives such as zone codes, city governments can attract new and greener businesses to their communities. Responsible business and responsible government initiatives are increasingly common in cities and towns of developed countries. In this context climate change adaptation plays a crucial role, with local governments required to implement protective regulations that can for example prevent flood damage to inner-city businesses close to rivers.

Most cities strive to have good relationships with the local business community, in support of developing the local economy. They can also learn from successful practices that the local businesses implement, determining what could be replicated by the local authority. This interest can help strengthen local capacity with a solid institutional framework that can reinforce the relationships between businesses and their associations. Various ICLEI cities have created innovative mechanisms to include business as key actors in reaching their GHG emissions reduction target (see box below).

BOX 2: ICLEI CITIES ACTIONS: WORKING TOGETHER WITH BUSINESS, PRIVATE AND UTILITY COMPANIES

The USA City of Fort Collins' Climate Wise programme engages businesses on a volunteer basis to achieve the reduction of GHG emissions by promoting waste reduction, energy savings, alternative transportation, water conservation and pollution prevention. For more information, see http://www.fcgov.com/climateprotection/climate-wise.php

In Germany, Heidelberg has closely co-operated with a local electric utility to provide 'green electricity' for the city and several municipal needs. Despite having a slightly higher cost, this has led not only to reducing its own electricity bill (through energy efficiency), but also contributed to the use of clean energy in local schools and 'kindergärten', with the reinvestment of the profits into local sustainable energy options.

San Francisco, California, recently formed the Business Council for Climate Change (BC3), a public–private partnership to engage local business in climate protection.

By addressing public- and private-sector issues simultaneously, interesting opportunities for a win-win situation can be considered. In the transport sector, for example, the promotion of sustainable public transport is a key area where the local authority, the business providers, and the public can benefit through increased user numbers on public transport, mandating improved services, lowering emissions and improving air quality. The City of Ann Arbor, Michigan, USA, implemented a discounted bus pass that brought more customers to the downtown area. The City of Freiburg, Germany, has a car-free city centre, extended its tramline, and encourages commuters to use the extensive transport network through the sale of a popular monthly regional travel ticket, thereby dramatically increasing the use of city transport as well as supporting regional bus and rail systems and reducing CO_2 emissions in the process.

Landfill gas recovery projects present interesting opportunities where private–public partnership can benefit a city that doesn't necessarily have the resources to build an infrastructure project. The City of Sao Paulo, in partnership with an engineering firm and a national bank, managed to build the first landfill gas recovery pilot plant generating 20MW to provide electricity for a nearby neighbourhood, illustrating how private investment can support public aims.

In conclusion, there are various models that city governments can implement to work with business and the private sector. In all public–private partnerships the common objective is to implement financially sound actions, effectively reduce GHG emissions and promote sustainability.

Global action: more than 800 local governments join forces

BOX 3: ICLEI – LOCAL GOVERNMENTS FOR SUSTAINABILITY

ICLEI – Local Governments for Sustainability, is a world-wide membership organisation of local authorities and their associations working to achieve tangible improvements in global environmental and sustainable development.

ICLEI was founded in 1990 as the International Council for Local Environmental Initiatives. The council was established when more than 200 local governments from 43 countries convened at our inaugural conference, the *World Congress of Local Governments for a Sustainable Future*, at the United Nations in New York. Since then the name has been changed to reflect the focus on sustainability.

The International Cities for Climate Protection (CCP) Campaign

One of ICLEI's core campaigns is the International Cities for Climate Protection (CCP) Campaign, started in 1993 as a worldwide movement. The CCP offers a framework for action to local governments to adopt policies and implement measures to achieve:

- Measurable reductions in local GHG emissions
- Improved air quality and public health
- Enhanced urban sustainability
- Improved resilience of local community infrastructure, and
- Costs savings.

The campaign provides its participants with a strategic framework, making available support and tools for the development and implementation of climate protection policies and actions.

Local authorities can use their public influence, decision-making responsibilities and remarkable purchasing powers to move towards sustainable energy practices in different sectors. This can lead to financial savings for communities in the short and long term.

A parallel approach of mitigation and adaptation must be taken by cities to effectively lead, protect and govern their communities as the consequences of climate change take root. The direct impact of rising sea levels, changing precipitation, and heat waves are but a few results of a changing climate that can cause deaths and damage and have activated many local authorities into moving climate change to the top of priority lists. Urban areas need to assess their resilience to identify weaknesses in their infrastructure (e.g. dam walls, sewage systems, canalisation, building structures) to ensure that increases in temperatures or changes in rainfall will not damage existing infrastructure to the detriment of the community.

The imperative for local leadership is here. By combining strategies and actions to address local community concerns, including security of energy supply, improved air quality and stimulating the local economy, and simultaneously influencing global climate change, local authorities can bring together diverse stakeholders at the local level to support effective implementation. Here business also has a large role to play, to provide services and products that will reduce energy requirements and help strengthen local resilience.

The 800-plus local governments from 29 countries participating in this campaign have identified respective emissions reduction targets, and implemented a diverse range of actions to achieve these in the energy, transport, urban planning, water and waste sectors.

A basic requirement for joining the CCP campaign is political commitment to respond to climate change. The political commitment can take form of a resolution, proclamation, etc. This is subsequently translated into action by identifying clear targets, setting a time frame and programme for action, and implementing a Local Climate Action Plan using the CCP five-milestone process to fulfil the commitment.

The CCP methodology provides a simple, standardised way of acting to reduce GHG emissions and of monitoring, measuring, and reporting performance.

- **Milestone 1:** Conduct a baseline energy and emissions profile and forecast
- **Milestone 2:** Set an emissions reduction target
- **Milestone 3:** Develop and approve a local action plan

- **Milestone 4:** Implement emission-reduction measures through the local climate action plan

- **Milestone 5:** Monitor and report progress to the campaign managers.

Each region and country has a different culture and political background which also influences the role of the local governments. As such, the CCP campaign in each country varies, to accommodate the requirements and realities of that area. The activities implemented are also dependent on available funding and specific projects developed, which means that the international CCP campaign reflects a rich diversity that supports productive technical and political peer exchanges.

Latest developments

A recent development to complement the CCP campaign is the emphasis on adaptation. In the USA a pilot initiative, Climate Safe Communities (CSC), has been launched in partnership with the National Oceanic and Atmospheric Administration (NOAA). Three pilot communities are assessing their vulnerability to climate change at the local level and developing specific action plans, through the CSC initiative. More information will be available at www.iclei.org/usa.

Furthermore, ICLEI launched the Reinforced Strategy for the CCP Campaign in Europe in May 2006 in Stockholm, Sweden, during the conference 'A Future with Zero CO_2 Emissions' (www.iclei.org/itc/stockholm2006). Here adaptation was added formally, to be considered by European CCP participants, in parallel to climate change mitigation. A central message presented at the conference is that cities and towns need to support ambitious CO_2 reduction targets and increase the rate of reduction measure implementation to achieve these targets, moving towards a zero carbon future in urban areas, while diminishing the current impacts from climate change to the extent possible.

More details about the campaign can be found under: http://www.iclei.org/ccp.

Specific CCP results and impacts – two city examples

Case study: A fossil fuel free Stockholm by 2050

Considering the future

Sweden's capital city, Stockholm is the largest city in the country with a population of 750,000 (out of nine million total Swedes). The City is the central municipality in the Stockholm metropolitan region. It is growing and faces a challenge in retaining and developing its unique character, also considering that it must be sustainable and an attractive place for people to live and work. It has long had the reputation of being one of the cleanest capital cities in the world. It also has to deal with many of the environmental threats that every large city in the world faces.

Taking steps against climate change – both in the areas of mitigation and adaptation – impact on different areas and sectors, including energy, transport, water and waste as well as urban planning. The first goals for environmental issues were set out in the mid 1970s. A comprehensive mitigation strategy was started in 1995, with the implementation of an action plan aimed at cutting CO_2 emissions by more than 25 per cent by the year 2006.

Having now reached this target, the city presented its next ambitious aim in 2006 – **achieving zero CO_2 emissions by 2050** and making Stockholm a **fossil fuel free city**. The ambitious 'target zero' links to and follows long-standing co-operation with ICLEI's CCP Campaign. Against this background, the Reinforced CCP Campaign in Europe was launched during the conference 'A Future with Zero CO_2 Emissions' held in May 2006 (www.iclei.org/itc/stockholm2006). An invitation from Stockholm's Vice-mayor Viviann Gunnarsson: 'We invite cities to join us in moving away from the rhetoric and day-to-day pragmatism and concentrate our discussions on the formulation of ambitious agendas and the adoption of radical targets to drastically reduce CO_2 emissions in our cities'.

Areas of action

The city works closely with various stakeholders, including business and the public. It also intends to co-operate more closely with other cities in order to provide mutual support. An example of this is the use of greener heating and electricity, with district heating attaining 70 per cent today, and estimated to reach 80 per cent by 2010. Furthermore, 65 per cent of the electricity used by the city administration is eco-labelled as being 100 per cent renewable.

Positive trends in the transport sector and co-operation with the private sector

The transport sector is one area that should be highlighted (as one of many areas where successful actions have been implemented, as the targets developed and reached are indeed ambitious:

Public transport percentages:

- Commuter trains 100 per cent renewable

- Subway 100 per cent renewable

- Buses 25 per cent renewable today (50 per cent by 2011 and 100 per cent by 2020)

- National trains 100 per cent renewable

Traffic is one of the major environmental problems in Stockholm, and a combination of 'carrots' and 'sticks' are used to change behaviour and reach effective CO_2 reduction goals in this sector. Ambitious investments in traffic management and congestion charging have made a big difference, but also small and inexpensive measures such as bus priority systems have been shown to be very effective.

Positive developments include an increase in cycling and use of public transport in the inner-city area, which has led to a decrease in air pollution and traffic noise levels. Congestion taxation, environmental zones for trucks and buses, as well as access restrictions in the city, are but a few examples of the 'sticks' used effectively. On the other hand the public transport network has been extended and is increasingly based on environmentally efficient vehicles and fuels.

Over the long-term, fossil fuels have to be replaced with renewable energy sources. Here the City is influencing developments, in its capacity as a major purchaser and producer. Through the long-standing work on Clean Vehicles Stockholm, the City works to promote the use of alternative fuels, both in the City's own car fleet, as well as among businesses and the general public (some 3,000 clean vehicles were sold to private companies). The target is to achieve a market breakthrough for clean vehicles. In 2006 this also was achieved: clean light vehicles' share of new sales went up to about 12 per cent the first quarter.

Stockholm also addresses environmental considerations in connection with transport procurement processes – seen as a useful area to ensure environmental goals are met. As a major purchaser in this field (the city's vehicle fleet composition and municipal fuel requirements), Stockholm can support efficient and co-ordinated distribution and the use of vehicles with good environmental performances.

The law on public procurement limits the possibility to include environmental requirements in the transportation of goods to the City's administration, schools, social care centers, etc. Therefore the City has now separated transport when procuring goods. All goods are now delivered to a logistical centre which only operates with light duty trucks using biofuels. This not only reduces pollution and GHGs, but also saves money, increases transport safety and ensures less work handling fewer deliveries to individual schools, administration centres etc.

Case study: Chicago's environmental action agenda – leading by example and encouraging the private sector

The Mayor of Chicago, Richard M. Daley, is committed to environmental initiatives and sees them as a key part of the city's competitive strategy in the future. Mayor Daley also understands the importance of sustainability and the responsibility that he has of being a steward of the city and its resources.

Located on the shores of Lake Michigan in the heart of the Midwest, Chicago is home to almost three million people.

Since taking office, Mayor Daley's green initiatives have been responsible for planting 500,000 trees, 72 miles of median planters, green buildings, and environmental code changes including the landscape ordinance and energy conservation code, and rooftop gardens. Chicago's world famous city hall roof-top garden is home to more than 150 types of flowers and plant species. Completed in 2001, the 20,000 square foot rooftop garden was designed to test different types of green-roof systems, the benefit of heating and cooling, and the success growth rates of native and exotic vegetation. The garden also addressed concerns of reduction in storm water runoff due to the debris, chemicals and other pollutants that flow into city storm sewer systems. Since the garden was installed, over 200 other rooftop gardens on public and private buildings have been constructed or are planned. Because it believes so strongly in the benefits of green roofs, the City recently adopted a policy that encourages and, in some cases, requires green roofs in private, not-for-profit and public developments receiving financial or other types of public assistance from the City, as well as planned developments and lakefront-protection ordinance developments.

The City of Chicago also has several green building initiatives. The City renovated four bungalow-style homes to determine if the benefits of green buildings, such as improved indoor air quality and energy efficiency, could be affordably achieved while remaining true to the original character of each home's design. Renovation of the homes was completed in 2002 and subsequent energy analysis showed that the four bungalows together saved 56 tons of CO_2 emissions. The City is also committed to building public buildings to a US Green Building Council LEED Standard. The Chicago Centre for Green Technology was the first municipal platinum-certified building in the country. Additionally, a green permit programme through the building-permitting department allows developers to receive their permit faster due to a dedicated review if their building is green.

The Environmental Action Agenda of Chicago aims to document all of the green policies and programs in the city and set goals for achieving Mayor Daley's vision of creating the greenest city in America.

The 2006 Environmental Action Agenda sets a course for continued environmental innovation within the City of Chicago and reaffirms Mayor Daley's belief that a healthy environment is not only consistent with a strong economy and improved quality of life for Chicagoans – it is essential to both. The Action Agenda commits the City to reduce its use of natural resources, invest in greener buildings, vehicles and materials, save tax-payer dollars through wise energy use and resource-conserving actions, and improve the quality of life in the City.

The Environmental Action Agenda documents Chicago's renewable energy and energy efficiency accomplishments and goals. The City has purchased 1.27 Megawatts of solar thermal capacity for installation on its facilities. Chicago also has over 1.5 Megawatts of solar photovoltaics installed on municipal and private buildings, more than any other city outside of California. The City is also installing four locally designed and manufactured 4kW wind turbines on the roof of the Daley Center in downtown Chicago in order to monitor and test the potential for small-scale wind production in the City.

The City has completed energy efficiency retrofits of over 15 million square feet of City and sister agency facilities saving 3,360,995 kilowatt-hours of electricity and removing 2,389 tons of air pollutants from the environment. And the City is also a founding member of the Chicago Climate Exchange, committing to reduce its GHG emissions, and has met its reduction commitments to date.

Cost-effective actions any local government can take – encouraging business to provide green services and products

These easy-to-implement actions are budget friendly ways to reduce energy use and greenhouse gas emissions.

1. Buy or invest in green electricity (clean electricity)

To cover electricity requirements in municipal buildings and facilities, buy green electricity generated from wind, geothermal, small hydro or solar energy. Alternatively invest in your own sustainable electricity generation by making use of available roof space to add photovoltaics or small wind turbines.

2. Be efficient in using energy (save costs) by:

- **Turning off the lights**
  Institute a 'lights out at night' policy, or ask staff to only switch lights on when needed. In City-managed buildings this is an easy and effective way to save electricity, reduce greenhouse gas emissions, and save municipal funds. Use a combination of educational campaigns and technology, such as timers and occupancy sensors.

- **Switching to LEDs**
  Light emitting diodes (LEDs) are 90 per cent more energy efficient and last 6–10 times longer than conventional lights. Save energy and maintenance costs by switching conventional bulbs to LEDs in traffic signals and exit lights. Because these lights function 24 hours a day, energy and cost savings accrue quickly.

- **Including street lighting**
  Switch off every second street lamp in areas (where it is technically feasible and safe) from midnight to 6am in the summer and from 11pm to 5am in the winter, reducing energy use for approximately 30 per cent of street lamps.

3. Be green by planting a tree and promoting green spaces

Create green spaces and keep people comfortable. Strategically planted deciduous trees and shrubs in urban areas can significantly reduce heating and cooling costs by shading buildings in the summer months and letting solar radiation through in winter. Shrubs planted around a foundation can also help insulate a building during the winter. Well-landscaped commercial buildings and residential neighbourhoods have lower heating and cooling costs, and are more pleasant for the users.

4. Be a wise local government business by:

- **Minimising printing**
  Send electronic messages to colleagues, instead of printed letters thereby saving paper, ink and printer maintenance costs. When printing documents one should consider their medium- to long-term use. If it potentially has a short life span, consider using a sustainable alternative.

- **Buying local**
  Buying local products can boost the local economy and minimises the need for transportation thus reducing harmful emissions.

- **Purchasing energy efficient equipment**
  Look for energy efficient labelling (e.g. ENERGY STAR or EU Energy Label) on equipment. Such computers can use up to 70 per cent less electricity than 'standard' equipment, copy machines reduce paper costs by around US$60 a month and fax machines can cut associated energy costs by 40 per cent.

5. Encourage sustainable transport by:

- **Buying bicycles for municipal staff**
  Bicycles are inexpensive and people-powered. Downsizing municipal car pools, and replacing, for example, police sedans with mountain bikes in dense urban areas will significantly cut fuel costs, reduce tailpipe emissions, and increase mobility in times of heavy traffic congestion.

- **Encouraging commuters to use public transport**
  Providing incentives for employees and commuters in the community to use sustainable transport options, such as the bus, tram or train, rather than drive a car to work is one way for cities to decrease traffic congestion and reduce emissions. Incentives can include subsidised or free transit passes, parking cash-out programmes, co-ordinated car or van pools, limiting inner-city parking options, providing bicycle parking garages and programmes such as a sustainable commuter challenge.

- **Promoting car pooling**
  Individual car use is one of the biggest sources of emissions. Measures taken to decrease the amount of cars on the roads reduce traffic congestion, thereby increasing productivity as well as reducing emissions and promoting public health.

6. Switch to green fleets by using more fuel-efficient and clean fuel vehicles

More efficient fuels include biofuels such as biodiesel, ethanol, biogas, and less carbon-intensive fuels such as natural gas. The use of more efficient fuels reduces greenhouse gas emissions and pre-empts future problems of shortages of traditional fuels.

7. Build clever by:

- **Using solar energy and environment-friendly designs**
When planning and constructing a new building or renovating an existing building, use passive solar architecture strategies to reduce your energy requirements. A combination of different strategies such as daylighting (natural light use through the correct placement of windows and doors), natural ventilation for a good air flow, flexible shading options, and using building materials that can contribute to the thermal mass to support heating or cooling your building will reduce energy consumption. Using active solar energy to provide electricity and hot water makes for solar building that can be used to demonstrate your municipality's commitment to sustainable energy.

- **Promoting smart growth (stopping urban sprawl)**
Stimulating the local economy to encourage growth is a standard approach, and new development ostensibly brings new revenues. However, uncontrolled sprawl is expensive as it requires costly outlays for new roads, water pipes, sewers, new services and other facilities often costing more revenues and producing more emissions due to increased energy and travel needs.

- **Colouring your rooftops**
Use your roof to adapt to your climate and either heat or cool your building. In a warm area add a highly reflective/emissive coating to a black or metal roof on a city building to reduce the need for air conditioning. Use the reverse of this action for a cold climate. Also, use insulation to support heat retention or cooling. This will produce huge annual cost and energy savings.

8. Don't waste, but rather:

- **Reduce, reuse, recycle**
Reducing your waste stream by minimising it, reusing it, composting the organics and recycling the inorganics (such as glass and plastics) reduces greenhouse gas emissions. Minimise the need for landfills and the burning of waste.

- **Convert waste to energy**
Collect and recover biogas generated at landfills. Just collecting and flaring the landfill gas reduces GHG emissions. If additionally it is used as energy source, fossil fuels can be replaced.

The way forward

ICLEI vision

Climate protection underscores the mission of ICLEI. As an association, ICLEI ensures that our local government members have the most advanced and effective tools to implement actions and contribute through mitigation and adaptation to combating climate change. Local governments should increasingly pursue opportunities to collaborate with the private and business sector in achieving greenhouse gas emission reduction targets through strategic alliances. ICLEI will continue creating opportunities for all members to learn from each other and exchange information on best practices, cutting-edge solutions and ways to overcome the common barriers cities face in addressing sustainability.

Furthermore, to ensure that the local government voice is heard, and that a united worldwide local authority response to climate change is taken into account during important international negotiations, ICLEI holds official observer status with the United Nations Framework Convention on Climate Change (UNFCCC), and is the lead organisation representing local governments at the Conference of the Parties (COP) to the UNFCCC that take place every year.

ICLEI partners with the Clinton Climate Initiative

In an exciting new development for the climate protection arena, ICLEI has joined the Clinton Climate Initiative (CCI) as a key partner, as its launches efforts to substantially reduce GHG emissions that cause global warming.

ICLEI President David Cadman, and ICLEI USA Executive Director Michelle Wyman attended former US President Bill Clinton's August 2006 announcement in Los Angeles of the Clinton Climate Initiative and its first project, a partnership with the Large Cities Climate Leadership Group, led by the Greater London Authority (GLA) and London Mayor Ken Livingstone, dedicated to fighting climate change in practical and measurable ways.

Through this partnership ICLEI will lend its expertise and experience working with more than 800 cities in 29 countries to the CCI as it endeavours to:

- Provide world-class technical assistance to a group of large cities taking action on climate protection

- Organise a purchasing consortium that will act as a buying club for cities to procure energy efficient and renewable energy technologies

- Deliver the Harmonised Emissions Analysis Tool (HEAT) to the group of large cities. HEAT is a dynamic, online software tool for cities to track greenhouse gas emissions and is built upon the existing quantification software being used within ICLEI.

'Working together with the Clinton Climate Initiative will enable us to deepen emissions reductions in the cities we engage with, increase the level of access to our tools, and broaden the base of technical expertise and assistance that we can provide to cities,' says Michelle Wyman, Executive Director of ICLEI USA.

28

Moving London Towards a Sustainable Low-Carbon Energy Community

Allan Jones and Tatiana Bosteels,
London Climate Change Agency

Introduction

With increased evidence and impacts of climate change and continuously growing emissions of greenhouse gases across the globe; with large cities emitting 75 per cent of the world's greenhouse gas emissions today and the United Nations' prediction that for the first time in history the world will see more than half of its population living in urban environments; in today's modern world can a society really be sustainable and self sufficient?

If runaway global climate change is to be avoided it will be at the city level that this will be achieved, not at the national government level, through cities innovating and progressing measures to tackle climate change. Cities emit most of the world's greenhouse gases that cause climate change, cities are most at risk to climate change events and cities have a vested interest in tackling climate change.

BOX 1: LONDON IN A NUTSHELL

With a population of around 7.4 million citizens, London's energy consumption equals that of countries such as Greece or Portugal, leading to carbon emissions above 43 million tonnes of CO_2 per year. London is a growing city and is expected to grow by the equivalent of the population of Leeds in the next 15 years, requiring an increase in residential accommodation of more than 30,000 units per year. This growth represents a great opportunity to transform the way the city works and ensure it moves to a low-carbon development path. Through its sustainable policies – the London Plan, the Further Alterations to the London Plan, the Mayor's Energy Strategy – London is putting climate change at the core of its development vision.[1]

This vision also represents a critical commercial opportunity as London's potential clean technology market generated as a direct result of deploying technologies, set out in the Mayor's Energy Strategy, have been estimated to be worth around £3.3 billion by 2010 and to lead to between 5,000 and 7,500 new jobs.[2]

This chapter summarises the London Climate Change Agency's practical strategy for a sustainable energy society deriving its initial energy needs from low-carbon energy resources whilst at the same time establishing a sustainable energy infrastructure to enable future energy needs to be derived from wholly renewable resources via a hydrogen economy. This approach will enable the Royal Commission on Environmental Pollution recommendation to reduce CO_2 emissions by 60 per cent by 2050.[3] These concepts can be applied to any community in the UK or indeed in the world.

Allan Jones, the Chief Executive Officer of the London Climate Change Agency, with his unique experience and expertise in local sustainable decentralised energy systems, was able to tease out the real issues and barriers to a sustainable energy future through the actual implementation of such systems, including sustainable and renewable energy systems, fuel cell technology and low-carbon transport systems.

London taking the leadership

London, as a large and wealthy world city, has taken the commitment to lead and show by example in taking action to avert catastrophic climate change. Key drivers to achieve this ambitious objective are political leadership and effective partnerships on the ground. The Mayor of London Ken Livingstone and the Deputy Mayor Nicky Gavron have made addressing the causes of climate change one of the main priorities of London strategies and have set ambitious targets and policies for both mitigating and adapting to climate change. The Mayor's Energy Strategy for London has a target of reducing carbon dioxide (CO_2) emissions by 20 per cent, relative to the 1990 level, by 2015, as the crucial first step on a long-term path to a 60 per cent reduction from the 2000 level by 2050.[4]

London is using its policy, strategic and planning powers to ensure the necessary policy direction and action to achieve its objectives of transforming London into a sustainable city. From using its Mayoral and planning powers to ensure that any new build will incorporate the best low-carbon sustainable designs with a minimum of 20 per cent of the development carbon emissions being further reduced by on-site renewable energy, through to the implementation of the congestion charge in 2002 and associated improvement of the public transport networks, to Greater London being designated as a low-emission zone in 2008 to improve air quality and reduce carbon emissions. The Mayor's powers to act further in this area are set to increase with government proposals to increase the Mayor's powers, including a new Climate Change Duty, the first time that any body has been granted such a power in the world.

BOX 2: LONDON'S CONGESTION CHARGE[5] AND LOW EMISSIONS ZONES[6]

The Congestion Charge was introduced in London in 2002 to address the worst traffic congestion in the UK and amongst the worst in Europe with estimated loses of £2–4 million every week in terms of lost time caused by congestion. The congestion charging requires a financial contribution, £8 per day, from users willing to continue driving in central London during the scheme's hours of operation. The scheme also encourages the use of public transport with revenues from the charging invested in making public transport easier, cheaper, faster and more reliable. Finally, the scheme is intended to make journey times quicker and more reliable for those who have to use the roads.

Building on the success of the scheme, in September 2006 the Mayor confirmed the extension of the central London Congestion Charging zone to include an additional area to the west, almost doubling the charging area.

To further improve the air quality of London the Mayor has announced the creation of the Low Emissions Zones where, from 2008, diesel heavy goods vehicles (HGVs), coaches and buses that fail to meet a minimum pollution standard will be charged to drive within the Greater London area. Such a charge is designed to act as an effective incentive for operators to modify or replace dirty vehicles.

This approach not only contributes towards tackling climate change, it also makes good commercial sense in stimulating London's economic and social development as well as creating businesses and jobs in London's new green economy. The London Development Agency's *Green Alchemy Turning Green to Gold: Powering London's Future – A Study of the Sustainable Energy Sector* identified that the sustainable energy sector is set for substantial growth.[7] The potential sustainable energy market generated as a direct result of deploying technologies as set out in the Mayor's Energy Strategy could be worth around £3.35 billion by 2010 and employ between 5,000 and 7,500 people.

Finally, strong and effective public and private partnerships and joint ventures are a key part of London's strategy that will deliver the effective implementation of these policies and achieve these targets on the ground. As the main delivery agency behind his strategies, the Mayor committed to establishing the London Climate Change Agency (LCCA) in his 2004 election manifesto to implement projects in the sectors that impact on climate change, especially in the energy, transport, waste and water sectors. The LCCA is playing a key role in helping to deliver the Mayor's Energy Strategy for London.

The Mayor of London appointed Allan Jones in November 2004 to set up and run the London Climate Change Agency to implement the experience he gained during his work changing Woking into a sustainable energy community to transform London into a leading low-carbon sustainable city. The LCCA was launched by the Mayor in June 2005 with the support of private sector founding supporters: BP, Lafarge, Legal & General,

HSBC, Sir Robert McAlpine, Johnson Matthey, and the City of London Corporation. The Agency is also being supported by the Rockefeller Brothers' Trust, KPMG, Greenpeace, the Climate Group, the Carbon Trust and the Energy Savings Trust.

The London Climate Change Agency Limited is a municipal company owned by the London Development Agency (LDA) and chaired by the Mayor. The LDA is one of the Mayor's functional bodies as well as one of the UK Regional Development Agencies whose purposes and powers include economic development and contributing towards sustainable development. The Deputy Mayor is the deputy chairman and Allan Jones, as CEO, is the executive director of LCCA Limited.

Case Study 1: Allan Jones at Woking – demonstrating the feasibility of a sustainable energy community

Allan Jones had the vision for an effective and economic low-carbon energy system for the UK. As Energy Services Manager at Woking Borough Council and Director of Thameswey Ltd (Woking's Energy and Environmental Services Company) he has been able to catalyse the necessary political commitment at cross party level to implement this vision including decentralised sustainable and renewable energy systems, fuel cell technology and low-carbon transport systems.

Woking Borough Council has implemented a series of decentralised energy projects in the past 15 years. These include providing the UK's first small-scale combined heat and power (CHP)/heat-fired absorption chiller or trigeneration system; being the first local authority with private-wire residential CHP and renewable energy systems; providing the largest domestic combined photovoltaic/CHP installations, the first local sustainable community energy systems and the first fuel-cell CHP system; and being the first public–private joint venture Energy Services Company or ESCO in the UK.

The Council is now recognised as the most energy-efficient local authority in the UK having achieved the greatest percentage reduction in both energy consumption and CO_2 emissions in the UK, as well as establishing Thameswey Ltd and Thameswey Energy Ltd (a public–private joint venture Energy Services Company or ESCO) and supplying itself with the highest proportion of on-site decentralised energy supplies in the UK. In recognition of this pioneering work, Allan Jones was appointed a Member of the British Empire in 1999 for services to energy and water efficiency. He was also instrumental in the Council gaining the Queen's Award for Enterprise, Sustainable Development 2001 in respect of its Energy Services activities in the development of Local Sustainable Community Energy Systems, the only local authority ever to receive a Queen's Award for Enterprise.

Since the Council implemented its energy efficiency and environmental policies in 1990 (the base year), it has achieved a 51 per cent reduction in energy consumption, a 44 per cent reduction in water consumption and a 79 per cent reduction in CO_2 emissions by 2005 in its own corporate buildings and housing stock. Complimenting this reduction in energy consumption, the Council receives more than 93 per cent of its electrical and thermal energy requirements from on-site, low- or zero-carbon decentralised energy sources, squeezing the carbon content of its buildings at both ends of the spectrum.

In addition, the Council has improved the energy efficiency of the housing stock in its area by more than 30 per cent, achieving its Home Energy Conservation Act target one year early. The impact of the Council's Climate Change Strategy has led to a 17.25 per cent reduction in CO_2 emissions for the whole of the Borough, in excess of the one per cent reduction a year necessary to achieve the Royal Commission's target.

London Climate Change Agency's vision and strategy

The LCCA[8] is implementing a project-led strategy to deliver real carbon reductions in London rather than a carbon offset strategy that does not deliver real reductions locally. The LCCA is establishing a new energy infrastructure landscape in London that tackles all sectors that impact on climate change, including energy, transport, waste and water, by taking advantage of all available mechanisms to create sustainable systems for London's businesses and communities.

The LCCA strategy embeds future proofing into the new energy infrastructure landscape. A prime example of this is combined heat and power (CHP) where the fuel may initially be a low-carbon fuel such as natural gas which can be replaced later by a renewable fuel or hydrogen. The important issue here is to future-proof the heat, chilled water and private-wire infrastructure, serving buildings on local decentralised energy systems. Those systems have a life time many times longer than the CHP plant. Such future proofing enables the easy replacement or refuelling of the CHP plant in the future with renewable fuels or hydrogen without impacting on the energy infrastructure which is impervious to the primary fuels supplying it.

Building on his experience at Woking Allan Jones adapted his practical strategy for a sustainable energy community to the specific characteristics of a large city such as London. The building blocks of the London Climate Change Agency strategy are to implement projects and to act as a catalyst promoting the development across London of low-carbon decentralised energy systems. The sustainable energy community approach needs to be holistic and to incorporate energy efficiency as an integral part of the strategy followed by on-site low- or zero-carbon sustainable/renewable energy systems and the capturing of sustainable waste resources to provide opportunities to transform waste into a valuable resource leading to the production of renewable gases and fuels for both buildings and transport and the collection of sustainable water (through the dewatering of waste and other currently uncaptured water resources) for non-potable water resources. These systems are future-proofed allowing for the emergence of renewable hydrogen in the form of renewable gases and liquids as the common energy carriers of the future for both buildings and transport.

As a public sector body with strong private sector support, the LCCA has captured the best of both worlds by integrating public and private sector strengths to ensure the efficient implementation of the LCCA's strategy. Among the key elements of the LCCA strategy is the establishment of the London ESCO, a public–private joint venture Energy Services Company or ESCO, with a large corporate partner with the experience and the capability to implement decentralised low-carbon energy systems. A similar strategy was followed in Woking with the creation of Thameswey Ltd (Woking's municipal company) and Thameswey Energy Ltd (Woking's public–private joint venture ESCO).

In March 2006, the Mayor announced that the London Climate Change Agency had selected EDF Energy plc as the preferred bidder to set up a joint venture energy services company (ESCO) whose remit is to develop decentralised energy schemes for London. EDF Energy,[9] one of the largest energy companies in the UK and the owner of London Energy and London's public electricity network, was selected as a result of a competitive negotiated procedure process from a very strong field of nine energy and utility companies (including two oil companies and a US energy services company) who had submitted bids in being the private sector partner in the London ESCO. The London ESCO has been incorporated in September 2006.

The London ESCO has been established to design, finance, build and operate local decentralised energy systems for both new and existing development. It has been established as a private limited company with shareholdings jointly owned by the London Climate Change Agency Ltd (with a 19 per cent shareholding) and EDF Energy (Projects) Ltd (with an 81 per cent shareholding). Project investment will be in the same shareholding proportions. This shareholding and project investment ratio ensures that the company is not controlled or influenced by the public sector and remains an unregulated private company under the Local Authorities (Companies) Order 1995, a key criteria for private sector participation.

Although the ESCO is run by the private sector as the majority shareholder in the company, the public sector was the procuring agency and selected the private sector partner against a specification. The best of the private sector bids was then further refined by negotiation. In this case, EDF Energy plc complied with the full requirements of the specification and was able to demonstrate the full technical, financial, construction and operational expertise and resources to enable a pan-London energy service to succeed in achieving and going beyond the Mayor's Energy and other Environmental Strategies. The LCCA is not a sleeping partner, it participates fully in the London ESCO in proportion to its scale. Full participation by the LCCA is necessary for the London ESCO to take full advantage of both public and private sector experience, expertise, technical know how and stakeholder engagement and management.

The company tackles climate change by developing local decentralised energy solutions to London's electricity, heating and cooling needs. It will also catalyse the waste, transport, energy and water low- and zero-carbon sectors leading to the establishment of Special Purpose Vehicle Companies. Utilising a completely different technical and commercial approach to such projects originally developed by Allan Jones in Woking, the London ESCO will identify and develop sites across London where investment in sustainable and decentralised energy technology would reduce carbon dioxide and other greenhouse gas emissions contributing to climate change.

However, the London ESCO does start with the advantage of the 50 projects pipeline established by the LCCA in advance of the procurement of the private sector partner in the London ESCO and included in the London ESCO specification. The initial tranche of short-term projects from the collection of short-, medium- and long-term projects in the project pipeline would deliver 170MW of CHP (mainly trigeneration), 8MW wind farm, other renewables and fuel cell CHP with an investment value of £100 million and a reduction in CO_2 emissions of 310,000 tonnes per annum.

This approach to project delivery will eventually lead to taking mega tonnes of CO_2 emissions out of the atmosphere as well as catalysing the ESCO market in London, the UK and even internationally as others seek to replicate the London ESCO's success in turning market failure in this area into a commercial success through tackling climate change. In this way, global climate change can be tackled simply by re-writing the rules of commercial engagement and capturing the true economic benefits of low- and zero-carbon technologies which are currently lost in trading within a vested-interest fossil fuel grid and fossil fuel extraction, delivery and supply systems.

Decentralised private-wire energy systems

The key to an economically viable low-carbon energy system in the UK resides in implementing decentralised private-wire distributed generation systems. This is achieved by taking advantage of the exempt licensing regime under the Electricity (Class Exemptions from the Requirement for a Licence) Order 2001[10] (see Figure 1), which enables exempt generators, distributors and suppliers to supply electricity that they generate and distribute themselves directly to customers rather than to a licensed supplier (the grid). This model was originally developed in Woking at a small-scale level and has now been adapted into a London model at a much larger scale.

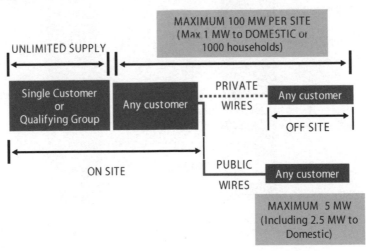

Figure 1: The Electricity (Class Exemptions) Order 2001
Source: London Climate Change Agency, 2006, based on Department of Trade and Industry, electricity Directorate, 2001

Most exempt generators are connected to the distribution networks but sell their electricity to a licensed supplier (the distribution grid) at very low wholesale electricity prices to which transmission use of system (TUoS), distribution use of system (DUoS), transmission and distribution losses and other charges are added to make up the supply or retail price of electricity. This exempt electricity makes very little use of the distribution network and no use of the national transmission grid at all. CHP and renewable energy generators are effectively treated as if they were 1,000MW coal-fired power stations in the Midlands incurring all of the transmission and distribution charges, transmission and distribution losses, etc. The embedded generation benefits and the true economic value of CHP and renewable energy are lost when they supply electricity to a licensed supplier (the distribution grid).

As can be seen from Figure 2, most of the grid supply price is not electricity but transmission and distribution losses and use of system charges, whereas most of the private-wire supply price is electricity. It is important to note that this is not the cost of generating private-wire electricity, but the value or price gap necessary to fund the decentralised energy generation and private-wire district energy infrastructure in the first place and still compete with the grid. The private-wire electricity competes with public-wire electricity by taking advantage of the true economic value of decentralised energy (sustainable energy or distributed generation) rather than losing it to licensed suppliers/grid.

Figure 2: Grid supply price and private-wire supply price
Source: London Climate Change Agency, 2006

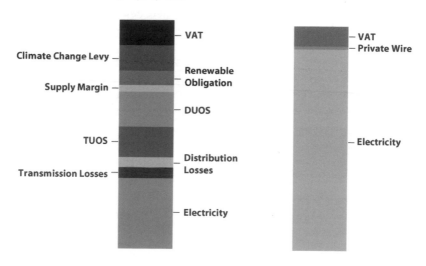

Even with a local decentralised energy system, grid connection (in practice the local distribution network, not the national transmission grid) would be required to provide standby and top-up supplies to guarantee energy supply to customers 24 hours a day all year round and to export surplus power over public wires to other customers or decentralised energy systems.

Private-wire decentralised energy systems enable island generation to be provided which means the energy stations can continue to operate independently of the national grid in the event of a failure of the national grid, even for prolonged periods. This contrasts with conventional CHP/renewables which have to be automatically disconnected from the grid to prevent reverse power flows into a 'dead' grid. This independence of the national grid in the event of disruption of the grid due to bad weather, damage or technical disconnection is particularly attractive to customers and a practical embodiment of what decentralised energy can achieve.

Further innovation has been implemented under the electricity law exemption order 2001 by establishing a trading system under an enabling agreement for exempt supplier operation (which the host utility is legally obliged to provide under their licence conditions). This enables the ESCO to trade each half hour of electricity imported/ exported over public wires (i.e. the local distribution network, not the national grid) between its own exempt private-wire decentralised energy sites to achieve virtual independence of the national grid and all of its energy from local sustainable energy sources.

The way that energy is generated and utilised on island generation sites, surplus/ standby and top-up energy transferred and traded between island generation sites under the private-wire decentralised energy system approach is similar to how the internet, arguably one of the most important inventions of the twentieth century, operates. The island generation sites are the Local Area Networks or the LANs and the local distribution network is the Wide Area Network or the WAN. With sufficient concentration and scale of island generation sites on a local distribution network transferring electricity between each other, the whole distribution network will change from a passive network with the national grid (as it is now) to become an active network independent of the national grid.

Therefore, the distribution networks will become of increasing importance to future energy systems as the value and the influence of the national grid declines along with the decline of large thermal power stations that require a very high voltage national grid and the non-renewable fuels on which they rely. The decentralised energy transfer and trading system developed and operated for the 80 island generation sites in Woking will be adapted for London into a London Energy Internet. See Figure 3.

Figure 3: Proposed London Energy Internet
Source: London Climate Change Agency, 2006

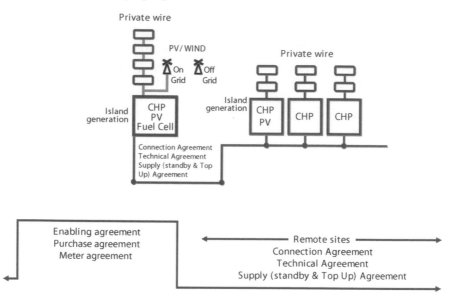

This approach is of key importance for the future-proofing of London's energy systems and to the future development of London ESCO energy stations in the licensed distribution area since energy stations can be configured to supply standby and top up to each other under an enabling agreement for exempt supplier operation. With the development of further London ESCO energy stations in the future it would be possible for such island networks to be completely independent of the national transmission grid. They would rely only on the interconnection between London ESCO energy stations via the local distribution network. This would enable the CHP units to be replaced by renewable cogeneration systems (most likely fuel cells because of the renewable fuel flexibility) by the time the generation prime movers require replacing, as the cost of such systems becomes economically viable.

A study sponsored by the Mayor, 'Powering London into the 21st Century', has shown that decentralised energy is capable of providing 35.5 per cent of London's energy demand by 2025 which would reduce CO_2 emissions by 33 per cent and natural gas consumption by 15 per cent. In the longer term it could provide up to 75 per cent of London's energy demand.[11] If the UK as a whole adopted a decentralised energy approach, the national grid could be reserved for connecting large-scale renewable energy supplies. This would allow thermal power station systems to be primarily reserved for the energy-intensive industries that currently connect directly to the very high voltage national grid system. By locating thermal power stations alongside energy-intensive industries, thermal energy could be supplied directly to the industries alongside electricity, thereby significantly increasing the overall efficiency of the energy system through combined heat and power (cogeneration and/or trigeneration). Such an energy efficiency strategy would require the location of thermal power stations at industrial locations like the Isle of Grain and not at rural locations like Didcot.

In any event, much of the national grid system would have to be replaced or refurbished within the Royal Commission's timescale for action. It would be folly to replicate the existing national grid system as this would not be suitable either for future energy systems or for most forms of renewable energy. The need will be for many thousands of decentralised or renewable energy stations where electricity flows will be dissipated at the nearest loads and not lost in heating up the wires and transformers in the national grid.

Decentralised energy will also avoid the unnecessary waste of the UK's water resources. Currently, 50 per cent of the UK's water resources are used for rejecting waste heat away from centralised power stations.[12] A typical 1,000MW power station consumes 2.5M litres of water per hour, 80 per cent of which is directly evaporated into the atmosphere from power station cooling towers. Displacing centralised power generation with local decentralised energy will have the biggest impact on reducing the UK's and London's water consumption, although other measures should also be taken to reduce water consumption – particularly potable water consumption – and to achieve a society with sustainable water resources and sustainable consumption.

Sustainable low-carbon energy systems: combined heat, cooling and power

Low-carbon sustainable energy systems must be implemented within every decentralised energy network. A sustainable energy system should provide the full range of continuous energy services required by customers while achieving a substantial reduction in CO_2 emissions. Sustainable energy systems enable energy supplies to be made sustainable, either now or in the future. It is important that the heat, chilled water and private-wire infrastructures serving local sustainable energy communities are future-proofed. The decentralised energy system may initially be fuelled by a low-carbon fuel such as natural gas which can be replaced later by a renewable fuel or hydrogen. The infrastructure will last many times longer than the primary generators serving the system so, when the system is refinanced at the end of its initial investment period, only the primary generators will need replacing. This will leave surplus finance that can be invested in a renewable fuel or hydrogen system.

Local community energy systems can be made viable by combining different types of buildings together on a predominantly thermal energy system, making use of thermal storage and heat-fired absorption cooling for air conditioning and refrigeration rather than supplying the community with unsustainable grid electricity and gas services. With the right mix of buildings and the different types of energy usage and duration, sustainability in electricity with surplus export available can be achieved. See Figure 4.

Figure 4: Combined cooling, heat and power (Trigeneration)
Source: London Climate Change Agency, 2006

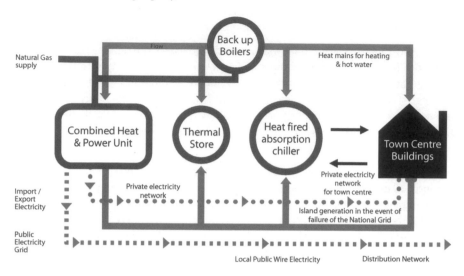

Combined heat and power (CHP) recovers the heat produced by the generation of electricity providing efficiencies of up to 90 per cent; centralised power stations and the national grid system can be as little as 33 per cent efficient at the point of use, most of the energy being wasted as heat from power station cooling towers, electricity losses through the national grid/local distribution systems, and through the inefficiencies of separate boiler heating systems. Conventional brown energy systems in the UK waste more energy than the entire North Sea annual gas output, enough energy to heat every home in the country. In the UK, the Regulator – the Office of Gas and Electricity Markets (Ofgem) – estimates that nearly $1billion worth of electricity is lost on UK distribution networks each year alone.[13]

The efficiency of the CHP can be further enhanced if the heat requirement of the energy plant is increased by use of a heat-fired absorption cooling system. In such a system, heat is provided by the CHP and low-carbon electricity is therefore generated from the requirement for cooling as well as heat. This displaces electricity that would have otherwise been consumed by electric air conditioning and refrigeration, generates more low-carbon electricity from the 'heat to cool' process and displaces very powerful greenhouse gas refrigerants that would otherwise be used by electric air conditioning and refrigeration systems.

Low-carbon decentralised energy systems and renewable energy

To ensure an effective and future-proofed sustainable energy community, renewable energy needs to be integrated with combined cooling, heat and power. Under the proposed 'Further Alterations to the London Plan'[14] currently under consultation, at least a 20 per cent contribution in terms of carbon emission reductions of the development will be required from renewable energy, compared to the 10 per cent currently required under the Mayor's Energy Strategy. Basing a policy on renewable energy delivering a 20 per cent reduction in carbon emissions rather than 20 per cent of the energy required teases out those renewable or partially renewable energy technologies, such as ground source heat pumps, that only reduce carbon emissions against coal, oil or electric heating but not against gas heating where emissions are increased due to the grid electricity required to run the technology.

Although any renewable energy technology can be considered for the London urban environment, only electricity-generating renewables (such as photovoltaics, wind or marine power, renewable gases, biomass or biofuels) used as the primary fuel for the CHP plant can complement a CHP system. This is because thermal energy renewables, such as solar thermal or ground source heat pumps, will reduce the thermal energy generation from the CHP and therefore reduce the electricity-generating capacity of the CHP, hampering its ability to reduce the amount of high-carbon grid electricity required. Integrating photovoltaics and/or wind energy with CHP provides a complementary reverse summer/winter electricity profile.

Renewable gas, biomass and biofuel energy technologies are key in integrating sustainable waste management in London's low-carbon energy systems strategy. Conventional waste management involves combining smaller local waste streams at larger disposal sites, with associated lorry movements and emissions. The use of alternative clean waste-to-energy technologies such as anaerobic digestion for organic waste and gasification/pyrolysis for residual waste produce renewable gases (biogases and/or syngases) and biofuels (sythethetic diesel) for use in both buildings and transport. The efficiency of such systems is increased significantly if renewable gases can be stored and pipelined off-site to where energy is required (e.g. CHP for buildings) rather than capturing only a small element of the energy through exclusively on-site electricity generation or pipelining more expensive heat networks off site. Where fuel cells are used, e.g. in molten carbonate fuel cell CHP, the whole energy chain can become non-combustion, increasing efficiency still further. Such systems would also obviate the need for expensive and environmentally damaging movement of waste, as most of this is recycled or recovered locally.

Indeed, the current growth of recycling implies moving away from large-scale waste disposal and towards modular, small-scale approaches to waste recycling and energy recovery. These would be versatile enough to deal with locally generated waste and maximise the supply of renewable energy from quite small communities to large cities. This avoids importing or exporting waste to or from the local community, thereby making significant savings in transport emissions as well as maximising energy recovery from renewable resources.

Microgeneration systems such as domestic CHP and/or renewable energy systems will play a valuable role in filling in generation gaps at the local domestic level (typically owner/occupier, small business units, isolated rural locations and so on). These smaller systems (which, though small individually, are large collectively) will be backed up by other local larger scale CHP/renewable energy systems, such as those Woking and London are developing. The electricity flows will be local and balanced out as part of a local mixed-technology, decentralised energy system. They will not be backed up by the grid and centralised power station generation, as these will become more unsustainable in the future.

Case Study 2: Palestra's photovoltaic and building-integrated wind turbines flagship project

As part of promoting the market penetration of low-carbon technologies, the London Climate Change Agency is implementing a series of flagship projects demonstrating the feasibility of implementing building-integrated renewable technologies in London. Among them, the LCCA has installed building-integrated renewable energy in its new office building, Palestra.

The Palestra building is the new home of the London Development Agency and London Climate Change Agency. The building was chosen following a detailed evaluation, negotiation and selection process of a number of buildings that met the location and accommodation criteria. One of the key criteria was the energy performance of the buildings and Palestra was the only building evaluated that had a very good Building Research Establishment Environmental Assessment Method rating (BREEAM). In order to improve the energy performance of the floors to be occupied by the LDA/LCCA still further and to contribute towards the Mayor's Energy Strategy the LCCA negotiated with the developer to allow the LCCA to include their own renewable energy system configured to supply the LDA/LCCA floors.

The project comprises an 84kW renewable energy system with 63kWp of photovoltaic panels on the roof and 21kWp of building integrated wind turbines (14 turbines) also on the roof. The combined renewable energy system will generate 3,397,000kWh of renewable electricity and reduce CO_2 emissions by 3,300 tonnes during its lifetime.

Source: London Climate Change Agency, 2006

The project is funded by the London Climate Change Agency and benefits from a grant of £155,276 awarded under the DTI Major Photovoltaic Demonstration Programme, managed by the Energy Saving Trust.

With the implementation of energy labelling under the EU directive on energy performance of buildings, this project is a good example of an occupier selecting the best energy performing building available then improving its energy performance and reducing its carbon emissions still further by implementing their own renewable energy system.

Removal of the regulatory barriers to decentralised energy

Government can take an easy first step to encourage the development of CHP, renewables, fuel cells and decentralised systems at the stroke of a pen – simply by increasing the supply limits for exempt generators/distributors/suppliers. The current low limits burden them with charges for centralised energy losses and high use of system which they are not contributing to, thus unnecessarily increasing the cost of low- or zero-carbon energy. Such legislative change will increase the economic value of low/zero-carbon energy and put it on a competitive footing with brown energy by taking away all those unnecessary charges that are added to electricity supplied from decentralised energy.

Although Woking has avoided centralised energy grid and penalty costs by utilising private-wire networks and a local trading system, the existing regulatory regime limits the size of decentralised energy and, more importantly, substantially limits the number of domestic customers than can be supplied with low-cost, low-carbon energy.

The current regulatory regime for exempt generators, distributors and suppliers should be changed to allow more customers to benefit from private-wire systems. At the moment, operators of decentralised energy stations as large as 100MW are exempt from generation licence requirements. However, of that 100MW only 1MW (about 1,000 households) is allowed to be supplied to domestic customers on private wire per generation site and only 5MW (of which only 2.5MW can be supplied to domestic customers) in aggregate export over public wires for all of its sites together (see Figure 1).

Although these barriers to low/zero-carbon decentralised energy do not prevent such systems for new development (where developers never build more than 500 dwellings per phase) or for existing non-residential development, it does severely limit such systems for existing residential development as a means to tackling fuel poverty and balancing between island generation sites, particularly for London. Given the interest in tackling fuel poverty and the need for local security of supply why have these limits been put in place?

The exemption limits should be further relaxed to enable the Royal Commission targets to be achieved.[15] A lot of the extra money needed to stimulate renewables and CHP could be found by relaxing the exemption criteria and allowing local generators/ suppliers to supply more electricity directly to local customers. Focus could then turn to bringing the Hydrogen Economy forward.

The LCCA has lobbied government for a review of the licence exemptions, as it sees the removal of the regulatory barriers to decentralised energy as crucial to enable large-scale decentralised energy systems to be implemented in London and the UK. The LCCA proposed amendments to the Electricity Order 2001 – Class Exemptions from the Requirement for a Licence – is detailed in Figure 5.

Figure 5: Proposed amendments to the Electricity (Class Exemptions) Order 2001
Source: London Climate Change Agency, 2006

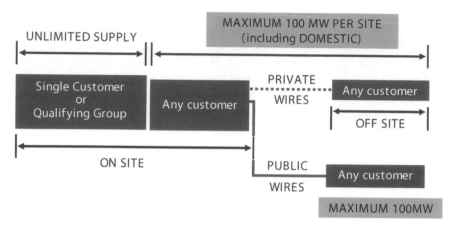

In environmental and sustainability terms, the more island generation and local discrete ('private wire') networks that you have interconnected to each other, the more a borough like Woking and a city like London becomes sustainable in energy. If other towns and cities did the same thing there would be no need for large centralised power stations and a very high voltage national grid system; these would be replaced by a network of local decentralised energy systems on local island networks interconnected to each other throughout the country. These can be backed up by large-scale renewable energy systems, particularly onshore and offshore wind and marine energy systems. The future grid would be very different from the one we know today operating on much lower voltage local island generation networks supplying more efficient energy directly to customer loads, overlapping with other local island generation networks and so on.

London's long-term strategy: renewable hydrogen energy economy

Renewable gases and liquids are the natural replacement for natural gases and non-renewable fuels. Hydrogen need only be extracted via a fuel cell at the point of use or energy load, thereby overcoming any hydrogen transportation and distribution issues.

Like electricity, hydrogen is an energy carrier not energy; but unlike electricity, hydrogen has zero carbon content, makes up 75 per cent of the known universe and can be generated from a variety of resources, including fossil fuels, renewables, biomass, waste and even algae. Using renewable hydrogen as an energy carrier in fuel cells for heat, power and cooling in stationary applications, or for transport applications, involves emissions only of pure water. The long-term development of renewable energy and of the renewable hydrogen economy will rely crucially on recognising and utilising the linkages between energy, water, waste and transport.

The greatest renewable hydrogen resource for a city like London is waste. Renewable gases and liquids rich in hydrogen could be developed from range of waste sources – sewage, municipal, commercial and industrial waste – that cannot be recycled, and biomass wastes. From these waste streams, biogases and/or syngases can be generated from environmentally safe technologies such as anaerobic digestion and gasification/pyrolysis.

The development of a renewable hydrogen energy economy based on these linkages has several benefits beyond the elimination of greenhouse gas emissions and toxic pollutants:

- Renewable energy and hydrogen from sewage, municipal, commercial, industrial and biomass waste does not suffer from limitations of intermittency

- The conversion of residual waste to energy using non-combustion technologies avoids waste going to landfill

- Dewatering of waste and pure water from hydrogen fuel cells will become important non-potable and potable water resources in the future, particularly in areas in which water is in short supply.

In the long term, we will only be able to meet our energy needs at minimal emissions through the use of hydrogen. Hydrogen will be the energy carrier of the future, deriving its energy from renewable fuels. Fuel cells and the Hydrogen Economy, used in conjunction with renewable fuels, is the only technology that can meet the UK's electrical, thermal and transport energy needs from renewable sources utilising a common energy carrier. Even if the long term environmental impact of nuclear waste is ignored, nuclear energy can only address a comparatively small portion of the UK's electricity needs, not the UK's thermal and transport energy needs. Only fuel cells and hydrogen can deliver all three of the UK's primary energy needs. If government looked at this issue in an innovative way, as Woking and London have done, then it would see that the Royal Commission on Environmental Pollution's CO_2 reduction targets could be met whilst, moreover, laying the foundations for a sustainable energy future. The barriers to this are not technical problems; they are regulation and vested interests.

Notes

1   Greater London Authority, 'The London Plan – the Mayor's Spatial Development Strategy', February 2004. See http://www.london.gov.uk/mayor/planning/strategy.jsp, accessed November 2006.
    Greater London Authority, 'Green light to clean power: the Mayor's Energy Strategy', March 2004. See http://www.london.gov.uk/mayor/strategies/energy/index.jsp, accessed November 2006.
    Greater London Authority, 'Draft Further Alterations to the London Plan', September 2006. See http://www.london.gov.uk/mayor/strategies/sds/further-alts/docs.jsp, accessed November 2006.
2   London Development Agency, 'Green Alchemy, Turning Green to Gold: Powering London's future – a study of the sustainable energy sector', November 2003.

3   The Royal Commission on Environmental Pollution, 'The Royal Commission on Environmental Pollution's 22nd Report: Energy – The Changing Climate', June 2002. See http://www.rcep.org.uk/newenergy.htm, accessed November 2006.

4   Greater London Authority, 'Green light to clean power: the Mayor's Energy Strategy', March 2004. See http://www.london.gov.uk/mayor/strategies/energy/index.jsp, accessed November 2006.

5   GLA Congestion Charge website, http://www.london.gov.uk/mayor/congest/index.jsp, accessed November 2006.
     London Congestion Charging website, http://www.cclondon.com, accessed November 2006.

6   GLA Low Emission Zone website, http://www.london.gov.uk/mayor/environment/air_quality/lez.jsp, accessed November 2006.
     Transport for London Low Emission Zone website, http://www.tfl.gov.uk/tfl/low-emission-zone/, accessed November 2006.

7   London Development Agency, 'Green Alchemy, Turning Green to Gold: Powering London's future – a study of the sustainable energy sector', November 2003.

8   LCCA website, http://www.lcca.co.uk, accessed November 2006.

9   EDF Energy Development Branch website, http://www.edfenergy.com/html/showPage.do?name=edfenergy.development.til, accessed November 2006.

10   DTI, Electricity Licence Agreement website, http://www.dti.gov.uk/energy/markets/electricity-markets/licence-exemp/page34529.html, accessed November 2006.

11   Mayor of London and Greenpeace, 'Powering London into the 21st Century', March 2006. See http://www.london.gov.uk/gla/publications/environment.jsp or http://www.uk.greenpeace.org.uk/climate/media/pressrelease.cfm?ucidparam=20061103180958, accessed November 2006.

12   Ibid.

13   OFGEM, 'International Power Generation', February 2003.

14   Greater London Authority, 'Draft Further Alterations to the London Plan', September 2006. See http://www.london.gov.uk/mayor/strategies/sds/further-alts/docs.jsp, accessed November 2006.

15   The Royal Commission on Environmental Pollution, 'The Royal Commission on Environmental Pollution's 22nd Report: Energy – The Changing Climate', June 2002. See http://www.rcep.org.uk/newenergy.htm, accessed November 2006.

29

Urbanisation in China: Designing the World's First Sustainable Eco-City in Dongtan

Peter Head and Alejandro Gutiérrez, Arup

Introduction

Dongtan, the world's first eco-city, illustrates perfectly how sustainability will be a cornerstone of future cities and the business opportunities that represents. It is also a city where the goal of cutting carbon emissions has shaped nearly every element of design. This visionary project, which is just beginning to take shape, could be a major milestone in the evolution of urban living.

This chapter discusses the principles, goals and objectives of the Dongtan project, as designed by Arup, the international firm of designers, planners, engineers and business consultants.

A day in the life of Dongtan

Shen Yijia finishes her bowl of breakfast and looks from the window of the family apartment to the clock then back again. Half an hour until school starts and it is another warm, bright summer's day. Outside, the heat is already rising, but inside the insulated and shady flat, the temperature is cool in summer and warm in winter with minimal need for central heating or air conditioning.

Her mother, Gu Yanbin, reminds her to put the rubbish out and clean her teeth before she leaves. Sighing, the twelve-year-old carries the individual colour-coded plastic bins one at a time out into the communal courtyard, saying good morning to a neighbour as she passes. Day by day, all the family's waste ends up in one or other of these bins – paper, packaging, food scraps, plastic and glass. The waste is collected from the block and taken for recycling, to be turned into fertilizer or to the power centre. Nearly everything in Dongtan is reused, and there is virtually no landfill.

In the bathroom she switches on the light, which is partly powered by electricity from the flat's tiny rooftop wind turbine and its photovoltaic panels. Crystal clear drinking water pours from the taps, and fills the basin. The water is taken from nearby the Yangtze and treated to the highest standards. However, after Shen Yijia has washed her face, cleaned her teeth and pulled the plug, the used water flows into another water system. Some of this used 'grey water', which also includes collected rainwater, will now be recycled and used to flush the toilet or irrigate the garden. The flat has two water systems: one for drinking water and one for grey water.

Looking at the clock with only fifteen minutes left, she kisses her mother, grabs her satchel and dashes out with her bike. Her school, like the shops and the other facilities, is only a five-minute cycle ride away. With few cars on the roads, Shen Yijia's parents need not worry about the dangers of traffic.

Her path weaves through housing blocks like her own, rising only five or six storeys high unlike the soaring tenements of her old home in nearby Shanghai. Some of the roofs and window frames of these blocks are lined with polished, gleaming photovoltaic panels. Other roofs are green with turf and vegetation, providing both rooftop gardens and added insulation. A barely audible hum comes from mini wind turbines on top of the blocks.

Picture reproduced courtesy of Arup

Every home has its own private garden or outdoor area and the blocks also open out onto communal space. Shen Yijia and her family know many of their neighbours well. Her neighbourhood is a mixture of homes, shops, leisure facilities and some small workshops and businesses. On one side of the path, the scenery opens out onto farmland and on the horizon she can see the majestic rotating blades of a towering wind turbine. On the other side she passes one of the numerous ponds and small lakes dotted around the area. As she approaches the school gates she pauses to watch a flock of birds fly towards the untouched wetland at the end of the island.

Meanwhile, with her daughter at school, Gu Yanbin finishes a load of washing before heading to work herself. The electricity powering the television, washing machine, dishwasher, lights and all the other gadgets, comes from the island's own power grid. The electricity flowing around Dongtan is a mixture of energy from the biomass, wind turbines, photovoltaic cells and from the Combined Heat and Power (CHP) plant. All the city's energy is generated within the city.

Though the family's electric appliances are all high-performance, energy-efficient models, with several of them running at once, the flat's computer information screen shows the family is using a lot of energy. With the system keeping an up to the minute tally of resources used, residents can adjust their energy use accordingly to keep their utility bills low.

Insulation, double glazing and energy efficient appliances mean the family use about a third of the energy they did in their old home in Shanghai. Closing the shutters to keep the midday heat out as suggested by the flat's computer, Gu Yanbin heads out to work at one of the research laboratories which thrive in the city.

The bus stop is just a few minutes walk away. No one lives more than five minutes from Dongtan's extensive public transport network. She boards the hydrogen-powered bus as it glides quietly up to the stop. At a junction, the bus approaches at the same time as an electric car. Traffic computers change the lights to halt the car and let the bus through. Petrol cars cannot access the city; only zero-emissions cars are allowed within Dongtan.

The journey to the science park passes along one of the many canals that criss-cross the island. Freight barges and water taxis ply the waterways. The roads are far quieter in terms of traffic and noise than in any other city. Not just buses, but also delivery vehicles and lorries are hydrogen powered. Between them weave hundreds of bicycles. The lack of congestion and emissions from cars makes the air in Dongtan as pure as it was before the city was built.

The bus glides past the city's Equestrian centre. This is one of a group of tourist attractions in Dongtan, which bring in thousands of visitors a year. Hotels, restaurants, bars and conference centres draw people from all over China and abroad and create employment for thousands of the city's residents.

Outside the compact town centre where Gu Yanbin lives, the scenery opens out more and includes fields and parkland. In the distance, she can see the power plant where her husband Shen Fang works. There, tons of waste rice husks are burnt as biofuel. Biogas given off by the city's organic waste is also burnt off to provide power.

The bus rolls on towards the science park, which is one of several owned by companies springing up around Dongtan. On its journey it passes thriving building sites as the world's first eco-city continues to grow.

China's urbanisation challenge

The site of this visionary development is currently a swathe of cultivated and flood-controlled agricultural land in the middle of the Yangtze delta. Chongming is the world's largest alluvial island, gradually formed from silt which drifts down the great waterway. At 100km long, it is getting bigger every year as more mud washes up on its banks. Soil washed from areas thousands of miles upstream means the island has doubled in size since 1950.

Despite its proximity to the bustling metropolis of Shanghai, until recently the island has remained a quiet backwater. Beyond the bustling streets of the island's two main towns, its only inhabitants have been wading birds and poor, peasant farmers who harvest reeds or grow food for their booming neighbour. The south-eastern end of Chongming, an area called Dongtan, is desolate except for farms and scattered fishing communities plying its growing coastline. At its furthest tip is an internationally protected nature reserve which is home to the endangered black-faced spoonbill and migrating wetland birds.

However, the face of Chongming is destined to radically change. Until now the island has been separated from the breakneck urbanisation of its neighbour by a 30km stretch of water. That isolation is soon to end.

The Chinese government has decided to urbanise Chongming as part of a wider scheme to develop the whole of the Yangtze estuary. To begin with, it is connecting Chongming to the mainland. Tens of thousands of workers are employed building a bridge and a tunnel to link the island to Shanghai's heart, the soaring Pudong district. When the building work is complete, this rural backwater will be a 30-minute drive from downtown Shanghai. Once connected, the island will gain a population of millions. But the government-owned corporation behind the development of the Dongtan area of the island has decided its development on Chongming needs to be different to the other cities sprouting up in the rest of China.

The extraordinary growth seen by China in the last 20 years means it must continue to develop land at an astonishing rate to keep up with the rate at which its rural population is moving to cities. However, at the same time the government has realised that its spectacular economic growth needs a completely new model of urban development. The fossil fuel-based urbanisation seen in the Western world since the industrial revolution is totally unsustainable in the world's most populous nation.

China, home to 1.3 billion, already has 90 cities with more than one million inhabitants. Around Shanghai alone, ten satellite cities are now being built, of which four will have more than half a million residents.

In the last 11 years alone, many millions of rural Chinese have left the countryside to head for jobs in the cities, and in the next 20 years, over 200 million more will make the transition from the countryside to cities. As its economy goes from strength to strength, this unprecedented migration will continue. Somewhere between 600 and 700 million people will follow them in the next 50 years.

Impact on the environment and resources

This shift is already having an immense effect on China's environment and resources. The ecological footprint of someone living in rural China – that is the area of productive land and sea needed to supply food, energy and resources while accommodating waste – is 1.6 global hectares.

The current model for China's booming cities is Shanghai, where that figure leaps to six or seven global hectares per capita – on a par with the footprint of Londoners. However, if you were to divide the total productive land and sea area of the earth by its inhabitants, each of us would have a fair earth share of only 1.8 global hectares.

The relentless march of urbanisation goes hand in hand with a relentless increase in energy consumption and pollution. China recently became the world's second largest consumer of energy, after the United States. Meanwhile, more than half of China's cities suffer the effects of acid rain. A third of major cities face falling levels of water and the groundwater they do have is contaminated. More than 40 per cent of the cities fail basic standards of air quality. The rush to the cities seems to be inevitable, but it is also completely unsustainable. The current, energy-wasting, resource-intensive way of city living cannot continue.

It is this realisation that has led China's third biggest developer, the Shanghai Industrial Investment Corporation (SIIC), to call on global design and business consultants, Arup. The corporation wanted to build a city that not only provided a healthy return on its investment, but also attempted to find a totally new paradigm for sustainable city living.

The fruits of that new urban paradigm will be the city of Dongtan to be built on the south-eastern tip of Chongming. One of the satellite cities being built around Shanghai, it will also be the world's first purpose-built eco-city. Not only will it be the first fully sustainable city, with a half a million people living there by 2040, but the innovations, new thinking and lessons of Dongtan could one day be the cornerstone of the way 21st-century cities are designed.

Designing the world's first sustainable eco-city

Designed from scratch, Dongtan has been guided from the beginning by profound and ambitious environmental goals. Some of these goals have been achieved singly in small communities and pilot projects around the world before, but taken together, nothing on this scale had ever been attempted. The aggressive Chinese construction deadlines are also faster than anything attempted in the West. Dongtan's first stage, a 'demonstrator' city of 20,000 people has to be ready in time for the Shanghai Expo in 2010.

Arup was initially hired to do a small consultancy for the project. Once involved, it realised that for such an ambitious scheme to work, SIIC did not need piecemeal advice on planning, energy and waste issues. To be successful, it needed a more holistic master plan.

The key to making the city sustainable was to understand how planning for transport, housing, energy and all the other factors fit together and influence each other. SIIC agreed and over the course of the next two years, Arup consultants from London, Shanghai, Hong Kong, the USA and all over the UK worked to develop an integrated and sustainable urban project where issues such as land use mix, transport, economics, water, energy and building design were thought through in a comprehensive framework.

It is this holistic, sustainable way of planning that will not only be the key to the project's success, but is also likely to be one of its most lasting legacies. Right at the start, SIIC and Arup set out their simple goals for Dongtan. These objectives, decided at a workshop at the beginning of the project, would then be constantly referred to during the design of the master plan.

The highest priority was to protect the island's precious wetland wildlife. Chongming is a crucial stopover for wildfowl travelling on the migration routes running across China. It was not enough just to try and minimise the effect of building a city on the delicate ecosystem, the plan had to try to improve the prospects of the wildlife living there.

Secondly, the whole city should run on renewable energy. All the energy needed to keep Dongtan going will be created in Dongtan. Transport is no exception. All the energy needed to keep Dongtan's fleet of vehicles moving will be generated from the city itself. All waste should be reused or recycled. There will be as little landfill as possible.

Dongtan will be designed to be self-sufficient in water. As well as improving the current supply and recycling water where possible, water will be collected from rainfall and then recycled and managed.

Picture reproduced courtesy of Arup

Another key sustainability goal was to ensure Dongtan produced as much of its own food as possible. Traditionally cities swallow farmland and grow at the expense of agriculture. In Dongtan food production would be kept within the city and with the use of new technology, the city should continue to produce as much food as the island did prior to development.

The overarching goal is to keep the sustainability of Dongtan as high as possible. In contrast to energy and resource-hungry modern cities, the planners want to keep the ecological footprint of Dongtan as low as possible.

Dongtan's sustainability goals

1. To protect the island's precious wetland wildlife

2. To ensure the whole city is run on renewable energy

3. To ensure all waste is reused or recycled

4. To be self-sufficient in water

5. To produce as much of its own food as possible

However, equally important alongside these sustainability goals is the desire to make the city work socially. Dongtan should be a city where people enjoy living. The design of the infrastructure, layout and facilities of Dongtan will all play their part in building the social capital of the city. As well as being a pioneering sustainable city the aim is to ensure it will have a friendly, tolerant and open sense of community. Community life should be harmonious and secure, while fostering a sense of belonging and responsibility to the environment. The city should have a sustainable mix of young couples, families, single people and older citizens, which should be well supported by shops, schools, jobs and leisure facilities.

As distinguished American architect Philip Johnson said: 'The development of Dongtan is surely ecological, but by no means at the sacrifice of the enjoyment of modern life.' Part of the social dimension of the planning process was to recognise that Dongtan would be a Chinese city, not a Western city transplanted into the heart of China. Chinese ideas of landscaping, design and community would all play fundamental roles in the how Dongtan grew.

An all-encompassing design approach – integrated urbanism

These goals cut right across all the disciplines of urban development. To draw up its master plan, Arup used more than 100 consultants with expertise in areas from urban design and planning, to water planning, to socio-economic planning. This all-encompassing approach to design has been dubbed 'integrated urbanism'.

Each individual aspect of the plan was quantitatively modelled to understand resource implications and to optimise the design. However, it soon became clear that these individual models had to be linked together. A small change in the plan for how food would be grown in the city could prompt a large shift in what was needed from Dongtan's transport network and that in turn could have a knock-on effect on the city's energy needs. By joining all the models into an integrated resource model, the designers were quickly able to see how the different aspects fitted together and affected each other.

Another key to the plan was to integrate the island's existing infrastructure and environment. The constraints of what already existed on Chongming, with its miles of canals and extensive waterfront could then be turned into opportunities for the future. The results of this master plan are about to take physical shape. The proposal for Dongtan was given outline planning permission in the summer of 2006 and building work will start at the beginning of 2007.

The low rise of Dongtan

Dongtan will be a low-rise and high-density waterfront. This post-industrial city will eventually spread over an area of 84 square kilometres. Starting from the site of the eco-demonstrator city on the southern coast of the island, facing Shanghai, approximately 6km east of where the new tunnel and bridge join the island, it will grow northward across the island to the opposite coast, forming a ribbon 2km wide and 16km long.

The wildlife reserve at the city's extreme eastern tip will be left untouched and be buffered from the rest of Dongtan by a band of eco-farming and controlled wetland. As more silt washes up on Chongming and extends the island, the natural reserve will get larger.

The economy will be driven by three different industries. Firstly, drawing on its agricultural roots, Dongtan will develop eco-agriculture in combination with modern urban service industries.

Secondly, Dongtan will become a major centre of leisure tourism. Visitors from Shanghai, the wider Yangtze delta and further afield will be drawn by sporting facilities, wildlife, hotels and theme parks.

Finally Dongtan will become a centre for knowledge industries such as research, development and education. The city will become home to research companies and institutions from around China and around the world.

Though the city of Dongtan will grow to cover an area of 84 square kilometres and have a population of 500,000 people, most of the land area will not be built up. Dongtan will be made up of three distinct but linked 'towns' set amid parkland and farmland. The three towns will be compact urban areas of living, bound together by a shared city centre acting as a reference point for the whole development. It is in this city centre that larger facilities such as hospitals, universities and theatres will be found.

This pattern of compact, urbanised towns plays a critical role in making the city sustainable. Housing will be mixed with shops, post offices, schools, nurseries and healthcare facilities. Population densities within these compact centres will be similar to those in London. By putting people and facilities close to each other, it will allow people to walk or bike to work or to school or the local shops. The design will cut down and even remove the need to use a private car.

Within these compact pedestrianised centres, public transport, walkways and cycle lanes will be plentiful. A compact, medium- to high-density design will also foster a village-like sense of community and identity in Dongtan – a social goal just as important as the environmental goals.

Green space will permeate the entire city. The condensed, pedestrianised centres will have easy access to farmland and parkland that will open out the city. Contact with green spaces will be an everyday feature of life in Dongtan and nowhere will be more than a few minutes from a park. This continuous network of green spaces will also create corridors for wildlife to move through the city.

The waterways and ponds that define Chongming island will also create open space, and continue to play a defining role in the character of the city. Dongtan will be the gateway to the whole of Chongming's canal network. Canals are a traditional feature of Shanghai developments and a bustling web, carrying freight, passengers and tourists, will serve Dongtan. Waterways will range in scale from the great main canal up to 80m wide to a network of smaller secondary canals, small inlets, docks, lakes, marinas and ponds.

Picture reproduced courtesy of Arup

Sustainable transport and energy strategy

The layout of Dongtan is a cornerstone of the strategy to make Dongtan sustainable and to cut carbon emissions. The worldwide burgeoning use of private vehicles is one of the most serious causes of fossil fuel consumption, carbon emissions and pollution.

That meant a key element of Dongtan's design must be to cut the use of cars. The aforementioned condensed nature of the three constituent towns will cut out the need for many vehicle journeys. Cycle paths and walkways will crisscross the city, meandering through parks and alongside canals and ponds. Dongtan will be designed for pedestrians, not for cars. Neighbourhoods will be accessible to pedestrians and cyclists, but will prevent through motor traffic. Visitors from the mainland will be encouraged to leave their vehicles at the edge of the city and continue by public transport. All of that public transport will be zero emission. Buses and trams will be hydrogen powered, as will the city's fleet of freight and delivery vehicles. Supplies from outside Dongtan will be delivered to a central depot and then distributed by clean vehicles.

The goal of low carbon emissions extends to all the other energy used by the city. The energy will be renewable and created in the city. The roofs of houses will be covered with solar panels. Wind farms will rise from open land in the city. Biofuels are another foundation of the energy strategy. Rice husks, a by-product of rice agriculture in China, are produced in vast quantities. The husks are usually rejected as waste after milling, but in Dongtan they will fuel a city. Barges will carry tons of the husks from all over Chongming and the Yangtze Delta to the city's energy plant. Organic waste from the city and from its inhabitants will generate bio-gas which will in turn be burnt to generate more electricity.

Food will be grown in fields around the city and at high density using new technology in the city's food centre. Though unlikely to be totally self-sufficient for food, Dongtan will produce as much food when it is built as the land did before.

All of this technology is currently available. The innovation in Dongtan is to bring it all together and to design the city with sustainability as an all-encompassing guiding principle.

Results so far

The results have so far been impressive. The ecological footprint of someone living in Dongtan is predicted to be around 2.8 hectares, less than half of that of current modern Shanghai. After all the planning, Dongtan is now becoming a physical reality. The demonstrator city must be ready for the Shanghai Expo in just over three years time and building starts at the beginning of 2007 in order to meet this ambitious deadline.

Echoing the three towns that will make up the finished city, phase one will start as three linked villages. Each village will have a distinct character and will provide all the facilities needed to support its residents. The first village will be built around a marina and a ferry port as well as a large lake for water sports and hotels and restaurants for visitors. This lake will boast restaurants, hotels and conference facilities, but will also be home to the Food Science Cluster. Drawing on the island's heritage of farming and fishing, the centre will focus on education alongside the research and development of agriculture and fish farming.

Picture reproduced courtesy of Arup

The master plan of Dongtan is flexible enough to allow the city to evolve over the coming decades, but lays down guidance for future development. As the city grows it will continue to be guided by the goals of sustainability.

Dongtan is not a rigid blueprint of a city for the future. The master plan for its development grew from the unique environment and situation of Chongming. However, the holistic approach to sustainable planning can be exported elsewhere and can be used to tackle problems in building sustainable cities anywhere. It is this approach that could one day form the cornerstone of new cities in the 21st century.

References

http://www.arup.com/eastasia/project.cfm?pageid=7047

http://www.arup.com

http://www.dongtan.biz

Managing the Risks and Opportunities of Climate Change:

A Practical Toolkit for Corporate Leaders

January 2006

A Publication of Ceres and the Investor Network on Climate Risk

Ceres

Acknowledgments

This publication was prepared as part of a presentation at the New York Stock Exchange by Mindy Lubber, Ceres President and Director of the Investor Network on Climate Risk, and Ken Sylvester, Assistant Comptroller for Pension Policy, Office of the Comptroller, City of New York. It was written by Miranda Anderson and David Gardiner of David Gardiner & Associates. Peyton Fleming, Chris Fox, Dan Bakal, Andrea Moffat, Meg Wilcox and Jim Coburn of Ceres offered valuable comments.

At the Yale School of Forestry & Environmental Studies 2005 conference, "Climate Change: From Science to Action," the Business Working Group developed draft principles for corporate engagement on climate change. This publication is derived in part from those draft principles. This toolkit is also based on the *Investor Guide to Climate Risk: Action Plan and Resource for Plan Sponsors, Fund Managers and Corporations and Corporate Governance and Climate Change: Making the Connection.* To download these reports, please visit www.ceres.org.

Ceres is a national coalition of investors, environmental groups and other public interest organizations working with companies to address sustainability challenges such as climate change. Ceres also directs the Investor Network on Climate Risk, a group of over 50 institutional investors managing nearly $3 trillion in assets.

For more information, visit www.ceres.org and www.incr.com.

Copyright 2006 by Ceres

Investor Network on Climate Risk
Ceres, Inc.
99 Chauncy Street
Boston, MA 02111
(617) 247-0700 ext.15

TABLE OF CONTENTS

About this Toolkit 2

What is Climate Risk? What is Climate Opportunity? 4

Developing a Corporate Climate Policy 6

10 Key Steps to Corporate Climate Action 7

PHASE 1: ASSESS

Step 1: Create a climate management team 8

Step 2: Measure, benchmark and inventory
greenhouse gas emissions 9

Step 3: Compute physical, regulatory,
and financial risk exposure 10

Case Study: American Electric Power 11

Step 4: Assess strategic, branding,
and product opportunities 12

Case Study: General Electric 13

PHASE 2 : IMPLEMENT

Step 5: Develop corporate policies and procedures 14

Step 6: Create absolute GHG
emission reduction goals and action plans 15

Step 7: Set goals to increase energy efficiency,
purchase/develop clean energy technologies,
and offset GHG emissions 16

Case Study: Bank of America 17

Step 8: Engage in public policy 18

Case Study: Ford Motor Company 19

PHASE 3 : DISCLOSE & ENGAGE

Step 9: Publicly disclose assessments
and implementation plans 20

Case Study: Chevron 21

Step 10: Engage shareholders, analysts,
staff and public interest groups 22

GOOD CORPORATE GOVERNANCE INCLUDES
MANAGING CLIMATE RISK & CAPTURING THE OPPORTUNITIES

During the last five years, climate change has emerged as a top tier concern of governments, companies, and investors. The validity of the science supporting climate change is no longer debated. The atmosphere is warming, and human activity—principally the burning of fossil fuels—is a primary cause.

Climate change is a governance issue, a regulatory issue, and a matter of strategic risk management. The corporate risks and opportunities are vast. Leading Wall Street analysts including Goldman Sachs, Merrill Lynch, Prudential Equity Group, and JPMorgan are studying the effects of climate change on shareholder value. Institutional investors who manage nearly $3 trillion in assets have formed the Investor Network on Climate Risk, proclaiming climate change as a key fiduciary concern and one of the greatest challenges of the 21st century. Corporate boards and executives simply cannot afford to ignore this issue.

Given the sweeping global nature of climate change, climate risk has become embedded, to a greater or lesser extent, in every business and investment portfolio in the United States. Investors have begun pressing corporations for more disclosure of climate risk and opportunities, including the impact of climate change on competitiveness and investment returns. Some companies with significant emissions of greenhouse gases or high energy use face risks from new regulations, while climate change poses direct physical risks to other firms. While each sector and company may differ in its approach to the risks and opportunities of climate change, the most successful corporations engage with concerned stakeholders, disclose their strategies to investors, and take concrete actions to manage risk and capitalize on opportunities.

WHO SHOULD USE THIS TOOLKIT

This toolkit is designed for any corporate leader with responsibilities related to risk management, governance, climate regulation, or investor relations, including CEOs, COOs, CFOs, EH&S executives and line managers. It should be read by executives to help set policy, and serves as a reference guide for management. Tackling the risks and opportunities posed by climate change must be driven by senior management and managed by dedicated teams.

Business leaders manage off-balance sheet risks and opportunities every day. However, climate changes poses unusual challenges due to the uncertainty of regulatory risk at all levels of government and to the unpredictability of climate change's impact on weather, markets, and trade issues. Climate change also belongs on the balance sheet in the many instances in which direct financial risks can be calculated.

This toolkit provides the basic stepping stones that all leading corporations should follow in order to respond to the actions of competitors, growing investor concern, and existing climate regulations globally and in over 30 states. The kit also helps companies prepare for the inevitability of a carbon-constrained future due to national and international emissions restrictions. Each sector and company will have unique needs beyond the scope of this toolkit; however, the kit outlines the fundamental building blocks to a best practice climate risk management program.

"Nothing will happen on climate change without the CEO and board directly involved."

Jim Rogers, CEO/Chairman of Cinergy

CLIMATE RISK

Regulatory Risk

State, national, and international regulations are putting increasing pressure on companies with emissions from operations or products to invest in emissions controls, purchase carbon credits, or face clean-up costs. The Kyoto Protocol has come into effect, and the European Union, Canada, China, Japan and others have emission reduction laws. Many U.S. states regulate emissions.

Given the growing interest of businesses and Congress in reducing emissions, it is only a matter of time before the U.S. enacts federal carbon constraints.

Physical Risks

Many businesses are at risk from the physical impacts of climate change, including the increased intensity and frequency of weather events, droughts, floods, storms and sea level rise. Changes in consumer habits as the weather changes will also affect profitability in a number of sectors.

CLIMATE OPPORTUNITIES

Regulatory Opportunities

Companies that are ahead of the curve on emission reductions will face fewer compliance and clean-up costs, and may increase revenue by selling carbon credits. Leading companies can help shape federal regulation as it develops.

Technological Opportunities

Companies in many sectors have the opportunity to increase profitability by developing emission-reducing technologies or new products that meet changing corporate and consumer demands. Companies can also implement energy efficiency strategies to reduce emissions and save money.

Competitive and Reputational Opportunities

Companies with clean technologies may seize new markets or market share. Recent studies demonstrate the financial benefits of being market leaders in this area.

TABLE 1: CLIMATE RISK & OPPORTUNITIES IN SELECTED INDUSTRIES

	Electric Power	Manufacturing	Auto & Transportation	Oil & Gas	Forestry	Agriculture	Fisheries	Health-care	Real Estate	Tourism	Water
Regulatory Risk	◆	◆	◆	◆	◆	◆					
Physical Risk (dependent on location)	◆	◆	◆	◆	◆	◆	◆	◆	◆	◆	◆
Competitive, Reputational Risk	◆	◆	◆	◆	◆	◆	◆	◆	◆	◆	◆
Regulatory Opportunity	◆	◆	◆	◆	◆						◆
Technological Opportunity	◆	◆	◆	◆	◆	◆					◆
Competitive, Reputational Opportunity	◆	◆	◆	◆	◆	◆	◆	◆	◆	◆	◆

THE 3 PHASES TO DEVELOPING A CORPORATE CLIMATE STRATEGY

There are three primary phases to developing a comprehensive climate change strategy:

1. **Assess** your company's risks and opportunities.

2. **Implement** policies and action plans to manage risks and capitalize on opportunities.

3. **Disclose** your findings and plans, while **engaging** stakeholders throughout the process.

The three phases are not mutually exclusive and may occur simultaneously. You will find more detail on each phase on the next page and throughout this toolkit.

While the kit provides the basic hammer and nails, as your company develops increasingly sophisticated climate strategies, more complicated tools—specific to your sector or company—will have to be developed.

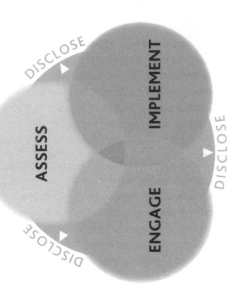

THE 10 KEY STEPS TO CORPORATE CLIMATE ACTION

ASSESS:

Assess risk and opportunities.

1. Create a climate management team and develop a board oversight committee.

2. Measure, benchmark and inventory greenhouse gas emissions from operations, electricity use, and products.

3. Compute physical, regulatory, and financial risk exposure in fixed assets, products and competitive positioning.

4. Assess strategic, branding, and product opportunities related to climate change.

IMPLEMENT:

Implement action plan for climate risk and opportunities.

5. Develop corporate policies and procedures to reduce climate risk and increase value.

6. Create absolute GHG emission reduction goals and deadlines, and an action plan to achieve results.

7. Set goals to increase energy efficiency, purchase or develop clean energy technologies, and offset GHG emissions.

8. Engage in policy dialogues about reducing climate risk and enhancing opportunities.

DISCLOSE & ENGAGE:

Disclose your findings and engage with stakeholders.

9. Publicly disclose assessments and implementation plans in annual financial reports and corporate responsibility reports.

10. Engage shareholders, analysts, staff and public interest groups to receive valuable feedback and develop proactive responses to climate change.

PHASE 1: ASSESS

Step 1: Create a climate management team to report to the CEO and develop a board oversight committee.

Why Take This Step?

This step establishes a commitment from the board to climate risk and opportunities, oversight by the CEO, and a dedicated team of managers and staff from all branches of the business. Step 1 shows investors, employees, and the public that your company is managing this important issue at all levels of the company.

The Board

Assign a committee of directors with direct oversight responsibility for climate change.

Take a clear position on the issue of climate change and the risks and opportunities it poses.

The CEO

Make attainment of greenhouse gas targets an explicit factor in executive compensation.

The Team

Create a multi-departmental steering committee to coordinate and communicate climate change and clean energy strategy to the board of directors and CEO.

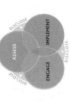

PHASE 1: ASSESS

Step 2: Measure, benchmark and inventory greenhouse gas emissions from operations, electricity use, and products.

Why Take This Step?

Before a problem can be managed, it must be measured. In order for your company to mitigate climate risk, you must have a solid understanding of how much greenhouse gas your company emits (i.e., your greenhouse gas "footprint").

1. Develop annual emissions inventory data for the past 10 years, based on WRI/WBCSD Greenhouse Gas Protocol.

2. Benchmark company performance to your peers on GHG emissions, mitigation strategies, and climate friendly technologies.

Direct Emissions:
Operations
Property holdings
Manufacturing

Indirect Emissions:
Consumer use of products
Electricity use
Employee travel

Note: Throughout the process of assessing emissions, companies should also disclose their findings to stakeholders through the Global Reporting Initiative and the Carbon Disclosure Project.

PHASE 1: ASSESS

Step 3: Compute physical, regulatory, and financial risk exposure in fixed assets, products and competitive positioning.

Why Take This Step?

Climate risk is broad and may affect every aspect of your business, from manufacturing to operations to products. Your company must understand how proposed regulations will affect fixed assets as well as future capital investments. Many businesses are at risk from the physical impacts of climate change, including the increased intensity and frequency of weather events, droughts, floods, storms and sea level rise. Companies that neglect their fiduciary duty, employee well-being, or community safety by disregarding climate risk may face reputational risks.

PHYSICAL RISK	REGULATORY RISK	FIXED ASSET RISK	PRODUCT RISK	COMPETITIVE RISK
✓ Changes in weather	✓ Effect of GHG regulations	✓ Physical exposure	✓ Direct and indirect GHG emissions	✓ Aggregate GHG emissions of operations
✓ Water availability	✓ Secondary effects	✓ Age and projected life	✓ Energy demand and fuel use	✓ Ability to respond to changing regulations and new markets
✓ Changes in temperature	✓ Changes in consumer demand	✓ Energy use and fuel mix	✓ Energy efficiency and clean energy design	
✓ Health effects on workforce	✓ Future cost of carbon, resulting from emission reductions	✓ Fuel switching capabilities	✓ Low GHG alternatives	✓ Introduction of new climate-friendly products
✓ Cost of adaptation		✓ Vulnerability to interruptions in power/water	✓ Low GHG R&D	✓ Corporate reputation, brand value, credit risk, and legal risk
		✓ Proximity to coastlines	✓ Supply chain issues	

CASE STUDY: AMERICAN ELECTRIC POWER ASSESSES REGULATORY RISK

A committee of independent directors of the Board of American Electric Power (AEP) recently completed a report to shareholders assessing the company's actions to mitigate the economic impact of emissions policies, especially for climate change (see www.aep.com/environmental/).

The report analyzes three potential policy scenarios – the Environmental Protection Agency's current proposal to regulate nitrogen oxides (NOx), sulfur dioxide (SO_2) and mercury (Hg), but not carbon dioxide (CO_2); the proposed McCain-Lieberman Climate Stewardship Act; and Senator Carper's proposed Clear Planning Act. AEP projects the costs of each scenario.

By carefully assessing risk, AEP was able to develop a strategic approach to addressing air pollution and climate change. Between now and 2010, for example, AEP expects to invest $3.5 billion in pollution control equipment to meet new EPA requirements for SO_2, NOx, and Hg. However, when the company assumes a constraint on CO_2 after 2010, it faces difficult choices about changes in the composition of its generation fleet, especially as these assets age.

AEP's report is detailed and comprehensive and establishes a new benchmark in corporate disclosure on the climate change issue.

PHASE 1: ASSESS

Step 4: Assess strategic, branding, and product opportunities as a result of climate change.

Why Take This Step?

Your company should examine whether it is well positioned to capitalize on the opportunities related to climate change. If you discovered in Step 2 that your company has particularly low emissions, your firm may profit from the growing multi-billion dollar carbon trading market. Or your company may develop low-carbon technologies that will be in high demand as new GHG regulations come into force.

Maximize strategic investments in climate-friendly technologies, products and manufacturing processes
Establish a business unit to collect GHG emissions data and engage in emissions trading to boost internal rates of return
Utilize leadership status on climate change to increase brand value
Factor costs of GHG emissions into major investment and operating decisions, and consider the physical effects of climate change in major facility siting decisions

CASE STUDY: GENERAL ELECTRIC ASSESSES STRATEGIC AND BRANDING OPPORTUNITIES

GE was quick to recognize the business opportunities posed by climate change and to seize the moment by launching "ecomagination," a company-wide initiative to aggressively bring to market new technologies to address environmental challenges, such as the need for cleaner sources of energy.

Through ecomagination, GE is establishing partnerships with its customers to reduce their carbon emissions, while doubling its research spending to develop new products anc services to fulfill its customers' needs. Specifically, GE has pledged to raise investment in R&D for cleaner technologies to $1.5 billion annually and double its revenues from the sale of ecomagination products to $20 billion by 2010.

Already a leader in energy-efficient power generation technologies, renewable energy, and energy-efficient consumer appliance and lighting products, GE has received substantial positive publicity by

branding these products with the ecomagination name. Less than a year after being launched, ecomagination has become an established part of the lexicon among energy and business professionals worldwide.

Seventeen GE products initially met the ecomagination criteria of significantly and measurably improving customers' environmental and operating performance, and GE plans to add more each year. The products include solar panels, wind turbines, fuel cells, hybrid locomotives, lower-emission aircraft engines, washing machines, lighter and stronger materials, and efficient lighting.

Several years in the making, the 2005 initiative grew out of a dialogue between GE and its customers in the energy and heavy industry sectors who were looking for cleaner and more efficient ways to operate.

"Increasingly for business, Green is Green."

Jeff Immelt, CEO of General Electric

PHASE 2: IMPLEMENT

Step 5: Develop corporate policies and procedures to reduce climate risk and increase value.

Why Take This Step?

After assessing your company's risk and opportunities, the board, CEO, and climate change team should develop clear policies and procedures to reach your goals. These action plans are signals to stakeholders and employees that you are looking toward the future by developing solutions that will protect and maximize your company's value.

Governance

✓ Describe corporate governance actions regarding climate change, including the Board's involvement and which executives oversee management of climate risk.

Policies

✓ Issue a clear, proactive policy about the company's climate change position and response plan.

✓ Disclose the company's greenhouse gas control strategy.

Operations

✓ Integrate climate policy into strategic business planning.

✓ Develop staffing structure for management of climate change operations throughout business units.

PHASE 2: IMPLEMENT

Step 6: Create absolute GHG emission reduction goals and deadlines, and an action plan to achieve results.

Why Take This Step?

A key component of a climate change strategy is setting goals to reduce GHC emissions, including total emissions and emission rates (e.g. tons of CO_2 per unit of production). The plan should have quantitative and temporal goals, and it should be certified annually by an external auditor.

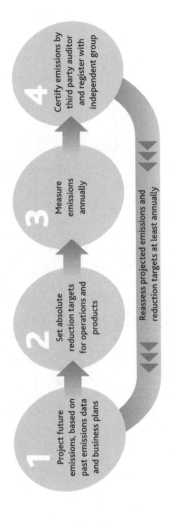

PHASE 2: IMPLEMENT

Step 7: Set goals to increase energy efficiency, purchase or develop clean energy technologies, and offset GHG emissions.

Why Take This Step?

In addition to reducing greenhouse gas emissions in step 6, which minimizes risks, step 7 helps reduce costs, maximize revenue, expand innovation, and develop new markets.

Set targets to improve energy efficiency and reduce carbon intensity in operations and products

Purchase or develop clean energy and climate friendly products and services

Participate in an external voluntary greenhouse gas emissions trading program

CASE STUDY: BANK OF AMERICA IMPLEMENTS CLIMATE CHANGE POLICIES

Bank of America is among a growing number of financial services companies that have set a corporate climate change policy and are integrating that policy into the company's operations (see www.bankofamerica.com/environment/). In 2004, it committed to specific goals for reducing greenhouse gas emissions resulting both directly and indirectly from its financing activities. Its initial goal is to reduce GHG emissions from its operations by 9 percent by 2009, and to realize a 7 percent reduction by 2008 of indirect GHG emissions from its energy and utilities portfolio.

Recognizing that forests play a key role in recycling carbon globally, Bank of America also introduced a new forests practices policy with due diligence measures to assure that lending proceeds are not used in resource extraction from old-growth tropical rainforests or logging in other sensitive forests. A similar policy is in place for sourcing paper for internal operations.

To ensure that environmental goals and objectives are achieved and reported, Bank of America created an environmental council comprised of senior and executive leadership, with the chair of the council reporting directly to the CEO. It also committed to meeting regularly with stakeholders to implement its policy and report on its progress. The bank began using the Global Reporting Initiative framework for sustainability reporting beginning with its 2004 report.

In the public policy arena, Bank of America is committed to using its position as a community and industry leader to elevate the public and private sector's commitment to addressing climate change. It recently issued a public statement in support of the Northeast states' innovative Regional Greenhouse Gas Initiative, a cap-and-trade system aimed at reducing greenhouse gas emissions from the region's power plants.

PHASE 2: IMPLEMENT

Step 8: Engage in policy dialogues about reducing climate risk and enhancing opportunities.

Why Take This Step?

Engagement in the public policy discussion shows stakeholders that your company is serious about climate change, and also positions your company to have increased influence on policy. Without clear federal mandates, U.S. companies are falling behind overseas competitors who are benefiting from tax incentives and subsidies for developing climate-friendly solutions.

Engage in policy dialogue at national, regional and state levels

Provide forward-looking, time-referenced disclosure of climate risk and opportunities in securities filings

Seek government support for energy efficiency and clean technology research and development to diversify the energy supply

" ...shareholders are increasingly asking about the risk as well as the opportunities associated [with climate change]."

Bill Ford, CEO/Chairman of Ford Motor Company

CASE STUDY: FORD CALLS FOR GOVERNMENT ACTION TO REDUCE RISKS OF CLIMATE CHANGE

The Ford Motor Co. has taken a strong public position that actions are needed today to address climate change and that developing vehicles with dramatically lower GHG emissions will be a key factor in the company's long-term competitiveness. (See www.ford.com/go/sustainability for the *Ford Report on the Business Impact of Climate Change*, released December 20, 2005.)

Ford has set aggressive targets to reduce greenhouse gas emissions at its facilities and was the first automaker to participate in GHG emissions trading programs in the U.S. The company also developed the world's first hybrid-electric SUV, the Ford Escape, and recently committed to build up to 250,000 hybrids a year by 2010, a 10-fold jump from current production levels.

CEO Bill Ford has advocated for closer cooperation between government and industry in confronting the country's pressing energy and manufacturing challenges. In a November 2005 speech to the Business Roundtable, Ford called for such cooperative measures as:

❖ Congressional action to dramatically increase the R&D tax credit to support companies working on advanced vehicles, components and fuel technologies;

❖ Congressional deliberation of tax incentives to help American manufacturers convert existing, outmoded plants into high-tech facilities;

❖ Increased government purchasing of hybrid or other alternatively-fueled vehicles by 2010;

❖ Expanding the infrastructure for ethanol fuels;

Ford stressed that government action on climate change could help America stay competitive in the face of globalization pressures, and that failure to invest in American innovation would concede the country's competitive edge in vital parts of the economy.

PHASE 3: DISCLOSE & ENGAGE

Step 9: Publicly disclose assessments and implementation plans in annual financial reports and corporate responsibility reports.

Why Take This Step?

Disclosure is a critical component of successful climate change governance. Transparent discussion of your company's strengths and weaknesses allows investors, employees, and stakeholders to engage in a meaningful way and help develop realistic solutions to ensure the maximization of shareholder value. Climate risk and opportunities that pose material risks to investors should be disclosed in securities filings.

Identify material risks posed by climate change and GHG emissions controls in securities filings.

Issue a sustainability report in accordance with the Global Reporting Initiative (GRI) guidelines.

CASE STUDY: CHEVRON DISCLOSES CARBON REDUCTION STRATEGY

Chevron is the first U.S. oil company to disclose its entire greenhouse gas footprint – including emissions both from its operations and the use of its end products – and to set an absolute reduction target.

Chevron's efforts to manage and reduce its greenhouse gas (GHG) emissions began in 2000 with the development of a software system to account for and report all known sources of GHGs and estimate energy use. After its merger with Texaco in 2002, Chevron developed a greenhouse gas emissions inventory protocol that defines emissions accounting principles, provides guidelines and establishes a scope for what to report.

Assessing its total emissions at 63.9 million metric tons equivalent CO_2 for 2003, Chevron set a reduction goal of a minimum of 900,000 metric tons for 2004. The company surpassed this goal, achieving a reduction of 1.4 million metric tons through divestiture of some production facilities and increased efficiency—even as refinery

throughput slightly expanded. Chevron also commissioned KPMG and the URS Corp. to conduct a third-party verification of its greenhouse gas emissions inventory for the years 2002 and 2003.

Beyond setting goals to achieve an absolute reduction in GHG emissions, the company has taken actions to disclose its potential financial exposure from climate change, and to develop strategies to improve its strategic positioning, including:

❖ factoring carbon costs into capital allocation decision-making and new investments

❖ developing a long-term greenhouse gas emissions profile based on assumptions of future growth

❖ investing over $100 million annually in wind, solar, geothermal and other renewable energies and publicly reporting on these investments

PHASE 3: DISCLOSE & ENGAGE

Step 10: Engage shareholders, analysts, staff and public interest groups to receive valuable feedback and develop proactive responses to climate change.

Why Take This Step?

Open dialogue allows your company to benefit from the latest climate change science, innovative solutions by industry peers, new approaches from executives of other sectors, and robust stakeholder management.

Provide information to the public through the Global Reporting Initiative and the Carbon Disclosure Project

Engage with shareholder proponents

Conduct regular two-way communication on climate change with employees, plan sponsors, fund managers, securities analysts, government policymakers and outside experts on climate change

Join multi-stakeholder groups like Ceres and other climate-related stakeholder networks

MORE INFORMATION

This kit provides the basic tools for building your climate change program. However, more detailed solutions have been developed by leading corporations, concerned investors, and climate change experts.

ASSESS	IMPLEMENT	DISCLOSE & ENGAGE
Investor Network on Climate Risk **www.incr.com**	**WRI/WBCSD Greenhouse Gas Protocol** **www.ghgprotocol.org**	**Ceres** **www.ceres.org**
Promoting a better understanding of the risks and opportunities of climate change among institutional investors.	Harmonizing GHG accounting and reporting standards internationally to ensure that different trading schemes and other climate related initiatives adopt consistent approaches to GHG accounting.	A national network of investment funds, environmental organizations and other public interest groups working to advance environmental stewardship on the part of businesses.
	Emissions registration initiatives:	*Disclosure initiatives:*
	World Economic Forum Global GHG Register www.weforum.org/ghg	**Global Reporting Initiative** www.globalreporting.org
	Climate Leaders www.epa.gov/climateleaders/	**Carbon Disclosure Project** www.cdproject.net
	California Climate Action Registry www.climateregistry.org	

Post-word

The Stern Review argued persuasively in my view that the benefits of strong early action on climate change outweigh the costs. Taking strong early action must be viewed as an investment, a relatively small cost to be incurred now to help avoid the risks of very severe consequences in the future.

If you are the chairman, CEO or on the board of a company, can you afford to take the risk? A 1 per cent investment now could avoid the severe consequences of a loss of up to 20 per cent in the future. If, having read in this book the list of global organisations taking early action now, can you afford the risk of leaving your company behind? If, having read in this book of your competitors in your sector addressing climate change in a strategic and comprehensive manner, can you afford not to?

If not, future shareholders of your company will be entitled to ask the simple question: why did you not take early action on climate change when it was still possible to shape the strategic direction of your company? Indeed will you have shareholders at all without action? They may be more enlightened than you!

Now you have read this book, let's put pen to paper and commit ourselves to the steps outlined in the book while it is still fresh in our minds. Order a copy of this book for all your senior managers. Call a board meeting today to discuss one key agenda item: how your company can cut carbon and grow profits!

Sir Martin Laing CBE
Trustee Emeritus, World Wide Fund for Nature (WWf-UK) and former Chairman, John Laing plc

Post-word

Climate change affects everyone – from major developed countries to the smallest developing nation-state, from big global multinationals to the smallest technology start-up companies, from the major cosmopolitan cities to the smallest village.

Climate change has emerged as a challenge faced by every citizen in the world. We are at a crossroads. We either face it now or we face it in the future at a much greater cost to ourselves, to the environment and to the health of future generations.

The involvement of business – as this book has amply demonstrated – is a must if we are to combat the extreme effects of climate change. It is business that will provide the sophisticated energy-intensive goods and services demanded by the voracious consumer appetites of the world's burgeoning population. It is business that deploys the world's production and logistical machinery that needs significant energy support and resource use. It is business that utilises the immense financial resources to fund the world's desire and pressure for year-on-year economic growth. It is business, therefore, that will be required to act innovatively and responsibly to combat ecological and environmental concerns. It is business, therefore, that needs to provide the myriad leadership examples to address the multi-faceted problems of climate change. Such leadership examples – as you have just read – provide hope that we are heading in the right direction.

I specifically urge the developing countries of the world, in particular its cities, businesses, leaders and citizens to address the issue of climate change as an immense opportunity. For its cities and businesses, a glorious opportunity to leapfrog the old economy and position themselves to develop the low-carbon products required in the new low-carbon economy and to address the effects of climate change such as access to water, food production, health and use of land; and, for its citizens, a one-off opportunity to address the issues of energy poverty, resource depletion and consumption without wholesale adoption of the resource-intensive and energy-exhaustive lifestyles of the developed world.

Gordon Brown, UK Chancellor of the Exchequer, said: 'Climate change is an issue of justice as much as of economic development. It is a problem caused by the developed countries whose effects will disproportionately fall on developing countries'. This is especially true as the impacts of climate change are not evenly distributed – the poorest countries and people of the world will suffer earliest and most.

The book you have just read provides hope for the future. It should change your life. Why? It records the endeavours of man in business and industry in rising up to the challenge of climate change. It shows in real life how corporations and cities can begin to address their responses to climate change. Numerous examples abound of great heroics performed by companies. Employee empowerment to change their lifelong habits figures highly in this book.

We fully endorse this first ever book of its kind: *Cut Carbon, Grow Profits*. Climate change must figure highly on the board agendas of all financial institutions, multinational companies, cities, local authorities, businesses and into the mainstream consciousness of every individual. It must become a strategic board issue for all businesses – one that engages top and senior directors and managers, not a strictly climate or environmental issue that is relegated to the narrow confines of a departmental manager!

We warmly welcome *Cut Carbon, Grow Profits* as a significant breakthrough to bring climate change into the mainstream consciousness of businesses and onto the boardrooms of financial institutions and corporations in both developed and developing countries. The developed world cannot do it on its own – it needs to win over and engage the emerging market countries with more than just technology transfer, technical assistance, financial expertise and international co-operation! This book is a key starting point for businesses and cities in developing countries.

Climate change brings a formidable challenge to the world to face the risks and to take advantage of the opportunities. The international community needs to be fully prepared for the challenge and to utilise its collective out-of-the-box thinking. This book is a significant breakthrough to propel climate change onto the centre stage of the business community. Every individual in any part of the world has a role to play if we are to successfully address the formidable challenges of climate change.

This book is not only instructive to read but should be an essential part of your educational process and library. I commend this book to every government, local authority, city, corporation, business and investor everywhere in the world.

Tan Sri Dr Francis Yeoh, CBE
Group Managing Director, YTL Corporation

Contributor Profiles

Editors

Dr Kenny Tang CFA is founder Chief Executive Officer of Oxbridge Climate Capital, leading experts in the low-carbon, cleantech and climate change area. Kenny has postgraduate degrees from the Universities of Oxford and Cambridge. He has written on sustainability, climate change, cleantech and entrepreneurship for the *Financial Times* and *Wall Street Journal*. He is on the Board of Governors at the University of East London (having just completed two years as Governor at Middlesex University).

He sits on the Global Judging Panel of the *Wall Street Journal's* Technology Innovation Awards and the *Asian Wall Street Journal's* Asian Innovation Awards. He is a Chartered Financial Analyst (CFA) charter holder from the CFA Institute. He authored the first book on financing university spinouts: *'Taking Research to Market – How to Build and Invest in Successful University Spinouts'* (Euromoney Books, 2004). His most recent book: *'The Finance of Climate Change – A Guide for Governments, Corporations and Investors'* was published to coincide with the UK presidency of the G8 Group of Nations and the Gleneagles Summit in July 2005.

Ruth Yeoh is Finance Director at YTL Holdings, a US$5bn corporation in the power, water, retail, hotel, leisure resorts, property, construction, cement, and e-solutions sectors. She graduated with a BSc in Architectural Studies at the University of Nottingham and has an MSc in Management from Cass Business School in the City of London. She is currently attached with Credit Suisse Singapore conducting research in renewable energy markets, commodities, clean technology and investments.

Contributors

Ricardo Bayon is the Managing Director of the 'Ecosystem Marketplace,' a news and information service covering the emerging environmental markets for carbon, water, and biodiversity. For nearly a decade he has specialised on issues related to finance, banking, and the environment. He has done work for a number of organisations, including Innovest Strategic Value Advisors, Insight Investments, the International Finance Corporation (IFC) of the World Bank, among others. His articles have appeared in publications such as *The Washington Post*, *The Atlantic Monthly* and the *International Herald Tribune*.

Henri-Claude de Bettignies is the AVIVA Chair Emeritus Professor of Leadership and Responsibility at INSEAD and Distinguished Professor at the China Europe International Business School (CEIBS) in Shanghai. He was educated at the Sorbonne, Catholic University of Paris, and Harvard Business School. He has published several books and more than 50 articles in business and professional journals including (with Le Menestrel M. and van den Hove, S.) articles on the oil industry and climate change – in *Climate Policy* (2002, 2, 3–18) and *The Journal of Business Ethics* (2002, 41, 251–266).

Tatiana Bosteels is Climate Change Manager at the London Climate Change Agency, a public company which is the driving force behind London's bid to tackle climate change. She is responsible for identifying and implementing the agency's programmes and low carbon developments projects. She has strong expertise in energy and climate change policy and in managing and implementing projects. She developed her skills as a project manager, engineer and consultant within the corporate and the public sector.

Dr Arlo Brady is Special Advisor at Freud Communications, an associate at the Judge Business School, Cambridge University, and a regular business commentator. He is author of the 2005 book *The Sustainability Effect*, contributor to the 2007 book *Corporate Strategies for Climate Change* and a co-editor of the forthcoming CIMA report *Who exactly is managing your reputation?*

Sophy Bristow manages The Climate Group's work with retail companies and consumer-facing brands. Previously she worked for five years in broadcasting and communications as an Assistant Producer and Director of specialist documentaries for the BBC and Channel 4 (UK). She has also been a Research Fellow at the UK Parliamentary Office of Science and Technology where she researched business responses to climate change. Sophy holds an MSc (with Distinction) in Environmental Technology from Imperial College.

Dr Tauni Brooker is Director, Sustainable Solutions for UK and Ireland at URS Corporation Ltd. She has experience in the development and advancement of corporate responsibility and governance strategy in the marketplace and a recognised expert in the fields of sustainable finance and sustainable development in the finance sector. Previous publications include: *Environmental Business*, *Sustain Magazine* and various academic publications. She has a PhD in Environmental Economics from University of St Gallen, Switzerland.

Douglas G Cogan is the research director for Environmental, Social and Governance Analytics at Institutional Shareholder Services, a division of RiskMetrics Group, based in New York City. His 1992 book, *The Greenhouse Gambit: Business and Investment Responses to Climate Change* was one of the first to examine the investment implications of global warming on major industries. More recently, in conjunction with the Investor Network on Climate Risk, he has developed a 'Climate Change Governance Checklist' by which to evaluate company response strategies. Mr Cogan graduated cum laude from Williams College, USA with highest honours in political economics.

Benjamin Diggins has worked for Ford Motor Company for over 20 years. In that time Ben has introduced a range of recycling systems and is a keen promoter of closed-loop recycling and the use of waste as a social enterprise vehicle. Currently heading Ford's sustainable energy programmes in the UK, he is a non-executive director of London Remade.

Fraser Durham has a BSc in Economics & Mathematics from Bristol University, after which he spent ten years advising global investment funds on derivative and alternative asset transactions, most recently for Deutsche Bank. He works for CarbonSense where his passion is to leverage his financial experience to provide innovative solutions for a low-carbon economy.

Cecilia (Sid) Embree is the founding member and majority owner of AtmosClear Climate Club (atmosclear.org), a business focused on retail marketing of branded voluntary emission reductions. She has a Bachelor of Environmental Studies (University of Waterloo, Canada), a Master of Environmental Studies (York University, Canada) and an MBA in Finance and International Business (New York University, USA).

Peter C Fusaro is a chairman of Global Change Associates in New York, and best selling author of *What Went Wrong at Enron*. Peter is an energy industry thought leader noted for insights on emerging energy and environmental financial markets, and has worked on global warming, cleantech and alternative energy since 1990. Peter holds the annual Wall Street Green Trading Summit in New York. He graduated from Carnegie-Mellon and Tufts Universities.

Alejandro Gutierrez is an Associate in Arup's urban design business and is currently design leader for the Dongtan eco-city project. He joined Arup in 2002 and has worked intensively in large scale urban design projects such as Stratford City, Battersea Power Station, Wembley Transport Link, Wembley Industrial Estates, Swindon Regeneration Framework, Ningbo and Guangzhou University in China. Prior to joining Arup he was director for the Cities Consultancy Unit at Catholic University in Santiago, Chile and director of the University's Cities and Environment area at the Architecture School. He was a special advisor to the Chilean Government's Minister of Housing and Urbanism on urban issues.

Katherine Hamilton is the Carbon Project Manager at Ecosystem Marketplace and co-author of the book, *Voluntary Carbon Markets: An International Business Guide to What They Are and How They Work*. She completed her Master of Environmental Management degree at Yale School of Forestry and Environmental studies and her undergraduate degree in International Relations at the University of Michigan.

Dana Hanby is a director at Ecofys International based in London, where she advises European financial clients and utilities on environmental and climate change markets. Previously in the power and gas sector, she has held a variety of responsibilities including origination, European expansion, strategy and transmission. Dana holds a Masters degree in Electrical Engineering and an MBA from Nottingham University.

Amanda Hawn is the Managing Editor at Ecosystem Marketplace and co-author of the book, *Voluntary Carbon Markets: An International Business Guide to What They Are and How They Work*. She has also written about ecology and economics for *The Economist*, *The New York Times* and *Conservation in Practice*. Amanda completed an MSc at the University of Cape Town through a Princeton Fellowship and a BA in Ecology and Evolutionary Biology at Princeton University.

Peter Head OBE studied civil engineering at Imperial College London and has worked for Freeman Fox, Maunsell and now Arup where he leads their Planning and Integrated Urbanism business. Peter received an OBE in 1998 for services to bridge engineering after he led the successful delivery of the Second Severn Crossing. He is a Commissioner on the London Sustainable Development Commission and champions integrated investment in cities.

Andrew Hoffman is the Holcim (US) Professor of Sustainable Enterprise at the University of Michigan; a position with appointments at the Ross School of Business and the School of Natural Resources & Environment. He has published four books and over 50 articles/book chapters on environmental and social issues as they relate to business. He holds a bachelors degree in chemical engineering from the University of Massachusetts at Amherst and a masters and joint doctorate degree in management and civil & environmental engineering from MIT.

Adrian Hosford is Director of BT's Corporate Responsibility activities responsible for co-ordinating BT's combined effort to have as positive an impact on society as possible. This includes BT's community programmes, environmental programme and social responsibility performance. His background is in marketing where he was BT's Brand Manager and ran their customer communication including 'It's good to talk'. He joined BT from ICL as part of the new marketing team after privatisation. Adrian's early career was in the advertising business working for DMB&B, McCann Erickson and Ketchum.

Allan Jones MBE is the CEO of the London Climate Change Agency (LCCA) which implements projects in the sectors that impact on climate change, especially energy, water, waste and transport. He also established the London ESCO (LCCA/EDF joint venture company), which designs, finances, builds and operates decentralised energy systems for both new and existing development. Prior to his Mayoral appointment, he was Woking Council's Director of Thameswey Ltd, and reduced CO_2 emissions by 77.5 per cent from 1990 and undertook groundbreaking projects, including 10 per cent of the UK's photovoltaics and the first fuel cell CHP in the UK. Allan was appointed MBE in 1999 for services to energy and water efficiency.

Mark Kenber is Policy Director of The Climate Group and an economist who has worked on environmental issues for over a decade in non-governmental organisations, the public and private sectors. Immediately prior to joining The Climate Group, Mark was Senior Policy Officer at WWF's International Climate Change Programme, focusing on carbon market and finance issues and co-ordinating the Programme's economics-related work. Mark is an occasional lecturer at Sussex University's Institute for Development Studies and also serves on the Editorial Board of Climate Policy and on the advisory boards of a number of environmental organisations.

Art Kleiner is editor in chief of strategy+business (www.strategy-business.com) and a writer on corporate environmentalism. He is the author of *Who Really Matters* (Doubleday, 2003) and *The Age of Heretics* (Doubleday, 1996); editorial director of The *Fifth Discipline Fieldbook* project and teaches on New York University's Interactive Telecommunications Program.

Jennifer Layke is Director of Business Engagement and Deputy Director of the World Resources Institute's (WRI) Climate, Energy and Pollution Program. She founded and directs the Green Power Market Development Group, a partnership with twelve major US businesses including Alcoa, General Motors, and DuPont with a collective goal of developing 1,000 MW of cost-competitive, new green power in the US by 2010. She earned an AB in Asian Studies and Political Science from Pitzer College in Claremont, CA, an MS in Natural Resource Policy and an MBA from the University of Michigan.

François Lépineux is Research Fellow at INSEAD, Associate Professor of Corporate Global Responsibility at Bordeaux Business School and co-founder and past-President of ADERSE. He graduated from HEC Paris School of Management (1990) and received a PhD in Organization Science at the CNAM (Paris, 2003). His main research areas are in the contribution of business to the common good and the integration of sustainability in the financial services industry.

Peter Martin is Research Director at CarbonSense. He leads work on corporate engagement in climate change, following fifteen years helping organisations integrate strategies for sustainability and cultural change into business development. He has an MSc in Environmental Change from Brunel University, has taught at Royal Holloway and other universities, is widely published on sustainable development and leadership and is a skilled facilitator.

Trevor Maynard is manager of emerging risks at Lloyd's of London and an author of their climate change paper *Adapt or Bust*. He is a fellow of the Institute of Actuaries and chairman of their working party on climate change. Trevor gained his Bachelor and Master of Science degrees in pure mathematics at Warwick University in 1992/93.

Margarita María Parra is a Senior Program Officer at the ICLEI USA Office in Oakland, California and supports the Cities for Climate Protection (CCP) Campaign global co-ordination. She started working for ICLEI in October 2001 in the Latin America Secretariat in Rio de Janeiro, Brazil. Margarita is a chemical engineer from the Universidad Nacional de Colombia. She was a United Nations scholar in India where she obtained a postgraduate diploma in sustainable development. She was also awarded a New Zealand Overseas Development Assistance scholarship for her master's degree in environmental engineering with emphasis in sustainability indicators from Canterbury University.

Jonathon Porritt CBE, co-founder of Forum for the Future, is an eminent writer, broadcaster and commentator on sustainable development. He was appointed by the Prime Minister as Chairman of the UK Sustainable Development Commission in July 2000. He is co-director of The Prince of Wales's Business and Environment Programme which runs senior executives' seminars in Cambridge, Salzburg, South Africa and the USA. In 2005 he became a non-executive director of Wessex Water. His latest book, *Capitalism as if the World Matters* was published by Earthscan in November 2005. He received a CBE in January 2000 for services to environmental protection.

Samantha Putt del Pino is a Project Manager in the World Resources Institute's (WRI) Climate, Energy and Pollution program. Samantha works on several projects that engage the private sector in developing effective corporate responses to climate change. She also manages the Institute's internal climate commitment. Publications that Samantha has authored or co-authored include: *A Climate of Innovation: Northeast Business Action to Reduce Greenhouse Gases; Hot Climate, Cool Commerce: A Service Sector Guide to Greenhouse Gas Management;* and *Switching to Green: A Renewable Energy Guide for Office and Retail Companies.*

Trewin Restorick is the Founder Director of Global Action Plan, a charity that runs a wide range of practical sustainable development initiatives. Previously, Trewin worked for Friends of the Earth where he established the Recycling City initiative and created Paper Round, a green business in London. He also worked for Plymouth City Council, the Dartington Trust and produced a BBC2 programme called 'Something Else'.

Georg Rosenbauer is Manager of Climate Change Business Development with Siemens Power Generation, a leading supplier of the whole spectrum of power generation technology, ranging from turbo machinery, large-scale and industrial turnkey plants to renewable technologies like wind, biomass and geothermal. Georg is an electrical engineer and received his PhD from the Research Institute for Energy Economy in Munich. Before he joined Group Strategy of Siemens Power Generation, he worked as an energy consultant for various branches of industry and in an energy related think-tank within the Siemens Corporate Technology Group.

Karl Schultz heads the climate practice for Energy Edge, a London-based strategic consultancy to the energy industry. His specialities include project-based carbon credits, energy sector responses to climate legislation, and coal sector greenhouse gas mitigation. He has over 50 articles published on these topics, and has degrees from the University of Chicago (history) and the University of Southern California (planning).

David Singleton is a Director and Group Board member of Arup, where he leads and chairs the firm's Global Infrastructure Business. He graduated in Civil Engineering at the University of Nottingham in 1971 and joined Ove Arup & Partners in Melbourne in 1973. He gained a Master of Engineering Science degree by research at the University of Melbourne, graduating in 1977. He is a Fellow of the Institution of Civil Engineers and an alumnus of the Harvard Business School's OPM program (Class of 1998).

Antony Turner is the founder and Managing Director of CarbonSense. He helped set up the 'Business & Sustainability' courses at Schumacher College, which he managed for five years. He wrote the industry submission on wave and tidal power for the House of Commons Science & Technology Committee, and has a successful track record in launching innovative technologies and solutions worldwide. He has a knack for making climate and carbon science and solutions engaging and understandable.

Maryke van Staden is a Project Officer in the Climate & Air Team at the ICLEI European Secretariat (Freiburg, Germany) involved in managing the European Cities for Climate Protection (CCP) Campaign. Prior to joining ICLEI she headed the Scientific Projects Unit of the International Solar Energy Society (ISES), in particular addressing international renewable energy policy issues. Maryke obtained her honours degree in international political science from the University of Pretoria, South Africa. She has extensive experience in the field of political and sustainable energy research and analysis.

Daniel Wells is a Manager in the Transaction Advisory Services of Ernst & Young. He specialises in the valuation of carbon and corporate finance in the low-carbon sector. He is completing an MSc in sustainable business development from CSEM with a dissertation on the carbon value chain. He studied Modern History at Bristol University and is a Chartered Accountant.

Andrew White is Managing Director in Innovest's London office. Prior to joining Innovest, he was Managing Director of Research for Core Ratings/Fitch, a successor company to Global Risk Management Services in London. Prior to that, Mr. White spent several years as a senior researcher on corporate governance and social responsibility at Pensions & Investment Research Consultants (PIRC). He has appeared on several cable TV business news programmes discussing climate change and has written many financial journal articles on CSR. He holds an MA in Environmental Management as well as a BA in European business studies.

Peter Williamson is Professor of International Management and Asian Business at the INSEAD in Fontainebleau, France, and Singapore. He was Dean of MBA Programmes at the London Business School and Visiting Professor of Global Strategy and Management at Harvard Business School. Formerly at The Boston Consulting Group, he has acted as consultant to numerous multinationals with particular focus on strategies in China. He serves on the boards of several listed companies as well as Energy Edge Ltd and Green Gas International Ltd. Peter holds a PhD in Business Economics from Harvard University.